The book contains very informative and relevant content on contemporary issues pertaining to environment and sustainable development and also its classroom transaction. It can empower the readers only in gaining knowledge and awareness, but also help one make informed choices and can be transformative in nature.
—**Jubilee Padmanabhan**, *National Council of Educational Research and Training, New Delhi, India*

This book provides an in-depth understanding of Environmental Education and Education for Sustainable Development in India. It showcases current trends and practices as well as future possibilities. It will be a good starting point for those trying to understand the field in India.
—**Sylvia Almeida**, *Monash University, Melbourne, Australia*

The book is a comprehensive assimilation of various issues and concerns related to environmental education. It raises pertinent questions on the way environment and its education is looked at in the contemporary world and critically analyzes the emergence of new ideas such as ESD in this context.
—**Yukti Sharma**, *Department of Education, Delhi University, India*

UNDERSTANDING ENVIRONMENTAL EDUCATION

The book establishes the importance of environmental education by tracing its history and the developments that have taken place subsequently to date. It provides basic understanding about environmental education as well as valuable suggestions for its effective incorporation in the school curriculum. The strength of the book lies in its content as all major areas of environmental education have been addressed such as school curriculum, professional development, and policies, especially in the context of India, thus making it a unique and go-to resource for all stakeholders working in the field of environmental education. The well-balanced content will help readers appreciate the nature of environmental education and its distinctiveness from other subject disciplines as well as environmental studies and environmental science substantiated with several examples and illustrations. What is striking about the book is its proposed road map which is critical for successful implementation of environmental education in India with the launch of the National Education Policy 2020 and the subsequent introduction of new curriculum frameworks.

The book will be useful to students, preservice teachers, and teacher educators. It will also be of much value to in-service teachers, practitioners in different settings, teachers, policy makers, curriculum developers, and researchers in the field of environmental education.

Chong Shimray is a faculty member at the Department of Education in Science and Mathematics, National Council of Educational Research and Training, New Delhi. She has come a long way to establish herself in the area of environmental education beginning her academic journey in 2006. Chong is also a two-time Fulbright-Nehru Fellow in the United States and a Chevening Research, Science and Innovation Leadership Fellowship (CRISP) Fellow, a program hosted by St Cross College at the University of Oxford in the United Kingdom.

UNDERSTANDING ENVIRONMENTAL EDUCATION

From Theory to Practices in India

Chong Shimray

LONDON AND NEW YORK

Designed Cover Image: Author

First published 2024
by Routledge
4 Park Square, Milton Park, Abingdon, Oxon OX14 4RN

and by Routledge
605 Third Avenue, New York, NY 10158

Routledge is an imprint of the Taylor & Francis Group, an informa business

© 2024 Chong Shimray

The right of Chong Shimray to be identified as author of this work has been asserted in accordance with sections 77 and 78 of the Copyright, Designs and Patents Act 1988.

All rights reserved. No part of this book may be reprinted or reproduced or utilised in any form or by any electronic, mechanical, or other means, now known or hereafter invented, including photocopying and recording, or in any information storage or retrieval system, without permission in writing from the publishers.

The views and opinions expressed in this book are those of the authors and do not necessarily reflect the views and opinions of Routledge. Authors are responsible for all contents in their articles including accuracy of the facts, statements, and citations.

Trademark notice: Product or corporate names may be trademarks or registered trademarks, and are used only for identification and explanation without intent to infringe.

British Library Cataloguing-in-Publication Data
A catalogue record for this book is available from the British Library

ISBN: 978-1-032-57295-6 (hbk)
ISBN: 978-1-032-60930-0 (pbk)
ISBN: 978-1-003-46113-5 (ebk)

DOI: 10.4324/9781003461135

Typeset in Times New Roman
by SPi Technologies India Pvt Ltd (Straive)

*Dedicated to
Henu (Mom) & Avi (Dad)—
Anem Shimray & A.V. Shimray
who are now watching me from heaven…*

CONTENTS

List of Figures — *xi*
List of Tables — *xii*
Preface — *xiii*
Acknowledgments — *xvi*
List of Acronyms and Abbreviations — *xviii*

Introduction: The Book at a Glance — 1

1. State of the Environment — 6
2. Introduction to Environmental Education — 28
3. Why Environmental Education? — 62
4. Responsible Environmental Behavior: Ultimate Goal of Environmental Education — 91
5. Environmental Education in the School Curriculum — 108
6. Tracing Environmental Education in India — 144
7. Global Trends in Environmental Education—Ramifications in India — 196

8	Teacher Empowerment in Environmental Education	232
9	Environmental Education vs Education for Sustainable Development	265
10	Climate Change Education	293
11	Way Forward	332
12	Afterword	357
Index		*362*

FIGURES

1.1	Effects of Human Activities	16
4.1	Traditional Thinking of Responsible Environmental Behavior: Model I (Adapted from Hungerford and Volk 1990)	94
4.2	Traditional Thinking of Responsible Environmental Behavior: Model II (Adapted from Hungerford and Volk 1990)	94
4.3	Model of Responsible Environmental Behavior	96
5.1	Separate Subject or Interdisciplinary Model	115
5.2	Infusion or Multidisciplinary Model	120
5.3	Hand-Print CARE Ethics-Led Learning in Subject Teaching	138
7.1	View of Vast Area under Jhum	222
7.2	A Lady Harvesting Ginger from Jhum Field	223
9.1	SD-Related Educations Done in Isolation	281
9.2	SD-Related Educations Taking the Form of ESD	282
10.1	Content Outline for Climate Change Education	314
11.1	Road Map for the Implementation of Environmental Education in India	346

TABLES

2.1	Chronology of Important Events in Environmental Education	55
3.1	Relationship of Environmental Education—Environmental Science—Environmental Studies	83
5.1	Grade-Level Emphases on Environmental Education Objective Categories	110
5.2	Interdisciplinary (Separate Subject) Approach	116
5.3	Multidisciplinary (Infusion) Approach	124
5.4	Interdisciplinary (Separate subject) vs. Multidisciplinary (Infusion)	127
6.1	Modalities for Implementation of Environmental Education in Different Stages/Grades as Envisaged in NCF-SE 2023	176
7.1	Chronology of Important Events in Environmental Education in India	212
8.1	Comparative Study of B.Ed./ B.Sc.B.Ed./ B.A.B.Ed. Syllabus in the Regional Institutes of Education, NCERT	247
9.1	Key Goals of the DESD	273
9.2	Ten Key Findings of 2014 Global Monitoring and Evaluation Report	274
9.3	Milestones in ESD	276
10.1	Integration of Environmental Education and Climate Change in the NCF-SE 2023	307

PREFACE

During the initial years of my exposure to the area of environmental education, beginning 2006, I remember going through a hard time, hunting for appropriate books on environmental education that would give me a comprehensive idea about environmental education, especially in the context of India. Surprisingly, even today such books are hard to find. It was the struggles that I went through in search of such material that instilled in me the 'burden' to write this book, a burden because it would be a challenge to take up such a task which was going to be one of the first attempts in the country, if not the first. However, considering the fact that lack of appropriate material for reference could deter young students especially in India, who would want to become teachers, educators, and researchers in the field of environmental education from pursuing it, I deeply felt that not writing this book was not even an option. The book, therefore, primarily targets those neophytes in the area of environmental education.

Another purpose of this book is to cater to the needs of the bunch of teacher educators throughout the country who have not had much of experience in terms of training or practice in environmental education, yet are assigned the task of completing courses on environmental education or related courses. This book will help them understand the basics of environmental education to deliver the courses meaningfully. This book will give those educators who have already received basic training in environmental education and who are already associated with it for a while some fresh ways of looking at the practices and the latest trends in the area of environmental education. The discussions contained in the book will also serve as a guide to policy makers.

Yet another pressing reason to come up with the idea of writing this book was because I had come across too many people, even those in the field of education, who, although had very limited understanding about environmental education could exalt it or write it off, just like that! All because environmental education is still such an unpopular discipline which people tend to associate only with 'pollution' and 'planting trees.' This book is an attempt to throw some light on the importance, the relevance and the expanse of environmental education so that learners in general and those in the field of education in particular are informed and are educated about it. If this book could induce some clarity on people's perception about environmental education, it would serve much of its purpose.

Readers will find that not a single chapter is complete in itself. It will probably leave them with more questions than answers. However, this is exactly how the book has been perceived to be. It throws open several new ideas and intends to provoke its readers to critically think and enquire about the situations and arguments provided in various chapters of the book. It is envisaged that the thoughts and ideas that emerge from such critical thinking will guide students to take up further research in their topic of interest or will be need-based and take the field forward in a country like ours where most of the areas in environmental education are yet to be explored. This aspect of the book, which encourages students to become researchers, also sets it apart from other conventional books on environmental education where the content is heavily theoretical and purely examination based.

Writing the book for a specific course or audience would have restricted the topics to be covered, and hence this book is not written around any specific syllabus or for any specific user. A book with limited content coverage would mean doing disservice to the readers as well as to the book itself. A major portion of the content, however, will still meet the requirements of all environment-related courses. This book is therefore unique in that its coverage is much beyond what would be found in a conventional book on environmental education.

In order to make the book reader-friendly, sincere efforts have been put in to make each chapter exclusive with necessary supporting illustrations, pictures, and tables. However, at certain places, cross-references have been given to chapters which are interlinked, which was unavoidable. Hence, readers may be required to read the book in its entirety so as to understand the connections between the chapters. Efforts were put in to ensure that sufficient opinions and findings of various professionals, researchers, experts, practitioners, and so on are reflected in the book, which will give the readers a balanced idea of the differing philosophies, concepts and opinions. Key references have been substantially cited and provided wherever necessary. Complete references have been provided at the end of every chapter so that readers can turn to the references for further detailed readings.

The book, in short, is a 'starter' for those who want to venture into the field of environmental education, especially those in India. And it is a 'booster' or an enrichment material for those who have already had exposure in the form of training or research in the area of environmental education. An attempt has been made to present the concepts and concerns related to environmental education in the most comprehensive and understandable way by tapping all possible resources at my disposal in the form of books, journals, websites, and so on, besides my personal experiences in India and abroad, and interactions with experts in the field.

During the process of writing this book, I was also able to form some ideas which could have possibly influenced the chapters to head in a certain direction. Such instances, wherever they might have occurred, were only to enhance the chapters and not to present any biased or prejudiced opinions. Readers might also at times find themselves struggling to juggle as they go through the chapters due to the somewhat lack of uniformity in the manner they have been presented—book-like as well as journal-like nature. However, in spite of all its limitations and failings, it is hoped that readers will be able to make the best use of the book and appreciate the humble endeavor to bring out a book of this nature, which has not yet been attempted by many in the country.

For readers who are acquainted with my book 'Teaching Environmental Education,' this book will be an updated version which has been revised and reorganized for better understanding with fresh new chapters and content.

ACKNOWLEDGMENTS

Several individuals have contributed in different ways during the course of the writing of this book. A very special person, Professor Jaishree Sharma, had patiently gone through the manuscript and suggested ways for improvements. Besides, Professor Jaishree has always been a pillar of support ever since she introduced me to the world of environmental education. And I cannot thank her enough for that. There are a few other names that deserve mention who might not be even aware that they had made a difference in the process of writing this book. They are those who have generously shared their valuable resources at various points of time: Martha C. Monroe, School of Forest Resources and Conservation, University of Florida; David Sobel, Antioch University, New England; and Jennie Lane Farber, Educational Sciences, Faculty of Education, Bilkent University, Turkey. I especially appreciate Martha for being there to guide me every time I needed to clarify a doubt or simply to share her opinion or patiently hear me out and critically comment on my views. I have been able to organize my thoughts on important fundamental issues related to environmental education through such interactions.

Others, including Asanna Gonmei, has worked tirelessly to go through the initial draft and give shape to the book. My brother, Alfred Shimray, has helped me out with the illustrations. I appreciate their significant contributions. Words cannot express the value of the 'you-can-do-it' boosters that I received from family and friends, especially Alana Golmei, Tannu Malik and Achan Mungleng. I express my utmost gratitude to mom and dad for their blessings. It breaks my heart knowing we cannot hold the book together as both left us barely a month before I submitted the final manuscript.

I thank Dr. Shamita Kumar, professor and principal, Bharati Vidyapeeth Institute of Environment Education and Research (BVIEER) and the concerned staff at WWF-India for their contributions in the section 'Stakeholders for the implementation of environmental education in India,' in Chapter 11: 'Way Forward.'

In this world of business, a reference book of this nature is seldom a priority for publication. I sincerely thank Taylor & Francis (Routledge) for publishing this book under their prestigious banner and tag. And I am grateful to Jubilee Padmanabhan, Sylvia Almeida, and Yukti Sharma for endorsing the book.

Above all, I thank God Almighty for the privilege and the favor He bestowed upon me to author this book. I could have never done it by myself. But His grace was indeed sufficient for me!

ACRONYMS AND ABBREVIATIONS

AECC	Ability Enhancement Compulsory Course
AI	Artificial Intelligence
B.A.B.Ed.	Bachelor of Arts and Bachelor of Education
B.Ed.	Bachelor of Education
B.El.Ed.	Bachelor of Elementary Education
B.Sc.B.Ed.	Bachelor of Science and Bachelor of Education
CBCS	Choice Based Credit System
CBSE	Central Board of Secondary Education
CISCE	Council for the Indian School Certificate Examinations
CoP	Conference of Parties
COVID-19	Coronavirus Disease-19
CPD	Continuous Professional Development
CRC	Convention on the Right of the Child
CTEs	Colleges of Teacher Education
D.El.Ed.	Diploma in Elementary Education
DEC	Distance Education Council
DESD	Decade of Education for Sustainable Development
DIET	District Institute of Education and Training
DIKSHA	Digital Infrastructure for Knowledge Sharing
DoSEL	Department of School Education and Literacy
DoYA	Department of Youth Affairs
DRR	Disaster Risk Reduction
EE	Environmental Education
EEARSD	Environment Education, Awareness, Research, and Skill Development
EEAT	Environment Education Awareness and Training

EEP	Environment Education Program
EFA	Education for All
ESD	Education for Sustainable Development
EVS	Environmental Studies
GAP	Global Action Program
GHG	Greenhouse Gas
GM	Genetically Modified
HEI	Higher Education Institution
IASEs	Institutes of Advanced Studies in Education
ICT	Information and Communication Technology
IDPs	Internally Displaced Persons
IDT	International Development Targets
IMPACT	Integrated Multidisciplinary Professional Advancement Course for Teachers
IPCC	Intergovernmental Panel on Climate Change
ITEP	Integrated Teacher Education Program
KVS	Kendriya Vidyalaya Sangathan
LiFE	Lifestyle for Environment
MDGs	Millennium Development Goals
MoE	Ministry of Education
MoEFCC	Ministry of Environment, Forest and Climate Change
MoWCD	Ministry of Women and Child Development
NAAC	National Assessment and Accreditation Council
NCATE	National Council for Accreditation of Teacher Education
NCERT	National Council of Educational Research and Training
NCF	National Curriculum Framework
NCF-FS	National Curriculum Framework for Foundational Stage
NCF-SE	National Curriculum Framework for School Education
NCF-TE	National Curriculum Framework for Teacher Education
NCTE	National Council for Teacher Education
NEAC	National Environment Awareness Campaign
NEP	National Education Policy
NGC	National Green Corps
NISHTHA	National Initiative for School Heads' and Teachers' Holistic Advancement
NPE	National Policy on Education
NPST	National Professional Standards for Teachers
NTA	National Testing Agency
NVS	Navodaya Vidyalaya Samiti
NYKS	Nehru Yuva Kendra Sangathan
ODF	Open-Defecation Free
ODL	Open and Distance Learning
PIL	Public Interest Litigation

RIE	Regional Institute of Education
RUSA	Rashtriya Uchchatar Shiksha Abhiyan
SARS-CoV-2	Severe Acute Respiratory Syndrome Coronavirus 2
SC	Scheduled Castes
SCP	Sustainable Consumption and Production
SD	Sustainable Development
SDGs	Sustainable Development Goals
SNA	State Nodal Agencies
SSA	Sarva Shiksha Abhiyan
ST	Scheduled Tribes
TET	Teacher Eligibility Test
UN	United Nations
UNEP	United Nations Environment Program
UNESCO	United Nations Educational, Scientific and Cultural Organization
UNFCCC	United Nations Framework Convention on Climate Change
UNGA	United Nations General Assembly
UT	Union Territory
WMO	World Meteorological Organization

INTRODUCTION

The Book at a Glance

Environmental education in formal education has been in practice for several decades now. Some countries have marched far ahead, as is evident from their curriculum of the primary, secondary and tertiary education, while other countries are slowly catching up. The sincerity with which it is implemented may vary. Nevertheless, every country has been doing their bit to incorporate environmental education in their curriculum.

I.1 The Context

Environmental education has become more relevant now than ever before. This is because while we are draining our exhaustible natural resources with all the technological advancements that we are making, at the same time we are filling our environment with all its ill-effects in the form of pollution, other forms of hazardous and toxic chemicals and the likes causing threat to our own survival. We have realized that laws and penalties imposed to tackle environmental issues is only topical treatment of the issues and is not sustainable. We know education will be instrumental in bringing about the change that we want to see and hence the importance of environmental education. However, for this to materialize in the school systems, environmental education has to be done in a systematic manner, with clearly defined goals and pedagogy. This will require an understanding of the specific concerns related to environmental education in terms of implementation, such as curriculum for schools and to-be teachers, skills and competencies of the teachers and teacher educators, challenges and barriers in implementation, and so on.

This book is about understanding environmental education with a focus on formal school education in India. Other forms of environmental education, informal and nonformal, if mentioned, have been done only on specific contexts.

1.2 The Structure of the Book

The book has 11 chapters with an Afterword at the end. A bird's eye view on how each chapter has been organized in the book is provided below.

Chapter 1, 'State of the Environment,' introduces the readers to the various benefits humanity has received as a result of developments in science and technology. At the same time, it also discusses the various environmental issues brought about by the use of such technologies and the need to come up with newer technologies so as to tackle the issues brought about by the use of technologies. Ample examples have been cited to explain the paradox that is encountered in solving environmental problems.

Chapter 2, 'Introduction to Environmental Education,' discusses how the growing concerns about environmental issues world over have led to the introduction of environmental education. It then discusses how the concept of environmental education has evolved over the years. Some landmark events and selected definitions of environmental education (EE) have also been provided in the chapter. The goals, objectives, and guiding principles of environmental education have also been discussed.

Environmental education could be the most misconceived discipline due to lack of consistencies in the presentation of what environmental education is. To explain this, the chapter explores the different views or perspectives on what is included under environmental education. Four different perspectives have been presented in the chapter—environmental education is all-inclusive, environmental education is moderately ecocentric, environmental education is purely ecocentric, and environmental education is purely anthropocentric. It elaborates the different perspectives with several examples. The chapter also touches upon in brief how Education for Sustainable Development (ESD) took over environmental education.

Why do we need environmental education when we are already learning about environmental issues in science is a question still asked by many. Chapter 3, 'Why Environmental Education?,' consolidates the status of environmental education as an indispensable area of study and therefore the need for its inclusion as an integral component in the school curriculum. The chapter explains the unique nature of environmental education and how it is different from other disciplinary subjects. For this purpose, the nature of environmental education and other disciplinary areas have been discussed. It goes on to explain the limitations to implement environmental education through Science–Technology–Society (STS) education. The possibilities and limits to implement environmental education through a science curriculum have also been discussed. At the end, the chapter discusses the relationships that exist between environmental education, environmental science, and environmental studies.

Chapter 4, 'Responsible Environmental Behavior—Ultimate Goal of Environmental Education,' discusses the importance of environmental responsible behavior through 'doing.' It elaborates on how, in spite of all the efforts that we put in, environmental education will not be meaningful unless we see some positive actions being taken, or observe some patterns of behavior (not inherited but learned) or, in other words, if only students display some kind of responsible environmental behavior (REB). It discusses several factors which contribute to REB. Several views on behavioral change are being discussed in the chapter while emphasis has been laid on a model of REB which illustrates the complexity of REB. The chapter also explains how it is impossible to get a perfect model to bring about REB while also bringing out the importance of understanding REB for practitioners and policy makers.

Chapter 5, 'Environmental Education in the School Curriculum,' gives the readers some idea of the different ways environmental education is done and can be done through the curriculum. It explains how the goals of environmental education can be achieved through the school curriculum. The chapter then discusses the two common approaches of implementing environmental education—interdisciplinary (separate subject) approach and multidisciplinary (infusion) approach. The pros and cons of both the approaches are discussed in the chapter. It then provides numerous examples on how environmental education can be incorporated in the teaching–learning of different disciplines. It also presents to the readers an approach introduced more recently—HandPrint CARE approach.

Environmental education has come a long way in India to be what it is today. As the title of the chapter suggests, Chapter 6, 'Tracing Environmental Education in India,' traces the evolution of environmental education in India by looking at the various school education-related documents such as educational commission reports, national policy on education documents, national curriculum frameworks for schools and teacher education, and other nationally important educational reports that were brought out in India since the beginning of the 1930s. How each document has reflected environmental education has been provided succinctly in the chapter. Significantly, the book critically and elaborately discusses the ideas, philosophies, and recommendations with respect to environmental education laid down in the National Education Policy 2020 and the curriculum frameworks subsequently brought forth such as the National Curriculum Framework for School Education 2023.

Someone who has just been introduced to the area would be naturally curious to know whether the initiatives taken at the global level on environmental education have any effect on the implementation or decisions taken in India. This aspect is discussed in Chapter 7, 'Global Trends in Environmental

Education—Ramifications in India.' The present status of implementation of environmental education in India, covering different aspects such as objectives, curricular materials, assessment, and implementation in different states and union territories, is then discussed in the chapter. This chapter also makes a special mention of how a public interest litigation (PIL) filed in the Hon'ble Supreme Court of India had an impact on the course of implementation of environmental education throughout the country. In view of the importance of project-based environmental education, as highlighted in the National Curriculum Framework 2005, the National Curriculum Framework for School Education 2023, and also in the affidavit submitted to the Hon'ble Supreme Court, the chapter incorporates a detailed pilot study undertaken to find out its practicability in schools.

The success of the implementation of environmental education totally depends on how prepared teachers are. Chapter 8, 'Teacher Empowerment in Environmental Education' focuses on the concerns related to the various aspects of teacher empowerment. It discusses the status of teacher empowerment in the area of environmental education and provides the basic content that should be incorporated in all teacher education courses. Issues pertaining to both preservice and in-service courses are discussed comprehensively in the chapter. A comparison of selected Bachelor of Education courses provided across the country is done in the chapter to find out how well the objectives of environmental education can be achieved through such courses. Besides these, issues concerning teacher educators with respect to environmental education are also discussed. At the end, some suggestions toward improving the situation and empowering teachers in the area of environmental education are also provided.

More than three decades after environmental education have been put into practice globally and also the United Nations Decade of Education for Sustainable Development (UNDESD) having been concluded, there is still lack of clarity on the similarities or the differences between environmental education and ESD. Chapter 9, 'Environmental Education vs Education for Sustainable Development,' introduces the concept of sustainable development and thence the goals of ESD. The chapter then discusses the different types of sustainability education. It also explains elaborately how ESD and EE can be considered similar and how they can also be considered different. The chapter also discusses the departure of ESD from environmental education and provides some of the possible implications and ramifications that such departure might bring about while dealing with environmental issues.

The unprecedented impacts of climate change have forced the world to come together to address this global challenge. Although climate change education is part and parcel of environmental education, keeping in view the urgency of the problem, Chapter 10, 'Climate Change Education,' has been especially included so that the issue can be presented systematically in the curriculum in addition to other environmental issues. Based on extensive review of literature, the chapter presents the broad picture of climate change education globally. A special emphasis is given on India keeping in view the new National Education Policy 2020 (NEP 2020) and the new curriculum frameworks that have been prepared in the light of NEP 2020. It highlights the positive aspects as well as the drawbacks of the documents. The chapter also provides an idea as to how climate change education can be systematically introduced in the curriculum.

Chapter 11, 'Way Forward,' provides an implementation strategy for the implementation of environmental education in India. However, successful implementation of such efforts will only be possible with the collective efforts of different agencies—both governmental and nongovernmental. While government bodies have put in much effort, the role of nongovernmental organizations has also been commendable. The chapter discusses the roles these bodies have played in the past and their anticipated efforts in the implementation of environmental education. Emphasis has been given on the role of the Ministry of Education (MoE) and Ministry of Environment, Forest and Climate Change (MoEFCC) along with some prominent NGOs and institutes working in the area of environmental education. The chapter also discusses the roles of other institutes and school systems which are indispensable. Lack of implementation strategies can be considered as one of the reasons why environmental education in India has not made much headway. The chapter, therefore, provides a roadmap which will help policy makers and implementers to come out with an appropriate plan of action for the implementation of environmental education in India. While these initiatives are undertaken, a component that necessitates special mention is that of research. Hardly any studies are available based on which strategic measures can be taken up for the implementation of environmental education. The chapter identifies the different areas where research can be undertaken. This will guide researchers to take up need-based research.

The book concludes with an Afterword, where the author tries to share a piece of her mind highlighting the one reason why things are the way they are (referring to environmental issues) and why nothing is likely to change in spite of all the most brilliant heads and the Heads of all powerful countries coming together for a solution. It also cautions all stakeholders about the danger of diverting all attention to climate change and ignoring other environmental issues. The author attributes the cause of the issues as well as the solution to the issues to one factor—Attitude! The issue begins with attitude and the solution also begins with attitude, the only difference in the two being whether it is the right attitude or the wrong attitude. Degradation of the environment begins with a wrong attitude and nurturance of the environment begins with a right attitude. The author concludes by highlighting the role of educators in addressing this issue and makes a clarion call to all educators to act, not based on the prescribed syllabus, but in response to their conscience.

1
STATE OF THE ENVIRONMENT

1.1 Chapter Overview

The chapter prepares the stage to delve into environmental education by engaging the readers in the various developments that have taken place over the decades and also informing the readers about the sustainable practices that were prevalent in India which are almost disappearing. It illustrates how the world has arrived at the current state of affairs where it is caught up with umpteen environmental issues, endangering the existence of different life forms—humans and nonhumans. The chapter begins by elucidating the contributions of technological advancements which transformed our way of living and at the same time attributing such technologies as the cause for the present-day environmental issues facing the world. The chapter then brings out some of the pros and cons of such technological advancements, especially with respect to environment, equity in the society, and health. It also discusses the complexity of addressing environmental issues and elaborates on how often a well-thought-of solution itself becomes an issue to be addressed. The major initiatives taken up in India and globally to address environmental issues are also provided in the chapter.

1.2 Introduction

Human civilization and technological developments are inseparable and hence can be considered as the two sides of a coin. In fact, different stages of human civilization are characterized by the level of technological developments. Such developments have been pretty much gradual throughout human civilization up until the first half of the 18th century. However, since the late 18th century, drastic and significant technological developments began to flourish across the globe.

All thanks to the Industrial Revolution that transformed the manufacturing processes which made industrial production easier, faster, cheaper, and less labor-intensive but not without a cost, a costly one at that, in terms of environmental degradation, natural resource exploitation, and health hazards. The consequence was so much so that it even impacted the course of evolution as in the case of peppered moth to adapt to air pollution, not to mention of what became of the global environment which today is manifested as climate change. Since then, there have been remarkable advancements in science and technology which have led to speedy growth and expansion of industries, numerous innovations, and great inventions of machines and tools for various purposes.

Development of new technologies and inventions has enabled increase in farm and industrial productions, including dairy products, agricultural products, and other food products such as genetically modified foods, lifesaving drugs, chemicals, household appliances, and electronic devices. Gone are the days when one has to struggle hard to survive or venture out in search of cooler clime and places or mechanically fan oneself to get some relief from the scorching summer heat or curl up around a fireplace to escape the freezing winter. Development and new technologies have made possible easier and comfortable life to a great extent. Healthcare is another sector which has seen developments beyond one's imagination. With the development of various diagnostic technologies and lifesaving drugs, diseases, and conditions such as smallpox, measles, influenza, malaria, tuberculosis, AIDS, etc., which took hundreds and thousands of lives can now be cured or controlled in most cases. Similarly, the development of vaccines for Polio, Influenza, Diphtheria, DPT, Tetanus, MMR (Measles, Mumps, and Rubella), Hepatitis B, etc., has provided protection from the associated diseases. The result of the recently introduced COVID-19 vaccines will be appreciated in due course of time. All these have surely contributed toward increasing life expectancy.

Through the process called 'progress,' humans have been successfully meeting almost all their requirements. For example, human ancestors invented papyrus, which they used to record information and events of their time which preserved history as they are discovered hundreds and thousands of years later. More recently, humanity witnessed more inventions and innovations in this area—papers and carbon papers, typewriters, pens for different purpose, photocopy machines, and 2D printers. The latest in this line being the invention of 3D printers, using which anything available digitally can now be obtained in its real life-size 3D form. In fact, 3D printed house is already a reality. India's first 3D printed house was completed at IIT Madras Campus, Chennai, in 2020.[1] One cannot even imagine what is up next. Advancements in science and technology has also enabled fast-paced new mode of transport and communication. This has made the world indeed smaller. Today, things that are available in any corner of the world can be made available in any part of the world. It is just the question of one's capacity to buy or afford. Destinations which took days and weeks or even months to reach can now be reached in a matter of few hours or few minutes. Distance no longer remains a reason to distance people. A person anywhere in the world can now be in contact with another person any day, anytime, anyplace, virtual of course.

The world has changed so much due to technological inventions and innovations. And humans have 'evolved' with the changes taking place around them, rapidly working toward creating a more comfortable living and at the same time changing their environment. A lifestyle sustained by using simple limited resources has now transformed into a more sophisticated lifestyle which is tremendously resource intensive. The traditional and indigenous practices that once prevailed in India is a good reference point—the way food was preserved, for example the leftover Indian bread is converted into *Khakra*, which can be stored for later consumption; how water has been conserved since ancient times, for example Stepwells[2] (which are known by local names such as *Baoli, Bavadi, Bawri* in Rajasthani, *Kalyani or Pushkarani* in Kannada, *Baoli and Barav* in Marathi, *Vav or Vaav* in Gujarati and Marwari languages) helped the community people overcome scarcity of water in arid regions with scanty rainfall; how seeds were stored for plantation in the next season; agricultural practices were sustainable including the age-old *jhum* cultivation; how houses were built using local sustainable resources suitable for the climate; how plants and animals used to be worshipped or looked after; nature was an integral part of their cultures and traditions and they were taken care of and protected in the form of sacred groves, etc. Sustainability used to be a lifestyle—a lifestyle that promoted the philosophy of *Vasudeva Kutumbakam* (a Sanskrit phrase meaning 'The world is one family'). Though such sustainable practices still prevail in pockets, unfortunately they are slowly but surely disappearing. However, fortunately, the value of such practices is being realized and they are being promoted because of the immense benefits that they provide—all contributing to sustainability. Yet the challenge remains to convince people to adopt a sustainable lifestyle when they have easier, quicker, and fancier options available at their disposal. The bigger question really is, how far can humans rely on technological advancements to enhance their life and livelihood or tackle environmental issues? What are its limitations?

1.3 Environment Issues

With new developments and great possibilities at humankind's disposal, life definitely appears better, easier, and improving. And much of the endeavors are toward developing newer technologies which would make life even better. However, it was hardly realized that the development and the great progress achieved so far and the changes taking place all over the world were at the cost of exploitation of the environment which is causing numerous issues—health hazards due to various toxic wastes released; deterioration of the environment, such as air, water, and soil pollution; scarcity of water, desertification, loss of biodiversity, and so on; destructions due to increase in natural disasters such as floods and cyclones; and issues related to social justice. Worse, most environmental problems and issues do not remain localized. The impacts are felt far and wide. It transcends boundaries as in the case of air pollution, water pollution, greenhouse gas (GHG) emissions, etc. And looking at the amount of waste that are produced today as humans buy more and throw away more, it almost appears as if technologies were invented to generate wastes. The fact is, the more technologies are developed, the cheaper and faster the production is; as a result, there is increased consumption which eventually results in increased waste generation.

During the past decade itself, India has witnessed numerous tragedies, which are associated with reckless developmental activities. The most recent one being the human-induced tragedy in the hilly Joshimath in Uttarakhand, India, in the beginning of 2023 that rendered many families homeless and hundreds of houses declared not safe to live due to various reasons such as unplanned construction, overpopulation, obstruction of natural flow of water, etc. Another incident is that of the landslide that occurred near the new Tupul railway construction site in Noney District in Manipur, India, in 2022, which resulted in 61 fatalities and 18 injuries (Zimik 2023), and at least more than two dozens remained missing. Though weak soil and excessive rainfall is to a large extent attributed for the landslide, human factors definitely played its part, such as extreme slope cutting of the hill to construct the railway station (Baruah, Dey, and Sanoujam 2023). Similarly, floods are not uncommon in different parts of India. However the scale or magnitude of its impacts are increasing. The catastrophic flood that happened in Kerala in 2018 is too recent to be forgotten. A mix of unusual heavy rainfall, the impact of global warming, leveling of wetlands, change in and use of land cover, mismanagement of forests, etc., together brought forth such disaster. Many of the concerns have also been mentioned in the Report of the Comptroller and Auditor General of India on Preparedness and Response to Floods in Kerala (Government of Kerala 2021). Even prior to that, an unusual heavy rainfall was experienced in Chennai in 2015, which led to the devastating flood. However, rainfall was not the sole reason for the flood. Much had to do with the replacement of natural sponge or recharge structures in the form of marshlands, riverbanks, lakes, tanks, ponds, and streams in the city by impermeable surface to facilitate rapid development in the city.[3] So then, should such developmental activities be avoided? None of those activities were taking place in secret. They were all happening in front of the eyes of the people and lawmakers, and most of those activities got clearance from the concerned department of the government. This suggests that checks and balances have failed at some point. One thing is certain that when it comes to choosing either environmental conservation or development, the latter wins hands down. In fact, environment is the last thing that is cared about when in dire situations. For example, during COVID-19 (Coronavirus Disease 19) pandemic, the amount of solid waste that was generated in the form of masks, PPE, gloves, caps, etc., was hardly a primary concern. Worse, such wastes were not even recyclable or could be reused.

Though it is true, rich or poor, ultimately no one can escape the hazards and disasters brought about by the downside of development, clearly there seem to be injustice in terms of bearing the brunt. Such disparity is not limited to development. When COVID-19 was at its peak, it was the poor who had to worry about many other needs such as livelihood, food, sufficient water to wash hands, sanitizers and soaps, face masks, etc., in addition to fighting the deadly virus. The poor apparently ends up paying more. Such disparities are also seen in the solutions that are proposed to address environmental issues. For example, the imposition of high parking fee for vehicles so as to discourage the public to use private vehicles—a measure to reduce air pollution. Such decisions have no effect on the rich. Only the economically weaker sections of the society will be impacted as they will have no choice but to avoid driving. While a set of people, or even nations for that matter, are enjoying the 'growth' and 'development,' another set is at the receiving end and are suffering the ill-effects brought about by the same. The ramifications of this in the lives of the people who suffer constitute another set of issues that need to be taken care of, such as health concerns, relocation, job, education, and so on. Should the society be content with such forms of development, the benefit of which is not shared equally by people belonging to different economic strata? Development will take a different form if guided by Mahatma Gandhi's *talisman* every time a new invention is being made or new technologies are being put to use or when developmental activities are initiated—"Recall the face of the poorest and weakest man you may have seen and ask yourself if the step you contemplate to take is going to be of any use to him. Will he gain anything by it?" Cautioning about the advances in science and technology, decades back, Nash (1976 in Schoenfeld and Disinger 1978, 9) had opined that unless science takes into consideration the ethical and humanitarian influences, it could turn out to be "mankind's greatest problem rather than its greatest blessing." However, this finds no place in today's science and society unfortunately, and hence the evident disparity and injustice prevailing everywhere. In short, humankind's progress has also resulted in bringing about serious threatening issues related not only to his biophysical environment but also to the social environment.

With the increasing disparity and injustice prevailing in the society, the world is seeing an ever-increasing number of different environmental groups and activists springing up to involve citizens in public environmental affairs which have resulted in the stalling or dropping of several developmental projects. While many would appreciate and support such initiatives, there are those who launch attacks on those groups labeling them to be anti-development who are ignorant about the importance of such projects. Often such attacks stem from vested interest—when personal or political benefits are associated with the projects.

An important area of concern is that of human health vis-à-vis economic growth and development. How far 'health' component should be taken into account in the arithmetic of economic index? If economic growth and development represents the well-being of a nation, the human health of its citizens should be considered as the most important index or indicator. And this is not just about human health and economic development. It has a lot to do with the environment as well. Everybody knows that all development activities, directly or indirectly, affect the environment. Pollutions of different kinds are all caused by such developmental activities or are the result of such developmental activities. And needless to say, such pollutions cause several health-related complications. In short, it reduces one's lifespan, and at the same time much of the earnings are spent in healthcare. Hence, it has become impossible to talk about health and not talk about environment and vice versa (Wenzel 1997). In 2015, a popular newspaper quoted a study by economists from the University of Chicago, Harvard, and Yale that was published in *Economic and Political Weekly*, which says:

> Over half of India's population—660 million people—live in areas where fine particulate matter pollution is above India's standards for what is considered safe… If India reverses this trend to meet its air standards, those 660 million people would gain about 3.2 years onto their lives.[4]
> *(The Hindu, 21 February 2015)*

The solution is not in using air purifiers. A huge chunk of the population cannot afford such appliances. In addition, even if it becomes affordable to all, imagine the kind of resources it would require to manufacture them, and the amount of waste it will generate from its usage. Hence, if one really wants to live healthier, longer, and be more productive, the only sustainable solution is in reducing pollution. This means that the whole approach to developmental activities and developmental policies need to change. Developmental activities for economic growth must necessarily take into consideration the impact on human health. If this is done seriously, the environment will also be automatically taken care of significantly. However, doing this will not be as easy as it sounds. It is a complex issue which will require great and committed minds coming together to work out appropriate strategies. Besides such complex issues, there are simple issues which continue to persist. For example, indoor air pollution due to the use of traditional high soot and smoke releasing *chulhas* or stove/hearth by a large number of households in the country is one of the causes for respiratory-related health issues in the rural areas and also among the urban poor.

As the connection between health and environment is being discussed, it is impossible not to talk about COVID-19 pandemic caused by severe acute respiratory syndrome coronavirus 2 (SARS-CoV-2). Although it is not confirmed that the virus reached from its wild animal host to human population due to developmental activities, it is agreed that nature cannot be exploited at will by being oblivion of its impact it could have on humans. It is not just about SARS-CoV-2 but zoonotic diseases in general are in the rise, and hence any form of interaction with, or interventions carried out in nature must be done so with utmost care.

Another battle, the most challenging one at that, the world is grappling with today is that of climate change which is caused by the greenhouse gases that have been pumped into the atmosphere since the boom of technological developments. It has been recognized that the developed nations are largely responsible for the high levels of GHG emissions in the atmosphere leading to global warming and the resulting climate change that have impacted every sphere of life—socio-economic, political, environment. Today, extreme weather events are no longer uncommon. Phenology is impacted with flowers blooming sooner in many places, population dynamics of plants and animals are changing, mosquito populations are increasing in the higher altitudes, so also the pest dynamics.

Specific negotiations about emission reduction have been taking place year after year at the Conference of Parties (CoP) since 1995 under the United Nations Framework Convention on Climate Change (UNFCCC). Yet it was always a matter of debate as to who should fix the problem. However, based on the principle of "differentiated responsibility and respective capabilities," it was at CoP 3 held in Kyoto, Japan, in 1997 that the Kyoto Protocol was brought out, and in 2015 at the CoP 21 held in Paris, a legally binding International treaty on climate change called the Paris Agreement was adopted by the parties. Although countries are now complying to it, it is now clear to all what it takes to get countries comply, and how cautious and reluctant countries are to take immediate climate actions in spite of already seeing the consequences of climate change. However, this should not surprise anybody because every developing country aspires to develop and the developed countries don't want to compromise. And the hard truth is that every development activity comes at a cost of GHG emission in some way or the other. Green technologies cannot replace the existing ones totally at least for now because of non-availability or cost-related issues. Hence, greener technologies need to be developed, if not green, so as to reduce GHG emission. Technologies alone cannot help. Lifestyle changes will be crucial—choices of food, clothing, accessories, appliances, devices, transportation, housing, energy consumption, recreation, etc., all of which will substantially contribute in reducing GHG emission.

There is another very complicated issue when it comes to environmental degradation. How can humankind's greed and craving for luxury be addressed? Mahatma Gandhi had said, "The earth provides enough to satisfy everyman's need but not for everyman's greed." The present-day unprecedented rate of environmental deterioration can be, to a great extent, attributed to people's greed and craving for luxury (Khoshoo and Moolakkattu 2009, 14). No doubt, need also changes with time, which is not a problem. It is greed that is causing all the problem. Everybody wants to have it all because 'possession' defines one's status in the society, and to be at the top of the pyramid defined by such possessions is every person's dream. Besides, once thought of to be a luxury is now considered a necessity. And who does not want to lead a comfortable life? But the question now is, where to draw the line between need and greed and also between comfort and luxury. For example, how many buildings or mansions does one need to own to lead a comfortable life or how many cars for that matter? How many trees need to be cut to be used as timber or firewood to lead a comfortable or luxurious life? How much food, water, energy, and so on? Is the society ready to act positively in this direction by taking some moral, social, and ethical responsibility? Such actions could be as simple and trivial-sounding as restricting buying that extra set of clothes if one can do without it, or extending the use of that pair of dress before discarding it, or holding on to one's urge a little longer to replace a perfectly working mobile phones or any gadget or appliances, or being mindful in terms of energy usage, or a simple car-pooling, or buying energy-efficient appliances, or depending on local produce as far as possible, or making sure that the discarded items are put to reuse or are recycled.

In short, indiscriminate use of resources and technology, environmental mismanagement, uncontrolled and short-sighted developmental activities, humankind's greed, unsustainable lifestyle, lack of compassion for others, etc., are responsible for environmental issues that have been discussed. Hence, tackling environmental issues will require interventions from all angles—international cooperation, appropriate technological innovations, elaborate life cycle assessment of new products before launch, a more robust assessment of developmental activities before clearance, strict compliance and implementation of relevant laws and policies, taking informed, responsible, and environment-friendly decisions in daily life, etc. Therefore, it is rightly said that environmental issues are complex in nature and complicated to deal with.

1.4 The Paradox of Environmental Issues

Environmental concerns are complex, deep, and widespread. However, what is being done to heal the damage that have been done and to prevent new ones from emerging seem to be a little too less for too long. Lack of awareness and growing human activities are also adding to the problem each day. As a result, nothing much seems to have changed even decades after extensive global efforts were initiated and pressed forward to tackle environmental issues. It is also being realized that environmental issues are much more complex than it was thought to be, and addressing the issues are more complicated and challenging than the issue itself.

Environmental issues range from exploitation of natural resources to all kinds of pollution—land, air, and water—to global warming, human rights to ecological justice to social justice to conflicts to issues of the 'commons' (any shared resources such as atmosphere, rivers, oceans, and so on) and much more. To address each of these issues, numerous aspects have to be considered—broadly, social, economic, and environmental concerns. Hence, often, if not always, addressing environmental issues is paradoxical. Even well-intended and well-thought-out decisions often lead to another more complicated problem. It appears that only the form of environmental issue changes but the issue remains. For example, the onset of the Green Revolution reduced farmer's dependency on forest resources. For this, the state provided water, electricity, fertilizers, and machinery at highly subsidized rates. This greatly increased food production, and the program was considered a great success. But, unfortunately, it also led to heavy destruction of forests with the building of large dams for irrigation and large power generation (Gadgil and Guha 2000, 222; Ramakrishnan 2001, 165–192). Therefore, it is not the development of new technology *per se* that is important but often to do with its appropriate use (Tortajada 2005, 12). Another example is the invention of plastic shopping bags of the 1960s and 1970s, which began to be used indiscriminately since the 1980s. Convenient as it is, it was not realized then that such a once-thought boon could someday turn out to be a bane and become such a serious environmental concern. Owing to its improper disposal, polythene bags, many other plastic products for that matter, are found to litter every possible place on earth—inhabited areas, soil, oceans, rivers, drains, mountains, and so on. One is aware of the presence of microplastics in the systems of many fishes and other aquatic organisms and other organisms that feed on them. Adding to the woes is the flouting of rules by manufacturers on the minimum thickness that has caused a major concern in terms of recycling. Another technology has to be developed now to address this issue. This cycle of solution-problem-solution brought about by invention of new technologies seem to have no end. Hirst (1977 cited in Schoenfeld and Disinger 1978, 9) holds such rampant technology responsible for environmental problems and blames engineers and scientists who are involved in the development of such technologies for the problems.

A huge chunk of the population of the world continues to glorify science and technology and believes it to be a *deus ex machina*. That is, they believe that all the problems facing the world can be solved by technologies, though this notion seems to decrease as educational levels increase (Silvernail 1978 cited in Disinger and Lisowski 1986, xi). Rightly so to some extent! For example, the latest innovations in negative emission technologies will do a world of good to tackle climate change. Similarly, inventions and innovations of new technologies to tap renewable sources of energy will drastically reduce our dependency on nonrenewable sources of energy. The Report of the World Commission on Environment and Development, *Our Common Future* (WCED 1987), also promotes management and improvement of technology to make way for a new era of economic growth. But the larger question that must be asked is, "can we in any way restrict our tendency to depend on technology completely" or "what are the practices that we can reinforce in our daily lives which will reduce our dependency on technology?" One needs to be reminded that invariably all the technologies that humans have invented for their welfare have adverse effects in some way or the other on the environment.

Tremendous efforts are being made to improve the human development index (which include indicators such as life expectancy at birth, adult literacy rate, and GDP per capita) by catering to different aspects of life such as literacy, healthcare, immunization, safe drinking water, sanitation, and so on, especially in developing countries like India. And all these are directly or indirectly connected with the use of energy. It has never occurred in history that a country has improved its level of human development without corresponding increase in per capita use of energy (Ghosh 2010, 182). At present, due to the issues of global warming and climate change facing the world, countries all over the world have to reduce their energy consumption, irrespective of their present level of per capita energy consumption. In this scenario, developing countries like India are in a Catch-22 situation. While they want to improve their human development index, the same will require increase in energy consumption. While such a move to reduce energy consumption worldwide is the need of the hour, it will not be fair to ask developing countries like India to reduce their energy consumption.

Wenzel (1997) also discusses about such paradox wherein development brings about individual benefits while at the same time in the process of doing so brings about threat to their own lives collectively. He puts down the same in the following words:

> Developed societies in uncontrolled ways have gone so far that individual life can be extended to limits never experienced before but simultaneously threatening collective lives in pursuit of their economic prosperity by establishing modes of production, manufacturing, housing codes, environmental pollution, and living standards hazardous to the health of the population rather than to the health of particular individuals.

Equity, affordability, fairness, justice—all these are nice sounding, and every effort is to be made to ensure that they are taken care in all developmental activities. However, in the process of achieving these, certain paradoxical situations could arise. For example, making air travel affordable so that every person can realize their dream of flying is a fair proposal at the face of it. In fact, introduction of low-fare airlines has increased the number of flyers by the hundreds and thousands. However, it is a known fact that GHG emission from aviation industry is enormous. According to a report,[5] aviation emissions account for about 2.1% of the global share, but when non-CO_2 effects are included, aviation contributes an estimated 4.9% to the global warming problem. This is what is seen even when about 80% of the world population do not fly[6] (or cannot afford to fly). Hence, a perfectly sounding proposal to make flying affordable could have its downside as well unless they are thought through—how and where to strike a balance between environment, development, and social justice. Another example is that of waste generation. In an attempt to make products affordable, the quality is being compromised. When products are affordable and cheap, they are less valued, not utilized to the maximum, and not maintained. As a result, the amount of waste generation also increases drastically compared to when products are higher priced. Respite, and perhaps a reasonable solution, could arrive when a circular economy becomes the norm.

The paradox seems to apply to almost every activity that humans are engaged in, for example land clearing, agriculture, and forestry, and for good intended results such as increase in food production, shelter, comfort, promote culture, and so on. However, such activities also in turn bring about negative unintended results such as habitat destruction, deforestation, desertification, etc., at high environmental costs (see Figure 1.1). Hence, the question, "Is the paradox associated with environmental issues inevitable or avoidable?" is not only a valid question but a crucial one at that.

1.5 Initiatives to Address Environmental Issues

Environmental problems and issues do not remain localized. Its impacts can be felt far and wide. For example, air pollution is not restricted by boundary. Such pollutions transcend state and national boundaries and have literally gone with the wind. Everybody is familiar with ozone layer depletion or the impacts of greenhouse gases on climate change, the consequences of which are felt by all,

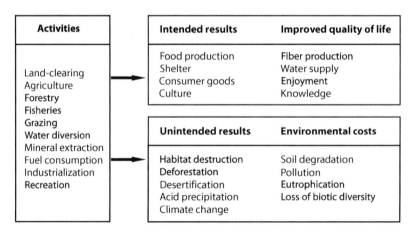

FIGURE 1.1   Effects of Human Activities.

Source: Adopted from Lubchenco et al. (1991: *Ecology*, 72: 371–412 in Ramakrishnan 2001, 16).

irrespective of whether they contributed toward it or not. Therefore, states and nations should not only address environmental issues which concerns them directly but also come together to tackle such issues collaboratively. In this regard, several initiatives have been taken up at the national and international level. This is done through negotiations, treaties, policies, schemes, program, laws, education, etc. Some of such initiatives are briefly discussed here.

1.5.1 Initiatives at the International Level

1.5.1.1 Environmental Education

The importance of education to tackle environmental issues was for the first time collectively agreed by global leaders at the United Nations Conference on the Human Environment held at Stockholm in 1972. Notably, it was subsequent to that conference, environmental education began to find a place in education and came to be what it is today. Details about the outcome of the Stockholm conference with respect to environmental education will be discussed in the next chapter.

1.5.1.2 Addressing Ozone Layer Depletion

The Montreal Protocol[7] was adopted on September 16, 1987, to regulate the production and consumption of nearly 100 man-made chemicals referred to as ozone-depleting substances (ODS) such as chemicals which are used as refrigerants, in aerosols, etc. It is one of the rare treaties to achieve universal ratification. ODS in the atmosphere damage the stratospheric ozone layer which is the Earth's natural sunscreen from harmful levels of ultraviolet radiation from the sun.

Under this treaty, all parties have specific responsibilities related to the phase out of the different groups of ODS, control of ODS trade, annual reporting of data, national licensing systems to control ODS imports and exports, and other matters. Developing and developed countries have equal but differentiated responsibilities, but, most importantly, both groups of countries have binding, time-targeted, and measurable commitments. Although not without issues, the steps taken under this treaty have been encouraging, which is resulting in ozone layer recovery. The World Meteorological Organization recognized this to be one of the environmental success stories[8] made possible by collaborative efforts globally.

1.5.1.3 Tackling Climate Change

The Intergovernmental Panel on Climate Change (IPCC) was created in 1988 by the World Meteorological Organization (WMO) and the United Nations

Environment Program (UNEP) to provide at all levels with scientific information that they can use to develop climate policies. Thousands of people from all over the world contribute to the work of the IPCC. It comes out with the assessment report occasionally since 1990 informing governments about the state of knowledge of climate change caused by human activities. It alerts the governments on various aspects—natural, economic, and social impacts, and the associated risks. As mentioned earlier, the two major international treaties to date on climate change are the Kyoto Protocol and the Paris Agreement. They are discussed in a little more detail here:

(i) Kyoto Protocol

The Kyoto Protocol[9] was adopted on December 11, 1997, but entered into force only on February 16, 2005. Currently, there are 192 parties to the Kyoto Protocol. It operationalizes the United Nations Framework Convention on Climate Change by committing industrialized countries and economies in transition to limit and reduce greenhouse gas (GHG) emissions in accordance with agreed individual targets. It only binds developed countries and places a heavier burden on them under the principle of "common but differentiated responsibility and respective capabilities," because it recognizes that they are largely responsible for the current high levels of GHG emissions in the atmosphere.

The Kyoto Protocol sets binding emission reduction targets for 37 industrialized countries and economies in transition and the European Union. Overall, these targets add up to an average 5% emission reduction compared to 1990 levels over the five-year period 2008–2012 (the first commitment period).

In Doha, Qatar, on December 8, 2012, the Doha Amendment to the Kyoto Protocol was adopted for a second commitment period, starting in 2013 and lasting until 2020. The amendment entered into force on December 31, 2020.

(ii) Paris Agreement

The Paris Agreement[10] is the first legally binding international treaty on climate change. It was adopted by 196 parties at COP 21 in Paris, on December 12, 2015, and entered into force on November 4, 2016.

Its goal is to limit global warming to well below 2, preferably to 1.5 degrees Celsius, compared to preindustrial levels (global temperature during the period 1850-1900).

To achieve this long-term temperature goal, countries aim to reach global peaking of GHG emissions as soon as possible to achieve a climate neutral world by mid-century. The Paris Agreement works on a five-year cycle of increasingly ambitious climate action carried out by countries. Countries were expected to submit their Nationally Determined Contributions (NDCs) by 2020. To date, two countries have submitted their fourth version of NDC while 26, 140, and 26 countries have submitted their first, second, and third versions, respectively.[11]

1.5.1.4 Conserving Biodiversity

The Convention on Biological Diversity[12] (CBD) is the international legal instrument for "the conservation of biological diversity, the sustainable use of its components and the fair and equitable sharing of the benefits arising out of the utilization of genetic resources" that has been ratified by 196 nations.

Its overall objective is to encourage actions which will lead to a sustainable future.

The conservation of biodiversity is a common concern of humankind. The CBD covers biodiversity at all levels: ecosystems, species, and genetic resources. It also covers biotechnology, including through the Cartagena Protocol on Biosafety. In fact, it covers all possible domains that are directly or indirectly related to biodiversity and its role in development, ranging from science, politics, and education to agriculture, business, culture, and much more.

1.5.1.5 Preserving Wetlands

The Convention on Wetlands[13] is the intergovernmental treaty that provides the framework for the conservation and wise use of wetlands and their resources. The Convention was adopted in the Iranian city of Ramsar in 1971 and came into force in 1975, and hence also popularly known as the Ramsar Convention. Since then, almost 90% of UN member states, from all the world's geographic regions, have acceded to become "Contracting Parties."

1.5.1.6 Managing Oceans

The United Nations Convention on the Law of the Sea[14] was adopted in 1982. It lays down a comprehensive regime of law and order in the world's oceans and seas establishing rules governing all uses of the oceans and their resources. It embodies in one instrument traditional rules for the uses of the oceans and at the same time introduces new legal concepts and regimes and addresses new concerns. The Convention also provides the framework for further development of specific areas of the law of the sea.

Protection of marine environment and biodiversity

The UN Environment Program (UNEP), particularly through its Regional Seas Program, acts to protect oceans and seas and promote the sustainable use of marine resources. The Regional Seas Conventions and Action Plans is the world's only legal framework for protecting the oceans and seas at the regional level.[15]

1.5.1.7 Handling Water

The Convention on the Protection and Use of Transboundary Watercourses and International Lakes[16] (Water Convention) was adopted in Helsinki in 1992 and entered into force in 1996. The Convention is a unique legally binding instrument promoting the sustainable management of shared water resources, the implementation of the Sustainable Development Goals (SDGs), the prevention of conflicts, and the promotion of peace and regional integration.

The Water Convention requires parties to prevent, control, and reduce transboundary impact, use transboundary waters in a reasonable and equitable way, and ensure their sustainable management. Parties bordering the same transboundary waters have to cooperate by entering into specific agreements and establishing joint bodies. As a framework agreement, the Convention does not replace bilateral and multilateral agreements for specific basins or aquifers; instead, it fosters their establishment and implementation, as well as further development.

Originally negotiated as a regional framework for the pan-European region, following an amendment procedure, since March 2016 all UN member states can accede to it.

1.5.1.8 Dealing with Plastic

In February 2022, a historic resolution was adopted at the United Nations Environment Assembly to develop an international legally binding instrument on plastic pollution, including in the marine environment with the ambition to complete the negotiations by end of 2024.[17]

The instrument is to be based on a comprehensive approach that addresses the full life cycle of plastic. The Intergovernmental Negotiating Committee (INC) will consider how to promote sustainable production and consumption of plastics from product design to environmentally sound waste management through resource efficiency and circular economy approaches.

1.5.1.9 Education for Sustainable Development

Education for Sustainable Development (ESD)[18] gives learners of all ages the knowledge, skills, values, and agency to address interconnected global challenges including climate change, loss of biodiversity, unsustainable use of resources, and inequality. It empowers learners of all ages to make informed decisions and take individual and collective action to change society and care for the planet. ESD is a lifelong learning process and an integral part of quality education. It enhances the cognitive, socio-emotional, and behavioral dimensions of learning and encompasses learning content and outcomes, pedagogy, and the learning environment itself.

The United Nations Educational, Scientific, and Cultural Organization (UNESCO) is the United Nations' leading agency for ESD and is responsible for the implementation of ESD for 2030, the current global framework for ESD which takes up and continues the work of the United Nations Decade of Education for Sustainable Development (2005–2014) and the Global Action Program (GAP) on ESD (2015–2019).

UNESCO's work on ESD focuses on five main areas:

- Advancing policy
- Transforming learning environments
- Building capacities of educators
- Empowering and mobilizing youth
- Accelerating local-level action

UNESCO supports countries to develop and expand educational activities that focus on sustainability issues such as climate change, biodiversity, disaster risk reduction, water, the oceans, sustainable urbanization, and sustainable lifestyles through ESD. UNESCO leads and advocates globally on ESD and provides guidance and standards. It also provides data on the status of ESD and monitors progress on SDG Indicator 4.7.1, on the extent to which global citizenship education and ESD are mainstreamed in national education policies, curricula, teacher education, and student assessment.

1.5.1.10 Sustainable Development Goals (SDGs)

In September 2015, the General Assembly adopted the 2030 Agenda for Sustainable Development that includes 17 SDGs.[19] Building on the principle of "leaving no one behind," the new Agenda emphasizes a holistic approach to achieving sustainable development for all.

The SDGs are the blueprint to achieve a better and more sustainable future for all, a call for action by all countries—poor, rich, and middle income—to promote prosperity while protecting the planet. They recognize that ending poverty must go hand in hand with strategies that build economic growth and address a range of social needs including education, health, social protection, peace, justice, and job opportunities, while tackling climate change and environmental protection. The goals also provide a critical framework for COVID-19 recovery.[20, 21]

1.5.2 Initiatives in India

India's role and contributions to address environmental issues are recognized globally. It has taken up several initiatives not only in compliance to international commitments but also to address its own challenges. Some of the initiatives are discussed briefly here.

1.5.2.1 Compulsory Environmental Education

Although environmental components have been part and parcel of the curriculum, it was the Hon'ble Supreme Court's directive of 1991 that mandated its teaching in all stages of education. This has played an important role in the implementation of environmental education in India. The details about this will be covered in several chapters of the book.

1.5.2.2 Swachh Bharat

To accelerate the efforts to achieve universal sanitation coverage and to put the focus on sanitation, the prime minister of India had launched the *Swachh Bharat Mission* on October 2, 2014.[22] Under the mission, all villages, gram panchayats, districts, states, and union territories in India declared themselves 'open-defecation free' (ODF) by October 2, 2019, the 150th birth anniversary of Mahatma Gandhi, by constructing over 100 million toilets in rural India. To ensure that the ODF behaviors are sustained, that no one is left behind, and that solid and liquid waste management facilities are accessible, the Mission is moving toward the next phase, Phase II of *Swachh* Bharat Mission (Grameen) (SBMG), that is, ODF-Plus. ODF-Plus activities under Phase II of SBMG will reinforce ODF behaviors and focus on providing interventions for the safe management of solid and liquid waste in villages.

1.5.2.3 National Mission for Clean Ganga

As part of the National Mission for Clean Ganga, the Government of India in June 2014 approved the 'Namami Gange Programme' as 'Flagship Programme' to accomplish the twin objectives of effective abatement of pollution, conservation, and rejuvenation of National River Ganga.[23]

The key tasks under this program include the following: creating sewerage treatment capacity; creating river-front development through construction, modernization, and renovation of ghats/crematoria; river surface cleaning for collection of floating solid waste from the surface of the ghats and the river and its disposal; biodiversity conservation for Ganga rejuvenation to restore viable populations of all endemic and endangered biodiversity of the river including breeding program of freshwater turtles and gharials; afforestation to enhance the productivity and diversity of the forests in headwater areas and all along the river and its tributaries; public awareness through a series of activities such as events, workshops, seminars, and conferences and numerous information, education, and communication (IEC) activities, and rallies, campaigns, exhibitions, *shram daan*, cleanliness drives, competitions, plantation drives, and development and distribution of resource materials for wider publicity via TV/Radio, print media advertisements, featured articles and advertorials; Industrial Effluent Monitoring and Ganga Gram to develop 1,674 model villages along the bank of River Ganga in five States (Uttarakhand, Uttar Pradesh, Bihar, Jharkhand, and West Bengal).

1.5.2.4 National Solar Mission

Solar energy has taken a central place in India's National Action Plan on Climate Change with National Solar Mission (NSM)[24] as one of the key missions. The NSM was launched on January 11, 2010. It is a major initiative of the Government of India with active participation from states to promote ecological sustainable growth while addressing India's energy security challenges. It will also constitute a major contribution by India to the global effort to meet the challenges of climate change. The Mission's objective is to establish India as a global leader in solar energy by creating the policy conditions for solar technology diffusion across the country as quickly as possible. The Mission targeted installing 100 GW grid-connected solar power plants by the year 2022. This is in line with India's Intended Nationally Determined Contributions (INDCs) target to achieve about 40% cumulative electric power installed capacity from nonfossil fuel–based energy resources and to reduce the emission intensity of its GDP by 33% to 35% from 2005 level by 2030. This is necessary because there is a positive correlation between growing per capital GDP and increase in carbon dioxide emissions.

1.5.2.5 Single-Use Plastic Ban

The Ministry of Environment, Forest, and Climate Change, Government of India, notified the Plastic Waste Management Amendment Rules, 2021, on August 12, 2021, to phase out single-use plastic items by 2022.[25] Thus marking a defining step to curb pollution caused by littered and unmanaged plastic waste being taken by the country. With this, ban on the manufacture, import, stocking, distribution, sale, and use of identified single-use plastic items, which have low utility and high littering potential, is effective all across the country from July 1, 2022.

The Government of India has taken resolute steps for mitigation of pollution caused by littered single-use plastics. The list of banned items includes ear buds with plastic sticks, plastic sticks for balloons, plastic flags, candy sticks, ice-cream sticks, polystyrene (thermocol) for decoration, plastic plates, cups, glasses, cutlery such as forks, spoons, knives, straw, trays, wrapping or packing films around sweet boxes, invitation cards, cigarette packets, plastic or PVC banners less than 100 microns, and stirrers.

The Plastic Waste Management Amendment Rules, 2021, also prohibit manufacture, import, stocking, distribution, sale, and use of plastic carry bags having thickness less than 75 microns with effect from September 30, 2021, and having thickness less than thickness of 120 microns with effect from the December 31, 2022.

1.5.2.6 Lifestyle for the Environment

The concept of 'Lifestyle for the Environment'[26] (LiFE) was introduced by the prime minister of India at the COP 26 in Glasgow on November 1, 2021, calling upon the global community of individuals and institutions to drive LiFE as an international mass movement toward 'mindful and deliberate utilization, instead of mindless and destructive consumption' to protect and preserve the environment. LiFE puts individual and collective duty on everyone to live a life that is in tune with Earth and does not harm it. Under LiFE, those who practice such a lifestyle are recognized as Pro Planet People.

Hinging on studies that suggest that practicing an action for a minimum of 21 days helps make it a habit, LiFE 21-Day Challenge was launched to enable Indians to take one simple environment-friendly action per day for 21 days and eventually develop an environment-friendly lifestyle. It is a challenge to change one small thing in one's life daily and become Pro Planet People.

1.5.2.7 Conservation of Biodiversity

In order to promote conservation of biodiversity in the form of crop varieties or seeds, India started a major effort at documenting traditional wisdom on biodiversity at the village level through People's Biodiversity Registers.

1.6 Conclusion

Technological developments and innovations are necessary to meet our ever-increasing needs. However, in the process it has brought about unprecedented degradation and deterioration of the environment endangering not only our own existence but also every life form. From the several examples provided in the chapter, it is clear that development or use of technologies which were meant to improve human life have resulted in various environmental issues and challenges. Similarly, a well-sounding proposal to bring about equity and justice in terms of opportunities and facilities could in turn aggravate environmental problems as discussed about making air travel affordable. This makes environmental issues complex. And invariably, the economically weaker section of the society is harder hit by the challenges posed by the deteriorating environment. Many of the efforts to address environmental problems seem to be unfair to them as in the case of hiking parking fees. This shows that environmental issues cannot be solved in isolation without considering the socio-economic aspects associated with the problems. Therefore, as complex as environment issues are, solving such issues are equally complex, if not more. Then what is the way forward to contain the enormous environmental challenges facing us? Several efforts have been made and are being made to tackle environmental issues nationally and collectively (globally) since the impacts are not restricted by physical boundaries. Such efforts will bear fruit depending on the sincerity, honesty, and integrity with which they are tackled.

The biggest takeaway in this chapter is that no matter how much the best technology is developed, natural resources will still be required to meet the needs of people and sustain life. And most of such resources are nonrenewable. Technology cannot create the land and the water or the atmosphere and the biosphere—at best, it can help manage. Therefore, the attempt should not be to develop technology to manipulate and manage natural resources; rather, it should be such that natural resources need no management by technology. At the end, the best solution lies in adopting a sustainable lifestyle that once used to be a way of life.

1.7 Summary

- Human civilization and technological developments go hand in hand.
- The role of science and technology in apparently improving life has also brought about other complications in life. Technological developments have not only made human lives comfortable but also increased life expectancy.
- Environmental issues are widespread.
- Many of the environmental issues facing the world are due to faulty development models, ecological mismanagement, and, most importantly, human greed.
- Many changes have taken place since the past two centuries which have impacted life and the environment.
- There exists a paradox surrounding the impact of technologies as well as those concerning environmental issues.
- Environmental issues are complex, and even a well-intended effort results into several other environmental issues.
- Environmental concern became a global issue due to the realization of the enormity of adverse effect of development on environment and brought the world together to collectively work toward addressing all environment-related issues facing humanity.
- Several initiatives have been undertaken at the national and international level to tackle environmental issues and challenges.

Notes

1 https://tvasta.construction/projects (Accessed on September 22, 2023).
2 https://static.pib.gov.in/WriteReadData/specificdocs/documents/2022/jun/doc202262267001.pdf (Accessed on September 24, 2023).

3. https://nidm.gov.in/PDF/pubs/ChennaiFlood_NIDM2021.pdf (Accessed on September 21, 2023).
4. https://www.thehindu.com/news/national/high-air-pollution-cuts-most-indian-lives-by-3-years/article6919346.ece (Accessed on September 23, 2023).
5. https://unfccc.int/sites/default/files/resource/156_CAN ICSA Aviation TD submission.pdf (Accessed on February 13, 2023).
6. https://ourworldindata.org/co2-emissions-from-aviation (Accessed on February 13, 2023).
7. https://www.unep.org/ozonaction/who-we-are/about-montreal-protocol (Accessed on February 13, 2023).
8. https://public.wmo.int/en/media/news/ozone-layer-recovery-environmental-success-story (Accessed on June 30, 2023).
9. https://unfccc.int/kyoto_protocol (Accessed on February 13, 2023).
10. https://unfccc.int/process-and-meetings/the-paris-agreement/the-paris-agreement (Accessed on February 13, 2023).
11. https://unfccc.int/NDCREG (Accessed on February 13, 2023).
12. https://www.un.org/en/observances/biological-diversity-day/convention (Accessed on February 13, 2023).
13. https://www.ramsar.org/about-the-convention-on-wetlands-0 (Accessed on February 13, 2023).
14. https://www.imo.org/en/OurWork/Legal/Pages/UnitedNationsConventionOnTheLawOfTheSea.aspx (Accessed on February 13, 2023).
15. https://www.un.org/en/global-issues/oceans-and-the-law-of-the-sea (Accessed on February 13, 2023).
16. https://unece.org/environment-policy/water/about-the-convention/introduction (Accessed on February 13, 2023).
17. https://www.unep.org/about-un-environment/inc-plastic-pollution (Accessed on February 13, 2023).
18. https://www.unesco.org/en/education/sustainable-development/need-know?TSPD_101_R0=080713870fab20000b7a00b9446939690830c6c4c2e9259ea818eea2f6db682539ed88580d1f76340833719d9b1430008c4e8833ad3d142d5253f20267fe00e76bc735f9da7b626eb9a6a9e5919f96f4cca630ff32e8d6cf4deefa41f4ec6b03 (Accessed on February 13, 2023).
19. https://www.un.org/development/desa/disabilities/envision2030.html (Accessed on February 13, 2023).
20. https://www.un.org/sustainabledevelopment/ (Accessed on February 13, 2023).
21. https://www.un.org/sustainabledevelopment/sustainable-development-goals/ (Accessed on February 13, 2023).
22. https://swachhbharatmission.gov.in/sbmcms/index.htm (Accessed on February 13, 2023).
23. https://nmcg.nic.in/NamamiGanga.aspx (Accessed on February 13, 2023).
24. https://mnre.gov.in/solar/current-status/ (Accessed on February 13, 2023).
25. https://pib.gov.in/PressReleaseIframePage.aspx?PRID=1837518 (Accessed on February 13, 2023).
26. https://www.mygov.in/life/ (Accessed on February 13, 2023).

References

Baruah, Santanu, Chandan Dey, and Manichandra Sanoujam. 2023. "Preliminary account on the 30th June 2022 Tupul, Manipur landslide of Northeast India." *Landslides* 20: 1547–1552. DOI: 10.1007/s10346-023-02074-y

Disinger, John F., and Marylin Lisowski. 1986. *Teaching Activities in Science/Society/Technology/Environment*. Columbus, OH: ERIC Clearinghouse for Science, Mathematics, and Environmental Education. Available at: http://files.eric.ed.gov/fulltext/ED282711.pdf (Accessed on July 2, 2023).

Gadgil, Madhav and Ramchandra Guha. 2000. *The Use and Abuse of Nature*. New Delhi: Oxford University Press.

Ghosh, Prodipto. 2010. "The Climate Change Debate: View from India." In *Dealing with Climate Change–Setting a Global Agenda for Mitigation and Adaptation*, edited by R.K. Pachauri. New Delhi: TERI.

Government of Kerala. 2021. *Report of the Comptroller and Auditor General of India on Preparedness and Response to Floods in Kerala*, Report No. 6. Available at: https://cag.gov.in/en/audit-report/details/114526 (Accessed on June 29, 2023).

Khoshoo, T.N., and J.S. Moolakkattu. 2009. *Mahatma Gandhi and the Environment—Analysing Gandhian Environmental Thought*. New Delhi: TERI.

Ramakrishnan, P.S. 2001. *Ecology and Sustainable Development—Working with Knowledge Systems*. New Delhi: National Book Trust.

Schoenfeld, Clay, and John F. Disinger. 1978. *Environmental Education in Action—II: Case Studies of Environmental Studies Programs in Colleges and Universities Today*. Columbus, OH: ERIC Information Analysis Center for Science, Mathematics, and Environmental Education. Available at: http://files.eric.ed.gov/fulltext/ED152557.pdf (Accessed on June 29, 2023).

Tortajada, Cecilia. 2005. "A Critical Assessment." In *Appraising Sustainable Development—Water management and Environmental Challenges*, edited by Asit K. Biswas and Cecilia Tortajada, 1–17. New Delhi: Oxford University Press.

WCED, World Commission on Environment and Development. 1987. *The Report of the World Commission on Environment and Development: Our Common Future*. New York: United Nations.

Wenzel, Eberhard. 1997. "Environment, Development and Health: Ideological Metaphors of Post-traditional Societies?" *Health Education Research—Theory & Practice*, 12(4): 403–418. Available at: https://www.researchgate.net/publication/249278804_Editorial_Health_Environment_and_Education (Accessed on June 29, 2023).

Zimik, Mungchan. 2023. "Himalayan Plunder: Manipur Landslides Raise Environmental Questions." *Down to Earth* (1–15 February 2023 issue). Centre for Science and Environment. Available at: https://www.downtoearth.org.in/news/urbanisation/himalayan-plunder-manipur-landslides-raise-environmental-questions-87595 (Accessed on June 29, 2023).

2
INTRODUCTION TO ENVIRONMENTAL EDUCATION

2.1 Chapter Overview

This chapter introduces the readers to the area of environmental education (EE). It elucidates the important role environmental education can play in our humongous task to tackle environmental issues. Environmental education has its roots in nature study, conservation education, and outdoor education. Such evolution of environmental education and the landmark events in its history is also discussed. Environmental education means different things to different people. In fact, there is a wide range of opinion about what makes up the term 'environment.' Such varied definitions of environmental education posited by experts and professionals in the field are also discussed in the chapter along with the challenges that arise in the implementation as a result of lack of clarity or agreement on the definition. The chapter also discusses the different perspectives that emerged due to the differences in the way 'environment' and 'environmental education' are conceived. Implementation of the different perspectives in the curriculum serves different purposes. Environmental education in the curriculum has largely focused on the bio-physical issues lacking holistic approach in its implementation. As a result, environmental education is considered to be 'insufficient' and 'outdated' in many countries and education for sustainable development (ESD) has been introduced. Such transition of environmental education to ESD is also discussed in the chapter in brief.

2.2 Introduction

It is being noted that since 1970s human beings have become increasingly aware and concerned about the deteriorating environment and the changing climatic conditions the world over. Environmental concerns are no longer restricted to a country or a few countries, but have become global issues that call for serious attention. It was realized that such environmental problems posed a threat to humankind's own existence. With this, there dawned a realization among world leaders that the issues are to be addressed with concerted efforts of all nations. The realization spread among all people and all communities in the world. Nations came together, and they agreed to collectively work toward nurturing the environment, more evidently, beginning the United Nations Conference on the Human Environment held at Stockholm in 1972. During this conference, the importance of education on environment to address the issues was strongly felt and highlighted. This was followed by the International Environmental Education Workshop held in Belgrade (formerly in Yugoslavia, now in Serbia), which brought out the Belgrade Charter of 1975 (discussed later in more detail) and the International Conference on Environmental Education held in Tbilisi, Republic of Georgia, which came up with the Tbilisi Declaration of 1977. Subsequent to these, several other global initiatives have been undertaken, and many are being carried out toward the same end.

Environmental education thus has been considered an important component of education the world over since the Stockholm conference. It is envisaged that EE will provide "the much needed foundation for a new international order which will guarantee the conservation and improvement of the environment" (NCERT 1981). However, it is important to note that EE developed due to man's perceived threat for its own survival and not out of concern or fascination for nature *per se* (Disinger and Howe 1990, 1; Lahiry et al. 1988, 20; Schoenfeld 1971, 41; Tilbury 1997). This could bring about, in fact it has brought about, selectively biased conservation practices which are purely anthropocentric as will be discussed in other sections of the book, more specifically in Chapter 9.

2.3 What Is Environmental Education?

Today, environment-related studies are being increasingly emphasized and promoted in school and college education throughout the world. In formal school education system, EE takes different forms of 'environment studies' depending on the environmental settings (not just the physical environment but the facilities in schools and the priorities and flexibilities in the curriculum)—as a subject by the name Environmental Studies, Environmental Science, etc., or as a set of out-of-classroom activities, etc. It is not uncommon to see schools or teachers 'do EE' through a wide range of activities—observation of environmentally important days; planting of trees; painting competition; slogan or essay writing competitions on environment-related themes; preparation of models of environment-friendly technologies, devices, blueprint of conservation strategies; holding rallies to create awareness and encourage public to take certain environmentally responsible actions or to promote certain environmentally sound practices; visits to biodiversity parks, national parks, botanical and zoological gardens, and museums; nature trails, and so on.

However, every curricular area has its own unique way of approach (Carter and Simmons 2010, 11) and definition. Hence, the questions that arise at this point are: What is environmental education? Is environmental education limited to the activities listed earlier, or is there more to it? How did environmental education take its present form? How is environmental education defined and what are its goals? These are the questions a person who has just been introduced to the field of environmental education would probably ask. Hence, the focus of the discussions will be on these questions based on various studies by several researchers and leading professionals in the field.

Based on different studies and views of experts, environmental education can be variously placed within the framework of education. The multiplicity of the meaning of the term 'environmental education' by different people, including environmental educators, was clearly pointed out by Disinger (1986). It "means many things to many people, including those who profess to be 'environmental educators'" (Disinger and Wilson 1986, 3). It can be considered an approach to education, a philosophy, a tool, and a discipline (Monroe, Andrews, and Biedenweg 2007), and a perspective—a way of looking at things, of analyzing, of evaluating (Sarabhai, Kandula, and Raghunath 1998). Tilbury (1997) calls it 'a new concept in education.' It is also considered a new approach in education which "not only gives a few pieces of information on environmental concerns but also brings about a new personal and individualized behavior based on a 'global ethic'" (Lahiry et al. 1988, 17). The National Council of Educational Research and Training (NCERT 1981) opines that environmental education can make a powerful contribution to the renovation of the educational process due to its very nature of being interdisciplinary and holistic. It has also been observed that practitioners and professionals have defined environmental education according to the goal(s) they want to attain. Some limit it to the study of nature and natural resources, while others stretch it wide open to include the total environment (biophysical as well as social). Besides the variations in the definition of environmental education, there exist issues due to lack of clarity as Lucas (1980) cited Wheeler (1975) as follows, "It is clear that different people mean different things by it, and also that some who use it are not really certain what they mean." The literature has also revealed that there exists cynical use of the term 'environmental' as a prefix to make a subject a better competitor in the academic marketplace such as using the title 'Environmental Physics' for a physics course which discusses topics such as work, energy, and the thermodynamic laws which has little to do with the concept of environmental education (Lucas 1980). However, the most widely accepted definition of environmental education seems to be that which was proposed in the Belgrade Charter:

Environmental education is a process aimed at developing a world population that is aware of and concerned about the total environment and its associated problems, and which has the knowledge, motivations, commitments, and skills to work individually and collectively toward solutions of current problems and the prevention of new ones.

(UNESCO-UNEP 1976; UNESCO 1984)

While some more definitions will be part of the discussion that follows, few others are provided in Box 2.1. As varied as the definitions may appear, all converge to one essence: environmental education is all about well-living and well-being of humankind.

BOX 2.1   DEFINITIONS OF ENVIRONMENTAL EDUCATION

Environmental management education is the process of developing a citizenry that is:

1. knowledgeable of the interrelated bio-physical and sociocultural environments of which man is a part;
2. aware of the associated environmental problems and management alternatives of use in solving these problems; and
3. motivated to work toward the maintenance and further development of diverse environments that are optimum for living.

Robert E. Roth (1970)

Environmental education is that education which develops in man a recognition of his interdependence with all of life and a recognition of his responsibility to maintain the environment in a manner fit for life and fit for living—an environment of beauty and bounty, in which man lives in harmony. The first part of environmental education involves development of understanding; the second, development of attitudes—a 'conservation ethic.'

Matthew J. Brennan (1970)

For the purpose of this act, the term 'environmental education' means the educational process dealing with man's relationship with his natural and manmade surroundings, and includes the relation of population, conservation, transportation, technology, and urban and regional planning to the total human environment.

Environmental Quality Education Act (1970)

From nature study, environmental education draws an emphasis on an understanding of our ecological system—man, culture, natural environment. From conservation education, environmental education draws a concern for the husbandry of the system. From outdoor education, environmental education borrows the concept that such issues should cut across the entire curriculum. From citizenship education, environmental education draws social dimensions and a commitment to action. From resource management education, environmental education draws a technological point of entry to public policy change.

Clay Schoenfeld (1971)

Environmental education is a way of implementing the goals of environmental protection. Environmental education is not a separate branch of science or subject of study. It should be carried out according to the principle of lifelong integral education.

Finnish National Commission for UNESCO, Report of the Seminar on Environmental Education, Jammi, Finland (1974)

Environmental education is an interdisciplinary, integrated process concerned with resolution of values conflicts related to the man-environment relationship, through development of a citizenry with awareness and understanding of the environment, both natural and man-altered. Further, this citizenry will be able and willing to apply enquiry skills, and implement decision-making, problem-solving, and action strategies toward achieving/maintaining homeostasis between quality of life and quality of environment.

Gary D. Harvey (1977)

To create an awareness and an understanding of the evolving social and physical environment as a whole, its natural, man-made, cultural, spiritual resources, together with the rational use and conservation of these resources for development.

Report of a Conference of African Educators, EDC and CREDO, Nairobi, African Social Studies Programme (1986)

The process of identifying an issue of concern, of researching and choosing the most appropriate solution, and of implementing a plan to make their idea a reality is environmental education.

Martha Monroe (1991)

Environmental education is essentially an education involving the head (knowledge), heart (responsibility) and hand (skills).

Daniella Tilbury (1997)

2.4 Roots of Environmental Education

The term 'environmental education' is considered to have been first used in 1948 by Thomas Pritchard, the then deputy director of the Nature Conservancy in Wales, during the meeting of the International Union for the Conservation of Nature and Natural Resources (IUCN) held in Paris. It was used to suggest an educational approach to the synthesis of the natural and social sciences (Disinger 1983).

However, over the years, different views and approaches of different philosophers, professionals, educationists, teachers, and practitioners have largely contributed and shaped environmental education to its present-day understanding. It may be mentioned that the pedagogy of environmental education was influenced by the following: educational philosopher Jean-Jacques Rousseau (1712–1778), who maintained through his writings that education should include a study on environment that encourages return to nature and discover nature as it is, rather than memorize scientific facts (Biedenweg, Monroe, and Wojcik 2013; McCrea 2006); Sir Patrick Geddes (1854–1932), an advocate of nature conservation; and John Dewey (1859–1952), who was a strong proponent of experiential education that included opportunities to explore, reflect upon, and apply newly learned concepts (Biedenweg, Monroe, and Wojcik 2013). Another renowned scientist, Louis Agassiz, strongly advocated learning directly from nature and not books (Disinger and Monroe 1994).

The primary antecedents of environmental education were nature study, outdoor education, and conservation education. The nature study movement in formal education, which took students outdoors to explore an indivisible environment with an integrated academic approach, began as early as 1891 with Wilbur Jackman's *Nature Study for the Common Schools*. Outdoor education has historically been defined as an educational method or approach—"the use of resources outside the classroom for educational purposes" (Swan 1975 cited in Disinger 1983). It has a very similar purpose as nature study. However, it differs in that outdoor education encouraged teachers to go outdoors for lessons in every subject area, not just science, and aimed to advance not only an appreciation for the natural world but also outdoor knowledge and skills. Its focus is in the place for learning—outside the school building, rather than a content area. Hence, it has been described as a potential vehicle for all subjects of the curriculum, including science, mathematics, English, art, and music.

Unlike nature study and outdoor education, conservation education was started in the United States by governmental agencies following the Dust Bowl of the 1930s, which resulted from irresponsible and indiscriminate use of natural resources. Conservation education was introduced to spread awareness about conservation issues, espouse the importance of wise use of natural resources, and encourage the public to understand and comply with environmental laws (Disinger and Monroe 1994). In 1949, the Commission on Education of the International Union for Conservation of Nature (IUCN) was established (Cook and Weider cited in Lahiry et al. 1988, 5) with a focus on environmental conservation education. But it was Rachel Carson's *Silent Spring* published in 1962 that triggered the environmental movement in America during the 1960s and 1970s. Although the book is exclusively about chemical pesticides and its impacts, it conveyed a larger message about the complexity of nature as Linda Lear (1998) wrote in the Afterword of the book "that everything in nature is related to everything else" and that "nature is not easily moulded."

2.5 Evolution of Environmental Education in the Modern Era

The first discussion on environmental education at a global platform took place in 1968 at the United Nations Educational, Scientific and Cultural Organization (UNESCO) Biosphere Reserve Conference held in Paris. A call was made at the meeting to develop curricula for all grade levels, promote technical training and increase awareness of global environmental problems. A subsequent meeting co-sponsored by UNESCO and IUCN in Nevada in 1970 set forth the following definition of EE:

> The process of recognizing values and clarifying concepts in order to develop skills and attitudes necessary to understand and appreciate the interrelatedness among man, his culture, and his bio-physical surroundings. Environmental education also entails practice in decision-making and self-formulation of a code of behaviour about issues concerning environmental quality.

In 1969, William B. Stapp[1] and his students at the University of Michigan formally developed and published the following definition of 'environmental education' in the first issue of *The Journal of Environmental Education*: "Environmental education is aimed at producing a citizenry that is knowledgeable concerning the bio-physical environment and its associated problems, aware of how to help solve these problems, and motivated to work toward their solution" (Stapp et al. 1969 cited in Disinger 1997).

Later, Lucas (1972, 1980, 1980–1981) characterized the perspectives of environmental education based on detailed analysis of early literature. He asserted:

> Uses of the term environmental education can be classified into education 'about' the environment, education 'for' (the preservation of) the environment, education 'in' the environment, and the classes formed by the combinations 'about' and 'for,' 'about' and 'in,' and 'about,' 'for,' and 'in.' Education 'about' the environment, which is concerned with providing

cognitive understanding including the development of skills necessary to obtain this understanding, and education 'for' the environment, which is directed environmental preservation or preservation for particular purposes, are characterized by their aims; education 'in' the environment…is characterized by a technique of instruction. In the 'in' case, environment usually means the world outside the classroom, and in the other usages it usually refers to the bio-physical and/or social context in which groups of people…exist.

(Disinger 1983, 1997)

Interestingly, a similar view is reflected in the Position Paper of the National Focus Group on Habitat and Learning (NCERT, 2006), which promotes a curriculum that focuses on learning 'about' the environment, learning 'through' the environment and learning 'for' the environment in order to achieve the objectives and goals of environmental education and sustainable development. This is discussed in more detail in Chapters 5 and 7.

In 1972, the United Nations Conference on the Human Environment was held in Stockholm, Sweden. This conference is considered one such landmark event in the history of environmental education. Its Recommendation 96 made a call for the introduction of environmental education as a means to address environmental concerns worldwide. The gist of the Stockholm Declaration (Declaration of the United Nations Conference on the Human Environment) is provided in Box 2.2. The conference also identified the need of "creating citizenries not merely aware of the crisis of overpopulation, mismanagement of the quality of human life, but also able to focus intelligently on the means of coping with them." Further, the Declaration of the conference proclaimed, "To defend and improve the environment for present and future generations has become an imperative goal for mankind." It subsequently led to the creation of the International Environmental Education Program (IEEP), jointly funded by the UNESCO and the United Nations Environment Program (UNEP). The IEEP aimed to promote reflection and action, as well as international cooperation in the field of EE. Its principal long-term objectives were: (a) facilitating the coordination, planning, and programming of activities essential to the development of an international program in environmental education; (b) promoting the international exchange of ideas and information pertaining to environmental education; (c) coordinating research to understand better the various phenomena involved in environmental teaching and learning; (d) designing and evaluating new methods, curricula, materials, and programs (both in-school and out-of-school; youth and adult) in environmental education; (e) training and retraining personnel to adequately staff environmental education programs; and (f) providing advisory services to member states in environmental education (UNESCO 1984).

BOX 2.2 DECLARATION OF THE UNITED NATIONS CONFERENCE ON THE HUMAN ENVIRONMENT

The United Nations Conference on the Human Environment, having met at Stockholm from 5 to 16 June 1972, *having considered* the need for a common outlook and for common principles to inspire and guide the peoples of the world in the preservation and enhancement of the human environment, proclaims that:

1. Man is both creature and moulder of his environment, which gives him physical sustenance and affords him the opportunity for intellectual, moral, social and spiritual growth...Both aspects of man's environment, the natural and the man-made, are essential to his well-being and to the enjoyment of basic human rights-even the right to life itself.
2. The protection and improvement of the human environment is a major issue which affects the well-being of peoples and economic development throughout the world; it is the urgent desire of the peoples of the whole world and the duty of all Governments.
3. Man has constantly to sum up experience and go on discovering, inventing, creating, and advancing. In our time, man's capability to transform his surroundings, if used wisely, can bring to all peoples the benefits of development and the opportunity to enhance the quality of life. Wrongly or heedlessly applied, the same power can do incalculable harm to human beings and the human environment.
4. In the developing countries most of the environmental problems are caused by under-development...the developing countries must direct their efforts to development, bearing in mind their priorities and the need to safeguard and improve the environment. For the same purpose, the industrialized countries should make efforts to reduce the gap themselves and the developing countries.
5. The natural growth of population continuously presents problems for the preservation of the environment, and adequate policies and measures should be adopted, as appropriate, to face these problems. Of all things in the world, people are the most precious... Along with social progress and the advance of production, science, and technology, the capability of man to improve the environment increases with each passing day.
6. For the purpose of attaining freedom in the world of nature, man must use knowledge to build, in collaboration with nature, a better environment. To defend and improve the human environment for present and future generations has become an imperative goal for mankind's goal to be pursued together with, and in harmony with, the established and fundamental goals of peace and of worldwide economic and social development.

7. To achieve this environmental goal will demand the acceptance of responsibility by citizens and communities and by enterprises and institutions at every level, all sharing equitably in common efforts...The Conference calls upon Governments and peoples to exert common efforts for the preservation and improvement of the human environment, for the benefit of all the people and for their posterity.

2.6 Initiatives by International Environmental Education Program

2.6.1 First Phase

The action of IEEP in the period 1975–1983 was conducted in three phases, centering successively on the following: (a) development of general awareness of the necessity of environmental education; (b) development of concepts and methodological approaches in this field; and (c) efforts for incorporating an environmental dimension into the educational process of UNESCO member states (UNESCO 1984).

In its first phase (1975–1977), the IEEP organized a series of regional workshops for education practitioners represented by governmental delegations toward creating environmental education policy. These workshops culminated in the final practitioner workshop held in Belgrade (formerly in Yugoslavia, now in Serbia) in 1975, which resulted in the Belgrade Charter of 1975 (UNESCO-UNEP 1976), and the same is reproduced in Box 2.3. The goal as mentioned in this charter is considered to be the most accepted definition of environmental education.

In 1977, the UNESCO together with the UNEP held the Intergovernmental Conference on Environmental Education in Tbilisi, Republic of Georgia. Sixty-six UNESCO member states and several NGO representatives took part. Delegates adopted the Belgrade statement and prepared the Tbilisi final report (the Tbilisi Declaration), which characterizes environmental education as a lifelong process; as interdisciplinary[2] and holistic in nature and application; as an approach to education as a whole, other than a subject; and about the interrelationship and interconnectedness between human and natural systems. The report also formalized the following goals, objectives, and guiding principles to guide UNESCO member states in the development of environmental education policies, which are reproduced here in its entirety (UNESCO-UNEP 1978).

BOX 2.3 THE BELGRADE CHARTER

A Global Framework for Environmental Education
   Adopted unanimously at the close of the 10-day workshop at Belgrade was a statement, subject to modification by subsequent regional meetings, of the framework and guiding principles for global environmental education, which became known as the Belgrade Charter.
   It follows:

A. **Environmental Situation**
   Our generation has witnessed unprecedented economic growth and technological progress which, while bringing benefits to many people, have also caused severe social and environmental consequences. Inequality between the poor and the rich among nations and within nations is growing; there is evidence of increasing deterioration of the physical environment in some form on a worldwide scale. This condition, although primarily caused by a relatively small number of nations, affects all of humanity.
   The recent United Nations Declaration for a New International Economic Order calls for a new concept of development—one which takes into account the satisfaction of the needs and wants of every citizen of the earth, of the pluralism of societies, and of the balance and harmony between humanity and the environment. What is being called for is the eradication of the basic causes of poverty, hunger, illiteracy, pollution, exploitation, and domination. The previous pattern of dealing with these crucial problems on a fragmentary basis is no longer workable.
   It is absolutely vital that the world's citizens insist upon measures that will support the kind of economic growth which will not have harmful repercussions on people and that will not in any way diminish their environment and their living conditions. It is necessary to find ways to ensure that no nation should grow or develop at the expense of another nation and that the consumption of no individual should be increased at the expense of other individuals. The resources of the world should be developed in ways which will benefit all of humanity and provide the potential for raising the quality of life for everyone.
   We need nothing short of a new global ethic—an ethic which espouses attitudes and behavior for individuals and societies which are consonant with humanity's place within the biosphere, and which recognizes and sensitively responds to the complex and ever-changing relationships between humanity and nature, and between people. Significant changes must occur in all of the world's nations to assure the kind of rational development which will be guided by this new global ideal—changes which will be directed toward an equitable distribution of the world's resources and more

fairly satisfy the needs of all peoples. This kind of development will also require the maximum reduction in harmful effects on the environment, the utilization of waste materials for productive purposes, and the design of technologies which will enable such objectives to be achieved. Above all, it will demand the assurance of perpetual peace through coexistence and cooperation among nations with different social systems. Substantial resources for reallocation to meet human needs can be gained through restricting military budgets and reducing competition in the manufacture of arms. Disarmament should be the ultimate goal.

These new approaches to the development and improvement of the environment call for a reordering of national and regional priorities. Those policies aimed at maximizing economic output without regard to its consequences on society and on the resources available for improving the quality of life must be questioned. Before this changing of priorities can be achieved, millions of individuals will themselves need to adjust their own priorities and assume a personal and individualized global ethic, and reflect in all of their behavior a commitment to the improvement of the quality of the environment and of life for the world's people.

The reform of educational processes and systems is central to the building of this new development ethic and world economic order. Governments and policy makers can order changes, and new development approaches can begin to improve the world's condition—but all of these are no more than short-term solutions, unless the youth of the world receives a new kind of education. This will require new and productive relationships between students and teachers, between schools and communities, and between the education system and society at large.

Recommendation 96 of the Stockholm Conference on the Human Environment called for the development of environmental education as one of the most critical elements of an all-out attack on the world's environmental crisis. This new environmental education must be broad based and strongly related to the basic principles outlined in the United Nations Declaration on the New International Economic Order.

It is within this context that the foundations must be laid for a worldwide environmental education program that will make it possible to develop new knowledge and skills, values, and attitudes, in a drive toward a better quality of environment and, indeed, toward a higher quality of life for present and future generations living within that environment.

B. **Environmental Goal**

The goal of environmental action is:

> To improve all ecological relationships, including the relationship of humanity with nature and people with each other.
>
> There are, thus, two preliminary objectives:

1. For each nation, according to its culture, to clarify for itself the meaning of such basic concepts as "quality of life" and "human happiness" in the context of the total environment, with an extension of the clarification and appreciation to other cultures, beyond one's own national boundaries.
2. To identify which actions will ensure the preservation and improvement of humanity's potentials and develop social and individual well-being in harmony with the bio-physical and man-made environment.

C. **Environmental Education Goal**

The goal of environmental education is:

To develop a world population that is aware of, and concerned about, the environment and its associated problems, and which has the knowledge, skills, attitudes, motivations and commitment to work individually and collectively toward solutions of current problems and the prevention of new ones.

D. **Environmental Education Objectives**

The objectives of environmental education are:

1. Awareness: to help individuals and social groups acquire an awareness of and sensitivity to the total environment and its allied problems.
2. Knowledge: to help individuals and social groups acquire basic understanding of the total environment, its associated problems, and humanity's critically responsible presence and role in it.
3. Attitude: to help individuals and social groups acquire social values, strong feelings of concern for the environment, and the motivation for actively participating in its protection and improvement.
4. Skills: to help individuals and social groups acquire the skills for solving environmental problems.
5. Evaluation ability: to help individuals and social groups evaluate environmental measures and education programs in terms of ecological, political, economic, social, aesthetic, and educational factors.
6. Participation: to help individuals and social groups develop a sense of responsibility and urgency regarding environmental problems to ensure appropriate action to solve those problems.

E. **Audiences**

The principal audience of environmental education is the general public. Within this global frame, the major categories are:

1. The formal education sector: including preschool, primary, secondary, and higher education students as well as teachers and environmental professionals in training and retraining;

2. The nonformal education sector: including youth and adults, individually or collectively from all segments of the population, such as the family, workers, managers, and decision makers, in environmental as well as non-environmental fields.

F. **Guiding Principles of Environmental Education Programs**
The guiding principles of environmental education are:

1. Environmental education should consider the environment in its totality—natural and man-made, ecological, political, economic, technological, social, legislative, cultural, and aesthetic.
2. Environmental education should be a continuous life-long process, both in-school and out-of-school.
3. Environmental education should be interdisciplinary in its approach.
4. Environmental education should emphasize active participation in preventing and solving environmental problems.
5. Environmental education should examine major environmental issues from a world point of view, while paying due regard to regional differences.
6. Environmental education should focus on current and future environmental situations.
7. Environmental education should examine all development and growth from an environmental perspective.
8. Environmental education should promote the value and necessity of local, national, and international cooperation in the solution of environmental problems.

Environmental Education Goals

- To foster clear awareness of and concern about economic, social, political, and ecological interdependence in urban and rural areas
- To provide every person with opportunities to acquire the knowledge, values, attitudes, commitment, and skills needed to protect and improve the environment
- To create new patterns of behavior of individuals, groups, and society as a whole toward the environment

Environmental Education Objectives

- Awareness: to help social groups and individuals acquire an awareness of and sensitivity to the total environment and its allied problems
- Knowledge: to help social groups and individuals gain various experiences in and acquire a basic understanding of the environment and its related problems

- Attitudes: to help social groups and individuals acquire a set of values and feelings of concern for the environment and the motivation for actively participating in environmental improvement and protection
- Skills: to help social groups and individuals acquire the skills for identifying and solving environmental problems
- Participation: to provide social groups and individuals with an opportunity to be actively involved at all levels in working toward resolution of environmental problems

Some Guiding Principles for Environmental Education

- Consider the environment in its totality—natural and built, technological, and social (economic, political, technological, cultural–historical, moral, aesthetic).
- Be a continuous lifelong process, beginning at the preschool level and continuing through all formal and nonformal stages.
- Be interdisciplinary in its approach, drawing on the specific content of each discipline in making possible a holistic and balanced perspective.
- Examine major environmental issues from local, national, regional, and international viewpoints so that students receive insights into environmental conditions in other geographical areas.
- Focus on current and potential environmental situations, while taking into account the historical perspective.
- Promote the value and necessity of local, national, and international cooperation in the prevention and solution of environmental problems.
- Explicitly consider environmental aspects in plans for development and growth.
- Enable learners to have a role in planning their learning experiences and provide an opportunity for making decisions and accepting their consequences.
- Relate environmental sensitivity, knowledge, problem-solving skills, and value clarification to every age, but with special emphasis on environmental sensitivity to the learner's own community in early years.
- Help learners discover the symptoms and real causes of environmental problems.
- Emphasize the complexity of environmental problems and thus the need to develop critical thinking and problem-solving skills.
- Utilize diverse learning environments and a broad array of educational approaches to teaching/learning about and from the environment with due stress on practical activities and first-hand experience.

Once environmental education objectives were set in place, nations across the world began to introduce and promote environmental education through the development of curricula, courses, and training programs (Biedenweg, Monroe, and Wojcik 2013, 16). The Tbilisi Declaration became 'the document' for implementers and practitioners all over the world.

2.6.2 Second Phase

The IEEP initiated several programs as part of its second phase (1978–1980) actions. This phase was primarily devoted to the conceptual and methodological development of environmental education with the view to provide member states with useful references for the incorporation of an environmental dimension into general educational practice. In this regard, the IEEP introduced a series of studies and activities concerning different pedagogical aspects of environmental education, launched a series of pilot projects in different countries of various regions of the world, and initiated a series of training workshops and seminars at the national, subregional, and international levels. Publications of a newsletter, *Connect*, and books such as *Trends in Environmental Education* (1977) and *Environmental Education in the Light of the Tbilisi Conference* (1980) were also the highlight of IEEP's activities in this phase (UNECSO-UNEP 1989).

2.6.3 Third Phase

In the third phase of the IEEP (1981–1983), emphasis was placed on the development of content, methods and materials for environmental education practices and training activities; experimental and pilot projects were intensified, with a view to facilitate member states' efforts concerning practical incorporation of environmental education into school and out-of-school education. As for educational contents, methods, and materials relating to environmental education, the IEEP developed a series of studies, research activities, and projects leading to the preparation of methodological guides concerning approaches for the inclusion of an environmental dimension into educational practice (UNESCO 1984).

2.7 Multi-Perspectives of Environmental Education

From the discussions above, it is clear that environmental education is interdisciplinary and holistic and encompasses the environment in totality, that is, biophysical, social, cultural, and economic. Yet, environmental education is still considered to be confined within the boundary of natural science or biophysical environment. Many would not even include the built or man-made environment and restrict their definition of 'environment' to the natural environment only. This, perhaps, has led to the marginalization of environmental education itself in the curriculum. Therefore, there needs to be clarity on how it is defined, or what will be the operational definition for 'environment' in environmental education and the definition of the term 'environmental education' itself. However, it may be noted that this lack of clarity is not surprising as the following discussion will reveal that the problem with this is as old as environmental education itself, which never got completely resolved universally. For example, referring to the range of meaning associated with environmental education, Lucas (1980) had pointed out, "Unless there is a clear change of perception, a developing consensus, a sense of unity and purpose, then environmental education will continue under a cloud of confusion."

In *Environmental Education's Definitional Problem*, Disinger (1983) quoted Hungerford et al. (1983) as follows:

> It is disconcerting (to say the least) for those involved in the implementation of environmental education goals to hear again the question: 'What is environmental education?'…We submit that environmental education does have a substantive structure that has evolved through the considerable efforts of many and that the framework has been documented formally in the literature. The question asked…has most certainly been answered. One would dare hope that this question could, at long last, be laid to rest…the field is quite definitely beyond the goal setting stage and into the business of implementation.

However, even after more than six decades of the first use of the term 'environmental education' in 1948 (Disinger 1983), the same question seems to be still relevant and prevalent today, especially with the 'environment' component of environmental education. There are basic questions that have not been answered. Whether the environment as is used in environmental education includes the entire biosphere or just the organisms, or whether it includes humans as part of the ecosystem, or does it include only 'nature' or 'wilderness,' or whether 'acculturated' human landscapes such as urban parks and gardens are to be considered 'natural environments' are still debated. Kopnina (2012) also mentions the inherent complexity and diversity of the use of the term 'environment' (what is and what is not included in it), wherein throughout the discussion 'environment' has been largely used to refer to the biophysical environment. According to the National Green Tribunal Bill of India, the term 'environment' includes water, air, and land and the interrelationship which exists among and between water, air, and land and human beings, other living creatures, plants, microorganism, and property.[3] This signifies that environment is represented more as an ecosystem in which all the components interact with each other. Social issues in themselves are not included as per the definition provided. Interestingly, a view that deviates from this definition of environment is presented in the recently brought-out National Curriculum Framework for School Education 2023 (NCF-SE 2023), which says, "Environmental Education critically addresses both social and natural concerns. Social concerns include issues of gender and marginalization, equity, justice and respect for human dignity and rights..." (NCERT 2023, 412). This suggests that every issue that a society goes through comes under the purview of environmental education. Such broad characterization of environment and, consequently, environmental education not only creates confusion but will also interfere in its implementation. Had the document clarified that the social concerns mentioned were with respect to environmental issues (i.e., bio-physical), then it would have been well-taken. However, in spite of including social issues under environmental education, when it lays down what should be included across different stages concerning environment as a cross-cutting area, the contents are found to be limited to nature or natural events and phenomena or bio-physical environment alone. When social aspects are included, it is with respect to the bio-physical environment (NCERT 2023, 177–179). The lack of clarity on what environmental education attempts to address is clearly evident in the document. Such a view of broad characterization of environment is not restricted to NCF-SE 2023. The term 'environment' has also been spoken of to include "social, personal, cultural, economic, political, and, of course, biological and physical environments" (Wenzel 1997). It may be noted that, in the context of India, the famous Hon'ble Supreme Court order of 1991 to make environmental education compulsory in all stages of education was based on a petition filed against the increasing issues related to environmental pollution, which is bio-physical in nature. One might wonder, how does it really matter if environmental education is considered to address even social issues which have little to do with bio-physical aspects? The problem is, if purely social issues are also considered under environmental education, it will become so broad that the whole purpose of environmental education will be defeated.

This lack of clarity on what 'environment' includes or excludes has brought about obscurity or vagueness in the understanding of the term 'environmental education' and, hence, impacts its implementation significantly. The lack of clarity on the part of teachers is bound to impact the understandings of the students. In one such study undertaken to find out what students conceive or consider the term 'environment' to be, it was found that most of the students consider only the components of nature (plants, animals, mountains, rivers, but excluding man or man-made environments) to be part of the environment (Shimray, Hoshi, and Sasidhar 2014). Disinger and Howe (1990, 1) discuss two ways by which the definitions of 'environment' can be presented: one in which humans are integral part of the environment (i.e., humankind in environment, as one participating species) and the other in which the environment is considered as the surroundings of humans (i.e., humankind and environment, humans being considered separately from environment, with 'environment' thus defined as 'everything else'). They maintain that the concept of 'environment' is also evolving with the increase in the scientific knowledge about the environment and the understanding of the interactions and interrelationships within the natural environment. This has broadened the original sense of the term 'environment,' which was limited to the biological study of plants and their environments, in an ecological sense to considering the totalities of complex environmental interdependencies which encompass the man-made physical environment and the political, economic, cultural, technological, social, and aesthetic environments, as well as the bio-physical natural environment (Disinger and Howe 1990). Liberty Hyde Bailey, noted botanist, writer, college administrator, educator, and proponent of nature study, had sent out a warning in this regard way back in 1905. He rejected the use of the term "environmental education" in his writing because he considered that it was "imprecise, theoretical, pompous, and would always need to be explained" (McCrea 2006). Rightly so, it still remains to be explained even today. Indeed, it is worth asking what we include in 'environment,' because all the activities and initiatives that would be taken up by the practitioners (used in the broader term to include teachers, teacher educators, curriculum developers, policy makers, and others) of environmental education, would heavily depend on how one envisions 'environment' in the composite term 'environmental education.' Therefore, the question, "How should we conceive the term 'environment' if we aspire to promote conservation and restoration of nature and natural resources through environmental education?" is a critical one and needs to be answered.

From the discussion, the variations in the views about 'environment' and 'environmental education' are clearly evident. Since implementation of environmental education will be shaped depending on the way those terms are understood, it is critical to categorize them. Therefore, what is being attempted in the following discussion is to group environmental education under four perspectives.

2.7.1 Environmental Education Is All-Inclusive

The first view is held by those who are of the opinion that environmental education includes a very broad area of studies which encompasses bio-physical as well as social dimensions. According to this view, the environment is not just about the bio-physical environment or nature but also includes the social as well as cultural and traditional environments. Here, the environment is spatial—anything (bio-physical or social) that is within a space. In their report on *Urban Environmental Education–Demonstration*, Glasser et al. (1972) clearly highlighted that "the environment is the totality of one's surroundings. It involves more than biological factors affected by problems like air pollution and solid wastes problems, it also includes social factors that affect problems like poverty and racism." Further in the same report, they defined the environment as, "Everything surrounding you. Generally, it's a system of forces that knowingly or unknowingly affects you. Specifically it includes a range of social and biological problems." They included recreation, class differences, open spaces, crime, dirt, drugs, solid wastes, housing, overcrowding, pollution, building codes, the consumer and the market place, unemployment, and transportation as part of environmental education. Stapp and Cox (1974, 1974a) also listed ecosystem, population, economics and technology, environmental decisions, and environmental ethics as the five major concepts to be included in environmental education and organized the activities under these themes. This indicated the all-inclusiveness of environmental education—bio-physical environment and social and economic dimensions. This view of environmental education is not held by them alone. Environmental educators such as Disinger and Monroe (1994, 13) also included drug abuse, homelessness, and teen pregnancy as environmental issues to be dealt as part of environmental education.

In an attempt to clarify the meaning of the term 'environment,' Lahiry et al. (1988, 26) include all nonliving and living objects, happenings, and forces—both natural and man-made—which influence the life of an organism. The man-made environment not only included man-made structures and technologies, such as means of agricultural and industrial production, transport and communication, and so on, but also social activities and institutions, such as the family, religion, education, the economy, and politics. Similarly, to humanists, environment is the place of existence, a habitat—with all its historical, cultural, political, economic, emotional, and other aspects as is reflected in place-based environmental education (Sauvé 2005). As mentioned earlier, the National Curriculum Framework for School Education (NCERT 2023, 359) also includes nature and socio-cultural life as part of the environment with environmental education addressing both social and natural concerns. And hence, all these views can be included under this category.

What could be gathered from these views is that all issues irrespective of whether environmental (in this context, meaning bio-physical), social, or economic, exclusively or involving either two or all of it combined, should be part of environmental education. In a sense, this view intends to signify that environmental education has no specific boundary suggesting that all issues that are encountered—from pollution, climate change, deforestation to drug abuse, discrimination based on caste, issues related to religion, dowry, etc.—are to be catered by environmental education. However, though plausible, there are valid concerns if this view were to dictate the curriculum. Making environmental education too broad will do little service in the attempt to restore and conserve the bio-physical environment which is undoubtedly the primary goal of environmental education. This is because, in trying to address all the aspects of environment, which essentially includes everything, focus on restoration and conservation of the bio-physical environment may not garner the attention that it critically demands.

To sum up, according to this view, environmental education is all-encompassing—bio-physical or social (economic and cultural aspects included) in nature. Under this category, examples that would be relevant in Indian context could include social issues such as dowry, female feticide, child marriage, migration, child labor, caste systems, racial discrimination, illiteracy, and poverty, which may not have direct relevance with the bio-physical environment, besides the many bio-physical issues such as those related to pollution, deforestation, wildlife, conservation, biodiversity, and energy.

Such description of an all-encompassing environmental education meets all the characteristics of ESD. The question then is, what was the need to introduce ESD when an all-encompassing environmental education was already existing?

2.7.2 Environmental Education Is Moderately Ecocentric

According to this view, environmental education focuses on addressing bio-physical issues along with its inherent social and economic issues. This view is supported by the fact that environmental education itself became established as a follow-up of the United Nations Conference on Human Environment held at Stockholm in 1972, which met to mainly discuss the issues of deteriorating environment resulting from degradation and pollution. The conference had pointed out that humans transformed the environment (bio-physical) so much so that it changed the balance of nature (more appropriately, the functioning of nature), which would in turn be dangerous for the living species. The declaration of the conference proclaimed the imperative goal for mankind "to defend and improve the environment for present and future generations" (UNESCO-UNEP 1978). In this context, it will be appropriate to recall some of the landmark decisions that were taken at the international level, particularly the Belgrade Charter of 1975 and the Tbilisi Declaration of 1977.

The Belgrade Charter was framed keeping in view the unprecedented economic growth and technological progress which, while bringing benefits to many people, had also caused severe social and environmental (bio-physical) consequences. It was a call to eradicate the basic causes of poverty, hunger, illiteracy, pollution, exploitation, and domination with an aim to improve the quality of life. The need for peaceful coexistence and cooperation was also emphasized. It specifically mentioned that environmental education should consider the environment in its totality—natural and man-made, ecological, political, economic, technological, social, legislative, cultural, and aesthetic. The Tbilisi Declaration voiced the same wherein it mentioned, "to foster clear awareness of, and concern about, economic, social, political and ecological interdependence in urban and rural areas" as one of its goals. Also, its guiding principles reiterated that environmental education should "consider the environment in its totality—natural and built, technological and social (economic, political, cultural-historical, moral, aesthetic)" (UNESCO-UNEP 1978).

Looking at this, there seems to be no difference in the views presented here and the views presented in the previous category. That is, both categories express the all-inclusiveness of environmental education. However, the following statement, which is the first recommendation of the Tbilisi Declaration, sets the two views apart. It mentions:

> Whereas it is a fact that biological and physical features constitute the natural basis of the human environment, it's ethical, social, cultural, and economic dimensions also play their part in determining the lines of approach and the instruments whereby people may understand and make better use of natural resources in satisfying their needs.

This suggests that the 'totality' that is being talked about here is in relation to the factors (ethical, social, cultural, and economic) that are connected to the bio-physical issues, and not just any issue. It does not include those factors which do not have direct relevance to bio-physical issues. For example, it will be difficult and would be stretching too far to relate issues like dowry or caste system with bio-physical issues. Hence, such social issues are not included in this category. On the other hand, social issues such as women walking miles to bring water are inherent to bio-physical issues such as scarcity of potable water. Therefore, while addressing scarcity of water, the problems faced by women will naturally be taken care of. Here is another example. It is known that poverty leads to misuse and exploitation of resources—natural and man-made. Therefore, if resources are to be conserved, then the issue of poverty needs to be addressed first. Hence, poverty, though considered to be a social issue, is included in this category.

Thus, the key difference between this and the previous category lies in the following: the former includes social or economic issues which do not have direct relevance to bio-physical issues under environmental education. The latter includes only those social and economic issues which have relevance or are associated with the bio-physical issues.

From these, it can be concluded that issues related to bio-physical environment is the key concern. At the same time, it is also clear that the approach suggested for tackling such environmental issues is not solely for the conservation of bio-physical environment alone but a holistic one. That is, based on this perspective bio-physical issues is the reason for environmental education. Social and other economic ramifications associated with such bio-physical issues are taken into account accordingly while addressing the bio-physical issues. In short, it takes into consideration the environment (bio-physical), society, and economy which are interconnected while dealing with environmental issues. For example, *jhum* cultivation as it is practiced today is causing environmental degradation in the form of deteriorating soil quality, loss of habitat, and biodiversity, etc. However, the solution is not to simply ban such an agricultural practice. Instead, in order to manage or regulate *jhum* cultivation, not only the adverse impacts of *jhum* cultivation on the environment are considered but other concerns which have direct relevance, such as alternative sources of livelihood, sustainable agriculture, development of vocational skills, and so on, are taken into consideration. Similarly, addressing soil pollution due to excessive use of harmful insecticides and fertilizers is not just about banning use of such chemicals, but other aspects such as impacts on health, crop production, bioremediation, and short-term and long-term economic loss are also taken into account. Hence, though the initial and central focus may be bio-physical in nature, the social as well as economic concerns inherent in it are essentially taken care of. Although the primary goal is to tackle bio-physical environmental issue, as seen in the examples, systems perspective is what is looked for in matters of environmental issues.

This perspective of environmental education, if practiced in letter and spirit in the curriculum, may meet the goal to tackle bio-physical environmental issues without compromising on the socio-economic aspects.

2.7.3 Environmental Education Is Purely Ecocentric

According to this view, environmental education caters only to bio-physical issues. It presents a one-sided approach to environmental issues and lacks the holistic approach to resolve them. That is, the only focus of environmental education is to solve environmental issues and problems with little concern for social and economic impacts that are associated with it. For example, the blanket ban of *jhum* cultivation without any consideration for the life and livelihood of people whose only means of sustenance is *jhum* cultivation since generations and many of their cultures and traditions have been around such practices. This view, in a sense, can also be related to those holding the view that every life has its intrinsic value, irrespective of whether they provide 'benefits' or not. Hence, environmental education should be about conservation or protection of every life form for which economic considerations should not get in the way.

Pro-ESD advocates label environmental education with this perspective and have strong objections to it, thereby justifying the need for ESD. They argue that since the focus of environmental education is on conservation of nature and natural resources, social and other related concerns are ignored. This is true to a certain extent if the focus of environmental education in the earlier days, such as during the 1970s and 1980s, is to be considered, which concentrated on mitigating pollution and conserving natural resources. Further, pro-ESD advocates maintain that if at all environmental education took care of social and other related concerns, it was insignificant. This point was also clearly highlighted in the UNESCO International Implementation Scheme (2005), which, while referring to environmental education says, "While some attention was attached to the social and economic issues inherent in these environmental issues the focus was largely on addressing the ecological impact of ever increasing unrestricted development."

Those who put environmental education under this category are of the opinion that issue resolutions as demonstrated by environmental education are biased toward the bio-physical environment (i.e., ecocentric) and not in favor of people or society at large.

Looking at the actual situation of how environmental education is practiced, the observations stated may be true in many instances. However, that is not what environmental education started off to be. If the roots of environmental education are explored, such viewpoints hold no ground. It may be recalled that social concerns have always been part of the debate and deliberations, even in the past, while addressing environmental issues. For example, in the Stockholm conference in 1972, Indira Gandhi, the then prime minister of India, had made a statement, "Poverty is the worst form of pollution," keeping in view the concerns of the developing country (Strong 1999). The statement may not be very appealing to many at the first instance. However, when it is dissected and expanded the real meaning of the statement can be understood. It is a fact that due to poverty there is often increased exploitation and abuse of natural and man-made resources. Poverty-associated problems also include littering, improper waste disposal, lack of proper sanitation, and so on, which lead to increased pollution of soil, water, and air. When the statement was made, there were staggering populations of people under poverty in developing countries like India. Therefore, it was suggested that if the environment is to be preserved, it is important to first address the issue of poverty. Doing this meant indirectly working toward the preservation of the environment. Also, Tang Ke, leader of the Chinese delegation to the same conference had stated, "We hold that of all things in the world, people are the most precious" (Sohn 1973, 444).

Keeping aside what environmental education started off to be, if this purely ecocentric perspective of environmental education is implemented in the curriculum wherein only the bio-physical environmental issues are addressed in isolation, it will have an unimaginable impact on the socio-economic aspect, thereby pushing sustainable development far away to a distant dream.

2.7.4 Environmental Education Is Purely Anthropocentric

This view assumes that the primary focus of environmental education is to cater to the needs of human beings, with little attention on the physical environment or other life forms. Looking at the pace at which developmental activities are taking place, many indiscriminately and haphazardly, everything seems to be about human beings, the privileged ones at that. This also seems to appear to be the case in sustainable development, or Sustainable Development Goals (SDGs) for that matter. Although caring for the planet is an integral part of sustainable development, it, more or less, revolves around people or humans. If environmental education aims to train students how humans can manipulate the environment for its well-being alone, then environmental education can indeed be considered purely anthropocentric. And if such a view of environmental education is held by teachers and curriculum developers, what implications it could have in the teaching–learning process, and thereby on the students, is a matter of huge concern. Such anthropocentric approach is considered dangerous and hence the promotion of deep ecology philosophy which advocates for equal and inherent worth of all living beings, and that humans are not above any other species in terms of worth.

From the above discussions, for successful implementation of environmental education, it becomes crucial to ask, "How should curriculum designers and developers decide which perspective of environmental education should be adopted in the curriculum?"

2.8 Environmental Education and Education for Sustainable Development

After numerous initiatives at every level, it was felt that environmental education has finally come of age. It was expected that such initiatives would soon bring about the much-anticipated change that was wished to be seen in the world. However, with time, inconsistency began to be seen in the way environmental education was understood, formulated, implemented, and practiced. One of the main reasons for this was that the approaches and priorities pursued through environmental education were strongly influenced by political power, existing environmental issues, social priorities, and trends in educational policy (Biedenweg, Monroe, and Wojcik 2013). At times, it was ecologically biased, while at other times advocacy was the priority. It was felt that environmental education did not address social and economic issues such as poverty, excessive consumption, underdevelopment, and so on, adequately. These compelled the world to think of a more holistic, all-encompassing approach on environmental education which will help tackle serious environmental concerns and which is, at the same time, socially viable.

It was in 1987 that the World Commission on Environment and Development first drew global attention in its report *Our Common Future* (Brundtland Report) on the concept of sustainable development. It highlighted how social and economic factors contribute to environmental problems. This concept was received well by all the nations during the Earth Summit held in Rio de Janeiro in 1992, and the Agenda 21 (meaning, agenda of the 21st century) was drafted, which consisted of 40 chapters (reproduced in Box 2.4). Chapter 36 of the Agenda focused on "reorienting education toward sustainable development; increasing public awareness; and promoting training." In addition, each of the 40 chapters included education as a component in the implementation strategy.

BOX 2.4 AGENDA 21–40 CHAPTERS OF SUSTAINABILITY

Chapter 1: Preamble
Section One: Social and Economic Dimensions
Chapter 2: International Cooperation
Chapter 3: Combating Poverty
Chapter 4: Changing Consumption Patterns
Chapter 5: Population and Sustainable Development
Chapter 6: Protecting and Promoting Human Health
Chapter 7: Sustainable Human Settlements
Chapter 8: Making Decisions for Sustainable Development
Section Two: Conservation and Management of Resources
Chapter 9: Protecting the Atmosphere
Chapter 10: Managing Land Sustainably
Chapter 11: Combating Deforestation
Chapter 12: Combating Desertification and Drought
Chapter 13: Sustainable Mountain Development
Chapter 14: Sustainable Agriculture and Rural Development
Chapter 15: Conservation of Biological Diversity
Chapter 16: Environmentally Sound Management of Biotechnology
Chapter 17: Protecting and Managing the Oceans
Chapter 18: Protecting and Managing Fresh Water
Chapter 19: Safer Use of Toxic Chemicals
Chapter 20: Managing Hazardous Wastes
Chapter 21: Managing Solid Wastes and Sewage
Chapter 22: Managing Radioactive Wastes
Section Three: Strengthening the Role of Major Groups
Chapter 23: Preamble to Strengthening the Role of Major Groups
Chapter 24: Women in Sustainable Development
Chapter 25: Children and Youth in Sustainable Development
Chapter 26: Strengthening the Role of Indigenous People
Chapter 27: Partnerships with NGOs
Chapter 28: Local Authorities
Chapter 29: Workers and Trade Unions
Chapter 30: Business and Industry
Chapter 31: Scientists and Technologists
Section Four: Means of Implementation
Chapter 32: Strengthening the Role of Farmers
Chapter 33: Financing Sustainable Development
Chapter 34: Technology Transfer
Chapter 35: Science for Sustainable Development
Chapter 36: Education, Training and Public Awareness

> Chapter 37: Creating the Capacity for Sustainable Development
> Chapter 38: Organizing for Sustainable Development
> Chapter 39: International Law
> Chapter 40: Information for Decision-Making

Following the World Summit on Sustainable Development (WSSD) held in 2002 in Johannesburg, the United Nations General Assembly in its meeting held in December 2002 proclaimed the period 2005–2014 as the UN Decade of Education for Sustainable Development (UNDESD). It designated the UNESCO as the lead agency to promote and implement the Decade. With this, there has been a transition in the approach to environmental education, and it took the form of ESD in many countries. Is this transition merely putting a new label on an old bottle as some believed in the case of transition from old conservation practices such as conservation education, outdoor education, citizenship education, or resource management education to environmental education (Schoenfeld 1971, 40)? Or is there a significant difference between the two? How different or similar is environmental education from ESD in philosophy and in effect is still being debated among professionals. This aspect is discussed elaborately in Chapter 9.

Today, the focus is shifting toward achieving the 17 SDGs, formulated and adopted in 2015 by the United Nations General Assembly to be achieved by 2030 and therefore also known as the Agenda 2030. It has 169 actionable targets. UNESCO is the leading UN agency in the implementation of the SDG 4—Quality Education. How environmental education can contribute toward achieving this goal and all other SDGs will be discussed in more detail in Chapter 9.

2.9 Chronology of Important Events in Environmental Education

A chronology of important events which shaped environmental education is provided in Table 2.1.

2.10 Conclusion

Dealing with environmental issues is indeed the most important concern for humanity today since its existence itself will be at stake if its ignorance about environmental issues continues. And rightly so, the world recognized that education would be an important tool for a sustainable solution to deal with the issues facing us. Environmental education thus began to be acknowledged in the curricula, without clarity on what it means or is intended to achieve, though. It is true that environmental issues are local specific and resolution will

TABLE 2.1 Chronology of Important Events in Environmental Education

Year	Event
1762	Jean-Jacques Rousseau published *Emile*, an educational philosophy written in the form of a novel wherein he maintains that education should include a focus on environment.
1807	Louis Agassiz was born. He grew up to become a renowned scientist who urged his students to learn directly from nature.
1891	Wilbur Jackman wrote the *Nature Study for the Common School*, which defined the nature study movement.
1930s	The "Dust Bowl" in the American heartland gave rise to the conservation education movement supported by state and federal natural resource agencies as well as many nongovernment organizations.
	John Dewey promoted a more student-centered and holistic approach to education by providing opportunities to explore, reflect upon, and apply newly learned concepts.
1948	Thomas Pritchard, deputy director of the Nature Conservancy in Wales, used the term 'environmental education' at a meeting in Paris of the International Union for the Conservation of Nature.
1949	The Commission on Education of the IUCN and Natural Resources was established to promote environmental conservation education.
1968	The first discussion on environmental education at a global platform took place at the UNESCO Biosphere Reserve Conference held in Paris.
1969	Dr. William Bill Stapp and his students at the University of Michigan formally developed and published a definition of 'environmental education.'
1972	Arthur M. Lucas classified environmental education as education 'about' the environment, education 'in' the environment, and education 'for' the environment.
	The United Nations Conference on the Human Environment in Stockholm, Sweden, was held.
	Recommendation 96 called for the provision of environmental education as a means to address environmental issues worldwide. The IEEP, jointly funded by UNESCO and UNEP, was created to promote reflection and action, as well as international cooperation in this field.
1975	The International Environmental Education Workshop was held in Belgrade (which was then in undivided Yugoslavia, now in Serbia). The delegates ratified the Belgrade Charter, which outlines the basic structure of environmental education.
1977	The International Conference on Environmental Education was held in Tbilisi, Republic of Georgia. The conference laid out the goals, objectives, and guiding principles of environmental education.
1987	The World Commission on Environment and Development published the Brundtland Report (*Our Common Future*), which introduced the idea of sustainable development.
1992	The United Nations organized the Conference on Environment and Development in Rio de Janeiro, Brazil. The Agenda 21 was prepared in which Chapter 36 focuses on "reorienting education toward sustainable development; increasing public awareness; and promoting training."

(*Continued*)

TABLE 2.1 (Continued)

Year	Event
2002	The WSSD was held in Johannesburg. It proposed that the United Nations should consider adopting a decade of ESD, starting 2005. The United Nations General Assembly proclaimed 2005–2014 as the UNDESD.
2014	World Conference on Education for Sustainable Development was held in Aichi-Nagoya, Japan, in November, which not only marked the end of UNDESD but an important milestone for pointing the way ahead.
2015	SDGs were formulated and adopted in the United Nations General Assembly. It includes 17 goals and 169 actionable targets. SDG 4 is on Quality Education.

also require local specificity. However, the larger goals and objectives of environmental education are the same as discussed in the Belgrade Charter and Tbilisi Declaration. And given the fact that environmental issues are very complex in nature as mentioned in the previous chapter, environmental education must be looked at with much seriousness and rigor. And it has been, and will remain, a challenge for teachers to implement environmental education in such a way that students are able to contribute in the actual resolution of environmental issues.

As much as it was important for different countries of the world to come together to collectively press the need to introduce environmental education in the education system, how effectively it can be implemented will also largely depend on the commitment and cooperation of these countries. While some countries are abounded with experts in different areas of environmental education, such as development of resource material, capacity building, advocacy, and so on, many other countries are still struggling to raise experts in these areas.

In order to effectively implement environmental education in the curriculum, it is crucial to understand the terms and perspectives related to environmental education. How one understands environmental education in general and 'environment' in particular will influence how environmental education is practiced or implemented which could be in terms of curriculum development, curricular material development, pedagogy, etc. The differing views of the experts, professionals, and practitioners about the meaning of the term 'environment' have already been mentioned. Such lack of clarity has brought about haphazard implementation of environmental education itself, which has also paved way for the introduction of other strategies such as introduction of ESD. As discussed in the chapter, the different perspectives of environmental education based on the differing views can be categorized into four views: (a) environmental education is all-encompassing, (b) environmental education is moderately ecocentric, (c) environmental education is purely ecocentric, and (d) environmental education is purely anthropocentric. Each view has a message of its own. Looking closely at these perspectives, one thing is clear. That is, the fundamental difference lies in the treatment of the bio-physical environment component. How much emphasis is given to this component categorizes the four views. Nevertheless, each category will serve a good purpose. For example, if the first view is predominant, then it will cater to all the issues facing a society which could be social, cultural, or bio-physical in nature. If the second view is predominant, then issues of bio-physical nature will be addressed holistically. And, if the third view is predominant, then focus will be on solving bio-physical issues, caring little about the socio-economic or cultural aspects. However, with the increasing damage that is meted out to the environment, which in turn has become a threat for the existence of humankind, a perspective with a little more inclination toward the bio-physical environment may be the need of the hour. This could bring about some hope in the restoration and conservation of the already-overexploited and degraded bio-physical environment.

The supposition that environmental education does not address social and economic issues, coupled with fragmentary or nonholistic practices of environmental education by practitioners, fortified the view that environmental education is ecocentric in its approach. This lack of clarity on the limits and boundaries has in a way paved the way for ESD to make its entry into the system. This ultimately led to the birth of the concept of ESD, which is considered to be holistic and more inclusive, encompassing the three dimensions of sustainable development—environment, society, and economy while resolving any issue. ESD could be done either through sustainable development–related education, which include peace education, global education, development education, HIV and AIDS education, citizenship education, and so on, or through full-fledged ESD, which essentially requires the integration of all the three dimensions (Wals, 2009), as it will be discussed in detail in Chapter 9. How similar or different environmental education and ESD are will also be discussed in more detail in that chapter.

An obvious tussle between environmental education and ESD exists. With the present trend heavily focused on ESD, environmental education seems almost redundant. However, in India's context environmental education is here to stay, at least till the Hon'ble Supreme Court's order of introducing environment as a compulsory subject is revoked. However, whether in its original intended form or whatever form environmental education might have taken, or might take, what is important to be recognized and acknowledged is that it remains an indispensable component of education which cannot be replaced or compromised with. This is because, as mentioned earlier, environmental education is all about well-living and well-being of humankind. As a matter of fact, with the unprecedented environmental issues facing us such as climate

58 Introduction to Environmental Education

change, environmental education has become more relevant and important today than ever before.

2.11 Summary

- Environmental concern became a global issue due to the realization of the enormity of adverse effect of development on environment and brought the world together to collectively work toward addressing all environment-related issues facing humanity.
- The necessity and importance of education on the environment to address the issues was highlighted at the United Nations Conference on the Human Environment held at Stockholm in 1972.
- Significant realization about the importance of education in addressing environmental issues led to the introduction of environmental education as an important component in the education system, in schools and colleges.
- The contributions of different pioneers in the field of environmental education as well as the important events that have happened over the decades gave shape to environmental education to be what it is today.
- There are definitely issues related to defining environmental education itself.
- The Belgrade Charter and the Tbilisi Declaration guided nations for effective implementation of environmental education by clearly defining its goals, objectives, and guiding principles.
- UNESCO and the UNEP were instrumental in setting up the IEEP, which strengthened different countries in carrying out environmental education.
- There are multiple perspectives of environmental education stemming from the difference in the view about the terms 'environment' and 'environmental education.' The perspectives are: (i) Environmental Education is All-inclusive, (ii) Environmental Education is Moderately Ecocentric, (iii) Environmental Education is Purely Ecocentric, and (iv) Environmental Education is Purely Anthropocentric
- The perspective held by stakeholders about environmental education will impact its implementation.
- The speculation and understanding that environmental education could not effectively address prevailing environmental issues largely resulted in the introduction of the concept of 'education' for sustainable development.'
- The focus eventually has shifted to the SDGs.

Notes

1 Dr William Bill Stapp, Professor Emeritus at the University of Michigan, Ann Arbor, Michigan, was one among a handful of individuals who had shaped the field of environmental education. He was the first director of the International Environmental Education Program (IEEP) at UNESCO. Bill spearheaded the first

international conference on environmental education held in Tbilisi, Georgia, in 1977. His environmental education program was the first to be unanimously accepted by all 135 UNESCO member nations. Bill was a true champion for environmental education. His contribution in the field is recognized worldwide and for which he earned numerous international, national, and regional awards.
2 The term 'Interdisciplinary' here simply means that environmental education should consider different disciplinary areas, and hence it should not be confused with the 'interdisciplinary or separate subject approach,' which will be discussed in Chapter 5. The term here, indicates the nature of environmental education and not the method. Therefore, it does not exclude the 'multidisciplinary or infusion approach,' which is mentioned in Chapter 5.
3 https://greentribunal.gov.in/sites/default/files/act_rules/National_Green_Tribunal_Act,_2010.pdf (Accessed on September 21, 2023).

References

Biedenweg, K., M.C. Monroe, and D.J. Wojcik. 2013. "Foundations of Environmental Education." In *Across the Spectrum: Resources for Environmental Educators*, edited by Martha C. Monroe and Marianne E. Krasny, 9–28. Washington, DC: North American Association for Environmental Education (NAAEE).

Carson, Rachel. 1962. *Silent Spring*. London: Penguin Books.

Carter, R.L., and Bora Simmons. 2010. "The History and Philosophy of Environmental Education." In *The Inclusion of Environmental Education in Science Teacher Education*, edited by Alec M. Bodzin, Beth Shiner Klein, and Starlin Weaver, 3–16. New York: Springer.

Disinger, John F. 1983. *Environmental Education's Definitional Problem*. ERIC Information Bulletin No. 2. Columbus, OH: ERIC Clearinghouse Science, Mathematics, and Environmental Education.

———. 1986. *Current Practices in Science/Society/Technology/Environment Education: A Survey of the State Education Agencies*. Columbus, OH: ERIC Clearinghouse for Science/Mathematics, and Environmental Education, Ohio State University. Available at: https://files.eric.ed.gov/fulltext/ED281709.pdf (Accessed on July 2, 2023).

———. 1997. Environmental Education's Definitional Problem. Reprinted from: *ERIC Clearinghouse for Science, Mathematics and Environmental Education Information Bulletin No. 2, 1983. An Epilogue EE's Definitional Problem: 1997 Update*. Columbus, OH: RIC/SMEAC.

Disinger, John F., and R.W. Howe. 1990. *Trends and Issues Related to the Preparation of Teachers for Environmental Education*. Environmental Education Information Report No. ED335233. ERIC Clearinghouse for Science, Mathematics, and Environmental Education Information Report. Columbus, OH: ERIC/SMEAC. Available at: http://files.eric.ed.gov/fulltext/ED335233.pdf (Accessed on July 2, 2023).

Disinger, John F., and Martha C. Monroe. 1994. *EE Toolbox—Workshop Resource Manual, Defining Environmental Education*. Ann Arbor, MI: University of Michigan, National Consortium for Environmental Education and Training.

Disinger, John F., and Terry L. Wilson. 1986. *Locating the "E" in S/T/S*. ERIC/SMEAC Information Bulletin No. 3. Available at: http://files.eric.ed.gov/fulltext/ED277547.pdf (Accessed on July 2, 2023).

Glasser, R., B. William Stapp, and J. James Swan. 1972. *Urban Environmental Education—Demonstration*. Final Report. Ann Arbor, Michigan: Michigan University, School of Natural Resources.

Hungerford, Harold R., R. Ben Peyton, and Richard J. Wilke. 1983. "Yes, Environmental Education Does Have Definition and Structure." *Journal of Environmental Education* 14 (3): 1–2.

Kopnina, H. 2012. "Education for Sustainable Development (ESD): the Turn Away from 'Environment' in Environmental Education?" *Environmental Education Research* 18 (5): 699–717.

Lahiry, D., Savita Sinha, J.S. Gill, U. Mallik, and A.K. Mishra. 1988. *Environmental Education: A Process for Pre-service Teacher Training Curriculum Development*. UNESCO-UNEP International Environmental Education Programme Environmental Education Series No. 26, edited by Patricia R. Simpson, Harold Hungerford, and Trudi L. Volk. Paris: UNESCO.

Lucas, A.M. 1972. *Environment and Environmental Education: Conceptual Issues and Curriculum Implications*, PhD Dissertation, Ohio State University. Available at: https://www.researchgate.net/publication/36112785_Environment_and_environmental_education_conceptual_issues_and_curriculum_implications (Accessed on July 2, 2023).

———. 1980. "Science and Environmental Education: Pious Hopes, Self Praise and Disciplinary Chauvinism." *Studies in Science Education* 7: 1–26.

———. 1980–1981. "The Role of Science Education in Education *for* the Environment." *Journal of Environmental Education* 12 (2): 33–37.

McCrea, E.J. 2006. *The Roots of Environmental Education: How the Past Supports the Present*. Environmental Education and Training Partnership (EETAP). Available at: https://files.eric.ed.gov/fulltext/ED491084.pdf (Accessed on July 2, 2023).

Monroe, M.C., E. Andrews, and K. Biedenweg. 2007. "A Framework for Environmental Education Strategies." *Applied Environmental Education and Communication* 6: 205–216.

NCERT, National Council of Educational Research and Training. 1981. *Environmental Education at the School Level: A Lead Paper*. New Delhi: NCERT.

———. 2006. *Position Paper of the National Focus Group on Habitat and Learning*, No. 1.6. New Delhi: NCERT.

———. 2023. *The National Curriculum Framework for School Education*. New Delhi: NCERT

Sarabhai, K.V., K. Kandula, and M. Raghunath. 1998. *Greening Formal Education— Concerns, Efforts and Future Directions*. Ministry of Environment and Forests, Government of India, Centre for Environment Education.

Sauvé, Lucie. 2005. "Currents in Environmental Education: Mapping a Complex and Evolving Pedagogical Field." *Canadian Journal of Environmental Education* 10 (Spring): 11–37.

Schoenfeld, Clay. 1971. "Defining Environmental Education." In *Outlines of Environmental Education*, edited by Clay Shoenfeld, 40–41. Madison, WI: Dembar Educational Research Services. Available at: http://files.eric.ed.gov/fulltext/ED050973.pdf (Accessed on July 2, 2023).

Shimray, C.V., A.N. Hoshi, and R. Sasidhar. 2014. "Preliminary Study of Environmental Awareness of Students with Implementation of Environmental Education in Schools in India." *School Science* 52 (2): 56–62.

Sohn, Louis B. 1973. "The Stockholm Declaration on the Human Environment." *The Harvard International Law Journal* 14 (3): 423–515. Available at: https://wedocs.unep.org/bitstream/handle/20.500.11822/28247/Stkhm_DcltnHE.pdf (Accessed on September 26, 2023).

Stapp, William B., and Dorothy A. Cox. 1974. *Environmental Education Activities Manual, Book 3: Middle Elementary Activities*. Dexter, MI: Thomson–Shore. Available at: https://files.eric.ed.gov/fulltext/ED119946.pdf (Accessed on September 26, 2023).

———. 1974a. *Environmental Education Activities Manual, Book 4: Upper Elementary Activities*. Dexter, MI: Thomson–Shore. Available at: https://files.eric.ed.gov/fulltext/ED119947.pdf (Accessed on September 26, 2023).

Strong, M.F. 1999. *Hunger, Poverty, Population and Environment*. The Hunger Project Millennium Lecture, 7 April 1999. The Hunger Project, Madras, India.

Tilbury, D. 1997. "A Head, Heart and Hand Approach to Learning about Environmental Problems." *New Horizons in Education* 38: 13–30.

UNESCO, United Nations Educational, Scientific and Cultural Organization. 1984. *Activities of the UNESCO-UNEP International Environmental Education Programme (1975–1983)*. Paris: UNESCO.

UNESCO-UNEP, United Nations Educational, Scientific and Cultural Organization-United Nations Environment Programme. 1976. "The Belgrade Charter." *Connect, UNESCO-UNEP Environmental Education Newsletter* I (1): 1–2.

———. 1978. "Tbilisi Declaration." *Connect, UNESCO-UNEP Environmental Education Newsletter* III (1): 1–8.

———. 1989. "Publications of the IEEP." *Connect, UNESCO-UNEP Environmental Education Newsletter* 14 (4): 7–8.

Wals, Arjen. 2009. *Learning for a Sustainable World: Review of Contexts and Structures for Education for Sustainable Development*. United Nations Decade of Education for Sustainable Development (DESD, 2005-2014), Paris, UNESCO. Available at: https://unesdoc.unesco.org/ark:/48223/pf0000184944 (Accessed on September 26, 2023).

Wenzel, Eberhard. 1997. "Environment, Development and Health: Ideological Metaphors of Post-traditional Societies?" *Health Education Research—Theory & Practice* 12 (4): 403–418. Available at: https://www.jstor.org/stable/45109002?seq=5 (Accessed on July 2, 2023).

3

WHY ENVIRONMENTAL EDUCATION?

3.1 Chapter Overview

The question as to why there is a need to have environmental education (EE) when all the concepts that come under its ambit are anyway part and parcel of the existing disciplinary subjects such as science, social science, and other subjects is not just a valid question but necessary to be understood by all and sundry associated with the field of education. The discussions in this chapter revolve around that question. It delves into the nature of different disciplinary subjects so as to bring out the uniqueness of environmental education. It further explains the limitations of other disciplinary subjects to address environmental concerns and hence the need to have environmental education which is interdisciplinary and holistic in nature. The addition of another subject in the school curriculum in the name of environmental education may not be appreciated in the present situation where there is competition for time slots for different disciplines. To address this, this section of the book also delves into the possibilities of converging environmental education with other subjects. It is also a common practice to use the terms such as 'environmental education,' 'environmental science,' and 'environmental studies' casually and interchangeably. Such carelessness can seriously impact its implementation since they serve different purposes. To overcome this, the chapter also attempts to clarify the relations and the distinctions between those terms.

3.2 Introduction

Today, environmental concerns no longer remain a local issue, but have become one big global issue. The world agrees in unison the necessity and the urgency to address the related environmental issues facing every country of the world and the ever-increasing environmental disasters, if not the impending doom. The urgency in the need to spread awareness and educate the entire world on environmental protection and conservation, and how to contain the already-existing problems facing humanity, began to be strongly felt since 1970s. In the light of these considerations, environmental education was introduced, and it gradually became an essential part of formal education world over. As a matter of fact, countries like India have made it mandatory to include environmental education in its curriculum throughout the different stages and levels of education. However, questions still arise in the minds of many about the nature of environmental education vis-à-vis other disciplinary subjects. Some of the questions most often asked include the following: "Why should we have environmental education?" "Is it not possible to address environmental concerns through the existing disciplinary subjects?" "Does it mean that we should have another school subject by the name 'environmental education' to add to the burden of the students?" "Is environmental education different from environmental science or environmental studies, for that matter?" The same questions will haunt those neophytes in the field of environmental education. These questions are not only relevant but are critical because one can only begin to value and appreciate environmental education when one is convinced of the answers to these questions. This chapter throws up some plausible discussions in an attempt to answer the questions. Much of the discussions in relation to other disciplinary areas centers around science education in view of the fact that science has been seen to take the dominant role to deliver environmental education.

3.3 Nature of Disciplinary Areas

As environmental education is introduced in the curriculum, it is expected that all disciplinary areas, including social science, mathematics, art, and language, should incorporate relevant environmental components which is the essence of environmental education. However, Disinger and Howe (1990, 5) reported that in nearly all instances, in both elementary and secondary schools, science courses were found to be 'hosts' for the infusion of environmental topics with social studies courses listed less frequently and other subjects only occasionally. While acknowledging that biology and geography are the subject areas that most are able to identify with environmental education, Fensham (1978 cited in Lucas 1980a) argued that:

> Subjects like literature, social studies, commercial subjects, physical sciences, and mathematics are much more likely to be the real bases that will get at the social values, political organizations, economic policies and structures, technological control and development, and national and international patterns of distribution that determine the environmental situation.

What is being argued here is that biology and geography may introduce environmental education at its best; however, such efforts will hardly be reflected when it comes to actual practices and priorities in the society or when it comes to taking economic or developmental policies and decisions. For example, prioritizing environmental concerns in economics discipline could help in bringing environment to prominence when economic or developmental decisions are taken. Therefore, environmental education is most likely to be effective in terms of impact on the ground when emphasis is given to 'other subjects,' referring to subjects other than biology and geography. This suggests the need to seriously consider integrating environmental education in the teaching–learning of subjects other than those 'traditional environmental education subjects' of biology and geography. However, it is not to be confused with the unique nature every disciplinary area carries with it and also that of environmental education (Carter and Simmons 2010, 11). To understand this better, the first task is to look at the nature of the disciplinary areas.

Some areas may be considered here for the purpose of discussion.

Science/scientific inquiry is based on the following:

1. 'Truth' (though not fixed but provisional and subject to modification in the light of new observations, experiments, and analysis), for example scientific laws and principles
2. Conclusions must be rationally justified by empirical evidence—observation and experiment
3. Objective (i.e., based on facts and not feelings or opinions)
4. Equality (there is no bias)

Speculation and conjecture may have a place in science or more specifically in natural science (biological or physical sciences), but, ultimately, a scientific theory, to be acceptable, must be verifiable by relevant observations and/or experiments. This involves "a systematic process of observing, questioning, forming hypotheses, testing hypotheses through experiment, analysing evidence, and thereby continuously revising our knowledge" (NCERT 2023, 294). However, the methodology of science and its demarcation from other fields continue to be a matter of philosophical debate. Its professed value neutrality and objectivity have been subject to critical sociological analyses. Moreover, while science is at its best in understanding simple linear systems of nature, its predictive or explanatory power is limited when it comes to dealing with nonlinear complex systems of nature. This clearly shows the limitations of science in dealing with complex issues, such as those related to the environment. Yet, with all its limitations and failings, science is unquestionably the most reliable and powerful knowledge system about the physical world known to humans (NCERT 2006a). This nature of science is what forms a very important aspect of environmental education which cannot be compromised with.

Similarly, other disciplinary subjects in humanities, such as language, literature, philosophy, religion, and so on, have its unique nature. It tries to answer to questions related to the following:

1. Meaning
2. Purpose
3. Value
4. Beauty
5. Moral/ethical
6. Equity

Unlike in natural science, answers to these questions are invariably not scientifically verifiable.

Social science, which generally includes economics, history, political science, human geography, psychology, and sociology, is a systematic study of society and its institutions and of the behavior of people as individuals and in groups within a society and their relationships. It carries a normative responsibility to create and widen the popular base for human values, namely freedom, trust, mutual respect, and respect for diversity. It aims at investing in children a critical moral and mental energy to make them alert to the social forces that threaten these values (NCERT 2006b). Although social sciences are considered to be 'scientific' as they involve a systematic and disciplined method of acquiring knowledge which is verifiable, unlike scientific enquiry in natural sciences where 'truth' is obtained, scientific enquiry in social sciences in many instances is able to provide only a factual base or a more general answer instead of a clear and precise answer as in natural sciences.

The above discussion makes it clear that each discipline has its boundaries. How strong or weak, how flexible or rigid, is beyond the purview of the discussion here. By nature, every discipline does not attempt or seek to answer every question or very kind of question. Science tries to answer a few things which are related to physical phenomena and natural processes; similarly, humanities and social sciences also have their limitations. Nevertheless, curricula of different disciplines go beyond their disciplinary boundary to make teaching–learning effective. However, this happens only to a certain limit and is practiced only by a few teachers, which could be because most teachers have expertise in only a specific subject, or simply because they do not feel the need to go beyond their discipline. If any subject or discipline was meant to address everything related to the topic, then there would not exist what is called 'disciplines' or 'subjects'. For example, if science, as a subject, was to address every detail and concerns related to water, such as properties of water, availability of water in different places, water cycle, water disputes, injustice on women as they walk miles to get water, pollution of water due to industries as well as traditional and religious practices, laws on water, and constitutional rights and duties related to water, then subjects such as geography and political science would not be required to address this topics. However, this does not happen due to the disciplinary nature of science. And, therefore, all that a science curriculum includes is the scientific facts and knowledge about water such as properties of water, availability of water, water cycle, and water pollution, while geography takes care of some other aspects and so also does political science. It is in view of the limitations of disciplinary teachings that interdisciplinary thematic approach is increasingly being employed by different educational systems. However, how far can the interdisciplinary nature of dealing with environmental issues through the teaching–learning of different disciplinary subjects be introduced is a valid question.

3.4 Nature of Environmental Education

In the previous chapter, it was seen that the Tbilisi Declaration emphasized the need to create awareness about the economic, social, political, and ecological interdependence through EE. The Declaration also characterized environmental education as a lifelong process; as interdisciplinary and holistic in nature and application; as an approach to education as a whole, rather than a subject; and about the interrelationship and interconnectedness between human and natural systems. It also identified five components to be addressed as part of its objectives—awareness, knowledge, attitude, skill, and participation. Environmental education being interdisciplinary draws upon the specific content of each discipline (Carter and Simmons 2010, 12) so as to make possible a holistic and balanced perspective. This interdisciplinary nature of environmental education makes teaching components of environmental education possible through science, history, language, and so on (Lahiry et al. 1988, 19). As this is done, an attempt is also made to integrate the inputs from different disciplinary subjects so that the learner is able to view the issue from a holistic perspective.

Often environmental problems are presented to students as the issue of depletion of natural resources which needs protection since it serves human interests, while the intrinsic value of nature (including all species) is not reflected (Kopnina 2014). Environmental education overrides such lapses as it addresses value education concerning ethical, social, or aesthetic values (NCERT 1981). This is especially important in the context of decision-making. While science may provide information related to the decision, it does not help in taking value choices (Holsman 2001). Environmental education puts the emphasis on developing environmental values such as inculcating a concern for the environment, a sense of ownership and responsibility, commitment and motivation to participate in improving the environment, and some even going to the extent of prescribing environmental 'morals,' a code of socially desirable behavior (Sauvé 2005). However, conventionally, it does not mean prescribing or teaching any particular set of values but about all of the values (Disinger 2009; Holsman 2001).

In situations where values or ethics are concerned, purely empirical treatment cannot be applied to environmental education. Whether clarifying positions or debating prospective solutions to moral dilemmas, environmental education activities give students an opportunity to develop their ideas of right and wrong and to accept the many 'gray' areas created by different viewpoints (Disinger and Monroe 1994). For example, while discussing about government's proposal to construct a dam in a location which is inhabited by an indigenous population in a classroom, an issue springs up. A set of students who hold the view 'development at all cost' is most probably likely to respond promptly in favor of the construction. However, there could be another set of students who understand the possible impacts on the local inhabitants in terms of their livelihood, rehabilitation, and occupation. The latter set of students in most probability is not likely going to take a stand or decision immediately but would like to be more convinced about the steps taken to avoid emergence of social issues as a consequence of such proposal by the government. There could be yet another set of students who are concerned about the impacts on the natural resources, ecosystem, and wildlife. As students share their views and justify their stands, it will help other students clarify their positions and enhance their understanding of other groups' opinions and values. Often the eventual choice may result from a compromise between conflicting positions and values, as in this case the construction of dam and the displacement of the inhabitants to an unfamiliar place. Environmental education provides such opportunity to explore various value perspectives which will help students understand that often issues are controversial because of different, not right or wrong, ways of looking at information (Monroe 1991).

Another conflicting position most commonly seen or most certainly to be seen is regarding setting up of factories or industries close to human inhabited locality or in forests, or in agricultural area. While factories or industries definitely provide job opportunities, it is also a source of pollution which could be that of air, water, or soil and environmental degradation in general. There will be other social issues associated with it. Taking positions in such a situation is not always easy, and it eventually leads to compromise (Disinger 1986, 1987; Patrick and Remi 1985 cited in Disinger 1986). However, it is not always about positions which are mutually exclusive (here as in this example, a choice between a pollution-free environment and factories), where one has to take a position either to have a pollution-free environment or have pollution-causing factories which also create jobs. There are ways to work out in most cases. Factories and pollution-free environment are not necessarily mutually exclusive. Although it is a fact that most factories always turn out to be polluters, it need not be the rule. There are possibilities that there could be factories with controlled or reduced emission technologies in place and at the same time have all the 'goods' (Kibert et al. 2012, 56). Thus, factories can be set up, jobs can be created, and pollution can be controlled without causing pollution-related impact on the lives of the local populace. These are the skills that environmental education teaches in decision-making about environmental issues. In the process, it prepares them to be independent thinkers.

Although environmental education does not always practice prescribing a value or a set of value or behavior, there are times when advocacy seems to be the best alternative. Such situation is encountered in those cases where conflicts are irreconcilable, as Caldwell (1980, 198–199) states in the following words:

> There are major policy areas involving, among others, questions of land use, transportation, energy, and species preservation, where no amount of joint problem-solving, mediation, or compromise can resolve differences… Where confirmed evidence points unmistakably to outcomes that would maintain or enlarge future options, or where the degradation of the biosphere is threatened, environmental education may appropriately assume an advocacy role. I cannot regard advocacy as inappropriate to environmental education when the destruction of the biosphere is clearly at stake.

Indeed, a fair understanding of social studies, mathematics, and the laws of science is essential to be able to comprehend environmental issues (Sarabhai, Kandula, and Raghunath 1998). And certainly, science is an indispensable component of environmental education since all environmental issues are invariably related to scientific concepts. But science by nature does not deal with such value clarification or taking positions as discussed above. Therefore, Disinger and Monroe (1994) maintained that "science is just one part of EE." While noting that a firm grounding in scientific information was critical to understanding the problems and potential solutions of many environmental issues, it was also noted that the answers to these problems must encompass other disciplines as well. They added that the challenge with environmental education "is to help non-science teachers tackle environmental subjects while helping science teachers cross disciplinary lines." This clearly signifies that, like science, humanities, and social sciences, environmental education has its unique nature—majorly composed of elements from all three, yet different from all three. Therefore, environmental education cannot be isolated from science, humanities, or social sciences, and vice versa. An isolated approach to environmental education will not bring out its holistic perspective since the 'whole' in environmental education is more than the sum of the parts (Sarabhai, Kandula, and Raghunath 1998). This holistic approach of environmental education sets it apart from other approaches used in the teaching–learning of disciplinary subjects and makes learning more meaningful, connects learners to their environment, and helps them in taking appropriate actions regarding environmental issues. Environmental education is therefore often said to be 'good education' (Athman and Monroe 2004; Disinger and Monroe 1994; NAAEE 2004, 1; Sarabhai, Kandula, and Raghunath 1998). A few simple examples to explain how an environmental education classroom could be different from a traditional classroom are provided in Box 3.1.

BOX 3.1   EXAMPLES TO ILLUSTRATE HOW ENVIRONMENTAL EDUCATION IS DIFFERENT

In a typical science textbook, say in Grade 9, a topic on deforestation will only discuss about the reasons for deforestation such as developmental activities, *Jhum* cultivation, etc., and the impact of deforestation such as soil erosion. However, if the same is to be discussed in an environmental education classroom, the teacher would take into consideration the following points:

1. Discuss what will happen to the animals living in such forests.
2. Discuss in terms of carbon sequestration, global warming, etc.
3. Discuss the possible long-term impacts.
4. Discuss if there are people who are dependent on such forests and how they will be impacted.
5. Discuss the concerns of people living in such forests and the problems they would face if they are forced to move out of the forests due to deforestation; how it would impact their livelihood. This will help students change their attitude toward forest dwellers.
6. Help students appreciate the self-sufficiency of forest dwellers and the implications brought about by developmental activities in and around the forests and the people living there.
7. Discuss how developmental activities will benefit the people living there and others after deforestation.
8. Help students critically think about the pros and cons of deforestation in terms of sustainable development.

A few more examples may be considered.

Ecosystem is a topic that is invariably part of the middle school or secondary school science or geography curriculum wherein food chain, food web, and interactions between the components of ecosystem are included. In a typical science or geography class, the focus is on the plants and animals but hardly on the role of human beings or people. However, an environmental education classroom on the same topic of ecosystem will ensure that there are discussions about human interventions resulting in degradation of ecosystems. What kinds of human activities are destabilizing the ecosystem and how they can be addressed will be part of the teaching–learning process. There will also be a focus on what students can do to contribute in the conservation of the ecosystem. An attempt will be made to convey the message that human beings are part of the ecosystem and that ecosystems without human beings will recover and stabilize at some point but human beings will not survive for long in a degraded ecosystem since human beings cannot adapt immediately to the rapidly degrading and changing environment. Most importantly, it will also encourage and involve students to contribute toward conservation of the ecosystem.

A discussion on enhancement of food production in a typical science classroom will focus on the different technologies, techniques, methods, etc. used to enhance food production. However, an environmental education classroom will also bring into the discussion the impacts of such approaches on the environment, how it can improve the economic condition of farmers, how it can help to meet food security, how it can be beneficial to cater to the needs of the population living in poverty, etc.

Similarly, in a biotechnology class where bioremediation is to be discussed the focus will be invariably on the techniques used in bioremediation. While in a classroom which is oriented toward environmental education, the discussion will also include about minimizing the release of pollutants/toxicants in the environment, the need for bioremediation in terms of social justice since those most impacted by toxics in the environment are the poor and the vulnerable population—elderly, children, and those with co-morbidities, etc., and how human beings need to change their lifestyle which is more sustainable, etc.

Unlike other disciplinary subjects, at the heart of environmental education is behavioral and attitudinal change. This feature also contributes to the uniqueness of environmental education. It envisages that the knowledge gained, skills developed, or values imbibed should translate into behavioral change or environmentally responsible behavior, that is, it should lead to certain positive actions. Without this, all attempts to protect and conserve the deteriorating environment can never be achieved. However, such behavioral change does not occur easily or naturally. It involves a complex array of factors which contribute to such behavioral change. The detail about environmentally responsible behavior is discussed in Chapter 4.

Finally, the million-dollar question is: Is there going to be another subject as environmental education? Or, is environmental education adding burden to the already-existing disciplinary subjects in schools? Several approaches on how environmental education can be implemented have been worked out by professionals and curriculum developers. Environmental education can be made a separate subject by incorporating inputs from different subjects or along with science, humanities, and social sciences or a combination of both. This option is left to the curriculum developers and teacher. As it will be discussed in detail in Chapter 5, each approach has its pros and cons. However, given the present situation where there is so much competition for time and space in the school time frame, besides the already-loaded curriculum, incorporating inputs into different disciplinary subjects might well be more acceptable to the stakeholders. But keeping in view the escalating environmental problems and issues emerging everywhere today, the choice should be based on what ought to be done and not on convenience. However, it is clear that having a separate environmental education subject is not the only option.

3.5 EE and Science–Technology–Society (STS) Education

The interactions of science and society are often implicitly or explicitly reflected in science and social studies education. Lucas (1980a, 1980b), in his review of literature related to science education, found that many science education programs carried an implicit view that science needs to be taught in a way that reflects the social issues that arise from the application of science, or which can be considered as candidates for an application of science. During the same time, due to the accelerating development and use of new technologies at the science–society interface, the problems of human society had exacerbated. This resulted in the STS movement which has been drawing attention since the 1970s. One of the earliest mentions of STS appears to be in 1971 by Jim Gallagher in *Science Education*, wherein he had predicted that in a democratic society it would be important to understand the interrelationships of science, technology, and society, as much as it would be important to understand the concepts and processes of science (Pedretti and Nazir 2011). STS education was proposed following the rationale that "understanding of the interactions of science and society, is of central importance to citizens individually and collectively, and that schooling can and should, perhaps must, address this concern squarely" (National Commission on Excellence in Education 1983 cited in Disinger 1986), and through which attempts were also made to raise environmental awareness by way of science and social studies education (Disinger 1986).

There is no denying that much of the goals of environmental education and STS approach are common or at least some direct crossover exists between environmental education and STS education, as Rubba (1987) puts in the following words:

> All science and technology-related societal issues impact the biosphere. Still, we tend to differentiate between 'environmental' and 'STS' issues. Those science and technology-related societal issues for which we recognize direct or overt ecological connections (e.g., energy consumption, land use, waste management, water quality) are referred to as 'environmental' issues. These so-called environmental issues have been the primary focus of environmental education over the past two decades. Science and technology-related societal issues for which the ecological connections are of a more extended and covert nature, and for which the science–technology aspects are more easily recognized (e.g., sexually transmitted diseases, the right to

life/death, technology in the workplace, organ transplantation) we tend to refer to as 'STS' issues. Societal issues with a strong STS flavor typically have not been dealt with in environmental education programs.

In fact, characterization of environmental education clearly indicates that it foreshadows STS emphases with its explicit and necessary interconnections with science and technology and the issues and problems of society (Disinger and Wilson 1986). Further, Volk (1984, cited in Disinger 1986) finds that environmental education and STS are identical in many respects and notes that much of the experience that educational community has had with STS education has been accomplished under the rubric of EE. As environmental educators practice serious issue-oriented education, the goals of STS can be achieved (Volk 1984 cited in Disinger and Howe 1990).

However, gaps that exist between theory and practice, which are described by some to be as wide as between 'science' and 'humanities' (Snow 1963 cited in Disinger 1986), are what makes it practically unsound to address environmental education through STS approach (as part of science education). For example, though the theory of STS existed, teachers had not been prepared toward that end accordingly so that it can be practiced. Thus, it was difficult for 'practice' to catch up with 'theory.' According to Harms (1981 cited in Disinger 1986), statistics indicated:

> Ninety percent of practicing science teachers emphasize goals directed toward preparing students for further formal study of science, that 99 per cent of science teachers have a philosophical orientation only toward a specific science discipline, and that more than 90 per cent of all science teachers use a textbook 95 per cent of the time, so that the textbook in effect sets the course outline, the framework, the parameters for student experience, testing, and their worldview of science.

Such facts revealed that teachers were neither equipped nor inclined to incorporate environmental issues or its inherent social issues through science curriculum. Besides, other factors such as use of purely science textbook and testing based on science knowledge alone acted as additional barriers to consider STS approach in the curriculum. As a result of these, actual implementation of STS programs has been found to be minimal (Yager 1984, 35–37 cited in Disinger 1986). Social studies educators also note a disparity between 'what should be' and 'what is' with respect to theory and practice, similar to that identified by the science education community (Disinger and Wilson 1986). The limitations of STS in achieving the goals of environmental education are also evident from the fact that science teachers use traditional instructional procedures such as discussions, lectures, audiovisual media, and labs which are limited to knowledge and awareness components only and do not empower students to take appropriate action, which is the ultimate goal of environmental education (Rubba 1987).

Pedretti and Nazir (2011) pointed out the fact that there exist widely differing discourses on science–technology–society–environment (STSE) education and that diverse ways of practicing have led to an array of distinct pedagogical approaches, programs, and methods. They revisited the orientation of STSE education in science education over the course of four decades of its implementation in *Currents in STSE Education: Mapping a Complex Field, 40 Years On* and identified six currents (used as a metaphor to represent ideas, principles, and practices) in STSE education:

1. Application/design (wherein it focuses on students on solving utilitarian problems through designing new technology or modifying technology)
2. Historical (wherein it focuses on extending students' understanding of the historical and socio-cultural embeddedness of scientific ideas and scientists' work)
3. Logical reasoning (wherein students are introduced to risk/benefit analysis, stakeholder analysis, and use of argumentation and decision-making models)
4. Value-centered (wherein it focuses on enhancing student understanding and/or decision-making about socio-scientific issues (SSIs) through explicit consideration of ethics and moral reasoning),
5. Socio-cultural (wherein it focuses on enhancing student understanding of science and technology as existing within a broader socio-cultural context, sometimes interacting with but, at other times, existing collaterally with other forms of knowledge)
6. Socio-ecojustice (wherein the focus is not simply on understanding the impacts of science and technology on society and environments, but on critiquing and solving these problems through human agency and action) currents

While currents such as value-centered, socio-cultural, and socio-ecojustice could very well mirror the concerns of EE, currents such as application/design (which could also encourage students to become solely reliant on technological solutions to all problems) and logical reasoning (which fail to address nonlogical factors such as feelings, values, spirituality, cultural norms, and politics, which are critical in issue-based education) could help little in achieving the goals of EE. Moreover, their focus of STSE education was in science education alone, as if STSE education was the subject matter of science curriculum only. How competent the science teachers are in the area of socio-cultural dimensions so as to be able to practice STSE education meaningfully is another question that demands serious attention.

With time, the possibilities of raising environmental awareness through science education have been acknowledged especially with the introduction of the STS approach and inclusion of SSIs. SSI is a field with similar principles as STS which "focuses on empowering students to consider how science-based issues reflect, in part, moral principles and elements of virtue that encompass their own lives, as well as the physical and social world around them" (Zeidler et al. 2005, 358 cited in Pedretti and Nazir 2011). However, in spite of such attempts, limitations that are inherent to science education remains to be an issue. Hadzigeorgiou and Skoumios (2013) also strongly raised their apprehension regarding the associated problems owing to the nature of science itself. They pointed out that science education fails to answer the 'significance' or 'purpose' or 'why should we know?' component, which is fundamental to raising environmental awareness. They argued that students might have studied science but they were not aware of what they had learned. In other words, students are not able to place what they have learned in the context of their life or reality. For example, students may know the detailed process of photosynthesis but they are not aware of the connection of the process with their life or in the sustenance and maintenance of life on earth. They seem to fail to recognize that as much as photosynthesis is important for the plant for their survival, it is also a life support for other organisms which depend on the oxygen and the food it produces. Students are unable to visualize the 'big picture.' There are also other concerns and drawbacks pointed out by Hadzigeorgiou and Skoumios (2013) regarding science education. For example, ethical/moral discourse and aesthetic appreciation of nature are not seriously considered in science education, which otherwise are indispensable in environmental education. They argued that such discourses and practices are very crucial since it help students become aware of the wider significance of environmental issue as well as mold their outlook toward such issues.

Environmental education, on the other hand, envisages letting students think 'differently' and more holistically. For example, when a child sees a tree, she does not merely understand it as a carbon dioxide-taking, oxygen-giving entity or does not merely visualize the cells and stomata present on the leaves, but also sees the shade it provides, the birds that perch on the branches and the nests they build, the insects that crawl on the trunks, the roots that hold the soil together, the water it absorbs from the soil, the water it releases from its leaves through the stomata in the form of water vapor by the process called transpiration, which contributes in water cycle, and so on. Similarly, when a child uses a computer, she understands that many resources such as water, chemicals, and metals have been utilized to manufacture it, many of which can be recycled, and, most importantly, it requires energy (mostly obtained from burning of fossil fuels which produces greenhouse gases during the process) to run it. She also understands that electronic wastes have become a major environmental concern, releasing hazardous chemicals such as mercury, lead, cadmium, etc., which impact the health, especially those of ragpickers, sorters, recyclers, and so on. She understands the scientific concepts along with the other concerns—social, environmental, or economic—associated with it. Such broader understanding is not brought out through the STS approach in science education or social science education.

The above discussions suggest that though it has been difficult to achieve the goals of environmental education by way of STS approach through science education, the issue is not with the nature of STS as such. The reasons include lack of implementation strategies such as preparation of teachers to integrate STS approach in science education and the nature of science itself which does not naturally accommodate social and economic concerns or value aspects in its discourses. Similar issues will be met in social studies education. Besides, it will not be the best consideration to encourage STS through science and social studies education at the expense of EE.

However, it is also a fact that the content to be provided through environmental education is to a significant extent subsumed in the STS education. Due to this, it has been argued that the inclusion of the term 'environment' in the title of the S/T/S (Disinger 1986; Lubbers 1986 cited in Disinger and Wilson 1986) such as S/T/S/E, S/S/T/E, and S/E/T/S, would make more sense (Disinger and Wilson 1986). Indeed, STS education gradually evolved to include the environment (E) component and subsequently came to be known with the acronym STSE (Pedretti and Nazir 2011).

3.6 Converging Environmental Education with Science Education: Possibilities and Limitations

As has been discussed, science education provides a favorable platform to implement environmental education since all environmental issues are invariably related to scientific concepts. And topics such as resource management, biodiversity, and other related topics have traditionally been addressed within science education (Feinstein and Kirchgasler 2015). However, it is a fact that implementation of environmental education through science education has been found to be limited to providing scientific information and content knowledge on environmental issues. This information-based transmission of environmental contents and facts is not environmental education at all.

In spite of the above facts and practices, converging environmental education with science education is not only a possibility but has become a necessity. However, this convergence should not impede or interfere with the possible convergence of environmental education with other disciplinary areas. Instead, other disciplinary areas should follow the same. There are several reasons for the need to converge environmental education with science education: (a) since environmental education is interdisciplinary in nature, it cannot be left out of science education, (b) to avoid introducing environmental education as a separate curriculum subject, and (c) the introduction of an infusion approach of environmental education. In fact, the long association of environmental education with science education is well known, and science has been the dominant subject for infusion (Gough 2013, 10). Studies suggests that such infusion benefits science education, surprisingly to an extent not thought of, though the underlying purpose of such infusion is to promote environmental education. The reason being that science education in itself is not able to draw students' attention anymore (Gough 2008). The various researches from the Proceedings of the World Conference on Science and Technology-2007 pointed out a widespread lack of student's interest in school science and technology education as manifested in their declining performance, the reasons for which are varied—lack of relevant, authentic contexts, inappropriate pedagogy, etc. This is consistent with other research findings, such as Othman (1999) cited in Petra (2007), which found the disconnect in the language and culture of science to be the cause, while Kanagasabai (1995) cited in Petra (2007) found the reason to be failure of teachers to stress the relevance and importance of the concepts of science to their everyday life.

Nevertheless, there are reasons to cheer about. Numerous surveys and research studies have shown that students are interested in the environment. Some of the topics that students are keen to learn about include the ozone layer and how it might be affected by humans, what can be done to ensure clean air and safe drinking water, the possible radiation dangers of mobile phones and computers, and how to protect endangered species (Gough 2008). Such environment-related topics find place in science curriculum and careful planning of pedagogy, and applying an appropriate approach can bring about meaningful environmental education and at the same time increase students' interest in the subject—in this case, science (Feinstein and Kirchgasler 2015). Thus, science education can play an important part in the implementation of environmental education, and the two can complement each other very well.

However, there are several questions that arise as an attempt is made to converge environmental education with science education. For example, can the goals of environmental education be really achieved through such initiatives as simply incorporating environment topics in science transacted by untrained teachers? Is environmental education being used to enhance learning in science? Is science course being made only 'environmental' as Lucas (1980b) mentioned, in the sense of using current environmental concerns as a vehicle for promoting the study of science or for developing themes 'about' science, particularly as a method of demonstrating or discussing the social relevance of science or the social responsibility of scientists? Or are the goals of environmental education proposed to be achieved through science? These are the questions to be considered more deeply by science educators. Unless science educators are sure of what they want to achieve, convergence of environmental education in science education in its true sense can never be expected. For this to happen, as Gough (2008) pointed out, it will require a major reconstruction of science education.

In 'Science and Environmental Education: Pious Hopes, Self-praise and Disciplinary Chauvinism,' Lucas (1980a) presented a thorough review of literature relating to science and environmental education where he concentrated on material written by science educators or scientists and published in journals, books, and pamphlets likely to be read by science educators. His review was based on his classification, or, rather, definition of environmental education as mentioned in Chapter 2 as education 'about,' 'in,' and 'for' the environment. In spite of science taking on the dominant role in environmental education, he found little evidence that science education had made any successful contribution to the goal of enhancing the preservation of man's environment. This, he said, was because science educators were fully not aware of the complete definition of environmental education, and hence their narrow focus was on the 'about' and 'in' components while ignoring the most important component, 'for.' In his review, he found that some literatures presented the view that science teachers are able to teach the content of other subject areas which is a sheer act of labeling science educators superior. The most extreme statement of this position that he came across was in McMichael and Strom's (1975) suggestion that high school 'science' courses should include topics on society; aesthetics; cultural heritage; freedom, justice, and responsibility; and economic systems. Lucas also found that science educators themselves feel that they are superior and hence do not need to draw upon literature available in other disciplines which focuses on the aims of, and issues in, environmental education. These educators seem to believe that science is 'the' vehicle for environmental education through which they can achieve all that environmental education looks to achieve. Lucas called this unjustified glorification of science by science educators as 'omnipotent disciplinary chauvinism.' Such glorification of science and science educators is unjustified because without any competence in the area of environmental education it is doubtful that these science teachers will be able to handle environmental issues appropriately. To substantiate this view, Lucas cited Arnsdorf, who commented as follows: "As a result, if social, political, geographical, economical and historical dimensions of environmental issues are taught, they are often under the tutelage of faculty with inadequate preparation." This indicates the dangers of resting environmental education entirely in the hands of science educators. Thus, sticking the field of environmental education just to science would also mean a disservice to a generation to develop the ability to critically evaluate issues and to apply skills in citizen action to resolve those issues (Holsman 2001).

However, his review also indicated that many science education programs and projects that were taken up in different countries showed some relevance to environmental education but in different ways, which he grouped under three categories: (a) such courses which are only 'environmental' in the sense of using current concerns as a vehicle for promoting the study of science, and hence environmental education is subsidiary; (b) those where science courses use an environmental organizing theme; and (c) those which have strong environmental education component (illustrating the impact of science on society and its interaction with other aspects of human life and hence most relevant). Lucas also maintained that the remarkable success of achieving the goals of environmental education through science education as claimed in many literatures is without any supporting or evaluative evidence. He found little evidence to show that science education can help achieve the goals of environmental education, especially the goals of educating 'for' the environment. The only evidence Lucas found were typically self-reports by teachers who describe their programs or a very small-scale study of the effects of particular teaching techniques. Hence, he labels the effectiveness of such environmental education programs as nothing more than 'self-praise' and 'pious hopes.' He also found very few science educators or scientists like Baer (cited in Lucas 1980a) suggesting the need to include values such as play, festivity, beauty, wonder, and praise in the understanding of and treatment of nature, an area which is not naturally reflected in the science curriculum, which otherwise is a very important aspect of environmental education.

The literature review of those pertaining to environmental education as well as science for environmental education revealed that development of attitudes has been given too much emphasis when it, without action, will not produce the desired environmental conditions (Lucas 1980b). Therefore, it is important that environmental practices and researches should also focus on the appropriate behavior or actions. Toward resolution of the impending issues on how education 'for' the environment can be best implemented, Lucas (1980b) cited the view of Fensham and May (1979), who suggested the concept of a core curriculum wherein environmental education forms one of the prime concerns with education 'for' the environment clearly elaborated.

A few years ago, Feinstein and Kirchgasler (2015) conducted a study to find out how the Next Generation Science Standards (NGSS) in science education approach sustainability, wherein they concluded that there are three major concerns on how sustainability has been projected in the NGSS: (a) Universalism, wherein sustainability issues are projected to be universal, the benefits and harms are equally shared by all. The fact however is that some humans are more responsible for existing sustainability challenges while others suffer the consequences more severely. (b) Scientism, wherein most questions related to sustainability issues can be answered by science. The fact however is that sustainability is a complex problem requiring multiple sources of knowledge. (c) Technocentrism, wherein sustainability issues are portrayed as a set of problems to be addressed with technical knowledge and technological solutions. The fact however is that sustainability issues have much to do with ethics, values, and decision-making. It is therefore important that science education looks into these concerns more seriously.

In spite of the many issues surrounding the convergence of environmental education with science education, the idea of convergence makes a lot of sense in the school curriculum. Such convergence will result in a win-win situation for both environmental education and science education, as Gough (2008) puts it in the following words:

> By bringing science education and environmental education together in the school curriculum, science content is appropriate to a wider range of students and more culturally and socially relevant. The convergence is also important for environmental education, because it needs science education to underpin the achievement of its objectives and to provide it with a legitimate space in the curriculum to meet its goals, which are very unlikely to be achieved from the margins. Adopting an environmental education approach might be just what science education needs. However, the task is to convince those who control the school curriculum and those who teach science in classrooms that science education needs to change.

3.7 Environmental Education–Environmental Science–Environmental Studies

The nature of environmental education and how it can be integrated in different disciplinary subjects have been discussed elaborately. However, there seems to be no clarity about whether environmental education is the same as environmental science and environmental studies, or whether each of these is distinct from the other. Concerns related to the lack of clarity of the terms have been pointed out by many (Filho and O'Loan 1996, 29 cited in Monde 2011; Harde 1984) and have been considered to be barriers in the successful implementation of environmental education (Monde 2011). It is seen that, more often than not, the terms 'environmental education,' 'environmental science,' and 'environmental studies' are used synonymously. While it is true that environmental education cannot make sense without having the basic understanding of the environment which is the concern of environmental science, the objectives of the two are different. Davis (1978a cited in Harde 1984) argues:

> Environmental Science largely is a disciplinary or multidisciplinary approach to the scientific and technical aspects of manipulating, modifying, or preserving our natural environment. Emphasis is generally placed on the physical sciences, on the ecologically-oriented biological sciences, on engineering and on statistical and computer modeling.

In an attempt to bring out the relationship between environmental education and environmental science, Carter and Simmons (2010, 12–13) assert the following:

> A major contributor to the EE knowledge base is environmental science. Environmental science is the engine of data collection and knowledge

creation, while EE is the vehicle for dissemination and application of that knowledge with environmental literacy as the ultimate goal…There can be no argument that EE and environmental science are very closely intertwined and interdependent, but to say that they are one and the same is to say that science and education are the same.

Further, the objectives of environmental science is restricted to focusing on the awareness and knowledge components of the environment, while environmental education includes the dimensions of attitudes, value, skills (Monroe 1991), and opportunities for participation in the issue resolution.

Similarly, environmental studies has its own objective. Nash (cited in Harde 1984) argues that the basic concept in environmental studies is the study of humans as they affect and are affected by their environments and further identifies the most distinguishing characteristic of environmental studies as its recognition that the welfare of the total environment may require a subordination of the parochial interests of humankind. As defined by Harde (1984), environmental studies is the interdisciplinary search for knowledge about and understanding of natural (physical and biotic) systems and of the dynamic interactions between these systems and humankind's social and cultural systems. In order to characterize environmental studies, the following factors or criteria mentioned in Disinger and Schoenfeld (1988); Schoenfeld (1971, 111–112); Schoenfeld and Disinger (1978, 8–9) seem to be implicit:

1. Concern with the environment of humankind: the concept in environmental studies is the study of humans as they affect and are affected by their environments.
2. Concern with the total environment: its social, cultural, economic, and aesthetic, as well as physical and biological aspects.
3. Concern with interdisciplinarity: contributions which can and must be made individually and collectively by all the arts, sciences, and professions.
4. Concern with problem-solving and the clarification of open-ended options, as opposed to 'ivory tower' studies (separated from real life problems).
5. Concern with configurations that transcend traditional lines of endeavor, with central focus on the relationships between humankind and the total environment.

Recognizing the importance of environmental sciences in environmental studies, Schoenfeld and Disinger (1978) label the former as the biophysical 'hardware' of environmental studies in contradistinction to the social science and humanities 'software.' Fields such as meteorology, climatology, plant and animal ecology, oceanography, agriculture, geochemistry, soil engineering, civil engineering, and many more are included under environmental science (Harde 1984; Lapedes 1974 in Schoenfeld and Disinger 1978). On the other hand, environmental studies seek to bring perspective to both the sciences and the arts (Schoenfeld and Disinger 1978), and it is "a new way of looking at a variety of old disciplines, their relationships, and their potential contributions" (Schoenfeld 1971, 112). Hence, though environmental sciences play a major role in environmental studies program, its contribution is only partial (Nash 1974 cited in Harde 1984).

Often, environmental science is deemed to be merely a subset of environmental studies and is considered to treat only the symptoms of man's dysfunction with his physical environment. It is also believed that the ultimate solution to environmental problems is to deal with those areas related to human values, attitudes, and policy which are in the purview of environmental studies. However, due to the accelerating environmental problems arising from uncontrolled technology and lifestyles such as air and water pollution, solid waste accumulation, wasted energy, and multiple pressures on the land, Frey (1978 cited in Harde 1984) argues that such are precisely the kinds of problems which can best be solved through the application of the principles found in the biological, physical, and engineering sciences, that is, programs in environmental science. He goes on to say that "Rather than to dwell on the differences between the concerns of environmental studies and environmental science, and perhaps unnecessarily develop internecine warfare, let me simply say we need both approaches."

Although environmental education, in its broadest sense, is the designation used to refer to all forms and levels of facilitating learning and disseminating knowledge about the environment and humanity's impact upon it, the terms 'environmental studies' and 'environmental education' have been often used interchangeable. Those which differentiate between the two consider environmental education as the process of acquiring, and applying, the content of environmental studies (Schoenfeld and Disinger 1978). It is also commonly observed that in many universities environmental education is the province of the school or department of education, while environmental studies is found to be associated with any or all other schools or colleges (Schoenfeld and Disinger 1978, 10). While schools and colleges of education developed courses in environmental education pedagogy and research, universities themselves tended to adopt the rubric 'environmental studies' as their umbrella term (Schoenfeld and Disinger 1978, 12). In spite of this segregation being adopted in the universities, environmental education or environmental studies has a basic message—interdependence—implying that everything is connected to everything else (Schoenfeld and Disinger 1978, 13).

It has also been argued that environmental education does not give importance to the content but emphasis is placed on developing effective methods and vehicles for presenting the content to school students and the general public. Hence, it is considered to be 'delivery-oriented' (Davis 1978 cited in Harde 1984).

While in the broadest use of the term 'environmental education,' environmental studies is enclosed under its umbrella, in the narrower sense of the term 'environmental education' is a distinct professional specialization that falls outside the field of generalized environmental studies. In that usage, environmental education is not synonymous with environmental studies, although courses from the curriculum of environmental education and environmental studies contribute to the curriculum of the other (Harde 1984). In contradistinction to the predominant thrust of EE, Craig B. Davis (1978 cited in Harde 1984) points out:

> Environmental studies is more than a series of instructional programs for training undergraduate and graduate students. It is also a field of scholarly pursuit. Faculty members engaged in environmental studies are, for the most part, keenly interested in examining the body of knowledge, sifting it, resorting it, and examining it again with the hope and expectation that their efforts will shed some light on the interrelationship of man, culture, society and the environment. It is this pursuit of knowledge that is the true raison d'etre for the field of environmental studies.

Notwithstanding its distinction from environmental science and EE, environmental studies is 'virtually synonymous' with Human Ecology, it being an effort to merge human sociology and ecology, and dealing with the interaction of human culture and the environment, drawing on the social and natural sciences, as well as on the humanities, to present a broad view of the phenomena of human culture. But it is not synonymous with Ecology, which is a systems approach to various specializations of the biological sciences. As such, Ecology does not draw sufficiently upon the other disciplines to achieve a total approach to the complex of activities defined as environmental studies (Harde 1984).

While environmental studies is offered as a course consisting of several areas/papers in general, in India, Environmental Studies (EVS) at the primary education is introduced as a composite area of study with insights drawn from sciences, social sciences, and environmental education and visualized as 'child-centered' (NCTE 2009, 2015). However, with the implementation of the National Curriculum Framework for School Education 2023, instead of Environmental Studies, The World Around Us will be introduced at the primary stage (NCERT 2023). The nature of the discipline will remain the same though.

Table 3.1 provides a better picture of the relationship among the three. The table shows that clear-cut differences are not seen in some of the points, clearly indicating that the three cannot be completely isolated from each other.

Further, when it comes to actual implementation or practice or in the teaching–learning process, the dividing lines among the three may not remain

TABLE 3.1 Relationship of Environmental Education—Environmental Science—Environmental Studies

	Environmental Education	Environmental Science	Environmental Studies
1	In preservice courses (courses for prospective student-teachers), deals with designing effective educational methodologies/pedagogies and communication strategies to transact environmental concerns. That is, 'how to teach' is given emphasis.	Designing educational methodologies/pedagogies is not part of the curriculum.	Designing educational methodologies/pedagogies is not part of the curriculum.
2	Addresses questions which are not scientifically verifiable such as those related to values and ethics. Not restricted to scientific enquiry method.	Restricted to scientific enquiry method. Addresses questions which are rationally justified by empirical evidence.	Addresses questions which are not scientifically verifiable such as those related to values and ethics. Not restricted to scientific enquiry method.
3	Process-oriented. It is an educational process aimed at building awareness, knowledge, attitudes, skills, and participation to tackle environmental concerns. It is holistic taking into account the social, environmental, and economic aspects.	Content-oriented. Its objective is to teach specified topics related to the environment through dissemination of scientific information and knowledge.	Content-oriented. Its objective is to teach specified topics related to the environment holistically by taking into account the social, environmental, and economic aspects.
4	Necessarily participatory.	Often one-way mode of transaction.	May be participatory.
5	Interdisciplinary and integrated in disciplinary subjects such as science, social science, earth science, environmental science, languages, mathematics, psychology, economics, and arts, or as a separate subject as environmental education.	Partially interdisciplinary and integrated in disciplinary subjects such as biological science, earth science, and physical geography, or as a separate subject as environmental science.	Interdisciplinary with contents drawn from science and social science. Taught as a separate subject.

(*Continued*)

84 Why Environmental Education?

TABLE 3.1 (Continued)

	Environmental Education	Environmental Science	Environmental Studies
6	As an approach, it is as much interdisciplinary as it is multidisciplinary. This is because it can be integrated in any subject and it can also be taught as a separate subject taking inputs from each.	As an approach, it is more interdisciplinary than it is multidisciplinary. This is because it can be integrated only in few subjects but can be easily taught as a separate subject.	As an approach, it is interdisciplinary.
7	Broad objective covering different components such as awareness, knowledge, attitude, skill, and participation to address environmental issues more effectively.	Deals with environmental facts about environmental processes and phenomena. Hence, it limits its discussion to spreading awareness and providing knowledge about the environment.	Deals with the natural environment and its associated social and economic issues.
8	Environmental education helps understand environmental issues and work toward resolution of such controversial issues.	Issues related to environmental problems are considered secondary. For example, cremation on river banks pollutes the water. Issue emerging from such practices as whether such practices should be permitted or not is not the concern of environmental science.	Environmental issues are discussed but resolution of such issues may be or may not be part of its objectives.

Why Environmental Education? 85

9	Focuses on developing process skills for issue resolution such as critical thinking, conducting survey, analytical skill, communication, value clarification, evaluating, and decision-making. For example, employs various skills to identify how such contamination by industrial waste is affecting the health of the people and how the same can be addressed holistically.	Uses established protocol for environmental problem resolution. That is, for issue resolution only scientifically verifiable answers are taken into consideration. For example, uses protocol to treat contaminated ground water due to industrial waste.	Problem resolution is flexible and can take any form.
10	Values are indispensable in decision-making.	Values—ethical, moral, social, or aesthetic—have little place.	Values are given emphasis.
11	Appreciates the differences of opinions about environmental issues, which brings about value clarification and encourage attitudinal change toward the environment and its issue.	Limits the discussion to scientific facts.	Discussions are democratic and open, encouraging value clarification and attitudinal change toward the environment and its issues.
12	Ultimate aim is to bring about citizens who are able to take conscious and informed decisions and display environmentally responsible behavior.	Restricted to imparting environmental knowledge. Environmentally responsible behavior is not the concern.	Encourages environmentally responsible behavior but not necessarily the ultimate aim.
13	Involves taking actions to protect the environment which sets it apart from environmental science and environmental studies.	Does not necessarily involve actions to protect the environment.	Does not necessarily involve actions to protect the environment.
14	Generally finds itself accommodated in the school or department of education.	Finds place in any other department related to science.	Finds place in any other department.

and tend to become insignificant. They can overlap so much so that one may not be able to make out whether teaching–learning in environmental education or environmental science or environmental studies is in progress. This suggests that, though the three may apparently be different, it all depends on how the teacher takes up the topic since teaching–learning process as such has no rigid boundary. A passionate environmental educator will deliberately make efforts to convert an environmental science classroom into an environmental education classroom by incorporating the concerns of environmental education in the teaching–learning process. The reverse is also true in that a teacher can turn an environmental education classroom into an environmental science classroom by focusing only on imparting environmental facts. For example, a teacher can emphasize value or behavioral change in an environmental science classroom. It may also so happen that a teacher in environmental education for some reason may fail to address the value or attitude component in the teaching–learning process.

3.8 Conclusion

Environmental education has now been established as an area of education that cannot be left out from the school curriculum. Yet, questions are still raised as to why there is a need to introduce another area of study to the already-loaded curriculum. From the elaborate discussions in the chapter, it can be concluded that environmental education is indeed important because no other subjects will be able to address all the concerns which it addresses or attempts to address all due to the nature of different subjects.

With the deteriorating environment that is increasingly being witnessed, environmental education must receive equal and corresponding attention, if not more, in the curriculum. The challenges and hurdles en route its implementation will be many but that should not diminish or marginalize its importance. As seen in the chapter, persistent and sincere efforts need to be made so that environmental education is reflected in the curriculum, as a separate subject or through the curriculum of different subjects. Which approach should be adopted or which subject is most appropriate to transact environmental concerns should hardly be a matter of dispute. Motivated teachers or teachers who feel morally responsible to take care of the environment will always find a way out wherever relevant to incorporate environmental concerns in their teaching–learning process and prepare environmentally conscious and responsible students.

3.9 Summary

- The uniqueness of environmental education necessitates its inclusion in the curriculum.

- The nature of different disciplinary areas is different, which makes it clear that different disciplines have their own limitations in addressing different topics of learning. Science can best bring out the 'truth' of the physical phenomena and processes while social science brings out the 'factual base.'
- Environmental education is holistic in nature as it takes into consideration the concerns of both science and social sciences. This aspect is important to address environmental issues which are transdisciplinary.
- Environmental education is also unique in nature in terms of value clarification.
- Environmental education concerns values–ethical, social or aesthetic, which is missing in the discourse of disciplinary subjects such as science.
- Environmental education provides an opportunity to explore various value perspectives which help students understand controversial environmental issues better.
- It is not necessary to have a separate subject by the name Environmental Education to implement environmental education in the curriculum.
- STS education has been used as a tool by many to achieve the goals of environmental education.
- Limitations of STS education to achieve the goals of environmental education are: science teachers prepare students for further formal study of science; philosophical orientation of science teachers only toward a specific science discipline; use of single textbook with limited and narrow worldview of science; it does not address the 'significance' or 'purpose' or 'why should we know?' component; science education does not give importance to moral/ethical discourse and aesthetic appreciation of nature.
- There exist possibilities and limitations of converging environmental education in science education. Convergence will be meaningful only if science educators have clarity on the goals of environmental education and are equipped to do it.
- Science educators have been acknowledged to be 'superior' and 'all-able,' and they are expected to know the contents of other disciplines. This harms the implementation of EE by these teachers.
- There is little evidence to show that science education had made any successful contribution to achieve the goal of EE.
- The emphasis needs to shift toward education 'for' the environment if we want to achieve the goal of preserving our environment.
- There is a lot of confusion in the understanding of the terms 'environmental education,' 'environmental science,' and 'environmental studies.' However, the terms do not restrict or limit their implementation.
- Teachers who are motivated or passionate about environmental education can make a difference in their classroom transaction, whether they are in their environmental education class or environmental science class or environmental studies for that matter.

References

Athman, Julie, and M.C. Monroe. 2004. "The Effects of Environment-based Education on Students' Achievement Motivation." *Journal of Interpretation Research* 9 (1): 9–25.

Caldwell, L.K. 1980. "Environmental Activism, Phase III: The Burdens of Responsibility." In *Current Issues VI: The Yearbook of Environmental Education and Environmental Studies*, edited by Arthur Sacks, (Selected Papers from the 9th Annual Conference of the National Association for Environmental Education), Columbus, OH and Troy: ERIC Clearinghouse for Science, Mathematics, and Environmental Education, and National Association for Environmental Education. Available at: http://files.eric.ed.gov/fulltext/ED197947.pdf (Accessed on July 4, 2023).

Carter, R.L., and B. Simmons. 2010. "The History and Philosophy of Environmental Education." In *The Inclusion of Environmental Education in Science Teacher Education*, edited by Alec M. Bodzin, Beth Shiner Klein, and Starlin Weaver, 3–16. New York: Springer.

Disinger, J.F. 1986. *Current Practices in Science/Society/Technology/Environment Education: A Survey of the State Education Agencies*. Columbus, OH: ERIC Clearinghouse for Science/Mathematics, and Environmental Education, Ohio State University.

———. 1987. "Environmental Education Research News." *The Environmentalist* 7 (2): 85–89.

———. 2009. "The Purposes of Environmental Education: Perspectives of Teachers, Governmental Agencies, NGOs, Professional Societies, and Advocacy Groups." In *Environmental Education and Advocacy: Changing Perspectives of Ecology and Education*, edited by Edward A. Johnson and Michael J. Mappin, 137–158. Cambridge: Cambridge University Press.

Disinger, J.F., and R.W. Howe. 1990 *Trends and Issues Related to the Preparation of Teachers for Environmental Education*. Environmental Education Information Report No. ED335233. ERIC Clearinghouse for Science, Mathematics, and Environmental Education Information Report. Columbus, OH: ERIC/SMEAC. Available at: http://files.eric.ed.gov/fulltext/ED335233.pdf (Accessed on July 4, 2023).

Disinger, J.F., and M.C. Monroe. 1994. *EE Toolbox—Workshop Resource Manual, Defining Environmental Education*. Ann Arbor, MI: University of Michigan, National Consortium for Environmental Education and Training.

Disinger, J.F., and C. Schoenfeld. 1988. "Environmental Education Research News." *The Environmentalist* 8 (4): 245–248.

Disinger, J.F., and T.F. Wilson. 1986. *Locating the "E" in S/T/S*. (ERIC/SMEAC Information Bulletin No. 3), Columbus, OH: ERIC Clearinghouse for Science, Mathematics, and Environmental Education. Available at: http://files.eric.ed.gov/fulltext/ED277547.pdf (Accessed on July 4, 2023).

Feinstein, N.W., and Kathryn L. Kirchgasler. 2015. "Sustainability in Science Education? How the Next Generation Science Standards Approach Sustainability, and Why it Matters." *Science Education* 99 (1): 121–144.

Fensham, P.I., and J.B. May. 1979. "Servant Not Master—A New Role for Science in a Core of Environmental Education." *Australian Science Teachers Journal* 25 (2): 15–24.

Gough, Annette. 2008. "Towards More Effective Learning for Sustainability: Reconceptualising Science Education." *Transnational Curriculum Inquiry* 5 (1): 32–50. Available at: https://researchrepository.rmit.edu.au/esploro/outputs/journalArticle/Towards-more-effective-learning-for-sustainability-Reconceptualising-science-education/9921860731801341 (Accessed on July 4, 2023).

———. 2013. "Historical, Contextual, and Theoretical Orientations That Have Shaped Environmental Education Research: Introduction." In *International Handbook of Research on Environmental Education*, edited by Robert B. Stevenson, Michael Brody, Justin Dillon, and Arjen E.J. Wals, 9–12. New York: Routledge.

Hadzigeorgiou, Yannis, and Michael Skoumios. 2013. "The Development of Environmental Awareness Through School Science: Problems and Possibilities." *International Journal of Environmental & Science Education* 8: 405–426.

Harde, R.B. 1984. "'Environmental Studies': Towards a Definition." In *Monographs in Environmental Education and Environmental Studies*. Vol. I, edited by Arthur Sacks, 31–54. Columbus, OH: ERIC Clearinghouse for Science, Mathematics, and Environmental Education; Troy, OH: North American Association for Environmental Education. Available at: http://files.eric.ed.gov/fulltext/ED251293.pdf (Accessed on July 4, 2023).

Holsman, R.H. 2001. "Viewpoint: The Politics of Environmental Education." *The Journal of Environmental Education* 32 (2): 4–7.

Kibert, C.J., M.C Monroe, A.L. Peterson, R.R. Plate, and L.P. Thiele. 2012. *Working Toward Sustainability—Ethical Decision Making in a Technological World*. Hoboken, NJ: John Wiley & Sons, Inc.

Kopnina, H. 2014. "Future Scenarios and Environmental Education." *The Journal of Environmental Education* 45 (4): 217–231. DOI: 10.1080/00958964.2014.941783

Lahiry, D., Savita Sinha, J.S. Gill, U. Mallik, and A.K. Mishra. 1988. *Environmental Education: A Process for Pre- service Teacher Training Curriculum Development*. UNESCO-UNEP International Environmental Education Programme Environmental Education Series No. 26. Edited by Patricia R. Simpson, Harold Hungerford, and Trudi L. Volk. Paris: UNESCO.

Lucas, A.M. 1980a. "Science and Environmental Education: Pious Hopes, Self Praise and Disciplinary Chauvinism." *Studies in Science Education* 7: 1–26. DOI: 10.1080/03057268008559874

———. 1980b. "The Role of Science Education in Education for the Environment." *Journal of Environmental Education* 12 (2): 33–37. DOI: 10.1080/00958964.1981.10801898

McMichael, D.F., and A. Strom. 1975. "Teaching Science for an Understanding of Our Total Environment and the Need for Conservation." *CAT Education Monograph* 12: 29–47, Macquarie University Center for advancement of Teaching.

Monde, P.N. 2011. *Barriers to Successful Implementation of Environmental Education in Zambian High Schools: A Case Study of Selected High Schools of Central Province*, PhD thesis. University of Zambia. Available at: http://dspace.unza.zm:8080/xmlui/bitstream/handle/123456789/809/Monde.pdf?sequence=1 (Accessed on July 4, 2023).

Monroe, M. 1991. "Meeting the Mandate: Integrating Environmental Education." *Clearing* 71: 8–9.

NAAEE, North American Association for Environmental Education. 2004. *Environmental Education Materials: Guidelines for Excellence*. Washington D.C.: NAAEE.

NCERT, National Council of Educational Research and Training. 1981. *Environmental Education at the School Level: A Lead Paper*. New Delhi: NCERT.

———. 2006a. *Position Paper of the National Focus Group on Teaching of Science*, No. 1.1. New Delhi: NCERT.

———. 2006b. *Position Paper of the National Focus Group on Teaching of Social Sciences*, No. 1.5. New Delhi: NCERT.

———. 2023. *The National Curriculum Framework for School Education*. New Delhi: NCERT.
NCTE, National Council for Teacher Education. 2009. *National Curriculum Framework for Teacher Education 2009*. New Delhi: NCTE.
———. 2015. *Curriculum Framework of Diploma in Elementary Teacher Education (D.El.Ed.) Programme*. New Delhi: NCTE.
Pedretti, E., and J. Nazir. 2011. "Currents in STSE Education: Mapping a Complex Field, 40 Years On." *Science Education* 95 (4): 601–626.
Petra, Fatimah. 2007. "Promoting Discussion in Lower Secondary Science Classrooms." In *2007 World Conference on Science and Technology Education CD Proceedings*, edited by Grady Venville and Vaille Dawson, 346–349. Perth. Available at: https://www.icaseonline.net/icase2007.pdf (Accessed on July 3, 2023)
Rubba, P.A. 1987. "An STS Perspective on Environmental Education in the School Curriculum." In *Trends and Issues Environmental Education: EE in School Curricula—Reports of a Symposium and a Survey*, Environmental Education Information Reports No ED292608, edited by John F. Disinger, 63–71. Columbus, OH: ERIC Clearinghouse for Science, Mathematics, and Environmental Education in cooperation with NAAEE. Available at: http://files.eric.ed.gov/fulltext/ED292608.pdf (Accessed on July 5, 2023).
Sarabhai, K.V., K. Kandula, and M. Raghunath. 1998. *Greening Formal Education—Concerns, Efforts and Future Directions*. Ministry of Environment and Forests, Government of India, Centre for Environment Education.
Sauvé, Lucie. 2005. "Currents in Environmental Education: Mapping a Complex and Evolving Pedagogical Field." *Canadian Journal of Environmental Education* 10 (Spring): 11–37.
Schoenfeld, Clay. 1971. "Environmental Studies Come to the Campus." In *Outlines of Environmental Education*, edited by Clay Shoenfeld, 111–112. Madison, WI: Dembar Educational Research Services. Available at: http://files.eric.ed.gov/fulltext/ED050973.pdf (Accessed on July 4, 2023).
Schoenfeld, Clay, and J.F. Disinger. 1978. *Environmental Education in Action—II: Case Studies of Environmental Studies Programs in Colleges and Universities Today*. Columbus, OH: ERIC Information Analysis Center for Science, Mathematics, an Environmental Education. Available at: https://archive.org/stream/ERIC_ED152557/ERIC_ED152557_djvu.txt (Accessed on July 4, 2023).

4
RESPONSIBLE ENVIRONMENTAL BEHAVIOR

Ultimate Goal of Environmental Education

4.1 Chapter Overview

Environmental education is about developing awareness, knowledge, attitude, skills, and opportunity to participate to solve environmental problems. The success of environmental education can be said to be meaningful only if it brings about certain pro-environmental behavior or action in the present and in the long run. Anything short of this will render the effort worthless. However, behavior change is not straightforward or linear but is complex, and several factors have to align so that it is conducive for one to take pro-environmental action. And the same set of factors may not apply to everybody. Therefore, it is very challenging to inculcate environmentally responsible behavior among people. This complexity is what makes it impossible to come up with a one-size-fits-all model of behavioral change. This chapter discusses the various factors and variables that contribute to fostering responsible environmental behavior (REB). Some models in this regard have been discussed in the chapter. The complexity on how the variables contribute to bring about behavioral change has also been highlighted.

4.2 Introduction

So far in the book, the discussions have covered the different environmental issues facing the world, the goals and objectives of environmental education, and the need for environmental education in the curriculum. However, all the efforts that is put in will be meaningful only if some positive actions are taken, or when some environmentally friendly patterns of behavior are observed (not inherited but learned and imbibed) or, in other words, only if students display some kind of environmentally responsible behavior, or REB, or pro-environmental behavior. This suggests that environmental education is all about promotion of REB (Bones 1994, 15; Disinger 1993, 35). Therefore, the importance of REB cannot be overemphasized. However, as important as it is, this aspect has not received much attention both in practice and in research. In this light, several researchers including Lucas (1980a, 20–21; 1980b, 36), Gough (2013, 16) and others pointed out the importance of considering behavior change as the focus of environmental education practices and research. Some, however, argue that such a goal to bring about behavior change is overstated (Jickling 1991 in Disinger and Monroe 1994). There has also been a lack of consensus among educators as to whether to teach explicitly for environmental action. It is because of this lack of consensus that this aspect has been brought into the formal curricula much later, after the introduction of environmental education itself (Disinger and Howe 1990, 15).

4.3 The Context of Responsible Environmental Behavior

Environmental education cannot be complete without 'action.' In other words, environmental education is not just 'knowing,' but environmental education will be complete only with 'doing,' which includes taking right choices. It may be reiterated that one of the goals of environmental education, as mentioned in the Tbilisi Conference on Environmental Education, is "to create new patterns of behavior of individuals, groups, and society as a whole toward the environment" (UNESCO-UNEP 1978). Whether an individual, a group, or a society has imbibed the new patterns of behavior will be known from the actions they take or the way they act while they are faced with different environmental situations. Hence, when it is said, 'new patterns of behavior,' it essentially refers to the 'action' that a person performs or undertakes. The importance of taking appropriate environmental actions so as to contribute meaningfully toward the betterment of the environment has also been highlighted in India's efforts to take environmental education forward. It may be cited that the syllabus for environmental education in schools developed in pursuance of the Hon'ble Supreme Court's order emphasized the importance of 'action' in environmental education, wherein it says, "a value based, action oriented course of EE would lead from knowledge to feeling and finally to appropriate action" (NCERT 2004). The National Curriculum Framework 2005 (NCF-2005) further reiterates that the main focus of environmental education should be "to promote positive environmental actions" (NCERT 2005). However, it may be mentioned here that this "creation of new pattern of behavior" is still considered debatable (Biedenweg, Monroe, and Wojcik 2013) with regard to whether or not educators should be teaching for the purpose of changing the environmental behaviors of their students (Disinger 1993, 36). This is not surprising, especially looking at the earlier understanding of REB which was authoritative in that environmentally responsible behaviors were considered to be those endorsed by professional resource managers and/or those championed by environmental advocates. Environmental educators were expected to teach students what those behaviors were and how to achieve them (Disinger 2009). It is argued that it is not right to inform the students about a particular pattern of behavior which, in many instances, could be biased and derived from the selfish motive of the educator and could turn out to be damaging and dangerous to the environment and do more harm than good in the long run. Volk (1993 cited in Disinger 2009), therefore, pointed out the necessity of including ecological knowledge, environmental sensitivity, knowledge of issues, investigation skills, citizenship skills, and feeling of effectiveness as part of the definition of environmentally responsible behavior. But the authoritative REB mentioned earlier should not be confused with the new pattern of behavior discussed later, which is the outcome of an impartial and democratic process which is not influenced by insincere motive. It is not about promoting specific behavior changes, but those behavior changes which the students exhibit of their own as a result of their informed choices. In fact, environmental educators should emphasize the maintenance of neutrality in their environmental education-related endeavors.

In order to achieve this goal of environmental education—appropriate action or behavior—several aspects were laid down in the Belgrade Charter, Tbilisi Conference, and the Habitat and Learning Position Paper of the NCF-2005. These can be broadly categorized under awareness, knowledge, attitude, and skill and opportunity to be actively involved in working toward resolution of environmental problems. It was envisaged that if these aspects were taken care of, appropriate environmental action or behavior would ensue. Whether this supposition works or not, or how it works, will be discussed elaborately in the subsequent sections.

As it will be evident in the ensuing discussions, irrespective of what the environmental issue is about, in general there are several factors which contribute to such pro-environmental behavior or REB. But how each factor contributes toward the process is difficult to be explicitly explained. In fact, it will not be possible to precisely quantify the factors that would bring about REB. Here, the discussion will be broadly on what it takes to trigger appropriate actions or behave in an environmentally responsible manner.

4.4 Traditional Thinking of REB

Based on the traditional thinking in the field of environmental education, it is envisaged that by making social groups and individuals aware of environmental issues and problems, and by imparting adequate knowledge about these issues and problems, appropriate actions or behaviors would follow suit. In other words, it is assumed that if students are properly taught about the environment, they will subsequently behave in an environmentally responsible manner and engage in pro-environmental actions (Disinger 1993, 35; Disinger 2009; Disinger and Howe 1990, 15). Two models related to such traditional thinking are presented here: First, wherein it is assumed that if human beings are made more knowledgeable, they will, in turn, become more aware of the environment and its problems and, thus, be more motivated to act toward the environment in more responsible ways (see Figure 4.1). Second, a model proposed by Ramsey and Rickson (1977 cited in Hungerford and Volk 1990) wherein it is envisaged that increased knowledge would lead to favorable attitudes, which in turn would lead to actions promoting better environmental quality. In other words, it was assumed that more knowledge will lead to more awareness, more awareness will bring about attitudinal change, and this will ultimately lead to appropriate action or behavior (see Figure 4.2).

The two figures provide linear models for appropriate environmental action or behavior. In both cases, knowledge may surely lead to awareness or attitudinal change. However, just because a person is aware about environmental problems, or has the right attitude toward the environment or environmental problems, it does not necessary lead to action. In fact, many researches that have been undertaken in this field do not find the linear relationships provided earlier to be valid. Instead, studies (Hines, Hungerford, and Tomera 1986/87; Hungerford and Volk 1990) reveal that there are numerous other variables that are at play simultaneously for bringing about appropriate action or behavior. Nevertheless, gaining environmental insights (the ability to understand and appraise the society's effects on the ecosystem) and environmental attitude (defined as all positive or negative attitudes and thoughts of individuals regarding environmentally beneficial behaviors, such as fears, resentments, uneasiness, values, and readiness to solve environmental problems) contribute and influence behavior toward the environment (Genc 2015).

FIGURE 4.1   Traditional Thinking of Responsible Environmental Behavior: Model I (Adapted from Hungerford and Volk 1990).

FIGURE 4.2   Traditional Thinking of Responsible Environmental Behavior: Model II (Adapted from Hungerford and Volk 1990).

4.5 Responsible Environmental Behavior: What Decides?

To begin the discussion, let us consider the following questions: Why do we do what we do? Why do we do how we do? What makes us do the way that we do? What is that, that influences us most? How do we decide how to do? What situations prompt us to exhibit environmentally responsible behavior and what are the situations that deter us? Do we even think that we 'decide' on the many things that we do every day? These are very relevant questions to ask when it comes to pro-environmental behavior. As a matter of fact, for every decision that is made—as big as buying a new house or as small as buying fruits—the actions people take are always associated with reasons, which they may or may not be even conscious about. In such cases, people use information that is stored in their memory, based on previous experiences. A number of studies have been done on what affects decision-making capacity or how people change their behavior. For example, Daniel Kahneman and Amos Tversky—two psychologists who developed a series of insightful experiments to test decision-making processes—found that decision-making could be affected, based on stored information, belief on initial fact, inappropriate use of logic and probability, and uncertainty (Kibert et al. 2012, 214–217). Social theorist Everett Rogers provides five successive steps that an individual goes through when changing behavior: knowledge (people must first become aware of the potential action, behavior, technology, or idea), persuasion (people form an attitude on how the innovation is presented to them—relevant and meaningful context), decision (people decide whether they wish to adopt or reject the change after they perceive the change to be good or bad), implementation (people engage in the actual activity), and confirmation (people seek additional information to confirm whether their decision was right; supportive information helps them to be firmly established in the change) (Kibert et al. 2012, 251–53). Rachel and Stephen Kaplan's Reasonable Person Model is another model which is about reasonableness in decision-making—in situations where the information is insufficient or excessive, or not understandable, or where a person lacks the skills to take actions, people are not able to take reasonable decisions (Kibert et al. 2012, 258). Umpteen studies have been undertaken to understand the criteria of decision-making in general and pro-environmental behavior in specific. One model in particular is being discussed more elaborately in the following section.

4.6 Responsible Environmental Behavior Model

The REB model proposed by Hines, Hungerford, and Tomera (1986/87) and Hungerford and Volk (1990) has been considered to discuss in detail the variables that can contribute to bring about pro-environmental behavior. Some modifications have been made by adding few more variables as it will be discussed further. An attempt has been made to present the model in a simplified manner. Figure 4.3 provides the detail of the model that is being discussed.

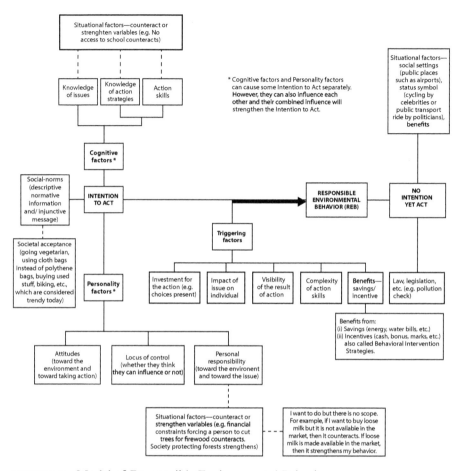

FIGURE 4.3 Model of Responsible Environmental Behavior.

Source: Modified from Hines et al. (1986/87) and Hungerford and Volk (1990).

The model presented in Figure 4.3 shows that REB results from 'intention to act.' Intention to act does not occur naturally but is influenced by factors such as 'cognitive' and 'personality factors.' Cognitive factors include variables such as 'knowledge of issues,' 'knowledge of action strategies,' and 'action skills.' Certain situational factors may counteract or strengthen these variables. For example, if students have no access to a school, this will counteract to the cognitive factor. Because in such cases students will not be able to gain knowledge about environmental issues, nor will they have knowledge of possible action strategies and action skills. This, in turn, will have a negative impact on the intention to act, which will ultimately reduce the chances to exhibit REB.

Personality factors include variables such as 'attitudes' (toward the environment and toward taking action), 'locus of control' (whether they think they can influence or not), and 'personal responsibility' (toward the environment and toward the issue). As in the case of cognitive factors, some situational factors can counteract or strengthen the personality factor variables. For example, even if people have the feeling of personal responsibility to take care of the environment, they may still cut down trees for firewood if they have no other means to get fuel for fire. Hence, in this case, financial constraint can counteract the variable. While in a society which believes in protecting forests, it will be easy for an individual to advocate for judicious use of firewood. This situation strengthens the variable. Thus, in the absence of situations which counteract the variables, there is positive impact on the intention to act which ultimately will increase the chances to exhibit REB. Similarly, some may want to reduce usage of plastic packaged products, and for this they may prefer to buy loose milk (unpackaged milk). But if loose milk is not available in the market, then it counteracts their intention to act, while if loose milk is made available in the market, then it will strengthen their behavior.

Intention to act responsibly can also be influenced by social norms. Such norms can be descriptive (perceptions of what is commonly done in a given situation) or injunctive (perceptions of what is commonly approved or disapproved within the culture) (Reno, Cialdini, and Kallgren, 1993). However, whether the normative information or normative messages, which could be descriptive or injunctive, will lead to desirable behavior or conduct is based on the situation. For example, a study conducted to examine the impact of an information campaign designed to increase recycling by combining the influence of injunctive and descriptive norms found that descriptive norm, in this case prevalence of recycling conveyed in the Ads, positively impacted intention to recycle even without the injunctive norm, in this case approval of recycling conveyed in the Ads, while the Ads for injunctive norm had to be very persuasive so as to positively impact intention to recycle (Cialdini 2003). That is, in this example, people tend to recycle more after seeing people recycle in the Ads compared to when the Ads only showed that it is a good and an approved practice to recycle. However, in a study conducted to compare the effectiveness of a descriptive norm signage and an injunctive message signage placed in the Arizona Petrified National Park to avoid theft of the fossil (Cialdini 2003), it was found that the descriptive norm signage that read, "Many past visitors have removed petrified wood from the Park, changing the natural state of the Petrified Forest," turned out to be detrimental, resulting in more theft compared to when the injunctive message signage read, "Please don't remove the petrified wood from the Park, in order to preserve the natural state of the Petrified Forest." This suggests that descriptive norms is detrimental when environmentally harmful behavior is prevalent while it is effective when the prevalent behavior is environmentally beneficial.

Also, the same descriptive information or message can be constructive or destructive depending on the behavior possessed by the group prior to the exposure to the normative information (Schultz et al. 2007). For those that do not possess desirable behavior, a descriptive message about a lesser desirable message is likely to have a positive impact on their behavior, while for those that already possess the desirable environmental behavior, the same descriptive message is likely to boomerang, that is, have a negative impact. However, adding an injunctive component to the message proved reconstructive as it buffers the boomerang effect (Schultz et al. 2007). For example, if my average monthly household energy consumption is 800 kWh and if I am told that the average energy consumption in my neighborhood is 500 kWh (descriptive norm), then I may try to reduce my energy consumption. However, if I was consuming 300 kWh and I am told about the same descriptive norm, then I am likely going to increase my consumption. If at the same time I am also told that reducing energy consumption is an approved behavior by the community (injunctive norm), then I may try to continue to consume less energy i.e., 300 kWh. Therefore, norm-based persuasive communications are likely to have their best effects when communicators align descriptive and injunctive normative messages to work in tandem rather than in competition with one another (Cialdini 2003). We can sum up the above discussions on norm-based persuasive communications with the following: (i) Descriptive norm is to be used only when such norm is the desired norm as in the case of recycling Ads. (ii) Injunctive norm is to be used when descriptive norm is not the desired norm as in the case of fossil.(iii) If the descriptive norm is not the desired norm then it should always be accompanied by injunctive norms to buffer the effect as in the case of energy consumption.

There is another factor that can bring about REB in spite of 'lack of intention' which has been designated 'no intention yet act.' In such cases, people do not actually want to act in an environmentally responsible way, but they do so to save their public image or because the government has imposed some law which compels the person to act environmentally responsible. For example, the punishment (fine or imprisonment) imposed for violation of pollution norms, burning solid waste, and leaves in the open, clearing or uprooting of trees without following norms, discharging untreated water in water bodies, and so on, more often than not, influences a person to act responsibly. However, this is further influenced by the nature of punishment. If the punishment is only fine in terms of money, a person who is wealthy will care little about abiding by the law. Such situation will be unfair to the people who are not financially sound, and, hence, it will turn into an issue of social injustice. However, if the punishment imposed is in terms of imprisonment, the law will seem fair to both the rich and the poor. Another very common example of REB, in spite of no intention to act, is the phony public display of certain pro-environmental behavior by celebrities or public figures such as taking ride in public transport systems, or becoming ambassadors for wildlife protection, or taking part in cleanliness drives. However, it is also a fact that REB, in spite of lack of intention, also appears to be effective in such situations when a person who is idolized or is considered a role model sets a trend for REB. For example, it is never easy to shell out money from one's pocket as donation, even when it is for a very good social cause. However, donation seems to suddenly start flowing in when the person making the call for donation happens to be a public idol or an icon.

4.6.1 Complexity of Responsible Environmental Behavior

While it is evident that awareness and knowledge of environmental issues and concerns are imperative to build environmental attitudes, almost always following a linear pattern, the situation is not as linear and becomes much more complex when it comes to attitudes translating into a behavior or action (Kopnina 2014). Lucas (1980a, 1980b), in his analysis of literature devoted to environmental education, found no strong evidence in support of the view that attitudes lead to appropriate behaviors or actions. He also found disparity in what a person believes 'people' ought to do and the same person's attitudes to the same question, and how a person's active concern for environmental issues dissipates when the costs include personal sacrifice. The question is, how 'strong' should an attitude be so that it is translated into action. Keeping this in view, Lucas suggested that environmental educators might instead concentrate on the direct modification of behavior rather than on intervention at the attitude level, which is matter of debate.

The complexity of REB is such that, even if all the variables of the cognitive and personality factors are favorable or positive, there are other factors, which are collectively called 'triggering factors' here (this term has been used for convenience) that greatly affect REB. These factors include the following: investment for the action (i.e., how much an individual has to invest to take the action, what are the choices present, and so on, for example an air conditioner which is more energy efficient but costlier versus one which is less energy efficient but cheaper); impact of issue on individual (i.e., how much the issue has direct relevance on the individual, for example dumping solid waste in the drain will impact an individual directly which will most likely trigger REB); visibility of the result of action (i.e., whether an individual will be able to see the positive result of his action immediately, for example one will not be able to see the result even if he gets pollution check of his vehicle, and, hence, he is not likely to readily exhibit REB); complexity of action skills (i.e., how difficult or inconvenient it will be to take the action, for example it will be difficult to take toxic waste to the assigned place for discarding if the place is located far away from one's locality, and, hence, it will act as a deterrent to REB), benefits—savings/incentive (benefits may be from (a) savings (energy, water bills) and (b) incentives (cash, bonus, marks), also called behavioral intervention strategies. Societal acceptance is also an important triggering factor. For example, turning vegetarian, using cloth bags instead of polythene bags, buying used stuff, biking, etc. are considered trendy today, and this influences people to adopt such behavior. In that case, what are the factors that bring about such trends in the society needs to be explored further.

4.6.2 Categorization of Variables

Hungerford and Volk (1990) distinguished the various factors which affect REB under different categories such as 'entry-level variables' (which include the prerequisite variables that would enhance a person's decision-making such as environmental sensitivity, basic knowledge of ecology, and so on), 'ownership variables' (which include variables which make environmental issues personal to the individual such as in-depth knowledge of issues, personal investment in an issue, and so on), and 'empowerment variables' (which include those variables which make an individual feel empowered or sense of competence to help resolve environmental issues such as knowledge of and skill in using environmental action strategies, locus of control, and intention to act). Chawla and Cushing (2007), in 'education for strategic environmental behavior', placed nature activities that an individual goes through during childhood and youth under the 'entry-level variables' since such activities predispose an individual to take an interest in nature, which enhances the possibility of the person to later work for its protection. Role models of children such as parents, other family members, and teachers who show an interest in nature are also included under this variable. Education programs and membership in environmental clubs and organizations where an individual gains increased knowledge about environmental issues and learns environmental action skills are included under 'ownership' and 'empowerment variables.' They maintain that a sense of competence, at an individual level as well as collectively, is the foundation of action, and, hence, it is considered as a strong ingredient in the 'empowerment variable.' An individual can develop such a sense of competence in many ways—observing the success of others, seeing the processes other people use to achieve their goals, assessing their own competence in comparison, being surrounded by role models who are very persuasive (Bandura 1982; Schunk et al. 1987 cited in Chawla and Cushing 2007), verbal encouragement, one's own experience of tasting success (Bandura 1997 cited in Chawla and Cushing 2007), opportunities to work for social and environmental change, and so on.

4.6.3 Other Factors/Variables

There are many other factors or variables that have not been mentioned here which contribute to or promote REB. For example, social marketing techniques such as understanding the motivations of the audience, removing real and perceived barriers to change, establishing social commitments, and avoiding approaches that can trigger unwanted reactions and persuasion also could be significant areas for promotion of environmentally responsible behavior

(Disinger and Monroe 1994). The mindset of the society is another factor that has not been accounted for in the model. How society looks at the people who exhibit REB in their daily lives or those who have no concern for it can also be a very important factor. In a society which does not commonly exhibit or encourage REB or which have no regard for people with REB, it is most likely that the situation is going to worsen. However, in a society which commonly exhibits or encourages REB or which has high regard for people with REB, it is most likely that even individuals who otherwise do not exhibit REB are most likely to change their environmental behavior so as to blend with the society—the impact of descriptive norm. Bamberg and Möser (2007) mention various studies which indicate that pro-environmental behavior could be pro-socially motivated, in the sense that they are hugely influenced by social norms, or could be guided by a rational evaluation of behavioral consequences in terms of rewards and punishments, in the sense that a person behaves in a certain way so as to be rewarded or in order to avoid punishment.

It is important to understand that any of the factors on its own does not bring about REB. For example, educational research does not support the optimistic assumption that acquisition of information and skills will lead to positive changes in social behavior (Stapp 1970 cited in Disinger 1983; Disinger and Monroe 1994, 9). It is also possible that some of the variables may not be relevant in the years to come. For example, at present, legislature helps in controlling environmental quality to a certain extent, and such legislature may not be necessary in the future if environmental education makes a meaningful impact in the society. Disinger and Monroe (1994) mention that environmental education can influence lifestyle choices and the students will be able to decide how to consider the environmental impact in their choices of electrical appliances, tools, gadgets, modes of transportation, and so on. However, as much as environmental education can influence society on lifestyle choices, society and its inherent or acquired cultures can also influence REB. For example, the inherent sustainable practices in certain cultures influence REB. Similarly, as mentioned above as one of the triggering factors, the changing trends in a society can also influence REB. For example, the present trend of not only acceptance but appreciation of using cloth bags, turning vegetarian, used or second-hand stuff such as vehicles, appliances, devices, furniture, furnishings, and clothes, biking, spending time in nature, etc., in a society influence and encourage people to follow such practices.

4.7 Different Levels of Activities for Behavioral Change

Several studies have come up with other details related to the categories of variables that contribute to behavior (Hungerford and Volk, 1990). A hierarchical approach involving the following four levels of activities was put forward by Hungerford (1987, 28–29), Disinger and Monroe (1994, 7):

1. Ecological concepts: This goal level attempts to provide the learner with the ecological knowledge that will permit him/her to make ecologically sound decisions with respect to environmental issues. This knowledge would include, but not be limited to, such concepts as individuals and populations, limiting factors, biogeochemical cycling, abiotic influences, homeostasis, and succession. Other educators may add companion goals in political, economic, psychological, and social concepts.
2. Conceptual awareness: This goal level attempts to develop a conceptual awareness of how individual and collective behaviors influence the relationship between quality of life and quality of environment, as well as how human behaviors result in issues that must be resolved through investigation, evaluation, decision-making, and action by citizens.
3. Issue investigation and evaluation: This goal level attempts to develop the knowledge and skills needed to permit learners to investigate environmental issues and evaluate alternative solutions for resolving these issues. It also provides opportunities for students to investigate and evaluate real-world issues.
4. Environmental action skills—training and application: This goal level attempts to develop those skills needed for learners to take positive environmental action for the purpose of resolving or helping to resolve environment-related issues. It also involves the development of action plans by students and provides them with the opportunity to implement those plans, if they desire.

Research studies have indicated that behavioral change will occur only if students are thoroughly exposed to all the four goal levels (Disinger and Monroe 1994, 7; Hungerford 1987, 28–29).

However, at the end, there is no model which is foolproof. It will also be local-specific depending upon the environmental settings—social and biophysical. Due to the number of variables that interact and influence each other to ultimately bring about REB, it is difficult to determine and specify which factors are the most important or the least important. As Sobel (2008, 145) says:

> Just because children know that burning fuel creates carbon dioxide and that this is bad for the planet, they do not necessarily develop ecologically responsible buying patterns. Increased knowledge and a change in attitude do not necessarily translate into different behavior. It's more complicated than that.

Nevertheless, it will never be wrong to say that every variable contributes in some way or the other. However, any and all of these will have some impact only if people give themselves some time to pause and consciously decide on every decision they make, however small or big it may be.

There are several success stories regarding behavioral change which have been exhibited by students throughout India. One such example would be regarding the burning of firecrackers. Of late, it has been observed that an increasing number of students have stopped burning firecrackers or reduced the use of it during festive seasons. Besides the dangers associated playing with it, firecrackers are known to increase air pollution drastically. Such behavioral change among the students is highly appreciated and encouraging when it comes to dealing with environmental issues. Similarly, there is an increasing trend in the number of people who use only biodegradable materials and colors to make Ganesh idols. The idols have also been known to reduce in size. Such decisions will greatly reduce water pollution when the idols are immersed as part of the ritual. It will be worth finding out what encouraged or led to such behavioral change so that similar strategies can be applied to other environmental issues such as consumerism, use of vehicles, and waste management.

4.8 Significance of REB Model

The discussion on the REB model gives us a fair idea on how it works. It was observed that there are numerous variables at play, each of which contributes toward REB. However, even when all the variables are favorable, it may not guarantee REB, indicating the complexity of how REB can be influenced. In spite of this uncertainty, the model definitely is significant as it provides a broad framework under which REB operates. This understanding of the impacts and importance of each variable will help policy makers and practitioners to identify the areas where they should focus while implementing environmental education. It will help them identify where the barriers are.

While trying to address any environmental issue, practitioners may begin by considering all the variables as mentioned in the model. They can also specifically focus on certain specific variables, as they can pick and choose depending on the requirements. For example, in the present trend of implementation of environmental education in the schools in India, it appears that the focus is largely on the cognitive factors, invariably on the 'knowledge of issues' component, and to some extent on the 'knowledge of action strategies' component. Adequate action skills are not provided, nor are opportunities given to apply the action skills. Hence, in this case, focus can be now on strengthening action skills by providing opportunities to participate in actual resolution of environmental issues. The model is not only useful in the teaching–learning process for students but the same can be and must be used for teacher preparation as well. The reason is that only when teachers themselves are familiar with the model through participation will they be able to implement it successfully in their teaching–learning practice.

The model can not only guide the policy makers in the area of formal education but also inform other government departments on their roles. For example, due to government's strict intervention, single-use polythene bags are now rarely used by shopkeepers in many places. Government has also imposed ban on single-use plastic since July 1, 2022, which includes items such as earbuds, plastic sticks for balloons, flags, candy sticks, ice-cream sticks, polystyrene (thermocouple), plates, cups, glasses, forks, spoons, knives, straws, trays, wrapping or packaging films around sweets boxes, invitation cards, cigarette packets, plastic or PVC banners less than 100 micron, and stirrers. If this is strictly implemented, it can make a huge impact. Similarly, concerned departments should also come up with appropriate strategies to bring about a larger change in the society. For example, Department of Animal Husbandry and Dairying can popularize the use of quality loose milk so that purchase of packaged milk can be reduced or consumers are given a choice. This could be an incentive to some families as well since loose milk is at least a few cents cheaper. Similarly, concerned department can strive for environment-friendly packaging of food items. Incentives may be given to innovators in this regard. Funders can also refer to the model to identify where (in which area) to put their money and resources. Researchers can also take up in-depth research on specific variables, based on requirement. This will be especially useful in India's context since, for successful implementation of environmental education, stakeholders will have to bank on the findings of such research which as of now is pretty much lacking.

4.9 Conclusion

The more the work in the area of behavioral change, the more complexities unravel. There are many variables that work simultaneously or otherwise. Yet, it is clear that without a pro-environmental behavior the positive impact on the environment can never be seen. Given this situation, what can be done is to try to address as many variables as possible while engaging with students in the teaching–learning process. Though having the right attitude does not guarantee REB, however, one can almost guarantee that without the right attitude REB cannot take place.

It is indeed fascinating to think how a certain variable can so dominantly control the mind in decision-making while at other times the same variable does not have any impact whatsoever in the decision made. Since it is a human mind that is at play, a bit of each of these—experience, knowledge, emotion, feelings, social acceptability, and social status—all play an important role in all such actions. It appears that, in India, much of the factors are all controlled by social acceptability. People buy a certain house, a certain car, a certain furniture, or a certain gadget, many a time, just to flaunt their social status. If this be the case, then addressing this aspect becomes a priority in the process to bring about REB.

Most important, how the factors and variables that influence REB and action are considered in the curriculum, especially in the teaching–learning process, will be crucial to nurture students who will take active part in the upkeep of the environment.

But the behavior change should not be limited to a few adjustments here and there in one's lifestyle such as giving up polythene bags, sorting of waste, or switching of lights. It's about time to look beyond such little tweaks. It should now be about responsible behavior in every aspect and stage of decision-making in one's life—as a consumer, commuter, farmer, industrialist, manufacturer, innovator, artist, healthcare provider, scientist, engineer, homemaker, chef, service provider, educator, student, priest, shopkeeper, builder, etc. That is, once-a-while pro-environmental behavior cannot be considered a behavior change. It has to be a continuous practice, a way of life.

In this regard, persuasive communication or messaging will play an important role to bring about pro-environmental behavior with challenges as daunting as climate change facing us (Kazdin 2008).

4.10 Summary

- Taking action—environmentally responsible behavior, or pro-environmental behavior, or REB —leading to environmental problem-solving is the ultimate goal of environmental education.
- Right action or environmentally responsible behavior does not come naturally to an individual.
- Numerous variables contribute in the process to bring about REB.
- Due to the complexity that is involved in bringing about REB, it is not possible to quantify or list the variables that will guarantee REB. The impact of the variables for different environmental issues will also vary.
- The sum of all the variables do not add up to the product, that is, environmentally responsible behavior.
- There is no foolproof REB model which can work for all situations and issues at all places at all times.

References

Bamberg, S., and G. Möser. 2007. "Twenty Years after Hines, Hungerford, and Tomera: A New Meta-analysis of Psycho-Social Determinants of Pro-Environment Behaviour." *Journal of Environmental Psychology* 27: 14–25.

Biedenweg, K., M.C. Monroe, and D.J. Wojcik. 2013. "Foundations of Environmental Education." In *Across the Spectrum: Resources for Environmental Educators*, edited by Martha C. Monroe, and Marianne E. Krasny, 9–28. Washington, DC: North American Association for Environmental Education (NAAEE).

Bones, David. 1994. *EE Toolbox: Getting Started—A Guide to Bringing Environmental Education Into Your Classroom*. Ann Arbor: MI: University of Michigan.

Chawla, Louise, and D.F. Cushing. 2007. "Education for Strategic Environmental Behavior." *Environmental Education Research* 13 (4): 437–452.

Cialdini, R. B. (2003). "Crafting Normative Messages to Protect the Environment." *Current Directions in Psychological Science* 12 (4): 105–109. DOI: 10.1111/1467-8721.01242

Disinger, J.F. 1983. *Environmental Education's Definitional Problems*. ERIC Clearinghouse for Science, Mathematics and Environmental Education Information Bulletin, 2. Columbus, OH: ERIC/SMEAC.

———. 1993. "Environment in the K–12 Curriculum: An Overview." In *Environmental Education – Teacher Resource Handbook*, edited by Richard J. Wilke, 23–43. New York: Kraus International Publications.

———. 2009. "The Purposes of Environmental Education: Perspectives of Teachers, Governmental Agencies, NGOs, Professional Societies, and Advocacy Groups." In *Environmental Education and Advocacy: Changing Perspectives of Ecology and Education*, edited by Edward A. Johnson, and Michael J. Mappin, 137–158. Cambridge: Cambridge University Press.

Disinger, J.F., and R.W. Howe. 1990. *Trends and Issues Related to the Preparation of Teachers for Environmental Education*. Environmental Education Information Report. ERIC Clearinghouse for Science, Mathematics, and Environmental Education Information Report. Available at: http://files.eric.ed.gov/fulltext/ED335233.pdf (Accessed on September 27, 2023).

Disinger, J.F., and M.C. Monroe. 1994. *EE Toolbox – Workshop Resource Manual, Defining Environmental Education*. Ann Arbor, MI: University of Michigan, National Consortium for Environmental Education and Training.

Genc, Murat. 2015. "The Project-Based Learning Approach in Environmental Education." *International Research in Geographical and Environmental Education* 24 (2): 105–117. DOI: 10.1080/10382046.2014.993169

Gough, Annette. 2013. "Emergence of Environmental Education Research: A 'History' of the Field." In *International Handbook of Research on Environmental Education*, edited by Robert B. Stevenson, Michael Brody, Justin Dillon, and Arjen E.J. Wals, 9–12. New York: Routledge.

Hines, J.M., H.R. Hungerford, and A.N. Tomera. 1986/87. "Analysis and Synthesis of Research on Responsible Environmental Behavior: A Meta-analysis." *Journal of Environmental Education* 18 (2): 1–8.

Hungerford, H.R. 1987. "Environmental Education and Student Behaviors in Trends and Issues." In *Environmental Education: EE in School Curricula*, edited by John F. Disinger, 25–38. Reports of a Symposium and a Survey. Environmental Education Information Reports. ERIC Clearinghouse for Science, Mathematics, and Environmental Education, NAAEE, Ohio, Available at: http://files.eric.ed.gov/fulltext/ED292608.pdf (Accessed on September 27, 2023).

Hungerford, H.R., and T.L. Volk. 1990. "Changing Learner Behavior through Environmental Education." *Journal of Environmental Education* 21 (3): 8–21. http://www.elkhornsloughctp.org/uploads/files/1374624954Changinglearnerbehavior-HandV.pdf. DOI: 10.1080/00958964.1990.10753743

Kazdin, Alan E. 2008. *Society's Grand Challenges—Insights from Psychological Science*. Washington, DC: American Psychological Association. Available at: https://www.apa.org/science/programs/gc-climate-change.pdf (Accessed on June 19, 2023).

Kibert, C.J., M.C. Monroe, A.L. Peterson, R.R. Plate, and L.P. Thiele. 2012. *Working Toward Sustainability–Ethical Decision Making in a Technological World*. New York: John Wiley & Sons.

Kopnina, H. 2014. "Future Scenarios and Environmental Education." *The Journal of Environmental Education* 45 (4): 217–231. DOI: 10.1080/00958964.2014.941783

Lucas, A.M. 1980a. "Science and Environmental Education: Pious Hopes, Self Praise and Disciplinary Chauvinism." *Studies in Science Education* 7 (1): 1–26. DOI: 10.1080/03057268008559874

———. 1980b. "The Role of Science Education in Education for the Environment." *Journal of Environmental Education* 12 (2): 33–37. DOI: 10.1080/00958964.1981.10801898

NCERT, National Council of Educational Research and Training, 2004. *Environmental Education in Schools—Syllabus for Environmental Education in Schools Submitted to the Hon'ble Supreme Court of India in Pursuance of its Order Dated 18th December 2003*. New Delhi: NCERT.

———. 2005. *National Curriculum Framework-2005*. New Delhi: NCERT.

Reno, R., Cialdini, R., and Kallgren, C.A. (1993). "The Transsituational Influence of Social Norms." *Journal of Personality and Social Psychology* 64: 104–112.

Schultz, P.W., Jessica M. Nolan, Robert B. Cialdini, Noah J. Goldstein, and Vadas Griskevicius. 2007. "The Constructive, Destructive, and Reconstructive Power of Social Norms." *Psychological Science* 5: 429–434. DOI: 10.1111/j.1467-9280.2007.01917.x

Sobel, D. 2008. *Childhood and Nature—Design Principles for Educators*, 144–146. Portland, ME: Stenhouse Publishers.

UNESCO-UNEP, United Nations Educational, Scientific and Cultural Organization-United Nations Environment Programme. 1978. "The Tbilisi Declaration." *Connect, UNESCO–UNEP Environmental Education Newsletter* III (1): 1–8.

5
ENVIRONMENTAL EDUCATION IN THE SCHOOL CURRICULUM

5.1 Chapter Overview

Inclusion of environmental education in the school curriculum is welcomed by all. However, how well has environmental education fared in the school curriculum? There is no consensus on how it should be reflected or implemented in schools. This chapter discusses the various ways in which environmental education can be implemented in the school curriculum so as to achieve its objectives. For this, two popular approaches have been discussed: separate subject (interdisciplinary) approach and infusion (multidisciplinary) approach. Keeping in view the limitations in the two approaches, a few other approaches have also been suggested which are discussed briefly in the chapter. The Hand-Print CARE approach will be especially interesting to readers. Irrespective of the approach adopted, every subject discipline can advance environmental education. Keeping this in view, for the benefit of teachers, several examples of how environmental education can be integrated in different subject areas are also discussed in the chapter.

5.2 Introduction

In the previous chapters, the objectives of environmental education have been discussed—to help students acquire awareness, knowledge, attitude, and skills and to provide opportunities to participate in the solving of environmental problems. However, how such objectives can be achieved by way of the school curriculum depends on the methods and strategies adopted in the teaching–learning process. It is no secret that, in the name of environmental education, only content and information are being added in the curriculum without any

DOI: 10.4324/9781003461135-6

serious efforts being put in to accomplish its objectives. And hence environmental education continues to be treated as a few side activities in schools such as sorting of garbage, switching off lights and fans, and planting of trees. However, there are definitely possibilities to meaningfully integrate environmental education in the school curriculum. For this, it is important to address all the three dimensions of environmental education, that is, education 'about,' 'in,' and 'for' the environment to successfully achieve its objectives.

There are at least a few approaches that can be used to integrate environmental education in the curriculum. How best environmental education can be implemented and which approach should be adopted has been a concern haunting environmental educators ever since environmental education began to be considered as part of the curriculum. All such approaches have their own pros and cons and it will be pretty much contextual to adopt the most appropriate approach depending upon various factors—availability of trained teachers, time, resources, state or national education policies, etc.

5.3 Environmental Education through the School Curriculum

In the light of the Tbilisi Declaration, the objectives of environmental education through the school curriculum is to help students acquire 'awareness' (of and sensitivity to the total environment), 'knowledge' (a basic understanding of the environment and its related problems), 'attitudes' (a set of values and feelings of concern for the environment, the motivation to actively participate in environmental improvement and protection, and so on), and 'skills' (for identifying and solving environmental problems) and provide students with an opportunity for 'participation' (to be actively involved at all levels in working toward resolution of environmental problems).

Although all the components—awareness, knowledge, attitudes, skills, and participation—are essential for a meaningful environmental education, Engleson (1987, 46) suggests that, due to the intellectual and moral developmental characteristics of children, some kinds of objectives should be emphasized more than others at certain levels and therefore suggests specific emphases for different levels (see Table 5.1).

Environmental education, today, has established itself in the formal school systems as an important component of the curriculum. However, when it comes to implementation, unfortunately, it seems to be more accepted than actuated in the schools (Lahiry et al. 1988, 1). In other words, environmental education has a presence in the curriculum, but remains marginalized in practice, as mentioned earlier in the introduction. In most cases, it is found that the curriculum addresses only part of the whole of environmental education. This is largely attributed to lack of understanding of the philosophy or concept of environmental education by the teachers (Lahiry et al. 1988, 16; Lucas 1980).

TABLE 5.1 Grade-Level Emphases on Environmental Education Objective Categories

Level	Major Emphasis	Minor Emphasis
K–3	Awareness, Attitudes	Knowledge, Skills, Participation
3–6	Knowledge, Attitudes	Awareness, Skills, Participation
6–9	Knowledge, Skills, Attitudes	Awareness, Participation
9–12	Skills, Participation, Attitudes	Awareness, Knowledge

Source: David C. Engleson (1987).

As a result of this, nothing much has changed on the ground. In the name of environmental education, additional scientific facts and information is provided about the natural environment through the curriculum, most commonly in science and geography curricula. This traditional way of handling environmental education is the easiest and most non-controversial way and continues to be practiced even today in most classrooms. Through this practice, students gain adequate environmental knowledge and become quite aware of environmental issues facing the world but it is never solution-oriented (Lahiry et al. 1988, 16). For example, students are taught in civic or social studies classes about decision-making by the government, but they fail to use such knowledge effectively as citizens in solving environmental problems, all because they were never taught how to use the knowledge in their daily lives (Hungerford and Peyton, 1994, 11). Considering Lucas' (1972) classification of environmental education as mentioned in Chapter 2, such practices in schools can be grouped as 'education about the environment,' which focuses on providing cognitive understanding including the development of skills necessary to obtain this understanding. Tilbury (1997) calls it a 'head' approach to environmental education. Students learn about the theories of how natural systems function, man–nature interactions, and various environmental issues—their causes, impacts, and so on. They also learn some of the skills in the classrooms or laboratories to tackle such issues—some process skills and technical skills such as testing water, soil, or air quality. These skills could be related to methods of collection of information or data and its analysis, investigation of environmental issues, problem-solving, and use of information and communication technology (ICT)—all in theory learned in the classroom. By addressing this dimension of environmental education, that is, education about the environment, at the most, students are able to acquire the 'awareness,' 'knowledge,' and 'skill' components of the objectives of environmental education. However, studies have revealed that this increase in cognitive understanding of the students about the environment does not, in any way, lead to attitudinal change nor does it encourage students to act on environmental issues. Moreover, it is also not uncommon to find that local environmental issues do not find place in such discourses. No connection between what is being learned about the environment and what is actually happening in their environment is reflected in the teaching–learning in schools. Therefore, such education 'about' the environment in itself is not complete and cannot achieve the objectives of environmental education.

What then needs to be done so that students can acquire a set of values and feelings of concern for the environment and the motivation to actively participate and contribute in the improvement of the environment and its protection? In short, how can they acquire environmental 'attitudes'? Going back to Lucas' (1972) classification of environmental education, the second dimension of environmental education is 'education in the environment.' This refers to education that takes place in a situation that best reflects what is being learned. Such education favors student-centered and inquiry-based learning facilitated by more open-ended and flexible teaching styles and often takes the form of outdoor education and experiential learning (Tilbury 1997). By way of doing environmental education 'in' the environment, students are able to link their curriculum with their environment which ultimately increases not only their awareness level but also their concern for the issue and their personal value toward the environment. It is through such experiences that students acquire environmental attitudes—a set of values, concern, a sense of responsibility, commitment, and motivation to participate in improving the environment. For example, learning about a degrading lake and its impact can be best done by taking the students to one such locations as it will not only help them connect real-world issues and their curriculum but will also help them acquire the much-needed attitudes toward the issue. Tilbury (1997) considers such attempts as a 'heart' approach to environmental education since it involves building of personal values and concern. However, the linear causality between educational experience (in the above example, visiting a degrading lake) and pro-environmental behavior has also been disputed with critics arguing that "people's environmental behaviors are too complex and contextually dependent to be captured by a simple casual model" (Kopnina 2014). Also, though development of environmental attitudes is important to achieve the goals of environmental education, Lucas (1980) warned that too much emphasis is given to it without focusing on the appropriate behavior or actions. He added that without action, attitude will not produce the desired environmental conditions that is envisaged to be achieved through environmental education. This aspect of environmentally responsible behaviors has been discussed elaborately in Chapter 4. Though such learning 'in' the environment may not always bring about pro-environmental behavior, it will definitely enhance the tendency toward such behavior. However, such practices hardly seem to be happening in the schools. What is being observed is, instead of doing environmental education 'in' the environment, most of the activities go on within the four walls of the classroom. It is found that there is still very inadequate exposure of the students to their 'habitat,' and there is little active learning from the natural and social worlds around them (NCERT 2006, 4; Shimray, Farkya, and Varte

2013). Schools make do with potted plants, mini-aquariums, movies, photographs, slide shows on environmental degradation, and so on to replace outside classroom activities and experiences. Such alternatives are not likely to help students develop environmental attitudes.

Education 'about' the environment and education 'in' the environment together still cannot achieve the objectives of environmental education. This is because education 'about' and 'in' the environment is mostly theoretical and not real situation-based. To bring about improvement in the environment, environmental education has to be action-oriented and participatory in real environmental issues. That is, it has to address environmental issues through action. This forms the third dimension of environmental education as proposed by Lucas (1972), that is, 'education for the environment' which has its focus on the values, ethics, problem-solving, and action objectives. It is about improving or protecting the environment. Therefore, although environmental education should encompass all the three forms or dimensions, for education to be 'truly' environmental so that ultimate goal of environmental well-being is achieved, then focus must be education 'for' the environment (Spork 1992). While addressing this dimension of environmental education, students are provided opportunities for 'participation' so that they can be actively involved in the resolution of environmental problems. This is necessary to achieve one of the goals of environmental education, that is, environmental education must develop problem-solvers and thus should itself utilize a problem-solving approach (UNESCO 1980, p. i). Tilbury (1997) considers it as a 'hand' approach to environmental education since it involves action. Through such activities, students feel empowered and believe that they themselves can be instrumental in bringing about change. Thus, it conveys the message that environmental issues can be resolved, it has been resolved due to involvement of committed people, and each one can participate in the resolution (Monroe 1991). Hence, this dimension of environmental education can be considered the most important, though it is dependent upon education 'about' and 'in' the environment to provide the skill, rationale, and knowledge to support its transformative intentions (Fien 1993 cited in Tilbury 1997). By ignoring the 'for' component of environmental education, the expected end result of environmental education, that is, resolution of environmental issues, cannot be realized, and the whole educational purpose of environmental education will be defeated. Chawla and Cushing (2007) went a step further by suggesting that it is not enough to promote action for the environment but the most strategic actions need to be emphasized. Yet, unfortunately, many researchers have found that education 'for' the environment has always received least coverage and support in the classroom, as reported by Spork (1992) in the case of Australian schools. As a result, the focus to nurture students to inculcate the appropriate environmental attitudes, such as values, ethics, morals, motivations, behaviors, and actions, receives little importance (Spork 1992). Also, students are not helped to develop skills necessary to act constructively for the environment. All that is done is to pass on information about the environment to build cognitive knowledge and increase awareness about environmental issues. Simply put, a passive form of environmental education is predominant instead of an action-oriented, socially critical, participatory form which is envisaged in environmental education. One of the reasons for this could be that since education 'for' the environment focuses on actual environmental issues, which are often controversial and action-oriented, many teachers either feel unconfident of handling such controversial issues or are fearful of being accused of bias or indoctrination (Tilbury 1997). Unless environmental education takes a socially critical or socially reconstructive orientation or encourages active involvement and participation in environmental problems and issues, education 'for' the environment can never be achieved (Spork 1992). Yet, what is observed is, critical discussions are predominantly lacking and rarely seen in classrooms (Spork 1992) and teaching is 'to the textbook,' as observed in a case study conducted in India by Haydock and Srivastava (2019).

As important as it is to address the 'for' component of environmental education, it is equally important to identify the 'actions' students could be involved in. It is felt that issue analysis and action may be appropriate to be taken up from the high school level (Lane 2006, 161). Nevertheless, there are actions that can be taken up by students at the primary level too. For example, for a kid in the primary stage, it could be as simple as closing taps properly, using water judiciously, turning off fans and lights when not in use, not littering, using paper judiciously, nurturing a sapling, and spreading awareness to friends in the locality to avoid using firecrackers. From the secondary stage onward, students may be engaged in resolving actual environmental concerns and issues in their locality. For example, they can look into the health and hygiene issues in slums, plights of ragpickers, waste disposal, scarcity of water, and lack of space for recreation. Once students have identified the issue of their concern, they can look for alternative solutions, choose the most appropriate, and apply it and see if it works.

As discussed, unless all the three dimensions of environmental education, that is, education 'about,' 'in,' and 'for' the environment are addressed, the objectives of environmental education, which fall under the five categories such as 'awareness,' 'knowledge,' 'attitude,' 'skills,' and 'participation,' cannot be achieved. However, the issues that exist in the implementation of environmental education are not new to us. Besides many other reasons, lack of professional development stands out prominently in the list, the details of which are discussed in Chapter 8.

5.4 Approaches in Environmental Education

So far, the discussions have been on the possibilities of implementation of environmental education in the school curriculum in general. As mentioned earlier, which approach should be adopted in its implementation has been a matter of debate among professionals and practitioners. Professional environmental educators have suggested several approaches or models, which include separate subject approach, infusion, insertion, and integration approaches. Some educators maintain the ambiguity in the latter three approaches keeping in view the lack of clear demarcation in the three as is practiced by teachers (Lane 2006, 167), while others treat them as distinct from each other in that environmental education is integrated into the curriculum by way of infusion (the incorporation of environmental concepts, activities, and examples into existing curricular goals) and insertion (the addition of an environmental unit or course to the class or curriculum; usually something else is removed) (Monroe and Cappaert 1994, 11). Much of the following discussions will focus on the two popular approaches or models that have been most commonly in use in environmental education curriculum development and implementation globally: Separate subject or 'Interdisciplinary' approach and infusion or 'Multidisciplinary' approach. These two approaches that have been put forward by many experts in the field will be discussed in detail. In addition, a third approach, which propagates the inclusion of both the infusion and separate subject approach in the curriculum, will also be discussed in brief.

5.4.1 Separate Subject (Interdisciplinary) Approach

The term 'interdisciplinary' (indicating the nature of EE) as used in the guiding principles in the Tbilisi Declaration and as it is being used here (as a method or approach to implement EE) has been clarified in Chapter 2. As the name suggests, separate subject or interdisciplinary approach is about teaching environmental education as a separate discipline. This approach reflects an important feature of the Tbilisi Declaration, which states that environmental education should be provided to all ages and at all grade levels and be interdisciplinary in its approach, drawing on the specific content of each discipline in making possible a holistic and balanced perspective (UNESCO-UNEP 1978). In this approach, environmental concerns are addressed by taking into consideration all possible perspectives from different subject areas (see Figure 5.1). In other words, a systems perspective or systems thinking (where the environment is visualized as a set of connected, interdependent objects that form a complex unity, that is, as a whole and not in compartments) (NCERT 2011) is employed while looking at environment-related topics, concerns, and issues which helps to understand the complex relationships within and between issues.

As shown in Figure 5.1, owing to its holistic approach, students using the interdisciplinary approach may show better understanding of environmental concerns and issues, compared to other students adopting different approaches.

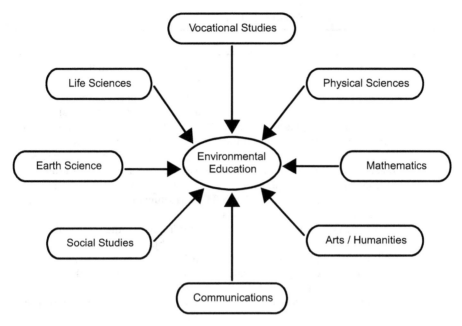

FIGURE 5.1 Separate Subject or Interdisciplinary Model.
Source: Adapted from Hungerford and Peyton (1994, 9).

The approach, however, has several disadvantages as well. Braus and Wood (1993, 35) provided a set of advantages and disadvantages of the approach, which is given in Table 5.2.

Several others have written in support of this approach while others have been critical. Views expressed by Feng (2012) show support of the approach. Feng maintains that interdisciplinarity enables learners to create links between individual disciplinary areas. They are able to have a holistic perspective of the concepts and hence make learning more meaningful and interesting. This, in turn, enables them to understand the complexity of the world better. This is especially important for learners at the lower stage of school education where they find it difficult to create links by themselves of the concepts they learn in different disciplinary areas (Sarabhai, Raghunathan, and Kandula 1998, 5). The interdisciplinary approach can help remove or reduce such gaps. For example, concepts related to water can be studied in different disciplinary areas. Properties of water, stomata and transpiration, evaporation, condensation, precipitation, water cycle, and rainwater harvesting, will be invariably part of the science curriculum. Water table, sources of water, rainfall, and so on will most probably be studied in geography. Water crisis in a society and acts and laws related to water are within the purview of another

TABLE 5.2 Interdisciplinary (Separate Subject) Approach

Sl. No.	Pros	Cons
1	Easier to implement as a single subject	Hard to get schools to 'buy' it (difficult to cull out time slot for environmental education in the already-congested schedule)
2	Allows teacher to present concepts that build throughout the course	Needs trained environmental education teachers (requires more in-depth knowledge of different subjects)
3	Teacher training is somewhat easier, although it requires teachers to have a more in-depth background of different subjects	Takes time from other standard topics (hard to squeeze in with other curriculum demands)
4	Easier to evaluate as a separate course	Might imply that the environment is its own subject and not interdisciplinary
5	Pulls everything together for students and can achieve greater depth and comprehension	Hard to find qualified teachers to design and teach courses
6	Puts a priority on the subject	Not as easy to see the connections with other subjects
7	Students' experience with interdisciplinary environmental education will go a long way	May limit the number of students exposed (especially if it is made optional)
8	The concerned teacher will be equipped enough to do justice to environmental education	May cause some teachers to assume environmental education 'is not my responsibility'
9	Teachers need not worry about what is included in the curriculum of other subjects related to environmental issues	Teachers will not care to bring out the relevance of environmental issues with other subjects

Source: Adapted from Braus and Wood (1993).

subject, that is, social science. Unless these concepts are linked together, learning will never be meaningful. Learners will not be able to view each issue from a holistic point of view. An interdisciplinary approach certainly helps to present the concepts holistically.

The key to interdisciplinarity is an open attitude, a willingness to learn, and an ability to engage with different ways of thinking on common issues faced. Such an approach exposes learners to the plurality of thinking and the limitations of particular perspectives. It will be especially useful in terms of taking positions on values and ethics. As a result, such learners are able to seize opportunities to disagree, to explore, to reflect, and to develop their own perspectives (Jickling 2003 cited in Feng 2012). It may be noted that learning does not take place in isolation but in connection with other disciplines and, hence, interdisciplinary courses provide students with 'a valuable model of lifelong holistic learning' (Stolpa 2004 cited in Feng 2012).

As discussed above in detail, the most common way to practice the interdisciplinary approach is by way of a separate subject wherein an individual teacher draws perspectives from different subject areas. In such cases, it is expected that the teacher must have a fair knowledge of different disciplines. However, this is not the only way to achieve the objectives of the interdisciplinary approach. There are several other different ways of employing this approach. Such strategies are most advantageous when an individual teacher does not have sufficient knowledge of different disciplines. A few of those will be discussed here. One predominant way of doing it is by having two or three courses taught separately yet ensuring that the contents are carefully designed by all the teachers to highlight significant connections among the disciplines. The success of such a practice lies in presenting a holistic picture to the learners in spite of the topics being taught at different times and space. Another way of doing it is by team-teaching. Two or three classes can be team-taught in a learning-community format where all the instructors who specialize in different disciplines are present at the time (Stolpa 2004 cited in Feng 2012). Learners are likely to understand complex issues better through this practice. And this practice seems to be more effective compared to the former. A possible drawback could be the difference in the style, language, and terms used by instructors from different disciplines which might affect learners in their process of learning.

Whatever be the model of interdisciplinary teaching and learning adopted, what is aimed for is to bring about systemic, relational thinking which emphasizes seeing contexts, connections, and developing integrative approaches. Systems thinking enables a learner to build up whole pictures of phenomena without breaking them into parts. Flood (2001, 133 cited in Feng 2012) qualifies such learning as 'valid knowledge and meaningful understanding.' It also helps "learners shift focus and attention from 'things' to processes, from analysis to synthesis, from detail to pattern, from static states to dynamics, and from 'parts' to 'wholes'" (Feng 2012). Sterling (2005 cited in Feng 2012) also presents a view that systemic thinking offers a "holistic approach through recognizing the complex interconnected nature of all aspects of the world around us from an individual to a global level."

The merits of interdisciplinarity are also clearly visible when it comes to real world situations. It is obvious that environmental and societal challenges are not defined by academic disciplines and, hence, when problematic situations arise—which is defined as a situation in which habitual responses to an environment are experienced as inadequate for continuing some activity that is aimed to fulfill needs and desires—the resolution of such a situation is initiated with inputs from a diversity of disciplines (Frodeman et al. 2007 cited in Feng 2012).

Although an interdisciplinary approach is ideal and desirable, practically it will not be easy to achieve it. Disinger (1997) in Environmental Education's Definitional Problem writes:

> Though environmental education is ideally interdisciplinary—an eclectic assemblage of interacting disciplines, its practitioners typically approach it as if it were multidisciplinary— an eclectic assemblage of discrete disciplines. Because environmental education practitioners typically are grounded in no more than one of the multiplicity of disciplines involved, logic leads them to approach environmental education through the intellectual filters of their own disciplines.

As a result, practitioners are unable to present environmental issues holistically. But instead of making efforts to fill this gap by discussing or collaborating with practitioners from other disciplines, Disinger (1997) adds:

> These practitioners in environmental education typically continue to talk past one another, rather than with one another; all say things approximating 'the right thing', but they apparently do not recognize the generally subtle, sometimes glaring, differences in meaning between their utterances and those of their colleagues.
>
> *(1997)*

Besides being grounded in only one subject, it has also been observed that teachers teaching a certain specific subject tend to think that they are superior to the others. Many science teachers are, in Lucas' (1980) terms, 'disciplinary chauvinists' who place a higher priority on teaching content from their own disciplinary specialization rather than engage the interdisciplinary or cross-disciplinary demands of environmental education. Such an attitude of teachers is a setback in the implementation of the interdisciplinary approach. Liu et al. (2007 cited in Feng 2012) further points out the challenges brought forth by the existing system of knowledge production fortified by disciplinary boundaries. Such practices do not prepare students to be adaptive or responsive to the real-world challenges and hence are a setback for the implementation of environmental education. This issue with the interdisciplinary approach exists because teachers and practitioners who have been trained in a disciplinary manner are engaged in the tasks. Hence, in order to address the challenge related to presenting an unbiased and holistic view of all aspects in environmental education, it will be crucial to have practitioners who themselves have been trained in an interdisciplinary manner. The common practice of entrusting the task to handle interdisciplinary environmental education to any science teacher has to be replaced by engaging teachers with interdisciplinary education background.

Besides the disadvantages of the interdisciplinary separate subject approach in terms of practicability as discussed, there is yet another reason that makes this approach undesirable in the school curriculum, and this needs to be highlighted here. It is agreed that the existing school curriculum is already loaded in terms of disciplinary subjects to be learned, vast content to be covered, and numerous curricular activities to be fulfilled, and even in terms of the time allotted to complete the course. Given this situation, adding another subject would be too much of a burden, not only for the students but also for the whole system, and the implementation of a separate subject under such circumstances would turn out to be only routine, lacking seriousness and without any meaningful impact. Moreover, even if the interdisciplinary separate subject approach is implemented, the curriculum of different subjects will still have environmental education components. For example, science curriculum will still include ecosystem, biodiversity, forest, energy, etc. Similarly, social science curriculum will continue to include sustainable development, mines, migration, population, etc. This means that students will be learning about similar topic twice, i.e., once in their regular subject of science/ social science etc., and once in the separate environmental education subject. The way it is approached will be obviously different, though. In a way, if availability of time in school was not an issue, such repetition could reinforce learning and may strengthen environmental education. However, the reality is, the school time table is already choked.

5.4.2 Infusion (Multidisciplinary) Approach

In education, infusion refers to the incorporation of a particular content of study in a different established course, with the focus on the new content, without affecting the unique nature of the course itself.

Infusion in environmental education is about incorporating environmental education into the curriculum of different existing subjects (multiple disciplines) rather than teaching environmental education as a separate discipline. In other words, in infusion approach, a single topic permeates many other disciplines (see Figure 5.2). Though environmental education has been traditionally infused mainly into science, history, and social studies classes, it can also be infused into all subject matters, including reading, writing, languages, mathematics, music, physical education, art, and other courses (Braus and Wood 1993). However, care is taken in such a way that the infusion process does not isolate the objectives of environmental education so extensively that the meaningful synthesis of experiences in the context of the discipline in which it has been infused is not possible (UNESCO 1980, 45). According to Hungerford et al. (1994, 11):

> Infusion refers to the integration of content and skills into existing courses in a manner as to focus on the content (and/or skills) without jeopardizing

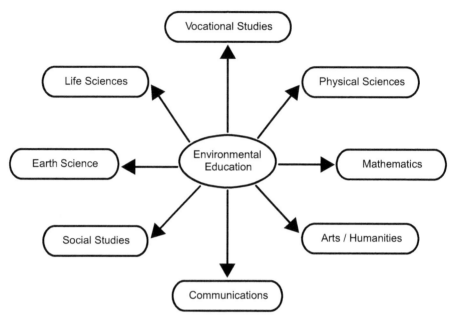

FIGURE 5.2   Infusion or Multidisciplinary Model.
Source: Adapted from Hungerford and Peyton (1994, 9).

the integrity of the courses themselves. In the case of environmental education, the professional educator carefully analyzes traditional courses for content and/or skills which could be 'environmentalized.'

While Monroe and Cappaert (1994, 11) equate infusion with thematic teaching, incorporating "environmental concepts, activities, and examples into existing curricular goals." However, in spite of the addition of content, the standard or the nature of the existing course/concept is not affected in any way. Ideally, the inclusion of a new content and skills in the process of infusion could enrich or enhance the existing courses or curriculum (Fellows 1980 cited in Lane 2006). For example, a study by Nam and Ito (2011) found that teaching climate science through history in an undergraduate course increased knowledge of climate change and human interactions as well as interest in the topic.

This approach is supported by professional environmental educators who believe that incorporating environmental education throughout the total curriculum at every grade level will bring about a more comprehensive treatment of environmental concerns (Simmons 1989 cited in Lane 2006, 12). It is also argued that "such an approach also recognizes that environmental issues cut across traditional disciplinary lines and that developing an environmentally responsible citizen involves acquiring knowledge, attitudes, and skills beyond that of a simple understanding of scientific or ecological principles" (Simmons 1989 cited in Lane 2006, 15). Such possibility was also pointed out by teachers in a study conducted by Glackin et al. (2018) in such a way that "Science can deal with the how it happens. Geography can deal more on the kind of impacts...and perhaps different strategies (to address problems)."

As discussed above, infusion is not merely adding certain environmental facts into the curriculum. But through infusion, different disciplines attempt to achieve the objectives of environmental education, that is, awareness, knowledge, attitude, skills, and participation, without jeopardizing the integrity of the concerned subject. Monroe (1991, 9) recommends the following four activities to turn environmental facts into environmental education and notes that each can be accomplished within existing subject areas and grade levels:

1. Include issues by extending the facts—the "often controversial edge between people and the environment" and solutions to these issues.
2. Carry out problem-solving skills with students: communications, group skills, leadership, creative thinking, and decision-making.
3. Find out suitable environmental feelings, attitudes, and values. Students may learn to appreciate and be responsible for others and the environment and compare their values to their ways of living.
4. Allow students to take part in the resolution of real issues.

Other professionals in the field have created certain steps that may be considered during infusion. For example, in A Guide to Curriculum Development in Environmental Education, Engleson (1985 cited in Lane 2006, 17) provides the following steps:

Step 1   Select the environmental topic to be infused into an existing subject area instructional unit...

Step 2   Identify the subject area units which relate to, or support the investigation of, the chosen environmental topic...

Step 3   Develop one or more environmental objectives for the subject-matter unit...

Step 4   Specify the environmental content to be added to the unit...

Step 5   Develop new instructional procedures as needed...

Step 6   Identify new process skills which might be used or developed in achieving the new environmental objectives...

Step 7   Identify new resources to be used in achieving the environmental objectives...

Step 8   Identify related activities and new topics for investigation which may be suggested by teaching the new infused unit.

(51–52)

However, the above steps may not be applicable in India as it is. Teachers will have to adapt to make the steps relevant in the context of their curriculum. In India, following the recommendation of the National Curriculum Framework 2005, environmental concepts and concerns have already been infused in the textbooks for different subjects and other textual materials, as in the case of materials developed by the National Council of Educational Research and Training (NCERT) as well as by states and union territories. In other words, contents on environmental issues and concerns have been added in the materials. However, in most instances, the content provided in subject textbooks is not sufficient to indicate environmental education objectives. In such cases, the subject teacher will have to identify the environmental concepts and concerns that have been incorporated in the textbooks and proceed from there. It will be interesting to see how infusion will be handled in the curricular materials which are being prepared based on the National Curriculum Framework for School Education 2023.

Drawing from the suggestions of Monroe (1991) and Engleson (1985 cited in Lane 2006), let us illustrate infusion approach by giving an example which will be relevant to schools in India. For this, let us consider a hypothetical passage from a Grade 8 science textbook in India:

You are familiar with coal and petroleum. But have you ever thought where did they come from? It will be interesting for you to know that coal and petroleum are fossil fuels. They are formed from dead organisms. It required millions of years for these dead organisms to be converted into fossil fuels. The coal and petroleum that is available today will not last for more than a few hundred years. It is not possible to speed up the formation of fossil fuel artificially. Therefore, the only way out is to use them judiciously and at the same time look for other alternatives to meet the world's ever-increasing energy needs. Using renewable sources of energy is the best option as it will also reduce air pollution, which is mainly caused by burning of fossil fuels. Burning of fossil fuel also releases greenhouse gases such as carbon dioxide which cause global warming.

The Government of India has set up the Petroleum Conservation Research Association (PCRAA) to promote energy efficiency in different sectors. Some of the tips given by PCRA to save petrol/diesel are:

- Check tire pressure regularly
- Keep the engine in good condition
- Drive at a steady speed
- Avoid clutch-riding
- Switch off engines while waiting at red traffic signal

In the above passage, a lot of information and environmental facts have been provided, such as 'fossil fuels are exhaustible,' 'burning of fuels causes air pollution which also causes global warming,' and 'important tips to save petrol/diesel while driving.' A teacher in a science classroom may follow the following steps so as to practice infusion approach of environmental education while engaging in such topics:

1. Explain how fast fossil fuels are being used compared to the rate that they are produced naturally.
2. Explain some of the air pollutants from burning of fuels.
3. Correlate air pollution with global warming convincingly while keeping in mind that it is Grade 8 students who are in the classroom. Hence, the concept should be simplified but not trivialized.
4. Identify some issues associated with the topics which could be the following: (a) people do not want to commute by public transport, (b) the public in general are not concerned about reducing air pollution, and (c) the steps undertaken by the government are not effective to reduce burning of fossil fuels or reduce air pollution.
5. Once the issues are identified, the teacher may choose appropriate steps to address the issues depending upon the skills that they want the students to learn. The following are some suggestions:

    (i) A debate can be initiated so that different perspectives of the students could be shared. Doing this will help students widen their perspective of the issue and introspect on their views.
    (ii) Group discussion may be conducted wherein different groups can discuss can come up with their suggestive measures.
    (iii) Students can also take up projects in their locality related to the issue such as investigating why people do not want to commute by public transport or conduct a survey on how often people give their vehicles for servicing, and so on. Based on their study they can come up with solutions from which they can choose the most appropriate option and act toward it. This will not only help students experience real issues surrounding them but also make them feel empowered to tackle such issues as responsible citizens.

The strategies presented above seem to suggest infusion approach as a sound practice to achieve the goals of environmental education. Students do not just acquire knowledge and gather information about fossil fuels and its impact but they also become aware about other associated concerns, thereby developing positive attitude; they also learn the skills needed to address relevant issues as they work on projects. Such multidisciplinary or infusion approach will allow students to apply environmental education concepts and problem-solving skills in a great variety of situations over a long period of time (UNESCO 1980, 15). For example, when students learn about how government functions in their civic or social studies classes, they can also learn how they can use such knowledge in solving environmental problems. Similarly, students can also learn to apply and connect the knowledge they obtain in different disciplines. If students learn long enough, year after year, to consider environmental consequences through different disciplines, it will do a world of good and bring about some attitudinal change in them at the end of their schooling.

However, in spite of its many advantages, the approach also has its disadvantages, as identified by Braus and Wood (1993, 35), which are shown in Table 5.3. One of the biggest concerns of the infusion approach as presented in the

TABLE 5.3 Multidisciplinary (Infusion) Approach

Sl. No.	Pros	Cons
1	Fewer resources are needed (do not need an environmental education specialist or a separate textbook)	Is difficult to infuse environmental education, and it requires extensive teacher training and effort
2	Does not compete with other standard subjects; does not compete for a slot in the curriculum	Often relies on motivated teachers for efforts to succeed
3	Can be done immediately, without core curriculum development	EE message can be so diluted to fit the objectives of a course that it can get lost/ students might not 'get it'
4	Many supplementary resources exist	Leaves too much to chance
5	Encourages transfer of learning and integrated problem-solving across the curriculum	Difficult to evaluate success
6	Appropriate for all age levels, although may be more difficult at upper grades	Subject specificity at upper grades seldom provides space for infusion
7	Allows all students at all levels an opportunity to get exposure	Exposure is often superficial
8	When done on a large scale, can continually reinforce and build upon key environmental concepts	Often brings about environmentally aware citizens but not environmentally committed warriors
9	Implemented easily in the subject/ discipline the teacher is teaching	Teachers may not be aware of what is included in the curriculum of other subjects related to environmental issues other than the subject/ discipline they are teaching; as a result, students may not get the opportunity to learn about all aspects of the issue

Source: Adapted from Braus and Wood (1993).

table is that, as a result of infusion, the message that is intended to be sent across may not be done so. For example, while discussing qualities of polluted water of different rivers and water bodies, the focus could be so much on the physical properties of the polluted water that the teacher might not be able to bring in the issues related to health hazards and other concerns, especially of those who are not able to afford pure drinking water and other social issues related to it. This could occur because of the 'it-is-not-my-concern' attitude of the teachers or due to disciplinary chauvinism as mentioned earlier. In some cases, the issue may be discussed, but if the teacher fails to make a deliberate effort to put forward the message clearly, the students will not grasp the message that is being attempted to be conveyed. In such a situation, the whole purpose of infusion approach will be defeated. Therefore, it is crucial for teachers to have an idea what other teachers are teaching in other subjects on the same environmental issue so that all aspects of the issue are covered and students can have a holistic view of those issue. However, Glackin et al. (2018) in their study observed that teachers did not know what is included in other subjects on different environment-related topics.

There are many others who are critical about the effectiveness of the infusion approach to achieve the goals of environmental education. For example, Feng (2012) writes: "In multidisciplinarity, learners may have studied, simultaneously or in sequence, more than one area of knowledge, without making connections between them or without collaborating as learners." The issue with this approach is that learners are unable to make connections or links between what they have studied in different disciplinary areas (Sarabhai, Raghunathan, and Kandula 1998). This will have serious implications on the implementation of environmental education since holistic understanding of environmental issues is fundamental to environmental education. In the absence of this, all other efforts related to environmental education will make little sense. Therefore, teachers must ensure that while they adopt the multidisciplinary approach, their attempt should be to make it as interdisciplinary as possible in the process which is the true nature of environmental education.

The concerns related to multidisciplinarity are not limited to the teaching–learning process alone, but it is also seen in the area of research. Godeman (2006 cited in Feng 2012) argues that in multidisciplinary teams, researchers are likely to carry out their analyses separately, working on "different aspects with their respective methods." The final result will tend to be a series of reports pasted together, without integrating synthesis (Max-Neef 2005 and Miller et al. 2008 cited in Feng 2012). For example, the impact of contamination of lake water can be studied by different researchers as a multidisciplinary team. One may study the impact on the economy of local people, another on the impact on the aquatic animals and plants, another on analysis of contaminants, and yet another on the health implications of people consuming fish and vegetables from the lake. If there is no synergy between the studies, the results obtained will not be meaningful and the report cannot be presented holistically.

Issues related to the infusion approach in India were already pointed out by Krishna Kumar (Kumar 1996; Sonowal 2009, 16). However, if the curriculum ensures that apart from the required knowledge of the discipline, other issues and concerns related to the topic also receive due importance, it would be the perfect way of approaching environmental topics. This is what is expected out of the infusion approach in the school curriculum. And given the curriculum load in the present education system where there is competition for space in the curriculum, this is a pragmatic approach to find room for environmental education (Disinger 1993, 39).

5.5 Comparisons between Interdisciplinary and Multidisciplinary Approach

The pros and cons of interdisciplinary and multidisciplinary approach have been discussed separately. Provided in Table 5.4 is the comparison of the two on some specific considerations, as mentioned by Hungerford and Peyton (1994, 10) and Hungerford et al. (1994, 11–15).

In spite of the several pros and cons inherent in both the models, multidisciplinary (infusion) model seems to have an edge over the interdisciplinary (separate subject) model because the former allows students to apply environmental education concepts and problem-solving skills in a great variety of situations over a long period of time. For example, if students consider ecological consequences of issues in a variety of situations, such as in economics, social studies, languages, or any other disciplines throughout their formal education, there is greater reason to expect them to use this knowledge in their own non-academic lives as well (Hungerford and Peyton 1994, 12). However, this does not mean discounting the many advantages that interdisciplinary model provides. For effective environmental education, all that is required is a sound educational procedure in either of the formats so that environmental education goals are achieved.

5.6 Examples of Environmental Education in Different Disciplines

Although environmental education comes naturally in the teaching–learning of science, it should not be a concern of science alone. It is but a challenge to the whole conventional subject-based curriculum and pedagogy since it requires a holistic accommodation of the personal, the social, and the economic, along with the scientific components (Jenkins and Pell 2006 cited in Gough 2008). This suggests that environmental education should be considered beyond

TABLE 5.4 Interdisciplinary (Separate subject) vs. Multidisciplinary (Infusion)

Sl. No.	Considerations	Interdisciplinary (Single Subject) Characteristics	Multidisciplinary (Infusion) Characteristics
1	Ease of implementation	Easier to implement as a single subject if time permits in the curriculum; teacher training is less of a problem.	Requires that more teachers be trained; greater coordination of curriculum necessary; requires less time/content in the existing curriculum
2	Teacher competencies	May require fewer teachers, but with more in-depth training in EE; thus, teacher training is less demanding in terms of teacher numbers but more demanding in terms of level of competencies required	Requires that teachers of all disciplines be competent to adapt and/or use environmental education materials, although perhaps not to the same depth as in single-subject approaches
3	Demand on curriculum load	Requires addition of this discipline to an already-crowded curriculum	May be effectively implemented with minimal demands on existing curricular load
4	Ease of curriculum development	Components easier to identify and sequence	Components must be effectively identified, sequenced, and accommodated by the existing curriculum
5	Evaluation	A comprehensive evaluation is much easier to accomplish in single-subject curriculum	Comprehensive evaluation difficult due to the number of variables involved
6	Age-level appropriateness	For a simple holistic approach, it will be more appropriate for lower age, but will be more appropriate at secondary level and above where greater depth of comprehension is required	Appropriate at all age levels
7	Effectiveness in teaching for transfer	More difficult to use in effectively teaching for transfer of learning; requires special efforts to do so	Teaching for transfer of learning is inherent in this approach when properly used; infusion permits decision-making to take place in other disciplines in an environmental context

(*Continued*)

128 Environmental Education in the School Curriculum

TABLE 5.4 (Continued)

Sl. No.	Considerations	Interdisciplinary (Single Subject) Characteristics	Multidisciplinary (Infusion) Characteristics
8	Ability to provide in-depth coverage of environmental issues	Budget considerations entirely depend on the nature of the course being developed; a highly sophisticated course demanding many field excursions or laboratory equipment could prove costly	Monetary considerations vary dependent on the nature of the curriculum being developed; monies required could be greater than in single-subject curriculum due to the number of learners involved across numerous grade (age) levels
9	Cooperation and collaboration among teachers	Is not necessarily required	Very much required for successful integration of different disciplines
10	Level of learning in students	Students are expected to learn better because issues are presented to them holistically	Largely depends on how well teachers of different discipline connect with the rest

Source: Adapted from Hungerford and Peyton (1994) and Hungerford et al. (1994).

disciplinary boundaries. Further, various studies have revealed that using the approach of environmental education in different subjects enhances learning and hence improves scores (Ernst and Monroe 2004; NEETF 2000).

In this chapter, as well as in the previous chapter, some examples to incorporate environmental education in the curriculum have been mentioned. Provided in the subsequent section are some more examples which have been presented rather crudely to illustrate how environmental education can make a difference in the teaching–learning process in different subjects. The examples represent only some of the ways environmental education can be done in every classroom, that is, all the examples provided here are not prescriptive but suggestive of how, through discussions, debates, sharing of experiences, and other teaching–learning strategies, a disciplinary teaching–learning can be extended or transformed to a more interdisciplinary and holistic approach as envisaged in environmental education. However, the approach to environmental education is not limited and should not be restricted to what is being presented in the following sections.

5.6.1 Environmental Education in Science

A science teacher prepares a slide of stomata of different plants—monocots and dicots—and tells the students about the structure, shape, number, and so on and explains its function in photosynthesis or connects it with the concept of transpiration. An environmental educator[1] takes it further to explain its role in water cycle and rainfall and how it is linked to conservation principles or how oxygen which sustains life is released by plants through these small pores called stomata. An environmental educator also enhances students' mathematics skills by involving them in simple arithmetic problems related to number of stomata, for example roughly counting the number of stomata in different trees, calculating the reduction in the number of stomata if trees are cut down, etc. In short, the teacher provides the larger picture which makes learning more meaningful and, at the same time, helps them understand the environmental problems that may arise due to deforestation.

A science teacher tells about the properties of mercury and its uses in blood pressure measuring instrument (mercury sphygmomanometers) or clinical thermometer. An environmental educator links its use in compact fluorescent lamps (CFLs) and the dangers of improper disposal of broken instruments or fused CFLs and how such carelessness can be hazardous, especially to ragpickers and sorters. An environmental educator can also narrate the incident that resulted in Minamata disease due to improper disposal of industrial mercury in the water bodies. She can explain how consumption of fish and other aquatic organisms from such water bodies led to the death of hundreds of people due to the disease and how hundreds are still suffering from the disease.

In a science class on the chapter forest, a science teacher discusses the types of trees, animals, shrubs, and the many services they provide in the form of timber, firewood, medicines, honey, and meat. An environmental educator purposely stretches the discussion to issues faced by forests dweller due to exploitation of forests and their products as well as developmental activities and their implications on their livelihood. An environmental educator can form groups in the class and ask each group to discuss whether forests dwellers should be rehabilitated to another place in the name of conservation of forests. Each group can then be asked to share the opinion of the group. The teacher can act as a facilitator of the discussion and intervene only when necessary. This will give opportunities to the students to hear differing views and understand other's point of view and help them rethink their opinion.

A science teacher explains how technology in the area of communication, healthcare, transportation, and agriculture has improved life. An environmental educator adds how much resources are used in the invention and production of such technologies and how the same can cause, and have caused, negative impacts such as pollution of air, water, and soil, health issues, and so on. For example, manufacturing industries for machine, tools, and chemicals, or thermal power plants for production of energy are major sources of pollution not only causing health hazards but also degrading the quality of the environment and impacting all life forms. An environmental educator emphasizes the practice of reducing, reusing, and recycling and brings in the concept of circular economy or zero waste.

A science teacher explains how food production can be increased to feed the ever-increasing population of the world by the use of genetically modified (GM) crops or fertilizers and pesticides. An environmental educator extends the discussion to the issues of farmers' inability to purchase seed for the next cropping season or how chemical fertilizers affect productivity, soil quality as well as health of the farmers owing to exposure to chemicals. An environmental educator also engages students in activities to find out if there are possible impacts of GM crops on biodiversity and also engages students in exploring the indigenous and traditional knowledge of seed conservation and their importance.

In a biotechnology class on bioremediation, the teacher explains the various types of wastes that requires bioremediation. The teacher also explains the strategies available for bioremediation of different kinds of wastes such as how microbes and plants are exploited to remediate the waste generated by humans. The teacher also explains why bioremediation is important and how it will pollute the soil, air, and water if bioremediation is not done to a safe level. An environmental educator emphasizes the importance of reduction in the amount of waste and at the same time brings in the aspect of social justice. It is to everybody's knowledge that the worst affected in a society due to environmental problems such as air or water pollution are those in the low economic strata or those belonging to a particular community, although they contribute the minimum to such problems. And the solutions available are not affordable to them in many cases. For example, indoor air purifier or RO water purifiers are not affordable to many. An environmental educator also discusses about the fact that people who die due to toxic air in manholes belong to some particular communities. Students are engaged in projects so that they can find out for themselves the social challenges pertinent to bioremediation. Similarly, students are also asked to find out the government initiatives related to bioremediation.

5.6.2 Environmental Education in Social Science

A social science teacher talks of industrial growth in terms of the kinds or types of industry, their number, and their production/manufacturing capacity. An environmental educator takes the discussion further and takes into account issues related to environmental justice to people who are most affected because of industrial developments. Industries are generally located in the outskirts of cities where in most cases, people with low-income group live. They are the most affected owing to pollution of air, water and soil, but they hardly get any benefit out of such industries. An environmental educator brings out such discussions in the classroom and gives opportunities to students to analyze such situations and share their views.

A social science teacher talks of demand–supply in terms of economic growth and development. An environmental educator also discusses that, with demand, supply also increases, and, in turn, increases the burden on the environment. This is because for every kind of production, natural resources are used in the form of raw materials, energy, water, and so on. In addition to utilization of natural resources in the process of production, it also generates wastes which could also be toxic or harmful to human beings and other life forms. Hence, emphasis on the maximum use of commodities in terms of duration and minimum extravagant purchase will reduce demand which in turn will reduce production at source, thereby decreasing exploitation of natural resources. Further, an environmental educator also makes students aware about the possible adverse impact on reduction in job opportunities, thus introducing a larger picture of the situation to the students.

A social science teacher talks about how development has made it easy for us to get anything from anywhere at any time of the year. For example, all kinds of imported food items are available everywhere. An environmental educator adds to the discussion on how such food products travel—the cost of transportation of such food items, how much fossil fuel is used in transportation, and how much carbon dioxide is released during transportation, and so on—taking the discussion to encourage the use of local products which will not only reduce harmful impacts to the environment but also improve the local economy. Students are engaged in projects related to local products and how consumption of such products by the local people can help the economy of the community and also the environment. Such education helps students become aware of the choices they can make as consumers and the difference they can make and at the same time makes them realize that the choices they make can have many negative impacts on the environment as well.

A social science teacher discusses where different kinds of mines are located in different parts of the country and the quantity in terms of production for different mines. An environmental educator takes the discussion further to its impact on the environment and also its implications for local people at the time of mining, and after since the problems and challenges faced by them are manifold. A social science teacher talks of the importance of the transport systems and the various ways of transportation—road, rail, air or water, and the developments that have happened in this sector in terms of area covered, transport vehicles, or the number of people traveling by different modes. An environmental educator takes the discussion beyond to include other aspects related to transportation such as the measures to be undertaken to avoid or reduce deterioration of the environment owing to such activities or impacts on the environment. For example, hundreds of hectares of forests are being cleared to make way for rails or vast stretches of lands are inundated under water due to construction of dams, displacing people and destroying their habitats, and disturbing the whole ecosystem. Of late, the increase in the number of air travelers is considered to be a sign of development. On the other hand, it is a fact that fossil fuel consumption is the highest in this mode of travel at the same time emitting the maximum greenhouse gas. An environmental educator brings in such aspects in the discussions.

A social science teacher discusses the GDP of the country. An environmental educator discusses the contribution of women to the society and how it can be improved if women are empowered. Besides, discussions also include the unpaid care work that women are engaged in and how such sacrificial contributions are not paid due recognition, or appreciated, or accounted for.

In a social science class, the teacher explains what sustainable development is i.e., "Development that meets the need of the present generation without compromising the ability of the future generation to meet their own needs." The teacher explains the different strategies for sustainable development. An environmental educator brings in the question of who would define 'needs' when the needs of different sections of the people are so different; what resources are required to meet the needs; how to ensure that the future generation can also meet their needs; how important it is to ensure that the balance in the functioning of the ecosystem is maintained for sustainable development. An environmental educator also emphasizes the value of nature in terms of aesthetic, spiritual, physical, or mental well-being which are not directly measurable and values nongeneration of wastes or reduction of wastes over technologies to treat waste by promoting circular economy or zero-waste economy. An environmental educator provides students an opportunity to critically think and explore these aspects and come up with their own views.

A social science teacher uses random example in the teaching–learning of economics, while an environmental educator takes examples of the economics of biodiversity[2] or the economics of climate change, economics related to insurance due to climate or environmental impacts, etc. using different economic models. For example, using the results from formal economic models, the Stern Review (2006)[3] estimates that if humans don't act, the overall costs and risks of climate change will be equivalent to losing at least 5% of global GDP each year, now and forever. This could rise to 20% if a wider range of risks and impacts is taken into account. In contrast, the Review reveals that the costs of action—reducing greenhouse gas emissions to avoid the worst impacts of climate change—can be limited to around 1% of global GDP each year. Students can be engaged in critical analysis of reports by different experts where there are disagreements especially due to differences in the treatment of risk and time in their evaluations of climate change as pointed out by Gollier (2006, 2008).[4]

A social science teacher discusses migration and other social issues associated with it. An environmental educator takes it further to include the environmental impacts associated with it, such as stress on the local resources which could be land, water, and food, which lead to scarcity, pollution, and other associated social issues such as reduction in job opportunities, social crimes, and conflicts. An environmental educator also brings in the aspect of migration due to environmental issues such as impacts of climate change causing a huge chunk of population in different parts of the world to migrate to other places and how such relocation affects their lives and livelihood, thereby jeopardizing sustainable development.

A basic necessity like housing will come up at some point in a social science class. A social science teacher discusses only in terms of availability, accessibility, and affordability. An environmental educator adds to the discussion other aspects such as environmental sustainability including the different kinds of resources used in the construction, waste generated, energy efficiency, air quality, sanitation and hygiene, etc. Students at the secondary stages may be engaged in designing eco-friendly, affordable, and sustainable housing for their geographical areas.

Resolving environmental issues is at the heart of environmental education for which an individual has to be prepared, not only intellectually but more importantly psychologically (Ernst and Monroe 2004; NEETF 2000). An environmental educator in psychology discusses the factors that influence the human mind to take certain environment-friendly decisions or behave in a particular manner that is pro-environment. For example, while discussing the principles of how the human mind can be influenced, an environmental educator deliberately uses an environment-related theme as a context for such deliberations as use of energy-efficient lighting system, equipment, or vehicle, construction of green building, use of solar energy, and so on. Such experiences will encourage students to have the right attitude toward the environment and also equip them to influence others in taking environmentally appropriate decisions.

5.6.3 Environmental Education in Mathematics

A mathematics teacher gives random data for analysis and plotting graphs. An environmental educator uses the real-world or local environmental problems or issues as a context of teaching such topics. For example, while teaching topics such as data handling an environmental educator asks students to collect data such as daily weather report, or temperature in different towns and cities and use it for plotting a graph, which could be a single-bar or a double-bar graph depending upon the data collected. The same can be used to study frequency distribution. This will not only make students aware about the weather pattern of different places but will also help them in the relation between different elements of weather. At the secondary stage, they may be engaged in more complex data, for example plotting a graph between greenhouse gases in the atmosphere and changes in the temperature over decades. Plotting such graphs will help students appreciate the phenomenon of climate change, and at the same time they will also be able to make rough predictions about future climate. While teaching topics related to comparing quantities, an environmental educator uses actual data of percentage increase in population or petrol consumption, or loss of biodiversity over the years. For example, students can be asked to calculate the amount of petrol that will be consumed in India in 2030 if the rate of increase in consumption per annum is 3.76% and the consumption in 2020 was 4.701 million barrels per day. Similar tasks are given related to an increase in population or petrol consumption. Drawing from the results of the calculations, an environmental educator also engages students to discuss further the impacts of biodiversity loss, petrol consumption, or increase in population. Engaging students in such exercise makes them aware about the issues related to the environment, such as challenges due to increase in population, biodiversity loss, or air pollution from burning of fossil fuels. Similarly, for calculation of direct proportion, an environmental educator uses the actual data of the current amount of carbon dioxide emission to calculate the expected amount in five years. Similarly, for calculation of indirect proportion, an environmental educator can use an example of rate of carbon dioxide emission with that of increased use of public transport or use of bicycle. Such teaching–learning experiences increase the awareness of the students about environmental problems and issues and at the same time connect the classroom with real-life experiences. It will also remind the students that the state of affairs of the environment is understood clearly only when it is represented mathematically. And these mathematical representations make sense when students are able to relate it with their real-life experiences.

5.6.4 Environmental Education in Languages

A language teacher often selects curricular material based on popularity or personal choice of authors/poets, while an environmental educator purposely chooses environment-related topics—stories and poems based on nature, such as rivers, clouds, snow, forests, and wildlife in the teaching–learning of language. As part of their letter writing skills, an environmental educator asks the students to write a letter to the municipal authorities putting forward the grievances about the waste issue in their locality. Similar letters can also be written to the editors of newspapers. An environmental educator can even take students out into the nature or into natural surroundings, let them experience the beauty of nature, make them hear the chirping of the birds, and use such experiences to improve their writing skills in the form of prose or poetry. This will not only improve the skills necessary to be learned as part of the curriculum, but it will also make students aware about the environmental issues in their locality and learn to appreciate the beauty of nature. This could also bring about some attitudinal change in the students.

The need to prepare and encourage students for environmental writing is also becoming increasingly important. It can be in the form of short stories, novels, poems, etc., which could be fiction or nonfiction. A good writing is always engaging. In today's world of unprecedented environmental challenges, the most worrisome being climate change, it is crucial to find ways to engage with people to convey necessary message. Environmental writers around the world are exploring different forms of writing. Rightly so, if climate change, or any environmental issue for that matter, is said to be threatening human existence, then it is only expected that all forms of writings—short, long, poem, prose, fiction, nonfiction—should reflect the threat whether as the 'story' (as the core or central idea of the writing) or in the 'setting' (as the background in the story). It is interesting to see Cli-Fi (climate fiction) becoming increasingly popular. Students can play with their imaginative capabilities and write on different areas of the environment. This will also reflect their understanding about the environment because fiction also stems from facts, after all. While it is important to convey environmental messages through writings, it is also equally important to preserve traditional and indigenous practices through writings. Terms and terminologies associated with many indigenous sustainable practices are likely to die out if such practices are discontinued.

5.6.5 Environmental Education in Arts

An environmental educator in an arts class engages students to meaningfully depict various environmental issues or environmental degradations that they have seen in their environment over the years in different art form such as through skits, paintings, songs, plays, making models such as sand arts, and so on. Students can also be encouraged to come out with their own ideas and experiences in different art forms. Paintings can be displayed in the school while songs, skits, and plays can be performed on occasions in the school or even in the locality or local events. Through such activities, every student can be engaged to bring out their aesthetic sense as well as their creativity, including students with any form of special needs. Such activities form an important means to spread awareness about the environment and its issues. Art has the power to tell complex stories, make them simple, and engage, engross, and immerse people in it. They can be a powerful tool to communicate to the public about environmental issues. Such approach to use art forms to communicate about environmental issues has become more important today because it takes different ways of persuasion for different people. To some a painting could turn out to be effective, to some plays could be effective, to some huge murals could just do the trick, and to others some other art forms will trigger their minds. Students not only learn about environmental issues through such art forms but also become advocates for the environment at the same time.

5.6.6 Example of Infusion of Environmental Education in Different Stages

The above suggestions for infusion in different disciplines do not indicate the stagewise considerations. Provided here is an example for the topic 'Conservation of water.'

Preparatory: Kids at this stage are easily influenced by what they see. They can be easily emotional. They are very persistent as well. For example, they will insist that what they know is followed by everybody around them such as parents or other family members. They are very effective advocates at this stage. A short video about hardships that kids of their age go through in different places due to scarcity or other related reasons may be an effective way to tell them the importance of conservation of water. They can be asked to share the difficulties they faced when there was no water at home or school.

Middle stage: At this age, kids can be given some calculations which will help them quantify the water that is wasted or saved. They can calculate for their school and for schools in the entire district, state, or even country and how such initiatives of conservation can help. For example, if each school can save 20 liters of water in a day, how much can be saved in other situations? Making issues quantifiable, measurable, or tangible is necessary for students to make sense of the issues and relate with them personally. They can be engaged in activities that will encourage them to find out how scarcity of water can impact them or their community, how they can save money by saving water (similarly energy and resources), etc. They can also be engaged in activities wherein they prepare simple models for water conservation as well as slogans and posters, etc. to create awareness among the masses about water conservation.

Secondary stage: At this stage, students are more calculative, apply reasoning and logical thinking, begin to weigh in the pros–cons for themselves, and begin to see and experience the larger issues in the society. Therefore, they need to be engaged in intellectual discussions and given opportunities to investigate the scientific evidences for scarcity of water that is available for use. They can be made to critically think and find out the larger need for conservation of water, how scarcity of water will impact every sector—domestic, industrial, or agriculture, how it will impact the economy of the country, how it will impact the poor more, how conservation of water is an ethical and moral issue, etc.

5.7 Integration of Different Approaches

Keeping in view the limitations of the interdisciplinary (separate subject) approach and the multidisciplinary (infusion) approach, Sarabhai, Raghunathan, and Kandula (1998) suggested a third approach, a three-pronged approach, which is an integration of the separate subject approach, the infusion approach, and the nonformal (outdoor, extra and, co-curricular) methods.

Meticulously implemented, this approach would be most appropriate to achieve the goals of environmental education. However, as in the case of the infusion and separate subject approach, the proponents of this approach point out that this too is not without challenges. For example, the challenges could include identifying the objectives for each of the three components, how synergy can be brought about, and how to accommodate them in the existing system.

5.8 Hand-Print CARE Ethics-Led Action Learning

Hand-Print CARE ethics-led action learning (O'Donoghue et al. 2020; O'Donoghue et al. 2022) will be a useful approach to meaningfully integrate the about, in, and for aspects of environmental education. This is a solution-oriented approach. As stated by Norris (2018), "Handprints are changes to environmental and social impacts that we cause outside of our footprints." When linked to CARE, a Hand-Print approach offers Concern for others, being Attentive to needs, Respect for all, and an Engagement with matters of concern related to sustainability. O'Donoghue et al. (2022) adapted the four-quadrant model of Edwards (2014), to expand and elaborate the Hand-Print ethics-led learning in subject teaching (see Figure 5.3). This model revolves around matters of concern that are linked to the subject that teachers teach and the knowledge they are expected to convey to their students for the common good. Hence, this approach can be adopted or adapted in the teaching–learning of any subject discipline.

The four quadrants of this approach are: start-up stories (Q1), deepening knowledge (Q2), critical thinking (Q3), and actions for change (Q4). In Q1, the teachers explore how real-world true stories are a useful way to start up story-sharing in subject teaching by students. Story-sharing enables students to begin to acquire relevant knowledge in real-life situations on local matters of concern that relates to their everyday life as they participate in collaborative action learning for social justice and future sustainability. In Q2, the teachers use the stories to enable students to raise questions which will take them into local depth inquiry. In Q3, empathy and concern commonly emerge in the learners; they clarify their ideas through mediated conversations, and students are able to design sustainable solutions related to the matter of concern. Students are then engaged in 'change projects' in Q4.

It is a shift from conventional 'teach–task–test' classroom routines to an open-ended, culturally situated, learner-led, co-engaged processes of depth inquiry, and action learning leading to significant learning. That is, it is a shift from interventionist to more co-engaged action learning. Such a teaching–learning process in which students are engaged in the learning transactions should make a difference as Pinker, discussing reason and the need for student engagement in learning transactions, notes that "people understand concepts

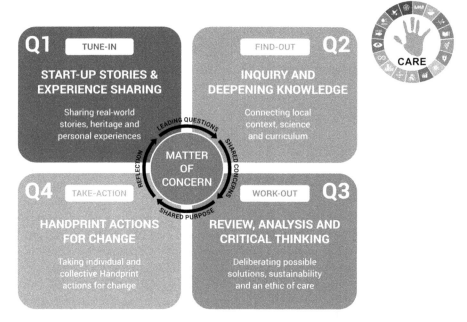

FIGURE 5.3   Hand-Print CARE Ethics-Led Learning in Subject Teaching.
Source: O'Donoghue et al. (2022).

only when they are forced to think them through, to discuss them with others and to use them to solve problems" (2018, 378).

As mentioned above, this Hand-Print CARE action-learning expansion in subject teaching also brings about significant learning, i.e., learning experiences resulting in "something that is truly significant in terms of the students' lives" (Dee Fink 2003, 6). Such learning also caters to a new social contract for education proposed by UNESCO wherein "How we learn must be determined by why and what we learn" (UNESCO 2021, 50).

5.9 Conclusion

Although the objectives of environmental education were identified which include awareness, knowledge, attitude, skills, and participation, the bigger concern has always been about how to achieve these objectives. All the five categories could be addressed if education 'about,' 'in,' and 'for' the environment is provided. A matter of debate has also been related to which approach will best suit to achieve these objectives. As discussed in the chapter, several approaches have been suggested, and each approach has its pros and cons. While one approach might work well in a particular setting, the other might work better in another setting. The third may work better still in yet another setting. Therefore, it is not as much about which one approach to adopt but about adopting any approach which works and working with it in the best possible way.

However, there definitely exist gaps in the actual implementation. The fact that education 'for' the environment has been neglected by teachers or other practitioners is doing little good to achieve the objectives of environmental education. It is, therefore, important to seriously address this aspect to see the environment actually being healed. For this, the concerns of teachers or other practitioners as to what the barriers are which hinder them to implement environmental education need to be first identified in toto. Based on this, appropriate measures need to be taken so that they are equipped in every aspect to address all the components of environmental education.

Separate subject (interdisciplinary) approach seems to be more holistic and meaningful for implementation of environmental education. However, there is no dearth of scope even in infusion (multidisciplinary) approach to infuse environmental education in the teaching–learning of any subject discipline. Clarity on the part of teachers and curriculum developers about the pros and cons of the separate subject or the infusion approach is all that is required. While all teachers teaching any subject for that matter will be able to incorporate environmental education as highlighted in the chapter, there will be times when they would feel that in certain topics environmental education can be highlighted more strongly as compared to other topics. What is most important is, they need to have the passion and commitment to grab all such opportunities to prioritize environmental education, irrespective of the subject they are teaching. Ultimately, they need to convey the message to students that environmental education is not the side activities that they do in schools like sorting of garbage or planting of trees, but it is about living an informed and responsible life for a sustainable world.

A fairly new approach, Hand-Print CARE ethics-led action learning has also been suggested in the chapter to meaningfully integrate the about, in, and for aspects of environmental education. This approach, which can be used in the teaching–learning of any subject discipline, focuses on matters of concern to the students (or matters which concern students in their life) and thereby leading to significant learning which will be for common good and for sustainability.

5.10 Summary

- Equal emphasis to the different components of environmental education such as 'about,' 'in,' and 'for' the environment during actual practice will help achieve the objectives of environmental education which include awareness, knowledge, attitude, skills, and participation.
- The most common and 'safest' way of doing environmental education is by focusing on the 'about' component of environmental education and to some

extent the 'in' component. With this, students become aware, acquire knowledge, and develop necessary skills and environmental attitudes.
- Environmental education cannot be implemented meaningfully because of the ignorance of the 'for' component by practitioners.
- For successful implementation of environmental education in the curriculum, a practitioner has to address all the five categories that define environmental education: awareness, knowledge, attitude, skills, and participation. And this can be achieved only when all the components such as 'about,' 'in,' and 'for' the environment are given equal importance.
- Two popular ways of approaching environmental education have been put forward by experts in the field: interdisciplinary and multidisciplinary approaches.
- Interdisciplinary approach appears to be appropriate to achieve the goals and objectives of environmental education, but there exists an issue of curriculum overload.
- Multidisciplinary infusion approach appears to be convenient to accommodate in the existing overloaded curriculum, but there exists an issue of linking what is learned in different disciplines.
- While a certain approach could work for a certain topic and in a particular setting, the same might not work in a different environmental setting.
- There is a third approach, wherein it is proposed to include both the interdisciplinary and multidisciplinary approaches and the nonformal methods in the implementation of environmental education.
- Hand-Print CARE ethics-led action learning is another approach to meaningfully integrate the about, in, and for aspects of environmental education.
- Educational planners, policy makers, curriculum developers, or practitioners will have to decide on the approach which will best suit different environmental settings.

Notes

1 An environmental educator, as mentioned here and also at several places elsewhere in the chapter or book, represents a teacher or educator (in elementary, secondary, or higher education) who deliberately uses environment, to the extent possible, as a context or incorporates environmental themes in her teaching–learning process, irrespective of whether she is a science, mathematics, social science, language, or arts teacher. In doing so, the teacher increases the students' awareness of the environment, leading them to adopt environmentally conscious attitudes and behaviors, and teaching them the knowledge and skills to make environmentally responsible choices (Bones 1994, 12).
2 https://assets.publishing.service.gov.uk/government/uploads/system/uploads/attachment_data/file/962785/The_Economics_of_Biodiversity_The_Dasgupta_Review_Full_Report.pdf (Accessed on April 18, 2023).
3 http://mudancasclimaticas.cptec.inpe.br/~rmclima/pdfs/destaques/sternreview_report_complete.pdf (Accessed on April 18, 2023).
4 https://www.oecd.org/greengrowth/greeneco/40133781.pdf (Accessed on April 18, 2023).

References

Bones, David. 1994. *EE Toolbox: Getting Started—A Guide to Bringing Environmental Education Into Your Classroom*. Ann Arbor, MI: University of Michigan.

Braus, J.A., and D. Wood. 1993. *Environmental Education in the Schools: Creating a Programme That Works!* Manual M0044. Washington, D.C.: Peace Corps Information Collection and Exchange.

Chawla, Louise, and D.F. Cushing. 2007. "Education for Strategic Environmental Behavior." *Environmental Education Research* 13 (4): 437–452. DOI: 10.1080/13504 620701581539

Dee Fink, L. 2003. *Creating Significant Learning Experiences: An Integrated Approach to Designing College Courses*. Published by Jossey-Bass. San Francisco: John Wiley & Sons.

Disinger, J.F. 1993. "Environment in the K–12 Curriculum: An Overview." In *Environmental Education – Teacher Resource Handbook*, edited by Richard J. Wilke, 23–43. New York: Kraus International Publications.

———. 1997. *Environmental Education's Definitional Problem*, Reprinted from: ERIC Clearinghouse for Science, Mathematics and Environmental Education Information Bulletin No. 2, 1983; An Epilogue EE's Definitional Problem: 1997 Update. Columbus, OH: ERIC/CSMEE. Available at: https://www.google.com/url?sa=t&rct=j&q=&esrc=s&source=web&cd=&ved=2ahUKEwj-rciEg8mBAxV-9jgGHdtoDhwQFnoECBAQAQ&url=https://canvas.umn.edu/courses/72128/files/3319177/download?download_frd=1&usg=AOvVaw1Jy6a-hk-n7DNgxFv1TW3b&opi=89978449 (Accessed on September 27, 2023).

Edwards, A. 2014. "Designing Tasks which Engage Learners with Knowledge." In *Task Design, Subject Pedagogy and Student Engagement*, edited by I. Thompson, 13–27. London: Routledge.

Engleson, D.C. 1987. "Environmental Education in the Curriculum: It's Already There!" In *Trends and Issues Environmental Education: EE in School Curricula—Reports of a Symposium and a Survey*, edited by John F. Disinger, 43–50. Environmental Education Information Reports. Columbus, OH: ERIC Clearinghouse for Science, Mathematics, and Environmental Education, NAAEE. Available at: https://files.eric.ed.gov/fulltext/ED292608.pdf (Accessed on September 27, 2023).

Ernst, J., and M. Monroe. 2004. "The Effects of Environment-Based Education on Students' Critical Thinking Skills and Disposition Toward Critical Thinking." *Environmental Education Research* 10 (4): 507–522.

Feng, Ling. 2012. "Teacher and Student Responses to Interdisciplinary Aspects of Sustainability Education: What do we Really Know?" *Environmental Education Research* 18 (1): 31–43. DOI: 10.1080/13504622.2011.574209

Glackin, M., Heather King, Rachel Cook, and Kate Greer. 2018. *Understanding Environmental Education in Secondary School in England: Report 2: The Practitioners' Perspective*. London: King's College London.

Gollier, Christian. 2006. "An Evaluation of Stern's Report on the Economics of Climate Change." IDEI Working Paper, no. 464. Available at: http://idei.fr/sites/default/files/medias/doc/wp/2006/stern.pdf (Accessed on February 24, 2024).

Gough, Annette. 2008. "Towards More Effective Learning for Sustainability: Reconceptualising Science Education." *Transnational Curriculum Inquiry* 5 (1): 32–50.

Haydock, Karen, and Himanshu Srivastava. 2019. "Environmental Philosophies Underlying the Teaching of Environmental Education: A Case Study in India." *Environmental Education Research* 25 (7): 1038–1065. DOI: 10.1080/13504622.2017.1402170 (Accessed on September 27, 2023).

Hungerford, H.R., and R.B. Peyton. 1994. *UNESCO–UNEP International Environmental Education Programme Environmental Education*, Series 22, Procedures for the Development of Environmental Education Curriculum (Revised). A Discussion Guide for UNESCO Training Seminars on Environmental Education. Paris: UNESCO.

Hungerford, H.R., T.L. Volk, W.J. Bluhm, B.G. Dixon, T.J. Marcinkowski, and A.P.C. Sia. 1994. *UNESCO–UNEP International Environmental Education Programme, Environmental Education*, Series 27, An Environmental Education Approach to the Training of Elementary Teachers: A Teacher Education Programme (Revised). A Discussion Guide for UNESCO Training Seminars on Environmental Education. Paris: UNESCO.

Kopnina, H. 2014. "Future Scenarios and Environmental Education." *The Journal of Environmental Education* 45 (4): 217–231. DOI: 10.1080/00958964.2014.941783

Kumar, K. 1996. "An Agenda of Incoherence." *Down to Earth* 4 (17): 32–34.

Lahiry, D., Savita Sinha, J.S. Gill, U. Mallik, and A.K. Mishra. 1988. *Environmental Education: A Process for Pre-service Teacher Training Curriculum Development*. UNESCO-UNEP International Environmental Education Programme Environmental Education Series No. 26. Edited by Patricia R. Simpson, Harold Hungerford, and Trudi L. Volk. Paris: UNESCO.

Lane, J.F. 2006. *Environmental Education Implementation in Wisconsin: Conceptualizations and Practices*. Unpublished PhD Thesis: Department of Philosophy, University of Wisconsin–Madison. Available at: http://www.uwsp.edu/cnr-ap/wcee/Documents/JennieLaneDissertation.pdf (Accessed on September 27, 2023).

Lucas, A.M. 1972. *Environment and Environmental Education: Conceptual Issues and Curriculum Implications*, PhD Dissertation, Ohio State University. Available at: https://www.researchgate.net/publication/36112785_Environment_and_environmental_education_conceptual_issues_and_curriculum_implications (Accessed on September 27, 2023).

———. 1980. "Science and Environmental Education: Pious Hopes, Self Praise and Disciplinary Chauvinism." *Studies in Science Education* 7 (1): 1–26. DOI: 10.1080/03057268008559874

Monroe, M. 1991. "Meeting the Mandate: Integrating Environmental Education." *Clearing* 71: 8–9.

Monroe, M., and D. Cappaert. 1994. *EE Toolbox: Integrating Environmental Education into the School Curriculum*. Ann Arbor, MI: Regents of the University of Michigan.

Nam, Y., and E. Ito. 2011. "A Climate Change Course for Undergraduate Students." *Journal of Geoscience Education* 59 (4): 229–241. DOI: 10.5408/1.3651405

NCERT, National Council of Educational Research and Training. 2006. *Position Paper of the National Focus Group on Habitat and Learning*, No. 1.6. New Delhi: NCERT.

———. 2011. *Teachers' Handbook on Environmental Education for the Higher Secondary Stage*. New Delhi: NCERT.

NEETF, National Environmental Education and Training Foundation. 2000. *Environment-based Education: Creating High Performance Schools and Students*. Washington, DC: NEETF.

Norris, G. 2018. "Footprints and Handprints: The Ripple Effects of our Presence." *Trim Tab* 35. Available at: https://trimtab.living-future.org/trim-tab/issue-35/footprints-and-handprints-the-ripple-effects-of-our-presence/ (Accessed on September 27, 2023).

O'Donoghue, Rob, Christa Henze, Chong Shimray, Kartikeya V. Sarabhai, and Juan Carlos A. Sandoval Rivera. 2020. "Hand-Print CARE: Towards Ethics-led Action Learning for ESD in School Subject Disciplines." *Journal of Education for Sustainable Development* 14 (1): 41–60. DOI: 10.1177/0973408220934647

———. 2022. *Handprints for Change A Teacher Education Handbook, Activating Handprint Learning Actions in Primary Schools and Beyond.* Ahmedabad, India: CEE.

Pinker, S. 2018. *Enlightenment Now: The Case for Reason, Science Humanism and Progress.* UK: Penguin Random House.

Sarabhai, K.V., M. Raghunathan, and K. Kandula. 1998. *Greening Formal Education— Concerns, Efforts and Future Directions.* Ministry of Environment and Forests, Government of India, Centre for Environment Education.

Shimray, C.V., S. Farkya, and S.L. Varte. 2013. *Study of Biology Curriculum at the Higher Secondary Stage: A Report* (Unpublished). New Delhi: NCERT.

Sonowal, C.J. 2009. "Environmental Education in Schools: The Indian Scenario." *Journal of Human Ecology* 28 (1): 15–36.

Spork, Helen. 1992. "Environmental Education: A Mismatch Between Theory and Practice." *Australian Journal of Environmental Education* 8: 147–166. Available at: http://www.jstor.org/stable/44668269 (Accessed on September 27, 2023).

Tilbury, D. 1997. "Environmental Education: A Head, Heart and Hand Approach to Learning About Environmental Problems." *New Horizons in Education* 38: 1–11.

UNESCO. 2021. *Reimagining our Futures: A New Social Contract for Education.* Paris: UNESCO.

UNESCO, United Nations Educational, Scientific and Cultural Organization. 1980. *Strategies for Developing an Environmental Education Curriculum: A Discussion Guide for UNESCO Training Workshops on Environmental Education.* Paris: UNESCO.

UNESCO-UNEP, United Nations Educational, Scientific and Cultural Organization-United Nations Environment Programme. 1978. "The Tbilisi Declaration." *Connect, UNESCO-UNEP Environmental Education Newsletter* III (1): 1–8.

6
TRACING ENVIRONMENTAL EDUCATION IN INDIA

6.1 Chapter Overview

Environmental education is thought to be a recent development in India. However, literature reveals that it is not so. Education related to environment has always been there since ancient times. It is just that it is now receiving much attention due to the urgency felt to take care of the environment and hence with a different approach. This portion of the book introduces the readers to the various documents brought out in the area of education in India beginning the 20th century and presents the elements of environmental education reflected in such documents. It begins with Mahatma Gandhi's Basic Education of 1937 followed by the reports, education policy documents, and curriculum frameworks brought out subsequently over the years. The latest policy, the National Education Policy 2020, brought out by the Government of India and subsequently the National Curriculum Framework for Foundational Stage 2023 (NCF-FS 2023) and the National Curriculum Framework for School Education 2023 (NCF-SE 2023) brought out by the National Council of Educational Research and Training (NCERT) will be especially interesting and crucial for different stakeholders since the strengths and gaps discussed in the chapter will be useful for consideration by the curriculum developers and other stakeholders.

6.2 Introduction

India has come a long way in the field of environmental education in the modern era, beginning with the Basic Education Movement started by Mahatma Gandhi in 1937 (Gandhi 1951). The country saw the first environmental

DOI: 10.4324/9781003461135-7

movement, the Chipko Movement, in the early 1970s in the remote villages of Uttarakhand (then, Uttar Pradesh). It is also important to note that basic tenets of ecology and environmental ethics were practiced even in the ancient periods. In the various texts of the Vedic period, humankind is exhorted to conserve the five elements such as air, water, fire, sky, and earth for their welfare and prosperity by scrupulously performing their duties prescribed in the texts (NCERT 2004b, 2). In fact, the earliest codified law traces back to the 2300 BCE when King Ashoka made a law in the matter of preservation of wild life and environment wherein killing of certain species of animals such as parrots, gees, rhinoceros, and so on were prohibited (NCERT 2011). Similarly, the National Curriculum Framework for School Education 2023 cites several literature studies in India from ancient times such as the Rigveda, Yajurveda, Tirukkural, and the Subhasitas to highlight "the intimate connection between nature and humanity and the interconnectedness of all creatures" (NCERT 2023, 171–172).

The previous chapters have discussed about the state of the environment, roots of environmental education, its objectives and goals, how it is different from other subjects, its need in view of the developments taking place in the world in different sectors, the approaches for practitioners, and their prospects and limitations. Following its expansion across the world in the changing global scenario and an increasing awareness on conservation of nature and protection of environment, environmental education has made a visible and formal entry into the Indian education system. While it is recognized as an indispensable component in the education process in India, environmental education continues to evolve and progress in the wake of the rapid developments taking place in the country. Such evolution can be seen in the national education documents brought out in the country just prior to independence and thereafter more frequently after independence to date. The focus on environmental education is pointed and clear in some documents, while in others, it is found to be discreet and left to the interpretation of the implementers.

6.3 Basic Education (1937)

As mentioned, Mahatma Gandhi started the Basic Education Movement in India in 1937. It was an earnest attempt at providing education in schools to meet local environmental needs. Following were the essential elements of Basic Education: productive activity in education; correlation of the curriculum with productive activity and the social environment; and a close contact between the school and the local community (NCERT 2006). In short, it was a holistic approach to life and education. This was in essence environmental and sustainability education, which remains the core principles of most school educational curriculum. For example, in an effort to connect the education system with the surrounding environment, Gandhi emphasized the activity of spinning thread as a basic and serious activity to be taught in a proper and scientific manner in schools. It was the best supplement to agriculture as it could be practiced by all, unlike other professions such as barber, carpentry, or shoemaking. He maintained that it should not only be taught mechanically, but also scientifically so that the child understood every step of spinning. This would be beneficial in many ways. It would help the child in understanding the functioning of the wheels, which essentially is the scientific aspect, and improving the wheels, the economic benefits of the skill, enhancing respect for manual labor, and benefiting the society at large. The importance of the laws of hygiene and sanitation was also envisioned, including waste management, such as proper disposal of food, excreta, and other wastes (Gandhi 1951).

6.4 Report of the Secondary Education Commission (1953)

This report was brought out by the Secondary Education Commission (1952–1953) (GoI 1953), the first commission on education appointed after the country's independence by the union government. It was set up to examine the prevailing system of secondary education in the country and recommend measures for its reorganization and improvement. The report of the commission is discussed below in relation to environmental education.

The commission recommended a step beyond Gandhi's ideas of 'dignity of labor' and 'self-reliance' to 'self-fulfillment' and 'national prosperity.' It stated the need to focus on enhancing the productivity or technical and vocational efficiency of students not only to appreciate the dignity of all work but also for self-fulfillment and national prosperity. It emphasized the proper utilization of the country's natural resources to add to the national wealth. For this, it suggested practical courses which would lead to equipping educated young people, psychologically and practically, to undertake technical professions and raise the general standard of efficiency, thereby helping to increase national wealth and ultimately to improve the general standards of living.

The commission felt that the existing secondary school curriculum was bookish and lacked provision for practical and other kinds of activities, for which it should reasonably find room for holistic education and proper development of the child's growth and personality. To shift from a narrowly conceived bookish curriculum to a more sustainable one, the commission suggested that students needed to take part in various kinds of intellectual and physical activities, practical occupations, and social experiences which is not possible through the mere study of books. It pointed out the importance of practical training in the art of living and showing students through actual experience how community life is organized and sustained. It maintained that the entire school life became the curriculum which could touch the life of the students at all levels and help in the evolution of a balanced personality.

The commission also pointed out the importance of holistic teaching of botany, climatology, and the nature of soils and seed and pests that affect agricultural plants. It suggested vocational education at the end of secondary education.

As far as social studies was concerned, the commission suggested a curriculum which viewed all subjects as a compact whole, whose object was to adjust the students to their social environment—which included the family, community, state, and nation—so that they might be able to understand how society has come to its present form and intelligently interpret the matrix of social forces and movements in the midst of which they were living.

In general science, the commission advocated that special emphasis be placed on demonstrations, field trips, and practical projects which could link school science with actual life problems and situations, such as poor local sanitation, short water supply, elimination of pests, and so on. The classroom, the home, the city and the village, the fields, woods, and streams, all offer rich resources and opportunities for science teaching that must be fully utilized by every science teacher. The teacher should aim at awakening in the students a lively curiosity about the natural phenomena around them, at developing their capacity for the practical application of their knowledge, and at appreciating the tremendous impact of modern science on all aspects of life. For this, the commission suggested the activity or project method as the basis of teaching, which would create opportunities for self-activity on the part of students and help them understand the relationship between their life and their lessons.

Overall, the Secondary Education Commission report reflected elements of environmental education such as learning by taking up locally relevant activity or project. It also brought out the importance of linking community life with the curriculum and economy.

6.5 Report of the Indian Education Commission (1966): Education and National Development

The union government appointed the Indian Education Commission (1964–1966) by a resolution, dated July 14, 1964, to advise the government on the national pattern of education and on the general principles and policies for the development of education at all stages and in all aspects.

The Education Commission Report in 1966, popularly called the Kothari Commission Report (GoI 1966), recommended the conception of education as an instrument of social transformation with a view to bringing education and national development together in a mutually supportive and interdependent relationship. It incorporated the best that basic education had to offer so as to relate it to the life, needs, and aspirations of the nation. For the primary stage, the report recommended that "the aim of teaching science in primary school should be to develop proper understanding of the main facts, concepts, principles, and processes in the physical and biological environment" (NCERT 2006).

The report also made a strong case for introducing 'work-experience,' which included manual work and production experience as well as social service as integral parts of general education at almost all educational levels. It stressed on moral education and inculcation of a sense of social responsibility, and the role of schools to recognize their responsibility in facilitating the transition of youth from the world of school to the world of work and life. The commission recommended making secondary education vocational oriented which conformed broadly to the requirements of the developing economy and real employment opportunities. Introduction of work experience and vocational education was significant in terms of environmental education.

With the aim of making a scientific outlook become part of everyday life and culture, the commission pointed out that, besides merely deepening the understanding of basic principles, science education should develop problem-solving and analytical skills and the ability to apply them to the problems of the material environment and social living and to promote the spirit of exploration, research, and experimentation. However, instead of moving toward interdisciplinary approach, the commission recommended that science from the post-primary stage should be taught as separate disciplines of physics, chemistry, and biology (NCERT 1970).

6.6 National Policy on Education (1968)

The Indian government took strong cognizance of the Education Commission's recommendations of 1964, and the same were reflected in this first National Policy on Education document (GoI 1968). Following are some of the recommendations, which is of significance in the context of the present discourse/discussion: to relate education more closely to life of the people; a continuous effort to expand educational opportunity; a sustained and intensive effort to raise the quality of education at all stages; an emphasis on the development of science and technology; and the cultivation of moral and social values. In short, the policy envisaged an education system that would produce young men and women of character and ability, committed to national service and development which would ultimately promote national progress, create a sense of common citizenship and culture, and strengthen national integration.

As recommended by the Education Commission of 1964, 'work-experience' and 'national service' was strongly emphasized in the document. It reiterated that the school and the community should be brought closer through suitable programs of mutual service and support. Work experience and national service, including participation in meaningful and challenging programs of community service and national reconstruction, should accordingly become an integral part of education. Emphasis in these programs should be on self-help, character formation, and developing a sense of social commitment. With a view to accelerating the growth of the national economy, science education and research should be given high priority.

As pointed out by the Education Commission, the document also reiterated the need to increase facilities for technical and vocational education at the secondary stage. Provision of facilities for secondary and vocational education should conform broadly to requirements of the developing economy and real employment opportunities. This should cover a large number of fields, such as agriculture, industry, trade and commerce, medicine and public health, home management, arts and crafts, secretarial training, and so on.

In all these documents, environmental concerns or issues were not specifically mentioned. During the time the documents were being written, the nation was in a phase when its sole focus was national development. The physical environment and the natural resources were largely unexploited. However, a closer look reveals that the inherent nature of environmental education is clearly visible in the programs it promoted such as 'work-experience' and other educational activities and projects. In addition, environmental concerns such as air and water pollution, pesticides, conservation of natural resources, and so on found place in the syllabi (Appendix 6.1) and the textbooks developed during the time.

6.7 Curriculum for the Ten-Year School: A Framework (1975)

It was the first national curriculum framework for school education of the country which was developed in the light of the National Policy on Education, 1968 (NCERT 1975). The document visualized a common curriculum with acceptable principles and values at the core which are in consonance with those enunciated in the Indian Constitution. This curriculum gave a thrust to curricular inputs related to social sensitivity which are fundamental to effective environmental education. It highlighted concerns such as social justice, national consciousness, national integration, and democratic values with the aim of including these issues in the discourse on curriculum construction (Yadav and Nikalje 2009).

The interdisciplinary nature of knowledge was also highlighted in the document. It reiterated the importance of the clustering of course content and its presentation through the teaching–learning method. It called for organizing course content in terms of 'units' rather than 'subjects.' This made a case for introducing students to the importance of seeing knowledge in an interdisciplinary way and appreciating its manifestation through specific situations as the document mentioned:

By this approach, the many-sided nature of knowledge will become self-evident to the learners, which is something that they completely miss while examining problems and situations from the narrow angle of a single 'discipline'. Another advantage is that areas such as health, sanitation, nutrition, population studies, pollution, water resources, elements of psychology, and culture, which have to find a place in the modern curriculum and which are multi-disciplinary, would be dealt with more easily through a unit approach.

This approach is aimed at better equipping students with abilities such as critical thinking, problem-solving skills, application of varied knowledge components, including skills and other competencies, and synthesis (Yadav and Nikalje 2009). This interdisciplinary approach provided immense scope for promoting environmental education.

At the Middle Stage, the document recommended that "environmental education, nutrition, health, and population education should be given adequate attention so that science was related meaningfully to life and living." Interestingly, this was the first time that the term 'environmental education' appeared in a national education document. The most significant recommendation in this document is that it emphasizes that a student at the Lower Secondary Stage which covers classes IX and X "should be able to contribute meaningfully to environmental conservation, the reduction of pollution, the development of proper nutrition and health and hygiene in the community."

In primary classes, sciences should be taught as environmental studies; in Classes I and II, as a composite course, including both the natural and the social environment, and later as two subjects, namely environmental studies I (natural science) and environmental studies II (social science). The purpose is to sharpen the senses of the students, to enable them to observe their environment, and to enrich their experience. The activities provided in the school should be based on the experience drawn from the child's environment. The fact that this document suggested a two-subject approach for environmental studies is quite contradictory to the interdisciplinary approach it attempted to proclaim.

This document reiterated the recommendations of the Kothari Commission Report, 1964–1966 and that of the National Policy on Education, 1968, on the importance of work experience. It pointed out: "For harmonious development of the child's personality, it is necessary not only to expose him to scholastic areas for intellectual development but also to put him in situations where he may get opportunities to work with his hands and develop proper attitudes towards manual labour."

It suggested that work experience should permeate the entire curriculum and proposed work experience as one of the curricular subjects in school.

Work experience provides the basis for the development of knowledge, skills, and attitudes, which are useful for later participation in productive work. It should cover production, maintenance, and the technological processes, as well as human relations, organization, and management and marketing. The areas of work chosen should have local significance and should be able to develop a sense of competency in the students. It is not just learning to do work; it is work education. This local specificity and 'activity'-based education provided a setting that was conducive for environmental education.

The document outlined the major objective of the study of social sciences in an attempt "to acquaint the child with his past and present geographical and social environment." It mentioned that teaching of social sciences should "inculcate attitudes and impart the knowledge necessary for the achievement of the principal values of a just world order, maximization of economic and social welfare, minimization of violence, and maximization of ecological stability." It suggested an integrated syllabus for social sciences wherein all the components of social sciences—history, geography, civics, and economics—can be integrated in the teaching in a way that students develop a proper understanding of the facts and problems in the right perspective without causing any damage to the totality of the individual disciplines. The document stressed the importance of relating the growing population to the available natural resources and the need for conservation.

For living well in a developing society where socio-economic changes are taking place at a fast pace, the curriculum suggested that it would be helpful if some rudimentary understanding of the economic forces that influence the citizens' daily life was provided even at the middle stage of education. Following this viewpoint, the need to introduce some elementary knowledge of consumer economics, such as earning and spending, controls, price rise, and the effects of increasing population, in a simplified form was felt. The document mentioned that the approach of the teaching of economics at the lower secondary stage should emphasize not so much the principles of economics as the current problems and issues that affect the everyday life of the common man, such as poverty, rising prices, agricultural stagnation, and so on. The course would throw some light on the future economic prospects of the country on the basis of its potential resources and the performance shown so far.

6.7.1 Syllabi for Classes VI–VIII (1976)

These syllabi provide ample scopes to address environmental concerns through different subject areas, including work experience (NCERT 1976). Some relevant topics under different subject areas for different classes are provided in Appendix 6.2.

6.8 Report of the Review Committee on the Curriculum for the Ten-Year School (1977)

The union government set up the Review Committee on the Curriculum for the Ten-Year School (Ishwarbhai Patel Committee Report) in 1977 to scrutinize the NCERT syllabus and textbooks, in the light of the review of the stage-wise and subject-wise objectives identified in the NCERT document: "The Curriculum for the Ten-Year School." It brought out a document: "Report of the Review Committee on the Curriculum for the Ten-Year School" (GoI 1977).

A major criticism of the committee was that work experience, which was intended to be an integral feature of the curriculum at all stages did not find a proper place in the teaching–learning process that followed the introduction of the new pattern, hence giving the impression that curriculum and the syllabuses developed by NCERT would perpetuate the same old system of 'bookish-education.' Programs of work experience were introduced following the Kothari Commission Report recommendations with the objectives of relating education to productivity. These programs, however, lacked the component of social usefulness and, in practice, were not even casually correlated to other subject areas. Work experience was thus assigned a much wider concept in the document to include social and cultural aspects, and it was renamed socially useful productive work (SUPW) (Yadav and Nikalje 2009).

The document maintained that SUPW must, therefore, be given a central place in the curriculum at all stages of school education and the content of the academic subjects should be related to it, as much as possible. The purpose of demarcating a distinct curricular area as SUPW was to emphasize the principle that education should be centered around work, as the concept of SUPW is to be developed in the light of the Gandhian philosophy of basic education, in and through work, the document added. It maintained that such work must not be performed mechanically, but must include practical planning, analysis, and detailed preparation at every stage so that it is educational in essence. It elucidated its view by providing the following examples: When children take part in an environmental cleanliness program by way of social service, they can prepare compost pits for manure. Similarly, if children conduct surveys of population, habitations, or cattle, they can use the information for planning programs for childcare and sanitation. During the harvesting season when the entire village is under pressure of intensive work, the schools, instead of remaining in isolation, can render valuable help to farmers.

The document expressed optimism that such work-based education would bring about at least some reduction in traditional book-knowledge and acceptance of the applied sciences taught through field experience, such as agriculture, accountancy, and soil science, with equal importance to fundamental sciences.

According to the document, the criterion for selection of activities should, thus, be that the work involved was productive, educative, and socially useful. It was felt that if SUPW was given a central and dominant place in the curriculum the gap between work and education would be reduced, the school would not remain isolated from the community, and the gulf that divided the affluent from the weaker and poorer sections of the community would be bridged. It expressed that such a scheme would provide equality of opportunity for working and learning to all children irrespective of caste, creed, sex, and economic status. To ensure that the educational objectives of this program are achieved, the document suggested that it was necessary to follow the problem-solving approach. These suppositions clearly indicated that the document was environmental education-friendly. The syllabus frames suggested by the committee for different subjects that are mentioned later substantiate and validate the view.

Some of the SUPW activities suggested by the committee for different classes include cleaning school campus or surrounding, gardening, maintaining compost pit, planting and care of shade trees, soil conservation, growing medicinal plants, soil conservation, desert control, beekeeping, poultry farming, and so on.

The committee also provided syllabus frames for different classes. It recommended no textbook for Classes I–II in EVS and one textbook for EVS for Classes III–IV/V. The concepts were spirally woven. Some of the chapters suggested in science, which directly relate to the environment, are as follows: food and health; man's dependence on plants and animals and the balance in nature; environment: adaptation to and manipulation of water; energy; oxygen; water; population; pollution; electric energy and power; atomic nucleus and nuclear energy; materials (metals, alloys, plastics, and glasses); agriculture; agriculture practices and implements; man's problems in agriculture; improvement and protection of crops; useful plants and animals, animal husbandry; conservation of natural resources; science in human welfare; agricultural practices and animal husbandry; combustion and fuels; chemistry in industry; man and his environment.

Some of the chapters that can be directly related to environmental education in social science include the following: trade, transport, and population (internal and external, land, water and air, population—distribution and density), social and economic challenges before our country, water and nuclear power, and industries production and output.

6.9 National Policy on Education (1986)

The major thrust of the National Policy on Education, 1986 (NPE-1986) (GoI 1986), was to relate education to 'development' and 'social change' in general (Yadav and Nikalje 2009). The policy document stated:

The National System of Education will be based on a national curricular framework which contains a common core along with other components that are flexible. The common core will include the history of India's freedom movement, the constitutional obligations, and other content essential to nurture national identity. These elements will cut across subject areas and will be designed to promote values such as India's common cultural heritage, egalitarianism, democracy and secularism, equality of the sexes, protection of the environment, removal of social barriers, observance of the small family norm, inculcation of the scientific temper.

The document clearly stressed the need to highlight environmental concerns in education wherein it stated:

> There is a paramount need to create a consciousness of the environment. It must permeate all ages and all sections of society, beginning with the child. Environmental consciousness should inform teaching in schools and colleges. This aspect will be integrated in the entire educational process.

The document also emphasized the need to highlight population growth and its related issues in educational programs.

Regarding work experience, the document laid down the following:

> Work experience, viewed as purposive and meaningful manual work, organized as an integral part of the learning process, and resulting in either goods or services useful to the community, is considered as an essential component at all stages of education, to be provided through well-structured and graded programs. It would comprise activities in accord with the interests, abilities, and needs of students, the level of skills and knowledge to be upgraded with the stages of education.

With its clear perspective on the environment, the NPE-1986 document is a major departure from the rest of the earlier documents and policies in terms of environmental education.

6.10 Science Education for First Ten Years of Schooling: Working Group Report (1987)

The Working Group was set up in 1987 by NCERT comprising distinguished scientists, science educators as its members, and Professor Yash Pal as its chairman to work out a viable action program for science education which will nurture and develop manpower for different levels of the economy (NCERT 1987).

Of the 20 points under "What is to be done?" laid down by the working group, those that need special mention in the context of environmental education include the following: "ability to understand and appreciate the joint enterprise of science/technology and society," "science curriculum in general education must be directed toward the development of concern about consequences and about people," and "certain thrust areas like energy, environment, social forestry, wildlife management, industry, which need immediate attention to avoid environmental crisis, should be highlighted."

6.11 National Curriculum for Elementary and Secondary Education: A Framework (Revised Version) (1988)

This curriculum framework was developed in the light of the NPE-1986 (NCERT 1988c). The importance of environmental consciousness, which was highlighted in the NPE-1986, is reflected in this document. Hence, environmental concerns received equal importance in this curriculum framework, as much as the social, economic, and political aspects.

The document clearly spelt out the urgency to tackle environmental problems and how a school curriculum can address them. Following is an excerpt from the document in this context:

> Protection of the Environment and Conservation of Natural Resources: The indiscriminate destruction of the environment and the use of the environmental resources, especially the non-renewable resources in nature by man have been upsetting the earth's ecological balance. Unfortunately, even some ambitious national developmental programs, when not based on careful consideration of their consequences in terms of the ecology in the long run, may become sources of serious hazards for the ecological balance. There is urgent need of tapping new alternative sources of energy and development of new technology aimed at the protection of environment.
>
> *(NCERT 1988c, 6)*

The document clearly points out the dangers that lie in developmental activities and the need to take precautionary measures. Toward this, the document highlights the utmost need to create consciousness of the environment among all sections of the society. It also identified the important role school education has in bringing about such consciousness as it states:

> The school curriculum, therefore, should attempt to create a commitment on the part of pupils to protect the environment and conserve nature and its resources so that the ecological balances, especially the balance between man and nature, could be maintained and preserved…promote an awareness of the need of counter pollution, whether caused by affluence or poverty, and of the impending energy crisis due to the ever increasing consumption of fuels available in nature and the exhaustion of these fuels at an alarmingly rapid rate…highlight the measures for protection and care of the environment, prevention of pollution and conservation of energy… highlight the inter-dependence between the material environment and the plant and animal (including human) life for survival, growth and

development. The significance of renewable and non-conventional energy resources should also form an important component of the curriculum.

(NCERT 1988c, 6)

The document also stresses that the significance of renewable and nonconventional energy resources should also form an important component of the curriculum. The need to take into account the interconnectivity among different areas has also been highlighted in the document. For example, it suggested that environmental education, energy management, and population education are to be seen as complementary to one another and they should be adequately reflected in the curriculum (NCERT 1988c, 7).

The document also included "understanding of the environment and its limited resources and the need for conservation of natural resources and energy" as one of the general objectives of education.

According to this document, school curriculum, on the whole, should aim at enabling the learners to acquire knowledge, develop concepts, and inculcate skills, attitudes, values, and habits conducive to the all-round development of their personality and commensurate with the social, cultural, economic, and environmental realities at the national and international levels. The document reiterated the perspective of the NPE-1986 on work experience.

6.11.1 Guidelines and Syllabi for Upper Primary Stage (1988)

Some of the relevant topics on environment for different subject areas and classes mentioned in the syllabi are provided in Appendix 6.3.

The syllabi clearly mentioned the importance of work experience to develop attitudes and values in an effort to "develop a deeper concern for the environment and a sense of responsibility and commitment to the community" (NCERT 1988b). The syllabi also suggested a list of activities for this stage, which is provided in Appendix 6.4. These activities are largely environmental in nature.

6.11.2 Guidelines and Syllabi for Secondary Stage (1988)

Appendix 6.5 provides a list of environmentally relevant topics in different subject areas and classes.

As in the syllabi for the upper primary stage, the syllabus for secondary stage also clearly mentions that the importance of work experience is to develop attitudes and values to "develop a deeper concern for the environment and a sense of responsibility and commitment to the community" (NCERT 1988a). The syllabus also provided a suggested list of essential activities which are essentially 'environmental' in nature. The list is provided in Appendix 6.6.

6.12 Learning without Burden: Report of the National Advisory Committee (1993)

The Ishwarbhai Patel Review Committee (1977), the NCERT Working Group (1984), and the National Policy on Education Review Committees (1990) made several recommendations to reduce the academic burden on students, to ease learning. But instead of getting mitigated, the problem became more acute, and hence the Ministry of Human Resource Development (now called Ministry of Education) set up a National Advisory Committee in 1992 to look into the issue of increasing academic burden on the students (GoI 1993). Its objectives included: "To suggest ways and means to reduce the load on school students at all levels, particularly young students, while improving quality of learning, including the capability for life-long self-learning and skill formulation." The committee came out with a report—"Learning without burden." This assumes significance in terms of environmental education as the decisions on environmental education curriculum subsequent to this report was guided by it to a great extent, especially in terms of the introduction of the infusion approach of environmental education in order to avoid addition of load by adopting a separate subject approach.

6.13 National Curriculum Framework for School Education 2000 (NCFSE-2000)

Responding to the phenomenon of globalization was considered to be one of the curricular concerns in this curriculum framework which would require the introduction of education toward active citizenship and human rights, environmental issues, and the promotion of consensus on a common core of universal values (NCERT 2000, 15). Keeping in view the diverse curricular concerns such as 'literacy,' 'family system,' 'neighborhood education,' 'environmental education,' 'human rights education,' 'tourism education,' 'AIDS education,' 'legal literacy,' 'peace education,' 'population education,' 'migration education,' 'global education,' and 'safety education,' which were making a case for separate place in the school curriculum, the NCFSE-2000 suggested that the best approach would be to integrate these ideas and concepts into the existing areas of learning in the curricula of different subjects.

Energy and environment were included in the "Frontline Curriculum" along with other areas, such as communication systems, space technology, biotechnology, genetic engineering, recent health issues, world geography, multinationals, archeological findings, and the like.

This curriculum framework reaffirmed that the common core components mentioned in the NPE-1986 as well as the fundamental duties as laid down in the Article 51-A of Part IV-A of the Indian Constitution, such as the history of India's freedom movement, the constitutional obligations, the content essential to nurture national identity, India's common cultural heritage, egalitarianism, democracy and secularism, equality of sexes, protection of the environment, removal of social barriers, observance of the small-family norm, and inculcation of scientific temper, should be integrated in school curriculum in a suitable manner.

In addition, "to help to generate and promote among the learners understanding of the environment in its totality both natural and social, and their interactive processes, the environmental problems and the ways and means to preserve the environment" were laid down in this document as one of the general objectives of education.

Relating education to the 'world of work' was another curricular concern of the NCFSE-2000. The document stressed on work education and vocational education being integral components of the school education system. Work education, it envisaged, would develop the understanding of facts and principles involved in various forms of work and to create a positive attitude toward work in line with Gandhi's philosophy of 'work-centered' education. A very important and interesting point made in this curriculum framework was that "All vocational education programmes and activities must stress the concept of sustainable development with a focus on fostering the awareness of the key environmental concerns and the rights of all to a decent standard of living."

The following points discuss in brief how the curriculum framework envisaged integration of environmental education in different subject areas:

Mathematics: The application of mathematics is an inherent part of every functioning and operation of daily life. Hence lies the importance of its study and its study is related to the immediate environment of the child at different stages and the world at large.

- Classes I–II: Content of mathematics to be built around the immediate environment of the child.
- Classes III–V: The child should gain familiarity with geometrical forms and figures and be able to appreciate patterns and symmetry in the environment.
- Upper primary: Should be confined mostly to the study of essentials of mathematics for day-to-day life.
- Secondary stage: Emphasis is to be laid on wider applications of mathematics by way of making data-based problems pertaining to actual data on population, agriculture, environment, industry, physical and biological sciences, engineering, defense, and so on. While developing the instructional material, the content and language of problems included in the textbooks should highlight core components like gender equality, protection of environment, removal of social barriers, observance of small-family norm, and so on.

Science and technology: Science must cut across traditional subject boundaries and open itself to issues such as gender, culture, language, poverty, impairment, future occupation, environment, and observance of small-family norm.

Classes I–II: Essentially, it has to be learned mainly through concrete situations related to immediate environment.

Classes III–V: Environmental studies (science) is introduced. The focus would, however, remain on objects, events, natural phenomenal, and the learner's environment. Children would continue to learn to observe, explore, and identify occurrences in their environment.

Upper primary: The environment should continue to be a major source of learning and students should try to understand the changes taking place all around. They would also gain an understanding of the living world, balance of nature, and the role of air, water, and energy. Due emphasis should be given to protection and conservation of natural resources.

Secondary stage: Learning of science would continue to be built around natural and social elements of environment. Science, technology, society, and environment would coalesce in teaching and learning of science at this stage. Teachers could help the learners devise appropriate experimentation and activities within the school and outside school, involving immediate environment, such as farming, factories, industries, and community.

Social sciences: It helps the learners in understanding the human environment in its totality and developing a broader perspective and an empirical, reasonable, and humane outlook. Food security, population growth, poverty, water scarcity, climatic changes, and cultural preservation are some of the major issues of the 21st century which have relevance for the social sciences curriculum. Hence, 'environment, resources, and sustainable development' and 'man–environment interaction' would be drawing their content mainly from geography, economics, sociology, and other related areas (NCERT 2000, 64).

Classes I–II: Children are introduced to the environment in its totality. No clear-cut distinction between natural and social environment has to be made.

Classes III–V: Environmental Studies (Social Science) introduced. Starting from the surroundings of the children—home, school, and neighborhood—they may be familiarized with their state and country in a gradual manner. Schools will be given full autonomy at this stage to use locally developed curriculum and locally available resources for teaching of environmental studies.

Upper primary: For example, students may be motivated to raise questions pertaining to various physical and human-made features, phenomena, and events; recognize simple patterns, such as rainfall distribution in the country and patterns of agriculture and urban land uses.

Secondary stage: It may include the processes and patterns of human–environment interaction and issues related to environment, its resources, and development.

6.13.1 Guidelines and Syllabi for Upper Primary Stage (2001)

Environment-related topics, concerns, problems, and issues have been included exhaustively throughout the document (NCERT 2001b). Hence, it is felt that no further detail on this is needed to be provided.

6.13.2 Guidelines and Syllabi for Secondary Stage (2001)

Environment-related topics, concerns, problems, and issues have been included exhaustively throughout the document (NCERT 2001a). Hence, it is felt that no further detail on this is needed to be provided.

6.14 Curriculum Framework for Teacher Education (2004)

This teacher education curriculum framework was developed in keeping with the spirit of the NCFSE-2000 (NCERT 2004a). Protection and conservation of environment was considered an important concern of this curriculum framework in the document. It also highlighted the importance of teacher education in order to bring about change in the general attitude toward the treatment of the environment. The document pointed out: "The content and processes of teacher-education programs will have to equip teachers with a proper understanding of love for the nature around and the skill of inculcating these among their students," which will not only result in a healthier society, both physically and mentally, but also bring about the much-needed replenishment and sustenance of natural resources affected by the unprecedented industrial development. Developing among teachers awareness and sensitivity toward environmental concerns was included as one of the thrust areas of teacher education.

At the pre-primary stage, the curriculum framework included the following: "Enabling teachers to inculcate among children a desire to know and understand their immediate natural environment, to love and respect it" and "preparing student teachers to use local resources and local contexts" as its objectives. The following curriculum content and transaction is envisioned by the document:

Teacher education curriculum at this stage needs to develop awareness about literacy programs, community dynamics, national and local customs, fairs and festivals, and community mode of social living. It may also develop awareness of forces affecting the environment, including pollution, appreciation of places of historical and cultural significance, and special educational features and developmental tasks contained in policies and programs.

At the elementary stage, the objectives included the following: "Developing among student teachers skills for teaching integrated environmental studies, integrated social sciences and integrated science and technology" and "enabling student teachers to inculcate among children a desire to know their immediate natural environment, to love and respect it."

As a part of the curriculum content and transaction for preservice teacher education, the document pointed out the need to sensitize teachers to the need for reducing curriculum load, organize appropriate learning experiences which are joyful in nature and related to immediate environment of the learner, and help them develop and imbibe desirable values. It further stated that teacher education programs at this stage needed to provide subject-based orientation. It added:

Teaching and learning of mathematics would be woven around the environment of the learners so that environmental concerns are properly integrated. The activities would focus on local culture and environment using the local specific contexts and resources. Student teachers shall have to be provided with experiences to help children develop socio-emotional and cultural aspects. A realistic awareness and perspective of the phenomena occurring in the environment will have to be linked with social or scientific events. This may be accomplished by emphasizing observation, classification, comparison and drawing of inferences, conducted within and outside the classroom.

"Developing among student teachers awareness and sensitivity toward environment concern and promoting skills for meeting environmental challenges" was included as one of the objectives at the secondary as well as at the higher secondary stage of school education. In addition, concerns, such as ecological imbalances and environmental degradation, also have to be studied in their socio-cultural-economic context in the academic stream.

This curriculum framework included "Enabling teachers to be sensitive to gender and environment-related issues" as one of the objectives for the in-service education of teachers (NCERT 2004a, 110–112).

6.15 Environmental Education in Schools: Syllabus (2004)

The syllabus for environmental education in schools was developed by the NCERT in pursuance of the Hon'ble Supreme Court of India order dated December 18, 2003 (NCERT 2004b, v–vi). In response to the writ petition No. 860/1990 by M.C. Mehta, the Supreme Court stated in its order dated

November 22, 1991: "We accept on principle that through the medium of education, awareness of the environment and its problems related to pollution should be taught as a compulsory subject." On December 18, 2003, the Hon'ble Supreme Court ordered, "We also direct the NCERT…to prepare a module (model) syllabus," and on July 13, 2004, the court directed that "the syllabus prepared by the NCERT for Class I–XII shall be adopted by every state in their respective schools." The Hon'ble Court also directed that "the NCERT be appointed as a nodal agency to supervise the implementation of the court's order."

Apart from its focus on bio-physical environmental concerns, the document visualized "EE as an instrument for inculcating healthy personal and social attitudes toward environment and development." It envisaged that a focus on the social environment would lead to better and healthier human relationships, which are vital for human survival and development.

This is a major departure from the earlier documents which largely focused on bio-physical environmental concerns. A comprehensive syllabus for Classes I–XII is provided in this document. The document discussed in detail the expected learning outcomes for every stage and listed the topics and concepts to be covered for every class. Exemplar activities to be considered during transaction of such topics, teaching–learning strategies, and evaluation methods were also provided in the document. The syllabus is, therefore, not just a syllabus but is in itself a curriculum.

The document suggested that the teaching–learning strategies "Are to be designed in keeping with the local environmental conditions, both natural and social. At the same time, it should aim at helping learners to develop a global perspective of the environment and problems related to it. The most important parameter, however, to be considered while designing teaching–learning situations would be to provide adequate emphasis on the development of positive attitude as well as love and respect for the environment" (NCERT 2004b, 58–59).

As for the evaluation methods, the document suggested: "The assessment of learners' achievement in environmental education would encompass all the three aspects of development, that is, cognitive, affective, and conative. Both process and product evaluation techniques will need to be used" (NCERT 2004b, 59–60).

6.16 National Curriculum Framework 2005 (NCF-2005)

This curriculum framework (NCF-2005) incorporated the views presented in the position paper of the National Focus Group on Habitat and Learning, which is about environmental education. The NCF-2005 elaborately discussed concerns related to the environment all throughout the document, keeping in view the unprecedented environmental degradation witnessed in the recent past owing to the emergence of new technological choices and lifestyles (NCERT 2005a). The document stated: "Humankind must, therefore, make an attempt to comprehend its roots, to reestablish links with its habitat, and to understand and take good care of it."

Reiterating the NPE-1986 recommendations, this curriculum framework considered making children sensitive to the environment and making the need for its protection an important curricular concern. It is believed that education can provide a necessary perspective on how human life can be reconciled with environmental crisis so that survival, growth, and development remain possible. Hence, the document stated that concerns and issues pertaining to the environment should be included in every subject and through a wide range of activities involving outdoor project work.

Like any other subject, environmental concerns can be best addressed in the school curriculum by linking knowledge to life outside the school, which is the first guiding principle of this document. The document stated that only when the living world becomes available for critical reflection within the school will the children come alive to the issues of the environment and nurture their concern for it. For example, apart from acquiring bookish knowledge, the children should examine water bodies and sources to know about water pollution.

However, the document did not limit environmental education to 'protection of the environment.' It stated:

> The main focus of EE should be to expose students to the real-life world, natural and social, in which they live; to enable them to analyse, evaluate, and draw inferences about problems and concerns related to the environment; to add, where possible, to our understanding of environmental issues; and to promote positive environmental actions to facilitate the move towards sustainable development. To achieve these goals, the curriculum may be based on: (i) Learning about the environment (ii) Learning through the environment, and (iii) Learning for the environment.

Holistic environmental perspective (which includes the physical, natural, and socio-cultural world) in terms of both their content and pedagogy, and which encourage flexibility to bring in locale specificities, are at the core of the curriculum. This curriculum framework emphasized the importance of working with hands and the need to encourage heritage craft traditions, which uses raw materials that are all indigenously available and are also environment friendly. The document mentioned that students should also be encouraged to learn local knowledge traditions such as harvesting and storing water, or of practicing sustainable agriculture through projects, and so on.

The NCF-2005 also stressed that projects and activities would be the backbone of any scheme aimed at effective implementation of environmental education in schools. This would engage the young minds in the excitement of first-hand observation of nature and of understanding patterns and processes in the natural and social worlds. It suggested that, for successful implementation, a separate time needs to be carved out for projects and fieldwork from the existing periods of SUPW, science, and other subjects. It pointed out that some of the information and understanding flowing from such projects could contribute to the elaboration of a publicly accessible, transparent database on India's environment, which would in turn become the most valuable educational resource.

The document maintained that, if well planned, many of these student projects could lead to knowledge generation. Various school-based programs and projects pertaining to the environment could help create the knowledge base for the Panchayati Raj institutions to better manage and regenerate local environmental resources. The document stated that such projects and activities would not only enrich the curriculum so that it goes beyond textbooks, but would also ensure that learning is shifted away from rote methods.

Although the Hon'ble Supreme Court emphasized the need to teach environmental concerns as a compulsory subject at all stages of school education (details about the Supreme Court order is discussed in the next chapter), the document recommended that these significant concerns are best realized by infusing the components of environmental education as a part of different disciplines. This would also help fulfill one of the concerns of the NCF-2005—reducing the curriculum load.

The document mentioned:

> This approach can be meaningfully employed in the treatment of content in Physics, Mathematics, Chemistry, Biology, Geography, History, Political Science, Health and Physical Education, Art, Music etc. Activities constructed for life situations become a meaningful means for the engagement of learners. Rainfall, for instance, exhibits intricate variations over space and time. Data on such variations are available and can be used to promote many interesting activities in Physics and Mathematics.

The document added that similar examples, such as effluents from sewage treatment plants in chemistry, biodiversity resources, medicinal plants, endangered fish, diets of tribal people, preparation of maps, water disputes, and so on, could form the raw data in different subjects.

The curriculum recommended by the NCF-2005 in Science and Social Science for different stages is discussed next.

Science Curriculum
At the 'primary stage,' the objectives should be to nurture the curiosity of the child about the world (natural environment, artifacts, and people). Science and social science should be integrated as 'environmental studies.' At

the 'upper primary stage,' the child should continue to learn more about the environment and health, including reproductive and sexual health, through activities and surveys. Group activities, discussions with peers and teachers, surveys, organization of data, and their display through exhibitions, and so on in schools and the neighborhood should be important components of pedagogy. At the 'secondary stage,' students should be engaged in activities and analyses on issues concerning the environment and health, including reproduction and sexual health. They should work on locally significant projects involving science and technology.

Social Science Curriculum

For the 'primary stage,' the natural and the social environment will be explained as integral parts of languages and mathematics. Children should be engaged in activities to understand the environment through illustrations from the physical, biological, social, and cultural spheres. For 'Classes III–V,' the subject EVS should be introduced. In the study of the natural environment, the emphasis would be on its preservation and the urgency of saving it from degradation. Children would also begin to be sensitized to social issues such as poverty, child labor, illiteracy, and caste and class inequalities in rural and urban areas. The content should reflect the daily experiences of children and their different worlds.

At the 'upper primary stage,' social studies would draw its content from history, geography, political science, and economics. The curriculum should take into account developments in different parts of India and the world; balanced perspective related to issues concerning the environment, resources, and development at different levels, from local to global; democratic processes of participation; and observe economic institutions like the family, the market and the state. There would also be a section that will indicate a multidisciplinary approach to these themes.

At the 'secondary stage,' the curriculum would focus on understanding the social and economic challenges facing the nation and concerns of scheduled castes (SC) and scheduled tribes (ST) and disenfranchised populations. It would enable students to understand their world better and also understand how their own identities came into being as shaped by a rich and varied past; inculcate in the child a critical appreciation for conservation and environmental concerns along with developmental issues; and engage in-depth discussion on equality, liberty, justice, fraternity, secularism, dignity, plurality, and freedom from exploitation.

Work and Education

The NCF-2005 elaborately discussed the meaning of 'work' in terms of productive activity and fulfilling their needs, contribution to the good of the society, an activity through which a person gains identity, and construction of knowledge. However, unlike the earlier curriculum framework where work-related education/work experience/SUPW was treated as a separate curricular subject, this curriculum framework recommended that work should form an integral part of the curriculum, not as a separate subject but as a pedagogical tool; that is, work-centered education, similar to the Gandhian philosophy and concept of work, and not just the completion of work. This is also because work is an interdisciplinary activity and it could be well-covered in all disciplines.

Work involves interaction with materials or people (mostly both), hence creating a deeper and wider comprehension and increased practical knowledge of natural substances and social relationships. The NCF-2005 believed that when academic learning and work are simultaneously collocated, there is a chance of greater creativity in academic pursuits and in the methods and approaches of working. At the same time, disciplinary boundaries that are normally drawn traditionally also diminish or disappear. The rich work knowledge base and skills of marginalized children can be turned into a source of dignity as well as of learning for other children through work-centered pedagogy.

6.16.1 Syllabus for Classes at the Elementary Level (2005)

Environment-related topics, concerns, problems, and issues have been included exhaustively throughout the document (NCERT 2005b). Hence, it is felt that no further detail on this needs to be provided.

6.16.2 Syllabus for Secondary and Higher Secondary Classes (2005)

Environment-related topics, concerns, problems, and issues have been included exhaustively throughout the document (NCERT 2005c). Hence, it is felt that no further detail on this needs to be provided.

6.17 National Curriculum Framework for Teacher Education (2009)

The NCFTE-2009 was prepared "towards preparing professional and humane teacher" (NCTE 2009).

The document elaborately discussed the context, concerns, and vision for teacher's education. It reflected upon the concerns related to environmental education.

The document observed:

> In order to develop future citizens who promote equitable and sustainable development for all sections of society and respect for all, it is necessary that

they be educated through perspectives of gender equity, the perspectives that develop values for peace, respect the rights of all, and respect and value work. In the present ecological crisis, promoted by extremely commercialized and competitive lifestyles, teachers and children need to be educated to change their consumption patterns and the way they look at natural resources.

It is encouraging to see environmental education discussed as part of contemporary studies under the foundations of education in the light of its critical perspective in sustaining a democratic social order.

The document also highlighted the importance of connecting community knowledge in education with formal school knowledge and inclusion of locally relevant content in the curriculum as well as pedagogy, conditions fundamental to environmental education.

As a part of its vision for 'teacher and teacher education,' the document stated that teacher education programs should broaden the curriculum (both school and teacher education) to include different traditions of knowledge; educate teachers to connect school knowledge with community knowledge and life outside the school; reconceptualize citizenship training in terms of human rights and approaches of critical pedagogy; emphasize environment and its protection, live in harmony within oneself and with natural and social environment; and promote peace, democratic way of life, constitutional values of equality, justice, liberty, fraternity and secularism, and caring values.

The curriculum framework also suggested that environmental hygiene should form an important component of teacher education curricula. As for pedagogic studies, this document suggested a departure from conventional teacher education which focused on a pure disciplinary approach of teaching individual school subjects such as physics, chemistry, biology, history, and geography to a more integrated approach of sciences and social sciences. All theory courses will need to be 'interdisciplinary' in structure and have 'field-based units of study' it maintained, which is a necessity in terms of environmental education.

It suggested that a pedagogy course on EVS should include the following: philosophical and epistemological basis of EVS as a composite area of study that draws upon sciences, social sciences, and environmental education; acquainting student-teachers with children's ideas of their physical and social world so that these can later be interpreted for classroom instruction; and helping student-teachers develop the ability to plan comprehensive units that do not compartmentalize knowledge but view it holistically. It also suggested that elementary school teachers needed to engage in research relating to different aspects of young children's learning in different areas, including environmental education in an effort to develop sound pedagogic understanding. The document added: "A 'critical examination of and engagement with teaching methods' such as concept formation, enquiry-based teaching, problem-solving, discovery, and activity-based learning and related terms can go a long way in making him/her a reflective teacher." Practical activities, such as workshops and course work, also form an integral part of the curriculum.

Many concerns related to environmental education have been addressed in the document. However, there still appears to be a sort of disconnect between this document and what the National Curriculum Framework 2005 for school education recommends for environmental education. For example, there is no mention of infusion approach of environmental education in the curriculum or the pedagogy component. It is felt that an explicit and clearer picture of environmental education would have been more appropriate instead of reflecting the concerns in patches.

6.18 National Education Policy 2020 (NEP 2020)

The National Education Policy 2020 (NEP 2020) is the first education policy of the 21st century and one that came around more than 30 years after the NPE-1986 was brought out (GoI 2020). It emphasizes the importance of integrating environmental education into the curriculum of schools, colleges, and universities. Some of the statements mentioned in the document with respect to environmental education are reproduced in the following:

> Certain subjects, skills, and capacities should be learned by all students to become good, successful, innovative, adaptable, and productive human beings in today's rapidly changing world…these skills include:…environmental awareness including water and resource conservation, sanitation and hygiene; … [4.23]
>
> Concerted curricular and pedagogical initiatives, including the introduction of contemporary subjects such as…Organic Living, Environmental Education, Global Citizenship Education (GCED), etc. at relevant stages will be undertaken to develop these various important skills in students at all levels. [4.24]
>
> The societal challenges that India needs to address today, such as access for all its citizens to clean drinking water and sanitation, quality education and healthcare, improved transportation, air quality, energy, and infrastructure, will require the implementation of approaches and solutions that are not only informed by top-notch science and technology but are also rooted in a deep under- standing of the social sciences and humanities and the various socio-cultural and environmental dimensions of the nation. [17.4]
>
> With climate change, increasing pollution, and depleting natural resources, there will be a sizeable shift in how we meet the world's energy, water, food, and sanitation needs,…resulting in the need for new skilled labour,

particularly in biology, chemistry, physics, agriculture, climate science, and social science." [Introduction]

All B.Ed. programmes will also…appropriately integrate environmental awareness and sensitivity towards its conservation and sustainable development, so that environment education becomes an integral part of school curricula. [5.24]

Some of the key recommendations of NEP 2020 that pertains to environmental education are listed below:

- The document emphasizes the need to provide environmental education to all the learners in India by integrating it in the curriculum from the foundational stage. This would enable learners to understand the importance of environmental issues and to appreciate the natural world.
- The policy emphasizes the need to train teachers adequately who will be able to meaningfully deliver so that environmental education is implemented effectively.
- It recommends the inclusion of environmental topics in the higher education curriculum, especially in the applied sciences, engineering, and social sciences. This would enable learners to understand the environmental implications of their professional area and make informed decisions. The policy also advocates environmental issues to be highlighted in the researches in higher education institutions (HEIs).
- Apart from teaching–learning in the classroom, the policy also recommends the inclusion of eco-clubs and experiential learning activities like field trips, nature walks, and eco-camps to enhance environmental education in schools, colleges, and universities.
- The importance of promoting environmental literacy and awareness at the community level has also been highlighted in the document. It recommends the establishment of community-based organizations to promote environmentally sustainable practices in local communities. These organizations would work toward creating awareness about environmental issues and encouraging communities to take collective action toward achieving sustainability.

While the key recommendations of NEP 2020 have been listed above, in the following section certain aspects highlighted in the document which relates to environmental education will be discussed in more detail.

(i) Sustainable Development Goals (SDGs): NEP 2020 reiterates India's commitment to achieve the SDGs and its targets, especially emphasizing Goal 4 (Quality Education), which seeks to "ensure inclusive and equitable quality education and promote lifelong learning opportunities for all" by 2030. The mention of this commitment in the policy document to achieve SDGs is significant as all the SDGs are related to environmental education in some way or the other, and, therefore, well-planned environmental education courses will be instrumental in achieving SDGs.

(ii) Global challenges and multidisciplinary learning: The document recognizes that the current issues facing the world such as climate change, increasing pollution, and depleting natural resources, energy issues, water, food, and sanitation, growing emergence of epidemics and pandemics etc. cannot be dealt with by a single subject alone but by way of multidisciplinary learning at all stages of education. For example, to address issues such as pandemic or epidemic due to zoonotic disease, it will require inputs from biologists, microbiologist, environmentalist, ecologist, population expert, epidemiologist, doctors, statisticians, bioinformatics specialist, chemist, social scientists, law makers, policy makers, economists, mathematician, etc. Similarly, climate change cannot be tackled by scientists alone. It requires inputs from people from different professions as well as contributions of different sections of people. Environmental education being multidisciplinary in nature, effective environmental education programs will play a crucial role to tackle such global challenges.

(iii) Curriculum in different stages: NEP 2020 recommends the introduction of environmental education at relevant stages as part of contemporary subjects in the school education. Environmental education is currently implemented by infusing in different subjects in all stages of education. If implemented as a separate subject, it will mark a departure from the current practice. This could be a boon since the present infusion approach lands itself into a lot of confusion since teachers have no clue what has been infused and how they are supposed to practice infusion approach in their teaching–learning. This is not unexpected, and teachers are not to be blamed for this. They have never been introduced to the infusion approach of environmental education. With a separate subject, that issue may not arise. However, it all depends on how the separate subject environmental education course is prepared and how teachers are prepared to teach the subject.

For HEIs, the document recommends a credit-based course in environmental education which will include areas such as climate change, pollution, waste management, sanitation, conservation of biological diversity, management of biological resources and biodiversity, forest and wildlife conservation, and sustainable development and living. As in the case of school education, students in HEIs are introduced to environmental education. We may recall that environmental education in the form of Environmental Studies is a mandatory one semester course for all students in the undergraduate course irrespective of the field, stream, or professional course. This is being done in compliance to the Hon'ble Supreme Court of India's order. Therefore, there is ample scope for environmental education in the existing system as well; the lack of seriousness in students and teachers alike is another matter.

(iv) Promotion and creating awareness about knowledge of India: The document mentions that promotion and creation of such awareness about knowledge of India will cater to both ancient and modern with regard to education, health, environment, etc., which will be achieved through specific courses in tribal ethno-medicinal practices, forest management, traditional (organic) crop cultivation, natural farming, etc. Such nature-based strategies are crucial for sustainable development, and these will form an integral part of environmental education.

(v) Moral/ ethical values: The document also highlights the importance of teaching students about "doing what's right" to enable them to embrace moral/ethical values and formulate a position/argument about an ethical issue from multiple perspectives. Such emphasis is the need of the hour since environmental issues are not so much a scientific or technological problem as it is about ethics and morality. For example, it is known to everyone that people who contribute the least to environmental issues and problems are the ones suffering the most. Many technological solutions are affordable only to a certain section of the society. As such, environmental degradation, their impacts, and the solutions available cannot be discriminatory. Therefore, ethical decisions which are environmentally, socially, and economically viable will go a long way while addressing the ever-increasing environmental issues and problems. However, it does not mean telling students what according to us is right, but instead they should be prepared in such a way that they are able to take into consideration moral/ethical values in their decision-making. It will not always be taking a decision between what is right or wrong. Sometimes it will be about the "better" decision at that point of time. For example, a turtle accidentally came out of the lake and is found more than 40 kilometers away on the highway. It will not be a straightforward decision whether to take the turtle back to its habitat, which would involve transportation at the expense of fossil fuel, or leave the turtle alone hoping it will find its way back.

(vi) Teachers and teacher education: The document emphasizes the importance of the role of teachers for quality education. Teacher education has always been a concern due to several lacunae in the existing system; the most serious and significant one, as pointed out in the document, is that of selling degrees for a price as mentioned by the Justice J.S. Verma Commission Report (2012).[1] NEP 2020 is seen to have sorted such issues and other associated issues and by revamping teacher education. Some of the solutions and recommendations of NEP 2020 in this regard are discussed below:

Teacher professional development (in-service)
NEP 2020 clearly lays down its vision for Continuous Professional Development (CPD) with 50 hours of CPD opportunities which will be driven by their own interest in numerous areas covering latest pedagogies,

learning outcomes, competency-based learning, etc. It is hoped that environmental education will also find a place in the CPD.

NEP 2020 recommends a common guiding set of National Professional Standards for Teachers (NPST) which will cover expectations of the role of the teacher at different levels of expertise/stage, and the competencies required for that stage. It will also comprise standards for performance appraisal, for each stage, which would be carried out on a periodic basis. It is to be seen how the Professional Standard Setting Body (PSSB), which will be responsible for the task, take into consideration environmental education in the whole gamut of the preparation of standards.

Teacher preparation (preservice)

Based on NEP 2020, by 2030, the minimum degree qualification for teaching will be a four-year integrated B.Ed. degree that teaches a range of knowledge content and pedagogy with strong practicum training in the form of student teaching at local schools. It also leaves scopes for a two-year B.Ed. program for those who have obtained bachelor's degrees in other specialized subjects and adaptation of one-year B.Ed. programs for those who have completed four-year multidisciplinary bachelor's degrees or who have obtained master's degree in a specialty and wish to become a subject teacher in that specialty. This proposal sounds encouraging as it will help the B.Ed. students to be equally strong in their content knowledge as much as they will be in their pedagogical knowledge.

The document also clearly mentions that environmental awareness and sensitivity toward its conservation and sustainable development will be appropriately integrated in teacher education programs so that environmental education becomes an integral part of school curricula.

In order to prepare quality teachers, it recommends establishment of multidisciplinary institutions, wherein teacher education will also be part of and will ensure education in high-quality content as well as pedagogy. It also mentions that HEIs offering teacher education programs will ensure the availability of a range of experts in education and related disciplines as well as specialized subjects. In addition, in order to maintain uniform standards for teacher education, the document suggests that admission to pre-service teacher preparation programs shall be through suitable subject and aptitude tests conducted by the National Testing Agency, and shall be standardized keeping in view the linguistic and cultural diversity of the country.

While several aspects of environmental education have been highlighted at different sections in the document, a clearly spelt-out vision of environmental education would have been much appreciated. It may also be noted that in spite of climate change being a critical global issue, the document did not make any specific mention about climate change education in school education.

6.19 National Curriculum Framework for Foundational Stage 2022 (NCF-FS 2022)

The National Curriculum Framework for Foundational Stage 2022 (NCF-FS 2022) is a comprehensive document that outlines the educational goals and objectives for students in the early years of their schooling, that is, up to age 8 or up to Grade 2 (NCERT 2022).

The NCF-FS 2022 aims at students' holistic and integrated development with a focus on different aspects such as physical and motor, cognitive, socio-emotional-ethical, cultural/artistic, and communication and early language, literacy, and numeracy. The curriculum emphasizes experiential learning that is based on supervised play, exploration, and discovery "to nurture and develop the child's innate abilities and capacities of curiosity, creativity, critical thinking, cooperation, teamwork, social interaction, empathy, compassion, inclusiveness, communication, cultural appreciation, playfulness, awareness of the immediate environment, as well as the ability to successfully and respectfully interact with teachers, fellow students, and others" (NCERT 2022, 16). These are skills and competencies essential to be developed to promote environmental literacy. It identifies five types of plays, which include "Environment/ Small World play" in which using miniature animals, nature walk to identify trees, plants, insects, birds, animals, sounds, and colors have been included as examples.

The document identifies five domains (physical development, socio-emotional and ethical development, cognitive development, language and literacy development, aesthetic and cultural development) under each of which a few curricular goals have been laid down. Competencies to be developed are listed under each curricular goal. Further, illustrative learning outcomes have been provided for each competency. In support of environmental education, the NCF-FS 2022 suggests various activities that are engaging and enjoyable for children. These activities include nature walks, field trips, hands-on activities such as gardening, etc.

Of all the curricular goals, one that prominently stands out to be directly related to the study of environment is provided below:

Domain: Socio-Emotional and Ethical Development

- CG-6 (Curricular Goal 6) Children develop a positive regard for the natural environment around them
- C-6.1 (Competency 6.1) Shows care for and joy in engaging with all life forms

(NCERT 2022, 50)

The document did not provide the learning outcomes for this competency and therefore, curriculum developers have to develop the associated learning outcomes for different grades.

While the environment has to be necessarily used to achieve the said curricular goal, the environment can also be used to achieve any other curricular goal, competency, or learning outcome. For example, many of the competencies under Curricular Goal 7 (children make sense of world around through observation and logical thinking) and Curricular Goal 8 (children develop mathematical understanding and abilities to recognize the world through quantities, shapes, and measures) may be achieved by using environment as the integrating context for learning. The document in fact suggests that "content in mathematics can reflect engagement with the local environment. Mathematical activities, whether understanding shapes or counting, can be integrated with engagement with the natural and human environments" (NCERT 2022, 141). The question is, how much the teachers will use or how aware teachers will be to use the environment in their teaching–learning process.

Successful implementation will depend entirely on how teachers are trained to integrate environmental concerns in the teaching–learning process, what facilities and infrastructures are available, how environmental components have been addressed in the teacher's handbook or in the textbooks of different subjects, what resources will be used, how flexible the classes and classrooms will be, etc. This is especially important because all teachers will not be naturally environmentally sensitive, oriented, and motivated.

6.20 National Curriculum Framework for School Education 2023 (NCF-SE 2023)

The NCF-SE 2023 was brought out in the light of the National Education Policy 2020. The document recognizes and emphasizes the need to nurture environmentally literate students given the unprecedented environmental problems facing us today. The aims of environmental education in the school curriculum as laid down in the document are reproduced here in verbatim:

- Create a strong foundation of environmental literacy, which includes understanding the interlinkages between ecological, social, economic, and political factors.
- Develop a more compassionate attitude towards the natural environment, drawing upon teachings from ancient Indian traditions and practices, the Indian Constitution, as well as scientific research on the effects of modern human activity on the environment.
- Develop an action-oriented mindset and skillset to promote environmental causes, with a solid understanding of how individual, societal, national, and

global actions can help us restore the balance between humans and nature and thereby save our planet and ourselves.

(NCERT 2023, 173)

NCF-SE 2023 envisages to address environment-related concerns in the school curriculum by including it as a cross-cutting theme as Learning about and Caring for the Environment and also as one of the school subjects under the Education in Interdisciplinary Areas—in Grade 10 as Environmental Education and in Grades 11 and 12 as Sustainability and Climate Change. While Environmental Education in Grade 10 is mandatory, Sustainability and Climate Change in Grades 11 and 12 is optional. This is a departure from the NCF-2005, which recommended the infusion approach, that is, as a cross-cutting area. Inclusion of environmental education as a school subject in Grade 10 may strengthen the infusion approach but at the same time this abrupt introduction of Environmental Education in Grade 10 defies logic and understanding.

NCF-SE 2023 mentions that 13 Curricular Goals and 20 Competencies that directly address learning about and caring for the environment have been included in the document across curricular areas and School Stages (NCERT 2023, 177). It also provides the key points to be considered for different stages. The modalities for implementation of environmental education in different stages/grades can be summarized as provided in Table 6.1.

Although environment is considered as a cross-cutting theme 'Learning about and Caring for the Environment' in the document, which means this aspect should be integrated in all disciplines across all stages, the document seem to contradict itself by specifically mentioning inclusion of learning about the environment only in specific subjects such as The World Around Us in the Preparatory Stage and in Science and Social Science in the Middle Stage (NCERT 2023, 178). The document falls short in elaborating how as a cross-cutting theme environmental concerns can be integrated in all disciplines, and not just in specific subjects such as Science or Social Science only. Another drawback of the document is that it fails to strongly recognize that unlike other cross-cutting themes, environmental education has a content and concepts of its own that needs to be delivered. A more comprehensive approach would have been achieved by adopting the approach employed as in the case of all other school subjects. A clearly laid-out curricular goals, competencies, and contents for different grades for environmental education would have made the task easier for the implementers. It will now be left on the expertise of the curriculum developers what aspect of the environment should be integrated in Science, Social Science, Mathematics, Languages, Vocational Education, etc.

Though well intended, the success of the implementation of environmental education will depend on teachers. This concern is not limited to teaching the subject Environmental Education in Grade 10 or Sustainability and Climate

TABLE 6.1 Modalities for Implementation of Environmental Education in Different Stages/Grades as Envisaged in NCF-SE 2023

SL. No.	Stage	Mechanism
1	Foundational	As a cross-cutting theme 'Learning about and Caring for the Environment'
2	Preparatory	1. As a cross-cutting theme 'Learning about and Caring for the Environment' 2. Through the curricular area "World Around Us"
3	Middle	As a cross-cutting theme 'Learning about and Caring for the Environment'
4	Secondary	
	Grade 9	As a cross-cutting theme 'Learning about and Caring for the Environment'
	Grade 10	1. As a cross-cutting theme 'Learning about and Caring for the Environment' 2. Through the Essential Course "Environmental Education" (under interdisciplinary areas as one of the curricular areas)
	Grades 11 and 12	1. As a cross-cutting theme 'Learning about and Caring for the Environment' 2. Through "Sustainability and Climate Change," which is one of the choice-based disciplines

Change in Grades 11 and 12, but more so when it comes to addressing it as a cross-cutting theme. It is a known fact that lack of trained teachers for environmental education has always been the biggest challenge, as is discussed in detail in Chapter 8.

6.21 Guidelines and Curriculum Framework for Environment Education at Undergraduate Level 2023

In June 2023, the University Grants Commission (UGC) brought out a new guideline and curriculum framework for a four-credit environmental education course at the undergraduate level titled 'Guidelines and Curriculum Framework for Environment Education at Undergraduate level.'[2] The preface says, "The document is expected to cater to students from diverse disciplinary backgrounds and to sensitise them about the commitment of our nation towards achieving sustainable development goals and addressing global environmental challenges." However looking at the course, there is hardly any scope for action-oriented, problem identification, or problem-solving scopes, which is the need of the hour (Shimray, 2016) except for fieldwork such as "Campus environmental management activities such as solid waste disposal, water management, and sewage treatment" (UGC 2023, 17). The course is heavily content knowledge-focused with eight units related to basic concepts on environment such as Humans and the Environment, Natural Resources and Sustainable Development, Environmental Issues: Local, Regional and Global, Conservation of Biodiversity and Ecosystems, Environmental Pollution and Health, Climate Change: Impacts, Adaptation and Mitigation, Environmental Management, and Environmental Treaties and Legislation and just one unit for Case studies and fieldwork. The first eight units on theory are allotted three credits, while only one credit is allotted for case studies and fieldwork. Learning outcomes are provided for each unit, which are all knowledge-based. One wonders how such a course will contribute in achieving SDGs as is envisaged when there is very little action required from students.

Nevertheless, what is encouraging about the new curriculum framework is that, unlike in the past where students just needed to pass, the new course carries four credits, and, therefore, the course will be approached with seriousness by students and teachers alike. However, an output-oriented course, which could be in the form of environmental problem-solving, innovative environmental solutions, environmental writings, authentic research on sustainable practices, traditional and indigenous knowledge, etc., would serve the environment better instead of acquiring more environmental knowledge. Students are introduced to environmental concepts and concerns throughout their school education, during which they acquire adequate awareness and knowledge about the environment. Therefore, instead of a knowledge-focused course, the four-credit course could have been prepared in such a way that students from diverse disciplinary backgrounds are engaged in fieldworks or projects in the area of environment but which are in tune with their backgrounds, such as persuasive messaging, essays, poems; audio, video, apps, etc.; green solutions in laboratories; mathematical modeling; tracing historical and indigenous practices; models, devices, appliances, etc. These could have been a group work as well. Imagine what it would be like if all undergraduate students in the country were engaged in such output-oriented problem-solving projects?!

6.22 Conclusion

Although the root of modern environmental education in India can be traced back to 1937, beginning with Gandhi's concept of 'basic education,' it was only since beginning the 1970s that its relevance is more evident in the education system. An interesting and important observation made in NCERT (1981, 21–22) regarding noninclusion of environmental education as an integral part of school education prior to 1975 is provided below verbatim:

1. Lack of comprehensive awareness of the importance of the earthly environment and the impact of its distortion and mutilation on man's present and future existence on earth along with other living beings from whom man is continuously deriving some form of benefit, directly or indirectly.

2. Inheritance of an old-fashioned and tradition education as a legacy of British rule over India, which was considerably divorced from the country's own environment.
3. Lack of expertise in developing an environment-related curriculum.
4. Traditional outlook toward education and societal unpreparedness to accept a new content of education, that is, environmental education.

Subsequently, the National Policy on Education-1986 (NPE-1986) provided a strong base to incorporate environmental education in the curriculum. This document can be considered a landmark for environmental education since all the programs and projects related to environmental education till the National Education Policy 2020 was brought out have in some way emerged and are being implemented based on this document. All the curriculum frameworks brought out after the NPE-1986 highlighted environmental concerns more evidently. Having seen the impact that a policy document can have, it becomes more important that such documents contain a more specific yet comprehensive content on concerns related to environmental education. This is necessary to prevent misinterpretation of the ideas and philosophies reflected in the document when different stakeholders begin 'deciphering' and 'decoding' the document during the process of implementation.

The Hon'ble Supreme Court's order of 1991 to make environmental education a compulsory subject in all stages of education, including schools, to a great extent promoted environmental education in the country and shaped environmental education into its present status. As evident from all the documents that have been discussed in the chapter, elements of environmental education are found implicitly or explicitly. However, for better and effective implementation of environmental education, a policy document which explicitly and strongly advocates environmental education is much needed. If such documents could accommodate a separate section purely for environmental education, it will make a world of difference in its implementation. This aspect is wanted even in the NEP 2020. The new curriculum frameworks—NCF-FS 2022 and the NCF-SE 2023—which have been prepared in the light of NEP 2020, signify a new dawn in India's school education. These documents introduced a somewhat different approach to environmental education recommending environment as a cross-cutting theme as well as introduction of Environmental Education as a separate subject in Grade 10 and Sustainability and Climate Change as one of the choice-based disciplines in Grades 11 and 12. As much as the shortcomings of the curriculum frameworks can be fixed during the implementation, the strengths of the documents can be weakened due to poor implementation strategies. Hence, implementation will be key to nurture environmentally literate students.

With regard to higher education, keeping in view the new guidelines and curriculum framework for environment education developed by the UGC for the undergraduate level, not much can be expected in terms of resolution of environmental problems and issues as the focus is on content knowledge with very little scope for opportunities to resolve or solve environmental issues and problems.

With the not-very-encouraging environmental education curriculum laid out for implementation in the country, its effectiveness rests in the hands of teachers, teacher educators, and other stakeholders.

6.23 Summary

- Root of modern environmental education in India can be traced as far back as 1937 with Mahatma Gandhi's concept of 'Basic Education,' where the focus was learning by/and doing. Education was envisaged not only for the sake of learning but the resultant product was also to add to the nation's wealth.
- After independence, the focus was shifted to building the nation and how to make the maximum use of the natural resources available, which could have resulted in a lot of exploitation of the environment.
- Beginning the 1970s, environmental concerns received more recognition and relevance in the education system, which was reflected in the national curriculum framework developed in 1975.
- The National Policy on Education-1986 (NPE-1986) provided a strong base to incorporate environmental education in the curriculum and can be considered a landmark for environmental education since all the programs and projects related to environmental education till today have in some way emerged and are being implemented based on this document.
- All the curriculum frameworks brought out subsequent to NPE-1986 highlighted environmental concerns more evidently.
- Increasing environmental pollution and degradation brought about the Supreme Court's order of 1991 to make environmental education a compulsory subject in schools. This order, to a great extent, promoted environmental education in the country and shaped environmental education into its present status.
- The NEP 2020 recognized and addressed environmental concerns quite adequately.
- The NCF-FS 2022 and NCF-SE 2023 brought out in the light of NEP 2020 failed to incorporate environmental education systematically.
- There is a disconnect between teacher education curriculum framework and what the curriculum framework for school education recommends for environmental education.
- The new guidelines and curriculum framework for environment education developed by the UGC for the undergraduate level is focused on content knowledge.

APPENDICES

Appendix 6.1 Syllabus of Science and Mathematics for the Middle School Level (1970)

Biology First Year (Part I, i.e., Class VI)

Part I: Section VIII: Plant as Living Organism—Conditions necessary for plant life—air, water, and light; role of soil; Importance of green plants in nature, an idea of conservation of plants—"Vana Mahotsava"

Biology Third Year (Part III, i.e., Class VIII)

Topic-wise Part IV: Man and his Environment—includes topics such as

1. Interdependence of the living and nonliving: Food chains, exchange of chemicals between living and nonliving, water, and other cycles
2. An agricultural field: Sun as energy source, environment in the field, daily and seasonal changes, drought and flood, animals and plants of the field, adaptations of animals for living in soil and litter layers, role of insect and other invertebrates—food chains, potential pests, aids to farmers as pollinators, nutrition of soil, and so on. Brief consideration of the chemical cycles (water, oxygen, and carbon and nitrogen) in the field. Dangers of disturbing the cycles by total removal of crop etc. Roles of fertilizers, rotation of crops, contour ploughing, fallow periods, proper crop, and herd arrangement.
3. Man and the conservation of nature: the need to conserve biological resources—soil, plants, and wildlife, methods of conservation, methods of preventing polluting of air and water, dangers of careless use of pesticides in disturbing the balance of nature, responsibilities of every citizen to practice conservation.

Appendix 6.2 Syllabi for Classes VI–VIII (1976)

Classes I and II

- Environmental Studies (Social Studies and General Science)—Integrated curriculum in environmental education
- Work Experience and the Arts

Classes III, IV, and V

Environmental Studies I (Social Studies)

- A separate subject where he/she would get an understanding of the geographical setting in which he/she lives and that of his/her social and cultural environment. In this course, the pupil would be gradually introduced to the life in his home and family, school, neighborhood, the state, the country, and the world at large.

Environmental Studies II (General Science)

- Work Experience and the Arts

Classes VI, VII, and VIII

Social Science (elements of history, geography, civics, and economics)

- Elements drawn primarily from history, geography, civics, economics, and sociology
- Taught as separate subjects as history, geography, and civics (economics and sociology to be integrated in these three subjects)
- Focus would be on interaction between man and his physical and social environment, and the relationship between man and his social and cultural heritage, and the community of which he is a part, which will help the pupil to understand various aspects of the contemporary problems in their totality.
- To develop an understanding of the economic forces that influence the everyday life of citizens.

Geography syllabus

Class VI

Unit 1: The Earth as a Globe: the earth and the solar system; rotation and revolution of the earth; latitude and longitude; globe and world map

Unit 2: Africa—Land and Peoples: land, climate, vegetation, wild life, gift of nature, peoples, and so on

Unit 3: Asia—Land and Peoples: land, climate, vegetation, wild life, gift of nature, peoples, and so on

Unit 4: Practical work: ideas of map

Class VII

Unit 1: Atmosphere and Hydrosphere: composition and layers of atmosphere; air and its changing temperature; pressure and winds; humidity and precipitation; ocean waters and their circulation

Unit 2: Australasia—Land and People: land, climate, vegetation, wild life, gift of nature, peoples, and so on

Unit 3: South America—Land and Peoples: land, climate, vegetation, wild life, gift of nature, peoples, and so on

Unit 4: North America—Land and Peoples: land, climate, vegetation, wild life, gift of nature, peoples, and so on

Unit 5: The Soviet Union—Land and Peoples: land, climate, vegetation, wild life, gift of nature, peoples, and so on
Unit 6: Practical work: night and day

Class VIII

Unit 1: Lithosphere and Landforms: crust, rocks, earthquakes, volcanoes, process of gradation and its agents: weathering, soil formation, running water, groundwater, moving ice, winds, sea waves
Unit 2: Europe—Land and Peoples: land, climate, vegetation, wild life, gift of nature, peoples, etc.
Unit 3: India—Physical Setting: relief features; climate, vegetation, and wild life
Unit 4: India—Its Agricultural Resources: soils, irrigation, crops, methods of farming
Unit 5: India—Minerals and Industries: mineral resources, industries
Unit 6: India—Trade, Transport, and Population: trade, transport, and population structure, distribution and density
Unit 7: Practical work: weather study

Science (elements of the physical sciences and the life sciences)

Integrated Science

Class VI

Unit 11: Man's dependence on plants and animals and the balance of nature: dependence of man on plants and animals; interdependence of plants and animals; dependence of plants and animals on environment; different uses of plants and animals to man; interactions of organisms with other organisms; interactions of organisms with physical environment
Unit 12: How do living species cope with the environment: changes in the environment; living organism can sense the change of environment; living organisms cope with the environment
Unit 13: Water: sources; purification of water for drinking; importance of water to living forms; some special properties of water like low melting point, high boiling point, density of ice, and good solvent and their importance of daily life
Unit 14: Energy: energy sources in nature—sun, water, wind, coal, petrol, etc.; relationship between work and energy; energy problems—social significance; various forms of energy; mechanical energy; chemical energy; transformation of energy from one form to another; use of energy in living systems

Class VII

Unit 27: Population and pollution

Sub-unit 27.1: Population: definition; characteristics of population; external factors affecting the population; population explosion and its problems

Sub-unit 27.2: Pollution: definition; environmental pollution—air, water, noise pollution; causes of pollution and its preventions; pollution and balance in nature

Class VIII

Unit 37: Agriculture

Sub-unit 37.1: Agriculture practices and implements: tilling leveling, manuring, sowing, transplanting, watering harvesting, water pump, spray pump

Sub-unit 37.2: Our Problems in agriculture: our problems in production and storage

Sub-unit 37.3: Improvement and protection of crops: nature and types of soil, treatment of soil; nutrient deficiency in soil; fertilizers (K, N, and phosphate), mixed fertilizers, and their composition; crop protection, use of insecticides, pesticides, and weed killers; precautions in the use of fertilizers, pesticides, and weed killers; different types of crops—their growth patterns, climate, and season; selection of seeds, water and irrigation, importance of crop rotation; hybridization, and crop breeding

Unit 40: Conservation of natural resources: what are natural resources—why conservation is necessary—how steps of conservation are taken for soil, water, air, forest, and wild life

Unit 42: Science in human welfare:—what made developments possible (with reference to industrial development in modern India)

Class IX and X

Social Sciences (history, geography, civics, economics, psychology); Science (the physical sciences and the life sciences)

Work Experience: No detailed syllabi are visualized for work experience. No 'syllabus' is really necessary in connection with work experience but ideas for implementing this aspect of education will be available through separate books.

Appendix 6.3   Guidelines and Syllabi for Upper Primary Stage (1988)

Science

Class VI

Unit I: Science in Everyday Life

Content: Role of science in solving many basic problems in our everyday life; misuse of science; scientific methods help us in making decisions, acquiring knowledge, and solving problems; contribution of scientists in the progress of science.

Unit 9: Air

Content: An envelope of air all around us; air—a mixture of various components; composition of air; oxygen—a supporter of combustion and life; necessity of air for sustenance of life; various uses of air to human beings

Unit 10: Water

Content: Importance of water for living beings; need of water for various purposes; sources of water; purification of water for drinking; some special physical properties of water; different forms of water; change of one form into another; water cycle in nature; hard and soft water; uses of water in day-to-day life; need of conservation of water

Unit 11: Energy

Content: Energy, relationship between work and energy; different forms of energy—mechanical energy, heat energy, light energy, sound energy; renewable and nonrenewable sources of energy; electric energy from coal; solar energy, wind energy, energy from water, energy from biomass

Unit 12: Balance in Nature

Content: Living and nonliving components of environment; interdependence; food and energy relations; balance in nature; essential for survival; indiscriminate human interferences are often harmful

Class VII

Unit 5: Sound

Content: Various types of sound; modes of production of sound; formation of echo; noise and its hazards; human ear

Unit 7: Energy

Content: Mechanical energy; potential and kinetic energies; transformation of energy; renewable and nonrenewable sources of energy; judicious uses of energy

Unit 9: Water

Content: Composition of water; electrolysis of water; some common physical properties of water, electrical attraction of water, some chemical properties of water; dissolution of various minerals and salts in seawater; hard and soft water; removal of hardness; water pollution

Unit 10: Air

Content: Various constituents of air; oxygen—an important constituent of air, air pollution; acid rain; uses of various constituents of air

Unit 12: Food, Health, and Diseases

Content: Food essential for human life; basic constituents, their main functions including water and roughage; different foods are rich in different constituents; balanced diet in relation to age and work; judicious choice of food; avoidance of fads; malnutrition; deficiency diseases; food preservation; contamination/spoilage; healthy living depends on hygiene, sanitation, and habits; diseases; disorders; role and spread of disease causing micro-organism; personal hygiene and environmental sanitation; noncommunicable diseases; smoking, alcohol, and drug addiction as health hazards

Unit 13: Soils

Content: Composition of soils—gravel, clay, organic matter; humus and living organisms in top soil, soil formed by weathering; soil as important natural resource; soil erosion and conservation; soil pollution

Unit 14: Agricultural Practices and Implements

Content: Management of plants and animals; usefulness, general methods; improved agricultural practices for increased food production; basic practices; sequencing; variation from crop to crop; practices common to gardening; agricultural implements and their uses and care; qualitative and quantitative improvement of crop yields; necessity and methods, improved practices and varieties; judicious use of soil, fertilizers and pesticides; animal management; need for keeping animals; general needs and maintenance of domestic animals with special reference to cattle, sheep, poultry; bee, and fish rearing

Class VIII

Unit 2: Alternative Sources of Energy

Content: Source of energy; fossil fuels; hydro-energy; bio-energy, wind-energy as renewable sources of energy; energy needs; development of alternative sources of energy; judicious use of energy

Unit 4: Man-made Materials

Content: Various types of materials and their applications; synthetic fibers; plastics and its uses in daily life; glass and its formation; ceramics; soaps and detergents; fertilizers; pesticides

Unit 8: The Microbial World Content: Micro-organisms have divers forms; fungi, protozoa, bacteria, viruses, and certain algae; causes of disease in man and animal bacteria (cholera, typhoid, TB); virus (cold, measles, polio, chickenpox), protozoan and fungi (malaria, dysentery, etc.); animal diseases (anthrax and foot and mouth), plant diseases (rust, bacterial wilt, leaf curl, mosaic); modes of transmission of diseases; vectors; control of microbial diseases; proper storage and preservation to prevent microbial damage to clothing, timber, and food

Unit 10: Adaptation and Organic Evolution

Content: Meaning of adaptation; adaptation caused by structural changes; adaptation of aquatic, terrestrial, and volant organisms; organisms have undergone continuous and gradual change since their evolution; origin of life from simple substances; origin of complex forms from simpler forms; slow process; evidence of evolution—external and internal structures; fossils; organic evolution through the process of natural selection

Unit 11: Useful Plants and Animals

Content: Plants and animals affect human life in many ways, harmful and useful plants of economic importance—wild and cultivated; useful animals; animals; animals products from wild and domesticated animals—(ivory, lac, horn, lime, pearls, leather, and honey)

Unit 12: Conservation of Natural Resources

Content: Necessity of natural resources of life; Matter or material from earth; energy from sun; living organisms get all requirements from nature; energy directly or indirectly from the sun; man requires more resources than other living organisms; proper distribution of resources; various types of natural resources; renewable and nonrenewable; depletion of resources and their causes; conservation of natural resources for human survival; conservation efforts at individual/community/governmental/international level is necessary

Geography

Class VIII

Unit IV India—Natural Resources

Major natural resources their distribution and utilization (a) soil; (b) minerals—iron, coal, petroleum, bauxite, and manganese; (c) forest and wild life; (d) water Conservation of natural resources

Unit V India—Human Resources

Population: density, distribution, growth rate and structure of population—sex composition, literacy, rural–urban ratio, employment, age–structure

Quality of life—economic and social development, health and nutrition

Unit VI India—Economic Development

(a) agriculture: predominance of monsoon, irrigation projects, food production, green revolution; (b) industries: heavy small-scale and cottage; few important industries—iron and steel textiles, sugar, oil refineries, heavy machinery and chemicals; (c) trade: internal and external; (d) transport and communications: land, water, and air transport; means of communications: land, water and air transport; means of communication and their development

Civics

Class VIII

> Unit IV: Our Economic Problems: poverty and unemployment, population growth; production and productivity in agricultural, industrial, and household sectors
>
> Unit VIII: World Problems: human rights; arms race; disparities between the developing and developed countries; environmental pollution (human activities and environmental pollution, types of environmental pollution, pollution of air, water, and land. Factors responsible for environmental pollution, impact of environmental problems on society, and the quality of life; ways and means to reduce environmental pollution at the local, national, and international levels)

Appendix 6.4 Guidelines and Syllabi for Upper Primary Stage (1988)

Work Experience: Essential Activities

1. Maintaining cleanliness at home
2. Cleanliness of the classroom and school premises
3. Keeping sources of water in the community safe and clean
4. Looking after sanitary disposal of waste material during festivals
5. Taking care of school dress
6. Helping in the cleaning of poultry house cattle shed in rural area
7. House/school decoration on special occasions such as festivals, marriages, birthdays
8. Organizing community service programs for road repairs, tree plantation, and cleaning of surroundings in a village slum area
9. Helping parents in looking after younger children in the family
10. Maintenance of personal and household accounts, payment of household bills (electricity, water, newspapers, etc.)
11. Making small purchases for self and family
12. Coaching primary school children including younger brothers and sisters who are weak in studies
13. Monitoring the weight of babies in the neighborhood to detect malnutrition.
14. Preparation of charts and posters indicating causes, symptoms, and prevention of common diseases
15. Carrying out environmental sanitation and tree plantation

Appendix 6.5   Guidelines and Syllabi for Secondary Stage (1988)

Science

Class IX

Unit 3: Ways of Living

Habitat and Organisms: habitat, types of habitat; classification of organisms based on habitats, habitat and organisms, interdependence including man; conservation of habitats

Adaptation: structural and functional potentialities of organisms, structural adaptation with reference to internal and external factors; functional adaptation refers to life processors

Unit 4: Human Beings

Continuous Efforts of Man to Reshape the Natural Environment; necessity and inventions; manipulation of environment to overcome limitations, for physical, biological and cultural needs; regulation of environment; use and exploration of needs; control and use of fire regulation of micro and macro levels, advantages and disadvantages of regulation

Unit 5: World of Work

Technology: meaning and application; evolution of technology and human society; development of new and improved technology—need, acceptance by the society, time gap between development and application; role of technology in harnessing energy

Impact of technology on society: influence of technology on individual needs, energy requirements of the individual and the society, energy crisis, impact of technology on physical, social, and cultural environment

Technology and science: interrelation between science and technology, application of technology in development of science, one technology creates need for another

Class X

Unit 6: Energy

Sun as a source of energy: absorption of solar energy by earth, photosynthesis, solar heaters, solar cells

Wind: windmills; hydroelectric generation, electricity from sea waves; bioenergy–bio-mass, bio-mass as fuel, biogas

Fossil fuels: sources of fossil fuels, coal; natu-fuels—conditions for combustion, heat produced during combustion, combustion of food in living organism

Types of fuels: energy from fuels, solid, liquid, and gaseous fuels, characteristics of fuels—conditions for combustion, heat product during combustion, combustion, food in living organisms

Nuclear energy: nuclear fission, energy released during fission, atomic power plants, radiation hazards; energy crisis—causes of energy crisis, trends in energy consumption of individuals; industry and agriculture, depletion in known stocks of fossil fuels, inefficient use of energy, industrialization and urbanization; possible solutions for overcoming energy crisis—population control, exploration of renewable sources of energy and emphasis on their use, reducing wastage of energy, use of energy efficient machines, judicious use of nonrenewable sources of energy

Unit 7: Food and Health

Necessity of balanced diet: diet and nature of work, need and functions of nutrients, vitamins, minerals; sources of dietary proteins, carbohydrates, and fats, vitamins, minerals; deficiency diseases and their symptoms; protein energy malnutrition, mineral malnutrition; symptoms of diseases, factors of insufficiency control, harmful effects of over intake; obesity, and other complications, cardiovascular disorder, mottling of teeth and fluorosis, hypervitaminosis

Wasteful food practices: type of wastage, defective practices—post harvesting, mode of storage and distribution, traditional systems, faulty methods of preservation, cooking, pre-marketing

Food yield: different practices—use of fertilizers and manures, proper irrigation, nitrogen fixation, crop rotation mixed cropping, use of good hybrids, protection of plants against diseases, animal husbandry, artificial insemination, care and management

Food spoilage: internal and external factors, control factors effecting human health: factors—use of spoiled food, organic failure, metabolic malfunctions, genetically transmitted diseases, malignancies of different organs

Environmental pollutants, contaminated water, causes, and transmission by physical contract or vectors

Disorders caused by addiction to alcohol, smoking, and drugs; essentials for good health—hygienic habits and control of environmental pollution

Unit 8: Environment

Biosphere: sources of energy, food chain, food web, flow of energy

Mineral cycles: carbon cycle, role of carbon and its compounds, nitrogen cycle, nitrogen fixation, oxygen cycle, oxidation processes, water cycle, role of energy in different cycles

Ecological balance: man's role in disturbing the balance, efforts for maintenance of ecological balance

Unit 9: Natural Resources

Water: water as a natural resource, origin of life in water, water as medium for the activity of the living, water as a solvent, saturated and unsaturated solutions, seawater as habitat of organism, salts from sea, use of water

Air: role of atmosphere in protection from radiation, composition of atmosphere, water, and particulate matter in atmosphere, carbon dioxide and its adverse effects on living organisms, role of trees, release of carbon dioxide from fossil fuels and automobiles, corrosion of metals, damage of historical monuments from acidic gases, effect of metallic particles, asbestos, etc. on living organism, carbon monoxide and its ill-effects, smog, air pollution, radioactivity, noise pollution and its effects on human beings

Dependence of man on natural resources: minerals from earth metals and nonmetals, use of metals.

Carbon and its compounds: properties of carbon and hydrocarbons, petroleum products

Extraction of metals: properties of metals and some alloys; uses of metals, nonmetals and some alloys at home and in industry

Living resources: renewable and nonrenewable resources, exploitation of resources, ecological crises due to deforestation, need for proper replenishment and management of living resources, means of replenishment through silviculture, conservation and monitoring of wild life parks and sanctuaries, wild life conservation, legislative measures for protection of living resources

Unit 10: Universe

Earth: physical and biological components, atmosphere, changes since its origin, evolution of life, role of solar energy in origin and sustenance of life

Space exploration: history of space exploration, applications of space science—satellite communication, weather monitoring, collection of information about other planets and outer space

Solar system: planets and satellites, structure of the solar system, age of planets including earth

Universe: solar system and Milky Way galaxy, universe, comprising galaxies, expanding universe, origin of universe—big bang theory

Recycling of waste material: waste materials, biodegradable and nonbiodegradable waste materials and their recycling, preparation of compost, proper disposal of nuclear and radioactive wastes, harmful effects of exposure to radioactive waste, technique for proper storage of radioactive wastes

Geography

Class IX: Man and Environment

Unit 2: Natural Environment (the totality of the environment; special place of human beings in the environment)
Unit 3: Natural Resources and Their Utilization

1. Resources and their classification; renewable and nonrenewable; potential and developed; classification of resources based on their source, for example, land and water
2. Land resources: land use patterns, soil formation, utilization, forest and wild life resources, animal resources, fisheries, mineral and power resources, water resources
3. Depletion and degradation of resources and their conservation

Unit 4: Human Interaction with the Environment

1. Human population: distribution, growth of population, density of population, man and ecosystem, and food supply
2. Human occupation: primary occupations—food gathering, hunting, fishing, animal rearing and mining; secondary occupations—industries; tertiary occupations—trade, transport, communication and other service.
3. Environmental degradation: nature of human intervention causing environmental degradation, depletion of resources, environmental pollution, environmental problems at local, regional, national and global levels; Need and efforts to improve the quality of environment
4. The natural regions: concept of natural region, major natural regions of the world, how natural regions help in the study of World Geography
5. Geography and area development: few case studies each of development from agricultural and industrial regions representing both developed and developing regions

Class X: Geography of India

Unit I: India: physical features, climate, natural vegetation and wild life (natural vegetation, wild life, conservation of wild life)

Unit 2: Natural Resources

a. Water resources: uneven and undependable nature of rainfall, the twin problem of floods and famine, flood control, irrigation and drainage, water budget, sources of irrigation, river valley, and multipurpose projects
b. Mineral and power resources: minerals—metallic and nonmetallic mineral fuels, hydroelectricity, their exploration, distribution and extraction, power development, wise use and conservation of mineral and power resources
c. Land use: forest lands, pasture, and farmlands, settlement and other uses, soil, forest and cattle wealth, fisheries
d. Agriculture: problems of Indian agriculture, post-independence development, major food, fiber and cash crops, food budget, yield per unit area

Unit 3: Developing our Resources

a. Manufacturing Industries: agro-based and mineral-based industries, iron and steel, heavy industries, large-scale, small-scale, and cottage industries, the need to step up industrial production and productivity
b. Transport and communications: road, railways, waterways, and airways, major ports, development of communication
c. International trade: major exports and imports, major trading partners, recent trends
d. People: the greatest resource of the country—population, size, distribution and density, composition in terms of age, sex and dependency, rural and urban, growth of population, quantitative vs. qualitative aspects of human population; need and efforts toward planned development of human resources in terms of education, health, occupational and vocational skills, productivity and employment opportunities, need and efforts to stabilize population growth
e. Area development: case studies from India

Plantations in Assam
Tribal area development—tribals in Andamans and Nicobar
Agriculture—Suratgarh Farm
Mineral—Neyveli
Industrial development—Jamshedpur

Unit 4: Field Study Project Work
Any topic of local/regional importance such as irrigation problem in and arid region; deforestation, soil erosion, and afforestation programs in hilly and mountainous areas, effect of cyclones in coastal areas, environmental degradation in an industrial/mining region, and so on

Civics

List of projects: study of some major developments in the national life, for example role of the nationalized banks in the development of the society, nuclear arms race, food, population, health and sanitation problem, environmental pollution and preservation, and so on

Economics

Unit I: Understanding an Economy (efficient use of Resources)
Unit II: An Overview of the Indian Economy (population situation in India: poverty, unemployment, consumer education)
Unit IV: Toward Economic Development (inputs in agriculture, new technology in agriculture, food problem in India, future outlook for agriculture, balanced industrial structure, future outlook for industrial development, foreign trade—exports and imports)

Appendix 6.6 Guidelines and Syllabi for Secondary Stage (1988)

Work Experience: Essential Activities

1. Use of bus and railway timetables
2. Milking of dairy animals
3. Reception work in school
4. Preparation and distribution of midday meal/snacks in composite schools
5. Preparation of teaching aids and equipment for self and lower classes
6. Helping school authorities in organizing exhibitions, picnics, tours, and excursions
7. First-aid activities like counting of pulse, taking of temperature, and bandaging of wounds after cleaning them
8. Helping traffic police in the regulation of traffic
9. Plantation of shady/fuel/ornamental/avenue trees
10. Preparation of family budget and maintenance of daily household accounts
11. Acquaintance with common fertilizers and pesticides and their application with appropriate equipment
12. Acquaintance with common pests and plant diseases and use of simple chemical and plant protection equipment
13. Handling farm animals for feeding, washing, or general examination
14. Preparation of soak pit for collecting liquid refuse from the cattle shed
15. Studying the nutrition and health status of people in a village/city/slum/tribal area
16. Helping community health programs for enhancing the nutrition, health, and environmental status of the community through door-to-door contact programs
17. Digging trench latrines during festivals and maintaining them hygienically
18. Participation in adult literacy program
19. Helping in child-care in crèches
20. Volunteer work in hospitals and fairs, during floods and famines, and in accidents

Notes

1 https://www.education.gov.in/sites/upload_files/mhrd/files/document-reports/JVC Vol 1.pdf (Accessed on September 18, 2023).
2 https://www.ugc.gov.in/pdfnews/4111559_Environment_Guideline.pdf (Accessed on June 15, 2023).

References

Gandhi, M.K. 1951. *Basic Education*, edited by Bharatan Kumarappa. Ahmedabad: Navajivan Publishing House.

GoI, Government of India. 1953. *Report of the Secondary Education Commission (1952–1953)*, Ministry of Education, Government of India.

———. 1966. *Report of the Indian Education Commission (1964–66)—Education & National Development*, Ministry of Education, Government of India.

———. 1968. *National Policy on Education—1968*, Ministry of Education, Government of India.

———. 1977. *Report of the Review Committee on the Curriculum for the Ten-Year School*, Ministry of Education and Social Welfare (Ishwarbhai Patel Committee Report), Government of India.

———. 1986. *National Policy on Education—1986*, Ministry of Human Resource Development, Government of India.

———. 1993. *Learning without Burden—Report of the National Advisory Committee appointed by the Ministry of Human Resource Development*, Government of India.

———. 2020. *National Education Policy—2020*, Ministry of Education, Government of India.

NCERT, National Council of Educational Research and Training. 1970. *Syllabus of Science and Mathematics for the Middle School Level*. New Delhi: NCERT.

———. 1975. *The Curriculum for the Ten-year School: A Framework*. New Delhi: NCERT.

———. 1976. *Syllabi for Classes VI–VIII*. New Delhi: NCERT.

———. 1981. *Environmental Education at the School Level: A Lead Paper*. New Delhi: NCERT.

———. 1987. *Science Education for the First Ten Years of Schooling—Report of the Working Group*. New Delhi: NCERT.

———. 1988a. *Guidelines and Syllabi for Secondary Stage*. New Delhi: NCERT.

———. 1988b. *Guidelines and Syllabi for Upper Primary Stage*. New Delhi: NCERT.

———. 1988c. *National Curriculum for Elementary and Secondary Education—A Framework (Revised Version)*. New Delhi: NCERT.

———. 2000. *National Curriculum Framework for School Education 2000*. New Delhi: NCERT.

———. 2001a. *Guidelines and Syllabi for Secondary Stage*. New Delhi: NCERT.

———. 2001b. *Guidelines and Syllabi for Upper Primary Stage*. New Delhi: NCERT.

———. 2004a. *Curriculum Framework for Teacher Education*. New Delhi: NCERT.

———. 2004b. *Environmental Education in Schools—Syllabus for Environmental Education in Schools Submitted to the Hon'ble Supreme Court of India in Pursuance of its Order Dated 18th December 2003*. New Delhi: NCERT.

———. 2005a. *National Curriculum Framework-2005*. New Delhi: NCERT.

———. 2005b. *Syllabus for Classes at the Elementary Level*. New Delhi: NCERT.

———. 2005c. *Syllabus for Secondary and Higher Secondary Classes*. New Delhi: NCERT.

———. 2006. *Position Paper of the National Focus Group on Habitat and Learning*. New Delhi: NCERT.

———. 2011. *Teachers' Handbook on Environmental Education for the Higher Secondary Stage*. New Delhi: NCERT.

———. 2022. *National Curriculum Framework for Foundational Stage*. New Delhi: NCERT.

———. 2023. *National Curriculum Framework for School Education*. New Delhi: NCERT.

NCTE, National Council for Teacher Education. 2009. *National Curriculum Framework for Teacher Education—Towards Preparing Professional and Humane Teacher 2009*. New Delhi: NCTE.

Shimray, Chong. 2016. "Redesigning Environmental Courses for Effective Environmental Protection." *Current Science* 110 (4): 499–501.

Yadav, M.S., and V.M. Nikalje. 2009. *National Curriculum Framework—A Historical Perspective*. New Delhi: NCERT.

UGC, University Grants Commission. 2023. *Guidelines and Curriculum Framework for Environment Education at Undergraduate Level*. New Delhi: UGC.

7
GLOBAL TRENDS IN ENVIRONMENTAL EDUCATION—RAMIFICATIONS IN INDIA

7.1 Chapter Overview

Environmental education (EE) has evolved over the decades in theory and practice so much so that today some countries find it outdated and prefer to opt for education for sustainable development (ESD). Even so, the need to nurture environmentally literate students can never be overemphasized keeping in view the unprecedented deteriorating state of the environment. With the changes taking place globally, the chapter attempts to bring out whether such global trends in environmental education have any semblance or corresponding impact on the trends in India. This is important to know since environmental issues are not restricted to, or limited by, political or geographical boundaries and hence need collective efforts. Besides, the details of implementation of environmental education in India highlighting the role of judiciary in the process of implementation are also discussed. Project-based environmental education has been specifically discussed keeping in view its importance, which is highlighted in different curriculum frameworks as well as pointed out by various researchers in their studies.

7.2 Introduction

In the preceding chapters, developments that have taken place in the area of environmental education and its evolution at the international as well as at the national level have been discussed. In this chapter, an attempt will be made to see if there is any connection between the developments that have taken place at the international and the national level and how India has adapted to the

DOI: 10.4324/9781003461135-8

changes at the international scenario. Further, trends in environmental education due to such adaptation and its present status in India will be discussed. For the sake of clarity in understanding, the discussions will be broadly in three sections. The first section will look into how the trends and approaches in the field of environmental education in India have changed in tune with the developments and changes that have taken place at the international scenario. The second section will focus on the status of the implementation of environmental education in India. Here, the discussion will include the intervention of the Hon'ble Supreme Court of India in the implementation of environmental education, its present nature of implementation, different areas of focus, and barriers in implementation. The last section of the discussions is devoted to project-based environmental education keeping in view its importance as envisaged in the National Curriculum Framework 2005 and, thereafter, as mentioned in the affidavit submitted to the Hon'ble Supreme Court as well as in the National Curriculum Framework for School Education 2023 (NCF-SE 2023). This section looks into how far project-based environmental education, as envisaged in these documents, is practicable or feasible in actual situations in schools.

7.3 Trends in India vis-à-vis Global Initiatives

To begin with, there is a need to understand how environmental education trends in India have changed (or appear to have changed) in the wake of the changes and developments that have taken place at the international level in the past few decades. For this purpose, a few selected programs and projects that have been initiated at the global level and have influenced the Indian scenario are briefly discussed. However, it is not claimed that the changes taking place in India, as will be discussed later, are purely the result of the developments taking place globally. In most instances, it presents the possible impact of global developments in India, while in some the actual impact leading to the changes in India is presented.

7.3.1 International Union for Conservation of Nature (IUCN)

Founded in 1948, IUCN is the world's oldest and largest global environmental organization. At the time of its foundation, it was named International Union for the Protection of Nature (IUPN), the main focus being the protection and conservation of nature and natural resources. Later, in 1956, the name was changed to International Union for Conservation of Nature and Natural Resources. Again in 1990, the organization was renamed World Conservation Union, although it continued to use IUCN as its abbreviation. In 2008, the name was reverted back to IUCN. The focus has now expanded to equitable use of natural resources and ecological sustainability.

The ideas promoted by IUCN appear to have influenced curriculum developers in India till the early 1970s. Although conservation of nature and natural resources did not appear in the Secondary Education Commission Report (1952–1953) or the Kothari Commission Report (1964–1966) and not even in the National Policy on Education 1968 (GoI 1968), some aspects related to conservation were reflected in the documents, such as local sanitation, water supply, concepts, principles, and processes in the physical and biological environment. However, the curricular materials developed subsequent to NPE-1968 were more explicit, in that, environmental concerns, such as air and water pollution, pesticides, conservation of natural resources, and so on, found place in the curriculum.

7.3.2 The United Nations Conference on the Human Environment, Stockholm, 1972

It was the world conference to make the environment a major issue.[1] Ecological management, economic growth, poverty alleviation, and pollution were the major issues that were discussed. This conference marked a milestone for environmental education. Recommendation 96 of the conference called for the development of environmental education as one of the most critical elements of an all-out attack on the world's environmental crisis.

The outcome of the Stockholm conference seems to have a significant impact on the development of India's first national curriculum framework for school education. Not only were the concerns and concepts added noticeably, but also, for the first time, the term 'environmental education' appeared in the national document related to education—the Curriculum for the Ten-year School: A Framework-1975. It may be added that concerns related to environmental conservation, reduction of pollution, maximization of economic and social welfare, and maximization of ecological stability also found space in the document which were the major concerns of the Conference. Soon after this Stockholm conference, the Water Pollution Control Act of 1974 came on the statute book in India. Interestingly, during the leadership of Indira Gandhi (the then prime minister of India), in the 42nd amendment of the Constitution in 1976, Articles 48-A and 51-A (g) were inserted. Article 48-A states "The State shall endeavour to protect and improve the environment and to safeguard the forests and wild life of the country," and Article 51-A (g) requires every citizen to protect and improve the natural environment including forests, lakes, rivers, and wild life, and to have compassion for living creatures. These amendments could well be considered the positive outcomes of the Stockholm conference, which was attended by the then prime minister Indira Gandhi, wherein she had strongly advocated the need to ensure protection of the environment without ignoring social issues such as poverty. These laid the foundation for the creation of Department of Environment in 1980, later renamed as the Ministry of Environment and Forests in 1985 and the Ministry of Environment, Forest, and Climate Change in 2014. It may be noted that subsequent to the conference many new acts came into being while several others were amended, such as the following:

- Water (Prevention and Control of Pollution) Act, 1974, Amended in 1988
- Air (Prevention and Control of Pollution) Act, 1981, Amended in 1987
- Wild Life (Protection) Act, 1972, Amendment in 1982, 1986, 1991, 1993, 2002, 2006, 2013
- Forest (Conservation) Act, 1980, Amendment in 1988
- Environment (Protection) Act, 1986
- Biodiversity Act, 2000

Among these, special mention may be made of the Environment (Protection) Act, 1986, which was passed by the Parliament based on Article 253[2] of the Constitution of India, as a result of the Stockholm conference. The National Green Tribunal Act, 2010, was enacted:

> To provide for the establishment of a National Green Tribunal for the effective and expeditious disposal of cases relating to environmental protection and conservation of forests and other natural resources including enforcement of any legal right relating to environment and giving relief and compensation for damages to persons and property and for matters connected therewith or incidental thereto.

The enactment of this act mentioned India being party to the decisions taken at the United Nations Conference on the Human Environment held at Stockholm in June 1972 and the UN Conference on Environment and Development held at Rio de Janeiro in June 1992, and also the Article 21 of the Constitution.[3]

7.3.3 International Environmental Education Program (IEEP)

As mentioned in Chapter 2, in response to Recommendation 96 of the Stockholm conference, UNESCO and UNEP initiated the IEEP in 1975 to promote reflection and action, as well as international cooperation in this field. IEEP carried out numerous activities from 1975 to 1983, during which it organized several meetings at the international and regional levels. Lasting for 20 years (1975–1995), the IEEP provided technical, advisory, and financial support to governments, civil society groups, and institutions of learning (UNEP 2005, 41). The International Environmental Education Workshop held at Belgrade (formerly in Yugoslavia, now in Serbia) during 13–22 October 1975 was one of the initiatives. The Belgrade Charter was the culmination of the workshop. Under the IEEP, the first intergovernmental conference on environmental education was held in Tbilisi, USSR (now in Georgia), from 14 to 26 October 1977.

The Tbilisi Conference laid the basis for the development of environmental education at the international level as well as strategies for the advancement of environmental education at the national level and the promotion of international cooperation. The challenges that environmental problems pose to the society and the role that education can and must play in solving such problems were highlighted more than ever. The conference laid down the goals, objectives, and guiding principles of environmental education.

Following the Belgrade Charter and the Tbilisi Conference, environmental education in India was elevated to another level in terms of importance and recognition. For example, the National Policy on Education 1986 (NPE-1986) more explicitly mentioned concerns related to the environment by reiterating and highlighting the 'fundamental duties' as laid down in the Indian Constitution, protection of the environment being one. It also stressed on the "paramount need to create a consciousness of the environment" and the need to integrate this aspect in the entire educational process (GoI 1986). The concerns laid down in this document were important because being a national policy document such concerns were subsequently reflected in all the national curriculum frameworks brought out by India, such as the National Curriculum for Elementary and Secondary Education—A Framework (Revised Version) (NCERT 1988), the National Curriculum Framework for School Education (NCERT 2000), the National Curriculum Framework (NCERT 2005), and the National Curriculum Framework for Teacher Education—Towards Preparing Professional and Humane Teacher 2009.

7.3.4 IEEP Activities in India's Context

The significant role played by the 23 pilot projects undertaken by the IEEP is irrefutable. These initiatives have greatly contributed to the incorporation of environmental education into the national education processes by facilitating the training of teachers and educators by developing educational and informational materials suitable to local environmental situations end conditions and by sensitizing the population in general (UNESCO 1984). Out of the 23 projects, two were specific to India which are:

- Pilot Project for Primary Schools, India (1979–1980): This project was developed by the National Council of Education Research (NCERT) of India. The project's main objective was preparation and experimentation of the implementation of environmental education modules in primary schools of several Indian states, including Assam, Punjab, Karnataka, and Tamil Nadu. In this connection, the pilot project organized workshops for teachers of the areas involved. During these workshops, teachers and specialists refined the modules prepared and provided appropriate guidelines for their use. The modules were implemented and evaluated on a national scale.

- Pilot Project on Environmental Problems of Urban Marginal Areas, India (1981–1983): This project aimed at developing multimedia educational materials related to major environmental problems of marginal urban settlements (hygiene, nutrition, pollution, and other aspects), the training of community leaders, and the experimental development of actions-oriented toward improvement of the environmental quality of the community concerned in India.

IEEP also conducted several trainings of environmental education professionals and activists. Participants/experts from India who attended it benefited from the following programs implemented through different periods:

- International Training Course in Environmental Education was organized on 1–28 September 1982 in Prague and other towns of the Czechoslovak Socialist Republic.
- Regional Training Workshop for Asia: This training workshop for Asia and Oceania was organized in September 1980 in Bangkok, Thailand. The workshop reviewed environmental education progress in the region and established concrete steps that may be taken to enhance environmental education for both in-school and out-of-school populations.
- Subregional Workshop on Teacher Training in Environmental Education for Asia was organized in March 1983 in New Delhi, India. The objectives of the workshop were to familiarize educators with the contents of the series of EE teacher training modules prepared by the International EE Program, explore ways for their local adaptation and use, and exchange information and experience on EE material development in the subregion.

7.3.5 Brundtland Commission Report, Agenda 21, Decade of Education for Sustainable Development

It may be noted that social and economic issues were inherent in all the initiatives undertaken to tackle environmental issues facing the world at large. The initiatives, however, focused largely on addressing only the ecological impact of the ever-increasing unrestricted development. A need was, therefore, felt to formalize a broader strategy to comprehensively address both the needs of the society and the environment. After an intense exercise which was initiated in the mid-1980s, the United Nations in 1987 brought out the Report of the World Commission on Environment and Development: Our Common Future, popularly known as the Brundtland Commission Report, wherein sustainable development (SD) was endorsed as an overarching framework or construct for future development policy at all levels of government.

Soon after the Brundtland Commission Report, from 1987 to 1992, the 40 chapters of the Agenda 21 on sustainability (see Chapter 2, Box 2.4) were written by different committees. The Agenda 21 was adopted by over 178 nations as the official policy at the UN Conference on Environment and Development, popularly known as the Earth Summit held in Rio de Janeiro, Brazil, during 3–14 June 1992 (UN 1993). One of the most important documents in the conference, the Rio Declaration on Environment and Development, sets out 27 principles (reproduced in Box 7.1) that aim to guide international actions on the basis of environmental and economic responsibility toward SD. Chapter 36 of the Agenda, "Promoting Education, Public Awareness, and Training," underlines global concerns related to education and sustainability. In addition, each of the 40 chapters includes education as a component in the implementation strategy.

The Johannesburg World Summit on Sustainable Development in 2002 deepened the commitments toward SD, especially by proposing that the UN should consider adopting a decade of education for SD beginning 2005. The UN General Assembly subsequently proclaimed the period 2005–2014 as the UN Decade of Education for Sustainable Development (UNDESD).

In view of the impressive efforts put forward for the implementation of the programs of action as laid down in Agenda 21, it was naturally expected that the National Curriculum Framework for School Education brought out in 2000 would center around or focus on SD. However, full-fledged ESD (which is different from SD-related education, as will be discussed in detail in Chapter 9), or SD as an emerging concern, was not reflected in the document. Many aspects related to SD, however, were spread all through the curriculum framework which could be comparable to SD-related education. For example, issues related to poverty, health, demography, population, and environment have been discussed, but without relating it to SD. Nevertheless, this lapse or gap was addressed to some extent in the documents published thereafter, including the Environmental Education in Schools—Syllabus for Environmental Education (2004) and the National Curriculum Framework 2005. These documents pointed out the importance and necessity of environmental education to facilitate the move toward SD. However, the focus remained on tackling environmental issues in isolation with little consideration of the society and economy aspects as is seen in science textbooks developed by NCERT such as in the chapters Natural Resources for class IX (NCERT 2006a reprint 2019), Sources of Energy for Class X, etc. (NCERT 2006b reprint 2019). Hence, a closer look revealed that the true essence of ESD was missing in these documents as well. Nevertheless, it may be noted that in the textbooks that were developed by NCERT based on these documents, the topic of SD was included in some subject disciplines such as in class XI Economics in the chapters Rural Development and Environment and Sustainable Development (NCERT 2006 reprint 2021) and in Fundamentals of Physical Geography for Class XI in the chapters Geography as a Discipline and Biodiversity and Conservation (NCERT 2006 reprint 2021).

BOX 7.1 RIO DECLARATION ON ENVIRONMENT AND DEVELOPMENT

REPORT OF THE UNITED NATIONS CONFERENCE ON ENVIRONMENT AND DEVELOPMENT
(Rio de Janeiro, 3–14 June 1992)
RIO DECLARATION ON ENVIRONMENT AND DEVELOPMENT
The United Nations Conference on Environment and Development,

Having met at Rio de Janeiro from 3 to 14 June 1992,
Reaffirming the Declaration of the United Nations Conference on the Human Environment, adopted at Stockholm on 16 June 1972, a/ and seeking to build upon it,
With the goal of establishing a new and equitable global partnership through the creation of new levels of cooperation among States, key sectors of societies and people,
Working toward international agreements which respect the interests of all and protect the integrity of the global environmental and developmental system,
Recognizing the integral and interdependent nature of the Earth, our home,
Proclaims that:

Principle 1. Human beings are at the centre of concerns for sustainable development. They are entitled to a healthy and productive life in harmony with nature.
Principle 2. States have, in accordance with the Charter of the United Nations and the principles of international law, the sovereign right to exploit their own resources pursuant to their own environmental and developmental policies, and the responsibility to ensure that activities within their jurisdiction or control do not cause damage to the environment of other States or of areas beyond the limits of national jurisdiction.
Principle 3. The right to development must be fulfilled so as to equitably meet developmental and environmental needs of present and future generations.
Principle 4. In order to achieve sustainable development, environmental protection shall constitute an integral part of the development process and cannot be considered in isolation from it.
Principle 5. All States and all people shall cooperate in the essential task of eradicating poverty as an indispensable requirement for sustainable

development, in order to decrease the disparities in standards of living and better meet the needs of the majority of the people of the world.

Principle 6. The special situation and needs of developing countries, particularly the least developed and those most environmentally vulnerable, shall be given special priority. International actions in the field of environment and development should also address the interests and needs of all countries.

Principle 7. States shall cooperate in a spirit of global partnership to conserve, protect and restore the health and integrity of the Earth's ecosystem. In view of the different contributions to global environmental degradation, States have common but differentiated responsibilities. The developed countries acknowledge the responsibility that they bear in the international pursuit of sustainable development in view of the pressures their societies place on the global environment and of the technologies and financial resources they command.

Principle 8. To achieve sustainable development and a higher quality of life for all people, States should reduce and eliminate unsustainable patterns of production and consumption and promote appropriate demographic policies.

Principle 9. States should cooperate to strengthen endogenous capacity-building for sustainable development by improving scientific understanding through exchanges of scientific and technological knowledge, and by enhancing the development, adaptation, diffusion and transfer of technologies, including new and innovative technologies.

Principle 10. Environmental issues are best handled with the participation of all concerned citizens, at the relevant level. At the national level, each individual shall have appropriate access to information concerning the environment that is held by public authorities, including information on hazardous materials and activities in their communities, and the opportunity to participate in decision-making processes. States shall facilitate and encourage public awareness and participation by making information widely available. Effective access to judicial and administrative proceedings including redress and remedy, shall be provided.

Principle 11. States shall enact effective environmental legislation. Environmental standards, management objectives and priorities should reflect the environmental and developmental context to which they apply. Standards applied by some countries may be inappropriate and of unwarranted economic and social cost to other countries, in particular developing countries.

Principle 12. States should cooperate to promote a supportive and open international economic system that would lead to economic growth and sustainable development in all countries, to better address the problems of environmental degradation. Trade policy measures for environmental purposes should not constitute a means of arbitrary or unjustifiable discrimination or a disguised restriction on inter-national trade. Unilateral actions to deal with environmental challenges outside the jurisdiction of the importing country should be avoided. Environmental measures addressing transboundary or global environmental problems should, as far as possible, be based on an international consensus.

Principle 13. States shall develop national law regarding liability and compensation for the victims of pollution and other environmental damage. States shall also cooperate in an expeditious and more determined manner to develop further international law regarding liability and compensation for adverse effects of environmental damage caused by activities within their jurisdiction or control to areas beyond their jurisdiction.

Principle 14. States should effectively cooperate to discourage or prevent the relocation and transfer to other States of any activities and substances that cause severe environmental degradation or are found to be harmful to human health.

Principle 15. In order to protect the environment, the precautionary approach shall be widely applied by States according to their capabilities. Where there are threats of serious or irreversible damage, lack of full scientific certainty shall not be used as a reason for postponing cost-effective measures to prevent environmental degradation.

Principle 16. National authorities should endeavour to promote the internalization of environmental costs and the use of economic instruments, taking into account the approach that the polluter should, in principle, bear the cost of pollution, with due regard to the public interest and without distorting international trade and investment.

Principle 17. Environmental impact assessment, as a national instrument, shall be undertaken for proposed activities that are likely to have a significant adverse impact on the environment and are subject to a decision of a competent national authority.

Principle 18. States shall immediately notify other States of any natural disasters or other emergencies that are likely to produce sudden harmful effects on the environment of those States. Every effort shall be made by the international community to help States so afflicted.

Principle 19. States shall provide prior and timely notification and relevant information to potentially affected States on activities that may have a significant adverse transboundary environmental effect and shall consult with those States at an early stage and in good faith.

Principle 20. Women have a vital role in environmental management and development. Their full participation is therefore essential to achieve sustainable development.

Principle 21. The creativity, ideals and courage of the youth of the world should be mobilized to forge a global partnership in order to achieve sustainable development and ensure a better future for all.

Principle 22. Indigenous people and their communities and other local communities have a vital role in environmental management and development because of their knowledge and traditional practices. States should recognize and duly support their identity, culture and interests and enable their effective participation in the achievement of sustainable development.

Principle 23. The environment and natural resources of people under oppression, domination and occupation shall be protected.

Principle 24. Warfare is inherently destructive of sustainable development. States shall therefore respect inter- national law providing protection for the environment in times of armed conflict and cooperate in its further development, as necessary.

Principle 25. Peace, development and environmental protection are interdependent and indivisible.

Principle 26. States shall resolve all their environmental disputes peacefully and by appropriate means in accordance with the Charter of the United Nations.

Principle 27. States and people shall cooperate in good faith and in a spirit of partnership in the fulfilment of the principles embodied in this Declaration and in the further development of international law in the field of sustainable development.

Setting itself apart from other documents, the National Curriculum Framework for Teacher Education—Towards Preparing Professional and Humane Teacher 2009, briefly, yet precisely, emphasized the need to educate future generations through perspectives of gender equity, the perspectives that develop values for peace, respect the rights of all, and respect and value work, and the perspective of the present ecological crisis to promote equitable and SD.[4]

7.3.6 United Nations Framework Convention on Climate Change (UNFCCC)

UNFCCC was adopted in 1992 with the ultimate aim of preventing dangerous human interference with the climate system. The 1997 Kyoto Protocol and 2015

Paris Agreement were developed under the Convention by the Conference of Parties (COP), the decision-making body responsible for monitoring and reviewing the implementation of the UNFCCC. In view of the existential threat to all life forms posed by climate change, enormous efforts are being made globally toward its mitigation and adaptation. As such, climate change education becomes more important, and this is being increasingly emphasized throughout the world. It may be mentioned that the term related to climate change was mentioned for the first time in the National Curriculum Framework for School Education 2000 as 'climatic changes' (NCERT 2000, 64). No other environmental issue has received so much attention and emphasis as climate change that today it is no more treated as part and parcel of environmental education but parallel to it. For example, at no point there has been biodiversity loss education, plastic pollution education, air pollution education, etc.; however, today climate change education not only exists, but is also greatly stressed upon. This explains the magnitude of the issue. However, in the context of school curriculum in India, such overt emphasis on climate change education is not evident. For example, systematic inclusion of concepts and concerns related to climate change is not seen in the curriculum to date. Even the latest National Education Policy 2020 does not specifically mention the need for climate change education. Similarly, even in the recently brought out National Curriculum Framework for School Education 2023 (NCF-SE 2023), a specific modality to address climate change in the curriculum is not provided. However, this is not to say that the curriculum ignored climate change. In fact, climate change–related topics have been included at several places in different grades such as in Grade 10 Environmental Education. The only concern is that without a systematic plan students may not be able to understand climate change meaningfully. It may also be mentioned that in the NCF-SE 2023, Sustainability and Climate Change has also been included as one of the optional courses in Grades 11 and 12 as already mentioned in Chapter 6.

7.3.7 Sustainable Development Goals

All member states of the United Nations in 2015 adopted the 2030 Agenda for Sustainable Development. At the heart of this Agenda, there are 17 Sustainable Development Goals (SDGs) (Box 7.2) with 169 associated targets which are an urgent call for action by all countries. They recognize that ending poverty and other deprivations must go hand in hand with strategies that improve health and education, reduce inequality, and spur economic growth—all while tackling climate change and working to preserve the oceans and forests. In short, the SDGs strive for peace and prosperity for people and the planet, now and into the future. SDGs have also been discussed briefly in Chapter 1, Section 1.5.1.10.

> **BOX 7.2 THE 17 SDGS TO TRANSFORM OUR WORLD**
>
> GOAL 1: No poverty
> GOAL 2: Zero hunger
> GOAL 3: Good health and well-being
> GOAL 4: Quality education
> GOAL 5: Gender equality
> GOAL 6: Clean water and sanitation
> GOAL 7: Affordable and clean energy
> GOAL 8: Decent work and economic growth
> GOAL 9: Industry, innovation, and infrastructure
> GOAL 10: Reduced inequality
> GOAL 11: Sustainable cities and communities
> GOAL 12: Responsible consumption and production
> GOAL 13: Climate action
> GOAL 14: Life below water
> GOAL 15: Life on land
> GOAL 16: Peace and justice strong institutions
> GOAL 17: Partnerships to achieve the goal

In the context of environmental education, due to its proximity with ESD, SDG 4 (Target 4.7) is especially important since this target requires that all learners acquire the knowledge and skills needed to promote SD through ESD and other forms of education. After more than 30 years of drawing from the National Policy on Education 1986 as a guiding document, India brought out the National Education Policy 2020 (NEP 2020) in 2020. As mentioned in the previous chapter, the document is definitely progressive and forward-looking. There are several recommendations which will favor strong and compelling implementation of environmental education, for example introduction of environmental education as a separate subject at relevant stages, adequate training of teachers, quality education to achieve the SDGs, etc. The mention of SDGs in the policy document is especially significant in the global context as the world has set a target of 2030 to achieve the 17 SDGs. Quality education, and effective environmental education programs for that matter, will be instrumental to address such concerns. Keeping in view India's adoption of the global education development agenda reflected in the Goal 4 (SDG4) of the 2030 Agenda for Sustainable Development, NEP 2020 points out the need to reconfigure the entire education system "to support and foster learning, so that all of the critical targets and goals (SDGs) of the 2030 Agenda for Sustainable Development can be achieved" (NEP 2020, 3). However, in the National Curriculum Framework for School Education 2023, which was prepared in the light of NEP 2020, details on how the SDGs will be achieved finds no mention except for stating ESD as a key enabler for SDGs in building a sustainable society (NCERT 2023, 171). There is no further mention of ESD in the document. It may be noted that the indicators for implementation of Target 4.7 will be decided by the extent to which (i) global citizenship education and (ii) ESD are mainstreamed in (a) national education policies, (b) curricula, (c) teacher education, and (d) student assessment. Such mainstreaming of ESD is also found wanting in the National Curriculum Framework for School Education 2023. It is to be seen how this gap is addressed in the syllabi, textbooks, and other curricular materials.

7.4 Implementation of Environmental Education in India

As discussed in the previous chapters, environmental education in India has gone through several changes and has evolved over the years to find a significant niche in different educational processes and curricula. The country has been trying to keep pace with the world in the field of environmental education, and its efforts are now beginning to be visible. There is growing awareness among the population across the country as today environment-related studies are being carried out at all levels of education in schools and colleges. Its promotion is gradually becoming widespread, though the country still has a long way to go. A survey of the World Health Organization and a similar result found in the IQAir site ranking India as the eighth most polluted country in the world,[5] and also the study by the Energy Policy Institute at the University of Chicago finding that an average Indian could lose 1.8 years of life expectancy and Delhi resident up to 8.5 years if the country's national ambient air quality standards are not met,[6] is a reminder of the need to increasingly focus on environmental education. Though there are criticisms to the survey report of WHO, one cannot really deny the fact that the air in many cities of India is indeed polluted beyond safe limits. A homemade App—SAFAR-Air—System of Air Quality and Weather Forecasting And Research (SAFAR) is in place, which is a national initiative introduced by the Ministry of Earth Sciences (MoES) to measure the air quality of a metropolitan city, by measuring the overall pollution level and the location-specific air quality of the city. More and more people, including young students, are increasingly becoming conscious of their environment and the need to protect it, which is encouraging. The number of environmentalists and NGOs contributing in the area of environmental protection and nature conservation is also multiplying and their contributions ever increasingly evident. Looking at the growing awareness among all sections of the society, it may be said that the country has made some progress in environmental education.

In the following section, the focus will be on how far environmental education has come to be what it is in India today and elaborating on the present status of its implementation.

7.4.1 Intervention of the Hon'ble Supreme Court of India

To initiate the discussion, it will be appropriate to recall M.C. Mehta's writ petition No. 860/1991. For it was this petition which resulted in the Hon'ble Supreme Court order that has shaped the present status of implementation of environmental education in the country, to a large extent. It may be mentioned that NCERT was the respondent in the case representing all school systems of the country.

The previous chapter as well as in the discussions so far in this chapter suggest that India has made considerable efforts to incorporate environmental education in the school curriculum. However, the initiatives taken so far seemed to be too little and ineffective as far as ground reality is concerned. It was found lacking to tackle the fast-deteriorating environment. Hence, in 1991, M.C. Mehta filed a public interest litigation (PIL) stating that environment should be made a compulsory subject in schools and colleges in a graded system so that there would be a general growth of awareness. Based on this, the Hon'ble Court, in its order dated 22 November 1991, stated:

> We accept on principle that through the medium of education awareness of the environment and its problems related to pollution should be taught as a compulsory subject…So far as education up to the college level is concerned, we would require every state government and every education board connected with education up to matriculation or even intermediate college to immediately take steps to enforce compulsory education on environment in a graded way. This should be done in such a manner that in the next academic year there would be compliance of this requirement.

Following the Hon'ble Supreme Court judgment, some steps were undertaken by states and other authorities concerned to comply with the court directions. Mehta, however, contended that the steps taken by many states and authorities were insufficient and not in conformity with the spirit and object of the court order. He submitted that the states and other authorities concerned should prescribe a suitable syllabus by way of a subject on environmental awareness, not only at the primary level of education but also in higher courses. He also submitted that in the absence of such uniform prescribed syllabus in educational institutions, in various states different institutions were adopting different methods, some of which are only basic and which do not fulfill the requirements of the Hon'ble Court's directions. Based on this, the Hon'ble Supreme Court, on 18 December 2003, directed the NCERT

> to prepare a module syllabus to be taught at different grades and submit the same to this court by the next date of hearing so that we can consider the feasibility to introduce such syllabus uniformly throughout the country at different grades.

In compliance to the Hon'ble Supreme Court order of 18 December, NCERT, in 2004, came up with the syllabus 'EE in schools,' so that environmental education can be studied as a separate subject. The court order dated April 22, 2004 stated:

> M.C. Mehta, the petitioner in this petition, submits that the directions should also be given to train the teacher in the subject, but for the time being we do not intend issuing any direction on such request of Mehta. It will be considered at an appropriate time.

The Hon'ble Supreme Court also, in its order dated July 13, 2004, directed that the syllabus prepared by the NCERT for Class I to XII be adopted by every state in their respective schools. The order also stated, "NCERT is appointed as a nodal agency to supervise the implementation of this court order."

However, in 2005, when NCERT was given the task of developing a new curriculum framework, the group consisting of experts in the field of environmental education, Focus Group on Habitat and Learning, had a different opinion regarding the implementing environmental education as a separate subject. The group was concerned about adding to the curriculum load if environmental education was included as a separate subject. The group recommended that environmental education could best be done by infusing environment-related concepts at appropriate places in different subjects. Considering this, NCERT, representing schools in India, filed a supplementary affidavit dated November 26, 2007, wherein it mentioned:

> The best way of accomplishing the order of the Supreme Court regarding the implementation of environmental education is to infuse the teaching of environmental education as a part of different disciplines while ensuring that adequate time is earmarked for pertinent activities.

In its affidavit, NCERT also provided the details of how environmental education would be implemented in different classes. The orders of the Hon'ble Supreme Court as well as the contents of the affidavit submitted by the NCERT to the Hon'ble Supreme Court are important since failing to implement by all the concerned parties (states, UTs i.e., union territories, different boards, NCERT, and so on) as mentioned will amount to contempt of court.

7.4.2 Chronology of Important Events in Environmental Education in India

A chronology of some of the important events in the evolution of environmental education in India is presented in Table 7.1.

TABLE 7.1 Chronology of Important Events in Environmental Education in India

Year	Event
1962	Article (51A) 'Fundamental Duties' of the Constitution was amended. Clause (g), thereof, requires every citizen to protect and improve the natural environment, including forests, lakes, rivers, and wild life, and to have compassion for living creatures.
1975	The word Environmental Education was reflected in the first national curriculum framework for school education entitled 'Curriculum for the Ten-year School: A Framework.'
1986	The National Policy on Education was prepared which highlights the importance of protection of the environment and to create a consciousness of the environment which should inform teaching in schools and colleges in the entire educational process.
1988	A centrally sponsored scheme of Environmental Orientation to School Education was launched by the Ministry of Human Resource Development (renamed as Ministry of Education) that will allow educational programs in schools to be fully harmonized with the local environmental situation and concerns.
1991	Writ petition (Civil) No. 860/1991 was filed in the Hon'ble Supreme Court of India by M.C. Mehta with a petition to make environmental education a compulsory subject.
1991 (22 November)	The Hon'ble Supreme Court of India directed all educational institutions to teach environment and its problems related to pollution as a compulsory subject.
2003 (18 December)	The Hon'ble Supreme Court of India directed NCERT to prepare a module (model) syllabus.
2004	NCERT submitted the module syllabus to the Hon'ble Supreme Court entitled 'Environmental Education in Schools: Syllabus for Environmental Education in Schools,' in pursuance of the court's order dated 18 December 2003.
2004 (13 July)	The Hon'ble Supreme Court directed every state to adopt the syllabus prepared by NCERT for Class I to XII in their respective schools. The Hon'ble Supreme Court directed NCERT to be appointed as a nodal agency to supervise the implementation of the court's order.
2007 (26 November)	NCERT submitted a supplementary affidavit before the Hon'ble Supreme Court to review model syllabus in consonance with the NCF 2005 and presented the details of implementation of environmental education in schools.
2010 (3 December)	The Hon'ble Supreme Court admitted the affidavit filed by the NCERT. The Writ petition (Civil) 860/1990 is disposed of.
2020	Introduction of environmental education as a separate subject at relevant stages.

(*Continued*)

TABLE 7.1 (Continued)

Year	Event
2022	National Curriculum Framework for Foundational Stage (NCF-FS 2022) mentions, "Children develop a positive regard for the natural environment around them" as one of the curricular goals.
2023	National Curriculum Framework for School Education (NCF-SE 2023) 1. Environment as a cross-cutting theme in all stages 2. In addition: In Preparatory stage: Through the curricular area 'World Around Us' In Grade 10: Through the Essential Course 'Environmental Education' (under Interdisciplinary areas as one of the curricular areas) In Grades 11 and 12: Through 'Sustainability and Climate Change' which is one of the choice-based disciplines

7.4.3 Status of Environmental Education in India

As syllabus, textbooks and other curricular materials are yet to be developed based on the National Curriculum Framework for School Education 2023, the status presented here will be largely in the light of the National Curriculum Framework 2005 and the affidavit filed by NCERT in the Hon'ble Supreme Court. However, relevant information will be provided wherever possible.

Environmental education is being implemented in India in accordance with the details mentioned in the affidavit filed by NCERT in November 2007 and admitted by the Hon'ble Supreme Court in December 2010. Accordingly, environmental education is being imparted at different levels in schools in the following manner:

- Environmental education for Classes I and II: EE concerns and issues transacted through activities
- Environmental education for Classes III to V: Environmental education is imparted through a subject, namely Environmental Studies (EVS)
- Environmental education for Classes VI to X: Environmental education is imparted through the infusion approach
- Environmental education for Classes XI and XII: Environmental education is taught as a separate and compulsory project-based syllabus

However, with the launch of the NCF-SE 2023, as mentioned earlier as well as in detail in Chapter 6, in addition to integrating environment as a cross-cutting theme, environmental education will be a mandatory subject in Grade 10 and Sustainability and Climate Change will be one of the optional courses in Grades 11 and 12.

7.4.3.1 Three-Pronged Focus of Environmental Education

The position paper of the National Focus Group on Habitat and Learning of the National Curriculum Framework 2005 stated:

> The main focus of EE should be to expose students to the real-life world, natural and social, in which they live; to enable them to analyse, evaluate, and draw inferences about problems and concerns related to the environment; to add, where possible, to our understanding of environmental issues; and to promote positive environmental actions in order to facilitate the move towards sustainable development. To achieve these goals, the curriculum may be based on: (i) Learning about the environment (ii) Learning through the environment, and (iii) Learning for the environment.

This three-pronged approach of achieving the goals of environmental education, that is, learning 'about,' 'through,' and 'for' the environment, follows the classification of environmental education by A.M. Lucas which is education 'about,' 'in,' and 'for' the environment. As it was seen at the international scenario as discussed in Chapter 5, even in India the focus of environmental education has been largely on the 'about' component, wherein only information is transmitted which enhances only the cognitive knowledge. The 'through' and 'for' components are yet to be seen to be considered in the school curriculum. In contradiction to what was envisaged in the position paper or the NCF-2005, neither is there exposure to real-world situation nor are students provided opportunities to participate in resolution of environmental issues. In a study conducted at the national level to analyze the status of the biology curriculum at the higher secondary stage (Classes XI and XII), it was found that students are very rarely taken out of the four walls of their classroom as part of their teaching–learning process, contrary to what is expected to be a regular feature in the transaction of Biology curriculum (Shimray, Farkya, and Varte 2013). This state of affairs indicates that meaningful environmental education is still a distant dream.

Although the NCF-SE 2023 did not define environmental education as learning 'about,' 'through,' and 'for' the environment, it presents almost the same essence as it advocates for strong foundation of environmental literacy, developing compassionate attitude and action-oriented mindset and skillset to save the planet and ourselves (NCERT 2023, 173). Details regarding pedagogy for environmental education based on NCF-SE 2023 have been provided in the document (NCERT 2023, 412–413).

7.4.3.2 Curricular Materials in Environmental Education

Following the infusion approach, environment-related topics and concerns have been infused at relevant places in all the textbooks developed by NCERT in the light of NCF-2005. While these are mostly information-based, relevant projects have also been incorporated at appropriate places in the textbooks. For Classes III to V, a separate textbook, namely environmental studies, is in use. Besides these, NCERT also brought out other supplementary and complementary curricular materials such as model project books for Classes VI to XII and a teachers' handbook for project-based environmental education at the higher secondary stage. Many state boards have adopted or adapted these books, while others have developed theirs in a similar line. These positive developments suggest that adequate measures have been taken with regard to the development of curricular materials.

However, one might wonder about the situation in private schools, although less than government or government-aided schools in the country accounts for more than 20%.[7] In most cases, these schools do not use the curricular materials developed by NCERT. These schools prescribe curricular materials developed by private publishers, which may or may not reflect the philosophies of NCF-2005 with regard to environmental education. It is yet to be ascertained whether environment-related concerns have been infused sufficiently in such materials. For example, in spite of the recommendation of the NCF-2005 and an affidavit that for Classes III to V there would be a single subject environmental studies, it is found that many private schools still use two subjects: environmental studies (science) and environmental studies (social science). This suggests that there is lack of awareness about the interdisciplinary and holistic approach, which is envisaged in the single subject approach which represents the basic philosophy of environmental education. It will be interesting to see the resources that will be prepared based on NCF-SE 2023.

7.4.3.3 Assessment-Related Concerns

NCERT committed in the affidavit submitted to the Supreme Court, dated November 26, 2007, that tests of environment-related concerns and components would be taken in the examination of the concerned subjects in which they have been infused. It also mentioned that all examination papers should compulsorily have questions pertaining to the environmental education component present in the text. It categorically mentioned that at the Class X-level examination, papers of different subjects should have compulsory questions on the concepts of environmental education and that 10% of the grand total of marks is earmarked for environmental education. The affidavit also mentioned that project work should receive enough importance in the evaluation, which should be evaluated orally by an internal evaluator along with an external evaluator. Similarly, for the project-based syllabus at the higher secondary stage, the affidavit clearly mentioned how the core syllabus as well as the projects would be evaluated.

The affidavit also stated that CBSE and other state boards should ensure that appropriate measures are taken to implement them.[8] In spite of such details presented the affidavit, it is yet to be ascertained how much of the court directions are being implemented in schools. Although there is no research study to back the claim, it is evident from interactions with teachers that the implementation falls much short of the expectations. There could be many reasons as to why it is not implemented. Is it because the affidavit submitted to the Supreme Court is not taken seriously by the boards? Is it because schools are not given strict instructions to follow the affidavit? Is it because schools are still not sure how exactly to go about as they have not been oriented to take up such task? One can only get the answers by exploring the reasons through intensive and extensive research.

However, such issues and discrepancies may be sorted at least for Grade 10 when the NCFSE-2023 is implemented with the introduction of a separate environmental education subject, which will be mandatory and treated at par with other disciplinary subject (NCERT 2023, 387, 409). Details regarding pedagogy and assessment for environmental education based on NCF-SE 2023 have been provided in the document (NCERT 2023, 414–417).

7.4.3.4 Monitoring Implementation of Environmental Education

Monitoring the implementation of environmental education in schools in India is another matter of concern. Some of the reasons are the countless number of schools and educational institutions spread out in all corners of the country, including rural and remote places, and the absence of a systematic monitoring system. Strict monitoring is necessary not only to ensure implementation but also to find out the issues faced by different schools in the implementation and to look for ways to resolve such issues. Only then environmental education will be meaningfully implemented. The Supreme Court had in its order dated July13, 2004 directed NCERT to be the nodal agency to monitor the implementation of environmental education in schools throughout the country.[9] As it has been contributing tremendously in the improvement of school education throughout the country, serious efforts by the NCERT will be very crucial to ensure effective monitoring of environmental education implementation, which will be a huge challenge given the vastness of the country.

7.4.3.5 Implementation in States and Union Territories

Following the NCF-2005 recommendations and the environmental education-related curricular materials brought out by NCERT, different states and UTs are adapting or adopting the exercise undertaken by NCERT. As the affidavit submitted by NCERT was for the entire schools and school systems throughout the country, the methods of implementation are essentially in tune with those suggested by NCERT. It is expected that states and UTs will likewise adapt or adopt the recommendations of NCF-SE 2023.

7.4.3.6 Barriers in Implementation

Despite the long history of environmental education in India, its formal introduction and implementation in the country's educational system is still at its nascent stage. Hence, it is difficult to say at this juncture whether environmental education has been successfully implemented in schools in India. A lot has been done, yet much remains to be done, especially through research in the area of environmental education to assess and analyze the existing status and to find out ways to overcome the shortcomings or limitations and loopholes. Since research in the area is wanting in India, researches undertaken in other countries at the international level may be referred. Most researchers admit that there is a problem in successful implementation of environmental education in schools owing to certain prevalent barriers. Ham and Sewing (1988) categorized the most prevalent barriers into the following:

- Conceptual barriers: Lack of consensus about the scope and content of environmental education. Several misconceptions about environmental education help to promote its lack of a consistent identity. One such misconception is that environmental education is relevant only to science curricula.
- Logistical barriers: Perceived lack of time, funding, resources, suitable class sizes, and so on.
- Educational barriers: Teachers' misgivings about their own competence to conduct environmental education programs. Teachers with a poor background in a discipline may lack the personal interest or commitment to provide adequate instruction in that subject area.
- Attitudinal barriers: Teachers' attitudes toward environmental education and science instruction often are found to hinder environmental education implementation. The supposition is that if teachers do not have positive attitudes toward environmental education, very little instruction in this area will occur in the classroom.

(Lane 2006, 17–19)

Similarly, Ballantyne (1995 cited in Monde 2011, 20) clearly identifies problems with management of cross-disciplinary approaches or infusion and shortage of qualified and experienced environmental teacher educators as important barriers. While Scott (1996 cited in Monde 2011, 20) adds lack of practice in terms of working with students and schools and the lack of opportunity to deliver environmental education goals through preservice courses as the additional limits for implementation of environmental education, little effort is being put in among the in-service teachers to make up for the gaps that exist in preservice courses. Many teachers have never been involved in in-service environmental education trainings, which ultimately hampers its implementation (Filho and O'Loan 1996 and Ketlhoilwe 2007 cited in Monde 2011).

Of late, a barrier of a completely different kind has come to be recognized. This is related to the lack of clarity on the part of curriculum developers, educators, or practitioners as to whether they are implementing environmental education or ESD. The documents do not specify explicitly what is expected of the course. Since SD is increasingly becoming popular, environmental education is considered to be redundant, and it has become a trend to 'practice' ESD even without understanding what ESD is. But at the end of the day, it so turns out that neither EE nor ESD is practiced in reality.

From the barriers mentioned above, one, some, or all of the barriers would invariably apply to teachers in India as well. Therefore, attempts to bring about successful implementation of environmental education should include adoption of measures to overcome such barriers. Of such barriers, one that stands out with regard to the implementation in India is related to the infusion approach which is prescribed by the curriculum framework. As discussed in Chapter 5 on EE approaches, infusion is not as simple as adding a few facts and information about environment-related concerns in different subjects. It involves an elaborate process of incorporating environmental concepts in the curriculum of different subjects for its successful implementation. Therefore, the success of implementation of environmental education largely depends on how well the infusion approach is understood. But unfortunately, it has been observed that practicing teachers in India are invariably not aware of or familiar with the term 'infusion' or the 'infusion approach' of environmental education. This inadequacy could be due to lack of coherence between the curriculum framework developed for schools and the curriculum framework developed for preservice course or the in-service courses for teachers. As a result, there is no mention of infusion approach in all the professional development courses. This will be dealt in detail in Chapter 8 when the issues concerning teacher education are discussed. Closely connected with the issue of infusion approach is the understanding that beyond Class V there is no more environmental education. Since the infusion approach is not discussed in the preservice courses or any other professional development courses, student-teachers or in-service teachers assume that environmental education is done only through EVS as a composite subject from Classes III to V. This is an issue which needs to be looked at very seriously. A study conducted among teacher educators from various District Institutes of Education and Training (DIETs) of the country revealed that much needs to be done to familiarize and strengthen educators on the infusion approach (Shimray 2015). Other important issues which hamper implementation of environmental education have also been listed by NCERT (1981, 56):

- The classroom teacher faces a problem in getting proper guidance to carry out some of the activities planned.
- Supplementary and reference materials are not easily available.

- The teacher does not get administrative support unless fellow teachers, headmasters, and supervisory staff are also properly oriented for the environmental education program.
- The teacher gets little time for proper planning of activities.
- The teacher loses interest in the new approach in the absence of regular follow-up action.
- The insistence on completion of the syllabus places too many constraints on teachers for them to be innovative.

These are only some of the practical barriers prevalent in schools throughout the country. There are many other barriers such as those relating to larger interest of the nation wherein environmental education might not be a priority, role of different stakeholders, lack of coordination and cooperation between different stakeholders, lack of accountability, and so on. Some of these issues are discussed in several sections of the book.

7.5 Practicability of Project-Based Environmental Education

The fact that education is the key element in preventing and solving environmental problems (Makki, Khalick, and Boujaoude 2003; Oweini and Houri 2006; Taskin 2005; Tuncer, Ertepinar, Tekkaya, and Sungur 2005 cited in Genc 2015) has led to environmental education gaining prominence of late. In the previous chapters, the importance of 'doing' or 'participation' for meaningful environmental education has been discussed quite elaborately. Studies have also shown that environmental courses administered with teaching methods that encourage more active student engagement enhance students' environmental attitudes and conceptual comprehension (Leeming and Proter 1997; Cheong 2005 cited in Genc 2015). An often-suggested activity toward this is getting students involved in meaningful projects, ultimately leading to resolution of environmental problems and issues.[10] Numerous researchers have pointed out the importance of action or direct involvement of students in investigations (Disinger and Monroe 1994) and their becoming problem-solvers so as to bring about quality environmental actions (Lahiry et al. 1988, 16; Lucas 1980; UNESCO 1980, iii, 15). The National Curriculum Framework 2005 (NCF-2005) is also a strong proponent of this approach. Besides, students also learn best about a situation in the situation (Tilbury 1997). Project-based learning has also been found to have a positive effect on students' environmental attitudes, and, at the same time, students find this approach "beneficial, enhancing creativity, encouraging research, and providing permanent learning" (Genc 2015). This helps them to define environmental problems more clearly and take on more active tasks in the solution process. However, it has been found that teachers are apprehensive to move in this direction. It is unclear whether it is because they think the outcome is not worth the effort or because they are not convinced that it is practical. One of the reasons could be because it demands efforts and investments on the part of the teacher as compared to the easiest way of providing more cognitive knowledge. Tilbury (1997) observes that often such action-oriented activities could be related to controversial issues, and hence teachers do not want to take the risk. It was mentioned earlier in this chapter about the recommendation of NCF-2005 to include projects and activities in the implementation of environmental education. Here, the focus will be on project-based EE in the present scenario in India and further explore the possibilities and advantages of taking up such projects by providing the details of a pilot study that was undertaken. It may be mentioned that NCF-SE 2023 also highlights the importance of project-based learning (NCERT 2023, 17, 282, 348, 465).

7.5.1 Project-Based Environmental Education in India

The NCF-2005 states that projects and activities will be the backbone of any scheme aimed at the effective implementation of environmental education in schools which should be as locale-specific as possible. It further says that in order to inculcate the desirable skills and competencies, it will be imperative to develop a basket of activities and projects that may vary in range in respect of their difficulty levels, coverage of skills, and parameters of environment, as well as the feasibility of carrying them out within the limitations of teacher competency, available resources, and time. The NCF-2005 also recommends the need to carve out separate time for projects and fieldwork from existing periods of SUPW, science, and other subjects, and develop tools and techniques for evaluation of projects and fieldwork. In addition, the task of developing project books along with other associated elements such as carving out separate time for projects and activities, assessment of projects, and so on were also part of the activities committed in the affidavit that was submitted by the NCERT to the Hon'ble Supreme Court,[11] as had been discussed earlier in the chapter.

In the light of the above, the NCERT in 2009 developed project books for Classes VI to X, entitled Project Book in Environmental Education, separately for each class. Subsequently, a project book for the higher secondary stage was also brought out by the NCERT in 2013. In order to connect the projects with the curriculum, the projects included were based on the concepts which were already discussed in the textbooks of different subjects. These projects were only exemplars, and the methodologies provided in the project books were also only suggestive. Keeping in view the physical and cultural diversity of the country, it is envisaged that teachers and students can develop their own projects which are locally relevant to them. All concerned stakeholders such as state and central boards and other school systems were also informed about the project books. NCERT had even initiated orientation programs on the use of these project books at regional levels. Some states have translated or adapted the project books in their state language. For example, Mizoram has adapted in its state language with modifications in order to contextualize it. However, it is uncertain as to how far these project books have reached the schools. Shome and Natarajan (2013) reported that such project books are neither known to all the schools nor are they implemented. The reason attributed by them is that the project books are not made mandatory. They did not, however, mention the details of their study. And whether or why the project books reach schools or not, or why they are not mandatory, though essential to find out, is beyond the purview of the discussion here. The focus here will be restricted to the practicability of the projects and how the possible barriers can be avoided or overcome. Though no scientific study has been undertaken to find out the issues facing the teachers and students in taking up such projects on environmental education, Shome and Natarajan (2013), in their article on project-based learning in general, pointed out issues such as lack of time on the part of teachers and lack of interest on the part of students and parents as the main barriers for project-based learning.

Keeping this in view, a pilot study was undertaken to figure out the realities existing in the schools, the possible barriers and difficulties in project-based environmental education, which could be academic or administrative in nature, so that appropriate measures can be worked out to tackle such issues. Since it is a pilot study, the experiences, observations, barriers, and possible suggestions provided will vary widely from place to place and project to project. Nevertheless, given the fact that school systems throughout the country follow a similar pattern in terms of periods and examination, the concerns in general will be comparable irrespective of the school or place.

7.5.2 Pilot Study on Project-Based Environmental Education

The following provides the details of the pilot study that was undertaken for one project. For the benefit of the teachers, the important points to be kept in mind at every step are provided as 'Note for teachers.' The procedure which is followed in this project need not and should not be duplicated, but should be modified according to the need and requirement of the place where the study is conducted.

Class for Which the Study Was Conducted: Class X

Forming groups: The class was divided into groups consisting of at least three students. A group consisting of three students took up this project.

Note for teachers: It will be more meaningful if a group could include people from different communities or races. This will be environmental education in itself. Disinger and Monroe (1994) call it multicultural education wherein different social and ethnic groups work together to resolve environmental issues, while Cole (2007) mentions the possible issues that may arise as a result of forming a group of mixed ethnicity.

Selecting topic: As mentioned earlier, the topics for the projects should be such that the concepts are already in the textbooks and are locally relevant.

One of the topics chosen for the project was Shifting Cultivation (*Jhum* cultivation) (Figures 7.1 and 7.2), not only because this practice is widespread in the state but also because this topic was a concept mentioned in the science textbook for Class X in the state. On the one hand, it is not ethical to simply do away with this age-old practice of agriculture—with no other plausible alternatives—and on the other hand, it is also a known fact that changes that have taken place in the shifting cultivation practices contribute to loss of habitat, global warming, loss of biodiversity, and loss of fertility of soil. Moreover, *jhum* cultivation is not just an agricultural practice, it is a cultural practice as well where community people come together, exchange helping hands often, enjoy the festivity during sowing and harvesting, etc., and therefore it binds the community together. This, therefore, is an important environmental issue that needs to be discussed.

Note for teachers: The topic for the project should be related to the existing curriculum. Let the students come out with their choice of project and try to find out why they chose that particular project. If need be, modify the topic by discussing with the group.

Objective: To understand the patterns of shifting cultivation and the issues related to it.

Note for teachers: Discuss with the group about the possible objectives of the project. It will be easier for the students if the objectives are made as specific as possible. This will give students directions as they carry out the project.

FIGURE 7.1 View of Vast Area under *Jhum*.
Photo Courtesy: David Buhril.

FIGURE 7.2 A Lady Harvesting Ginger from *Jhum* Field.
Photo Courtesy: David Buhril.

Methodology:

1. For their field study, the group identified a village located about 20 kilometers from their school where shifting cultivation was practiced.

   Note for teachers: Field for the study should not be located very far from the school or from where the students reside. It should also be easily accessible. Problem-prone or conflict-prone locations should be avoided. This is not to be confused with the addressing of issues which are controversial or challenging. Environmental education prepares students to handle such issues and develop problem-solvers (UNESCO 1980, i). Hence, environmental education is sometimes referred to as problem-oriented teaching (UNESCO 1991, 36). Martha (1991 cited in Lane 2006; Monroe 2012) also emphasized the importance of dealing with controversial and challenging issues so as to make environmental education complete, that is, issue resolution. She attributes the lack of eagerness of educators for their learners to venture into the territory of controversial and challenging issues to be the cause of environmental education being perceived as a narrow version of what it actually is. Cole (2007, 35–36) also mentions resolving controversial local environmental issues as part of environmental education.

2. A questionnaire was developed to obtain information on the following from 20 households:

(i) Since how many years they have practiced shifting (*jhum*) cultivation.
(ii) Whether there has been difference in the availability of land for shifting cultivation. If so, the reason thereof.
(iii) Whether there is any difference in the number of cycles in their grandparents and their parents' generation and now.
(iv) Varieties of crops planted.
(v) Whether there has been decrease or increase in productivity.
(vi) Whether there has been increase or decrease in pests or plant diseases.
(vii) Whether they use fertilizers or pesticides to increase productivity.
(viii) In what ways shifting cultivation benefit them.
(ix) Whether they have other sources of livelihood.
(x) Whether they can survive without practicing shifting cultivation.
(xi) Whether they know about the negative impacts of shifting cultivation.

3. Information on the above Was Collected by the Students over a Couple of Weeks through Interactions with the Farmers in the Village

Note for teachers: Developing a good questionnaire is very crucial for taking the study in the right direction. Students may find difficulty in obtaining the information for some questions. In such cases, the questionnaire needs to be modified accordingly. When different groups in the class work on different projects, the teacher will be required to carve out separate time or period so that the doubts and other issues related to the project faced by the students can be addressed.

Results: Students compiled the information they had obtained during their field study based on the questions. A simple analysis was done for each question so that they could summarize all the information question-wise. The students then prepared a report of their study.

Note for teachers: Students might need guidance on how to analyze their studies and come out with their reports.

Presentation in class: The group presented their study before the class besides sharing their experiences in the field study such as about transportations to reach the village, the socio-cultural aspects, technologies available, and so on. The group also responded to the queries raised by the rest of the students in the class about their study.

Note for teachers: It might be necessary to intervene at times especially when other students might come up with irrelevant questions not with good intent but otherwise. The presentation should be divided among the group members so that every student of the group gets the opportunity to present. This will build their confidence in public speaking.

Discussion: It was the most important part of the study. After the presentation by the students, further discussions followed. This was done to make sure that all the issues related to shifting cultivation were discussed. Students had only collected the data and did not get much out of it by themselves. For example, students had presented that they found the number of years for shifting cultivation cycle had reduced. Therefore, it was important to discuss the ecological implications of this reduction in the number of years in the *jhum* cycle. It was also important to clarify some of the misconceptions regarding shifting cultivation. Shifting cultivation operates on a basic principle of the following:

> Alternation of short crop phases (usually one or two years of cropping) with phases of natural (or slightly modified) vegetational fallow...The key for the stability of the system, thus lies in retaining a minimum agricultural cycle length (length of the fallow period before the farmer returns to the same site for another cropping phase). It is during the fallow phase that soil fertility recovery occurs, which in turn determines economic yield. In the north-east Indian hill areas, where shifting agriculture is the major land use, a minimum of 10-year cycle was found to be necessary for its sustainability—for both economic efficiency and ecological efficiency, as evaluated through energy efficiency, and fertility sustainability...
>
> *(Ramakrishnan 2001, 85–89)*

Some textbooks also give blanket statement that '*jhum* cultivation must be completely banned' or 'shifting cultivation must be completely banned' without discussing the circumstances under which this statement is applicable. Even the government appears to believe the views that shifting agriculture destroys the ecological balance and results in substantial soil erosion which subsequently leads to flooding of rivers and drying of hill springs (Gadgil and Guha 2000, 218). However, this is not true under conditions of stable population growth and maintaining long fallow allowing sufficient time for the forest to rejuvenate and recuperate (Savyasachi 1986 cited in Gadgil and Guha 2000, 219). In fact, shifting cultivation can be considered an eco-friendly method of cultivation since agricultural ecosystem functions such as nutrient cycling and pest population dynamics are controlled through both the complex cropping and the fallow phases. It is considered to be dangerous only because of the reduction in the average cycle length which has been found to be less than five years (Ramakrishnan 2001, 87). Similarly, discussions were also undertaken on the trends of productivity and chemicals used, benefits of shifting cultivation to the farmers, other source of livelihood, and so on, by correlating it with their findings.

Before these discussions were undertaken in the class, the activity did not make much sense to the students. But once they were able to relate the findings of their study to the discussions that followed, students were able to understand shifting cultivation holistically. Not only the students who had conducted the study but the whole class benefited out of the study.

Note for teachers: This is one of the most crucial parts of the project. While the groups present their results and experiences, it is very important to discuss the results they have obtained. Some of the points to be focused broadly in the discussion may include the following: (a) the scientific concept, (b) the social ramifications, (c) the economic issues.

Assessment: Assessment began from the time of selection of topics for the study till the presentation was over. Marks were given based on their overall performance.

Note for teachers: Some of the areas for assessment may include clarity about the project, planning and designing, collaboration skill within the group throughout the project, recording of observations, compilation of the project, conclusion, presentation or communication of the findings of the project, and so on. But every group who completes the project should not be failed.

Outcomes: Students' environmental knowledge, here, shifting or *jhum* cultivation, increased, there were some impacts on their attitudes, they had good experience of learning, and they will be able to communicate to others effectively about shifting cultivation.

In spite of the issues teachers/students/school may face, project-based EE is definitely helpful for the students. It was observed in this pilot study that students were not only able to understand the connection or relation between society, environment, and economy but they also learned various process skills such as communication, comparison, analysis, design, interpret, relate, connect, reason, and organize. Monroe (1991 cited in Lane 2006, 16) listed the following skills necessary for problem-solving such as communications, group skills, leadership, creative thinking, and decision-making which students could learn through environmental education. Such a study conducted by the students themselves enables them to learn better. The most important outcome of project-based environmental education is that the learning that takes place is holistic and interdisciplinary in nature and thus is able to bring out the essence of environmental education.

One cannot imagine how much learning would take place if there were ten groups of students in a class working on different projects.

Note for teachers: The number of groups may not be less than ten in a class, and it might sometimes be difficult to handle the situation. It is for this reason separate time needs to be carved out for this activity. Since environmental problems and issues are not restricted to a specific discipline, it will be advisable to discuss with teachers teaching other disciplines about connectivity of the topic with their disciplines and get their inputs as well. This will promote interdisciplinarity of environmental education as had been discussed earlier under an interdisciplinary approach. The whole activity will definitely be more time consuming compared to the chalk and talk method. However, at the end it will be worth it!

Follow-up actions: Through the discussions that followed, students were able to gather much information about shifting cultivation; thus, 'learning about the environment' is achieved. From their personal field visits, students were able to understand the actual situation, and, thus, 'learning in the environment' is achieved. Perhaps such an experience has helped them build an attitude toward shifting cultivation. Hence, the 'awareness,' 'knowledge,' 'attitude,' and 'skill,' components of environmental education can be said to have been fulfilled. However, it is clear from the previous discussions that without action environmental education cannot be complete. This will at the same time help achieve the 'learning for the environment' goal. Therefore, this step of follow-up actions has been included as the concluding step of this project-based environmental education. The possible follow-up actions for this project were discussed such as educating the farmers about the various environmental impacts of shifting cultivation through small group meetings, through *nukkad natak* (street play), and so on, so that *jhum* or shifting cultivation can be practiced sustainably.

Note for teachers: Follow-up actions should be action-based and easy to perform. It could be as simple as sensitizing people using word of mouth, posters, rallies, etc., or it could be organizing a cleanliness drive in the locality, or writing to the authorities highlighting the issues, or it could be inculcating a pro-environmental lifestyle.

7.5.3 Why Did It Work?

Given the busy time table throughout the year, one may be curious to know what made this activity work. The key to its success was that the marks obtained by the students through this project were to be counted for their final board examination. The state board allots marks for internal assessment in science. The school administration agreed to reflect the marks obtained through this project as internal assessment marks. As a result of this, students took keen interest and worked seriously and sincerely for the completion and success of the project. This reminds us of the importance given to marks in the school systems. The craving for marks is clearly evident. Therefore, in the present circumstance, it is critical to link activities with marks or assessment so that the activities are taken up seriously and effectively. This was the strategy that was adopted for the pilot study, and it worked.

However, for this to happen in every school, the role of the school administrators is very important. They should work out the plausible way with the teachers. For those schools which are under the umbrella of a bigger system such as Kendriya Vidyalaya, Navodaya Vidyalaya, Central Board of Secondary Education, and so on, the decision can be taken at the highest level and instructions passed on to every school. But passing on instructions does not guarantee that the activities will be undertaken. Teachers will be key to the success of this activity. Or else this project-based environmental education will receive the same fate as other internal assessment activities where students are simply given marks based on 'nothing' or 'anything.'

7.6 Conclusion

The initiatives undertaken in the area of environmental education at the international level have visible impacts in the way environmental education is implemented in India. However, the trends are not always the same. Some have stronger impact such as the Stockholm conference, while others, not so much, such as the Decade of Education for Sustainable Development or the introduction of ESD with India continuing to adhere with environmental education. As a signatory to various international initiatives, it is expected that similar developments are taking place in other countries as well. This suggests that nations of the world need to meet regularly and not only chalk out ways for collective responsibilities but also share their resources and expertise to build each other up for the successful implementation of environmental education.

Implementation of environmental education in India has taken a proper shape. Beginning with a random and unsystematic manner of implementation till the 1990s, today there is a clear mandate and objectives for implementation of environmental education throughout the country. Even the latest National Education Policy 2020 and the National Curriculum Framework for School Education 2023 also highlights the importance of environmental education. A more systematic approach could have been adopted, though. There are barriers that have to be tackled and they are many. While in the chapter the barriers have been grouped under conceptual, logistical, educational, and attitudinal barriers, it cannot be contested that all such barriers stem from marginalization of environmental education itself in the school curriculum and in teacher education. As a result, there is complete lack of coherence between the school curriculum and teacher education courses in the area of environmental education. Unless such issues are fixed, the barriers will remain.

As environmental education is implemented, more effective ways of implementation need to be explored so that its objectives are achieved. Project-based environmental education can be one such approach that can be successfully carried out in schools. As there is less and less interaction of students with their environment, such project-based environmental education will be a good opportunity to take them back to the real world and learn by themselves. Such project-based learning is also advocated by the National Education Policy 2020 and the National Curriculum Framework for School Education 2023.

7.7 Summary

- Changes and developments have been brought about in environmental education in India in tune with the developments taking place at the international level.
- Developments at the international level also led to the enactment of several environmental laws and effected even the amendment of the Constitution.

- Initiatives undertaken especially by IEEP have strengthened the implementation of environmental education through its various resource materials and training of personnel in India.
- The most recent global development is the evolution of environmental education in the shape of ESD, which is fast catching up in India as well.
- M.C. Mehta's PIL made a significant impact in the implementation of environmental education in India.
- At present in India, environmental education is implemented through the infusion approach throughout the country. However, with the implementation of recommendations of the National Curriculum Framework for School Education 2023, in addition to having environment as a cross-cutting theme, a separate subject will be introduced in Grade 10 which will be mandatory for all. In Grades 11 and 12 Sustainability and Climate Change will be offered as one of the choice-based courses.
- Environmental education, more or less, have finally seeped into the school curriculum though meaningful implementation is yet to be seen.
- There exist several barriers in the successful implementation of EE—conceptual, logistical, educational, and attitudinal barriers—which could be related to issues of infusion approach, assessment, or those related to teacher empowerment due to systemic issues.
- Working on projects is an opportunity for students to actually understand some of the environmental problems and issues around them. Project-based environmental education richly enhances learning.
- Learning that takes place through projects is holistic and students are able to relate their curriculum with what is actually happening around them, thus making sense of their curriculum. It provides opportunities where education or learning about, in, and for the environment can be accomplished as students acquire the awareness, knowledge, skills, attitudes, and opportunity to participate.
- As opposed to general views, project-based study is certainly doable and, if linked with marks, will motivate the students and teachers as they carry out the projects. The role of concerned government departments, the central and state boards, the school administration and the practicing teachers is important.

Notes

1 https://www.un.org/en/conferences/environment/stockholm1972 (Accessed on May 2, 2023).
2 Article 253 of the Constitution of India (1949): "*Legislation for giving effect to international agreements*—Notwithstanding anything in the foregoing provisions of this chapter, Parliament has power to make any law for the whole or any part of the territory of India for implementing any treaty, agreement, or convention with any other country or countries or any decision made at any international conference, association, or other body.".

3. The Gazette of India, Ministry of Law and Justice (Legislative Department): https://greentribunal.gov.in/sites/default/files/act_rules/National_Green_Tribunal_Act,_2010.pdf (Accessed on September 27, 2023).
4. https://ncte.gov.in/website/PDF/NCFTE_2009.pdf (Accessed on September 21, 2023).
5. The Weather Channel: https://weather.com/en-IN/india/health/news/worlds-50-most-polluted-countries-20140513 (Accessed on September 21, 2023); http://www.abc.net.au/news/2014-05-08/10-countries-with-the-worlds-dirtiest-air/5438872 (Accessed on September 21, 2023); https://www.iqair.com/in-en/world-most-polluted-countries (Accessed on April 14, 2023).
6. https://epic.uchicago.in/indians-lose-5-years-life-to-air-pollution-delhi-worst-at-12-years-chicago-university-study/ (Accessed on September 1, 2023).
7. https://educationforallinindia.com/highlight-udise-2021-22-data-all-india-level/#:~:text=AccordingtotheUDISE+databreakdownofschoolsbymanagement. (Accessed on September 22, 2023).
8. https://ncert.nic.in/desm/pdf/environment-edu/Affidavit.pdf (Accessed on September 21, 2023).
9. https://ncert.nic.in/desm/pdf/environment-edu/13.07.pdf (Accessed on September 21, 2023).
10. An environmental problem is a situation in which something is at risk, such as an endangered species, lack of clean air, and habitat destruction, whereas an environmental issue is more broad, and refers to the difference of opinion among people as to how the situation, that is, the environmental problem, should be managed (UNESCO 1991, 36).
11. https://ncert.nic.in/desm/pdf/environment-edu/Affidavit.pdf (Accessed on September 21, 2023).

References

Cole, A.G. 2007. "Expanding the Field: Revisiting Environmental Education Principles through Multidisciplinary Frameworks." *The Journal of Environmental Education* 38 (2): 35–44.

Disinger, John F., and Martha C. Monroe. 1994. *EE Toolbox—Workshop Resource Manual Defining Environmental Education*. Ann Arbor, MI: University of Michigan.

Gadgil, M., and R. Guha. 2000. *The Use and Abuse of Nature*. New Delhi: Oxford University Press.

Genc, Murat. 2015. "The Project-based Learning Approach in Environmental Education." *International Research in Geographical and Environmental Education* 24 (2): 105–117. DOI: 10.1080/10382046.2014.993169

GoI, Government of India. 1968. *National Policy on Education-1968*. Government of India.

———. 1986. *National Policy on Education-1986*. Government of India.

———. 2020. *National Education Policy 2020*. Ministry of Education, Government of India.

Ham, S., and D. Sewing. 1988. "Barriers to Environmental Education." *Journal of Environmental Education* 19 (2): 17–24.

Lahiry, D., Savita Sinha, J.S. Gill, U. Mallik, and A.K. Mishra. 1988. *Environmental Education: A Process for Pre-service Teacher Training Curriculum Development*. UNESCO-UNEP International Environmental Education Programme Environmental Education Series No. 26, edited by Patricia R. Simpson, Harold Hungerford, and Trudi L. Volk. Paris: UNESCO.

Lane, J.F. 2006. *Environmental Education Implementation in Wisconsin: Conceptualizations and Practices*. Unpublished PhD Thesis: Department of Philosophy, University of Wisconsin-Madison. Available at: http://www.uwsp.edu/cnr-ap/wcee/Documents/JennieLaneDissertation.pdf (Accessed on September 27, 2023).

Lucas, A.M. 1980. "Science and environmental Education: Pious Hopes, Self Praise and Disciplinary Chauvinism." *Studies in Science Education* 7 (1): 1–26.

Monde, P.N. 2011. *Barriers to Successful Implementation of Environmental Education in Zambian High Schools: A Case Study of Selected High Schools of Central Province*. Unpublished PhD Thesis, University of Zambia. Available at: http://dspace.unza.zm:8080/xmlui/bitstream/handle/123456789/809/Monde.pdf?sequence=1 (Accessed on September 27, 2023).

Monroe, M.C. 2012. "The Co-evolution of ESD and EE." *Journal of Education for Sustainable Development* 6 (1): 43–47. DOI: 10.1177/097340821100600110

NCERT, National Council of Educational Research and Training. 1981. *Environmental Education at the School Level: A Lead Paper*. New Delhi: NCERT.

———. 1988. *National Curriculum for Elementary and Secondary Education – A Framework (Revised Version) (1988)*. New Delhi: NCERT.

———. 2000. *National Curriculum Framework for School Education 2000*. New Delhi: NCERT.

———. 2005. *National Curriculum Framework-2005*. New Delhi: NCERT.

———. 2006a. reprint 2019. *Science Textbook for Class IX*. New Delhi: NCERT.

———. 2006b. reprint 2019. *Science Textbook for Class X*. New Delhi: NCERT.

———. 2023. *National Curriculum Framework for School Education 2023*. New Delhi: NCERT.

Ramakrishnan, P.S. 2001. *Sustainable Agriculture in Ecology and Sustainable Development—Working with Knowledge Systems*. New Delhi: National Book Trust.

Shimray, C.V. 2015. *Meeting of DIET Functionaries to Assess the Status of D.El.Ed. Syllabus in the Context of Environmental Education—Report* (Unpublished). New Delhi: NCERT.

Shimray, C.V., S. Farkya, and S.L. Varte. 2013. *Study of Biology Curriculum at the Higher Secondary Stage: A Report* (Unpublished). New Delhi: NCERT.

Shome, Saurav, and Chitra Natarajan. 2013. "Ideas of and Attitudes Towards Projects and Changing Practices: Voices of Four Teachers." *Australian Journal of Teacher Education* 38 (10): 64–81.

Tilbury, D. 1997. "Environmental Education (EE) A Head, Heart and Hand Approach to Learning about Environmental Problems." *New Horizons in Education* 38: 1–11.

UN, United Nations. 1993. *The Earth Summit—Agenda 21: The United Nations Program of Action from Rio*. Rio de Janeiro, Brazil.

UNEP, United Nations Environmental Programme. 2005. *UNEP Strategy for Environmental Education and Training—A Strategy and Action Planning for the Decade 2005-2014*. Nairobi, Kenya: UNEP.

UNESCO, United Nations Educational, Scientific and Cultural Organization. 1980. *Strategies for Developing an Environmental Education Curriculum: A Discussion Guide for UNESCO Training Workshops on Environmental Education*. Paris: UNESCO.

———. 1984. *Activities of the UNESCO-UNEP International Environmental Education Programme (1975–1983)*. Paris: UNESCO.

———. 1991. *Environmental Education for Our Common Future: A Handbook for Teachers in Europe Prepared by Faye Benedict on Behalf of the Norwegian National Commission for UNESCO*. Norwegian University Press: UNESCO.

8
TEACHER EMPOWERMENT IN ENVIRONMENTAL EDUCATION

8.1 Chapter Overview

The chapter brings out the importance of teacher preparation in environmental education. Keeping in view the need for teachers to have clarity in environmental concepts so that they are able to engage in the teaching–learning process effectively and meaningfully, the chapter discusses the basic contents that should be included in all teacher empowerment courses in environmental education. The existing scenario of teacher preparation in the area of environmental education in India in general is presented. A broad comparison of content in preservice courses such as B.Ed./B.Sc.B.Ed./B.A.B.Ed. syllabus in the Regional Institute of Education, NCERT, located in Mysuru, Ajmer, Bhopal and Bhubaneswar, is also provided to depict a national picture since these institutions are affiliated to universities located in different regions of the country. The disparities observed in the existing preservice programs are also discussed in the chapter. Further, opportunities available for in-service teachers as well as concerns related to lack of qualified teacher educators in environmental education are also discussed. The chapter specifically attempts to bring out some of the issues related to teacher education in the area of environmental education in India and suggests some measures to address such issues. Environmental education is also mandatory in higher education, and, therefore, the chapter also briefly touches upon concerns related to teacher preparation in higher education.

8.2 Introduction

Effective and meaningful classroom transaction can happen only when teachers are empowered. That is, teachers need to have appropriate knowledge, skills, and competencies. Hence, the quality of teacher preparation[1] courses becomes extremely crucial in terms of the course content, its delivery, etc.

In the previous chapters, how environmental education has evolved over the years have been discussed. It has also been discussed how such changes have been reflected in India in the policy documents and national curriculum frameworks and, ultimately, in the school curriculum. The intervention of the Hon'ble Supreme Court in the implementation of environmental education in India have also been thoroughly discussed. Together, they shaped environmental education to the form it is today in India. With the changes in the school curriculum there will be ramifications on teacher preparation and professional development courses for teachers—preservice and in-service. In fact, changes in the preservice professional development course is beginning to be seen with the launch of the National Education Policy 2020 which recommended that a four-year integrated B.Ed. degree will be the minimum degree qualification for teaching from 2030 onward. Accordingly, courses in line with that are being prepared and introduced. Changes are also likely going to be seen in the preservice courses especially with the introduction of Environmental Education as a separate in Grade 10 in addition to inclusion of environment as a cross-cutting area as per the National Curriculum Framework for School Education 2023.

Indeed, teacher empowerment must form an integral part of any reform in school education. The National Focus Group on Teacher Education for Curriculum Renewal states, "the hope of revitalising school education in India, via an idealistic or ideologically driven attempt at revising curriculum will probably meet with little success, if the central agency of the teacher remains unrecognised" (NCERT 2006, 26). Teachers form the key factor in all educational development, and hence they need to be professionally equipped. Some statistics as mentioned in National Curriculum Framework for Teacher Education (NCFTE) 2009 (NCTE 2009, 5) related to professional development is provided verbatim in Box 8.1. The message is loud and clear that teacher education is vital for the successful implementation of 'reformed' curriculum. However, in spite of the recognition of the importance of professional preparation of teachers for qualitative improvement of education since the 1960s,[2] very few concrete steps have been taken in the last three decades to operationlize this (NCERT 2006). Chattopadhyaya Commission also notes, "If school teachers are expected to bring about a revolution in their approach to teaching…that same revolution must precede and find a place in the Colleges of education" (Chattopadhyaya Committee Report cited in NCERT 2006, 2). Yet, teacher education programs continue to train teachers to 'adjust' to the needs of an education system in which education is seen as the transmission of information

> **BOX 8.1 SOME STATISTICS RELATED TO PROFESSIONAL DEVELOPMENT**
>
> The number of courses offered at different stages—pre-primary, elementary, and secondary—face-to-face and distance modes of teacher education; programs of M.Ed., face-to-face and distance modes, C.P.Ed., B.P.Ed., and M.P.Ed. have increased from 3,489 courses in 3,199 institutions in March 2004 to a whopping 14,428 courses in 11,861 institutions in March 2009. The student intake has likewise increased from 274,072 to 1,096,673 during this period. This expansion has taken a heavy toll on quality parameters of infrastructural provision, faculty qualification, learning resources, and student profile.
>
> Till December 2009, as many as 31 Institutes of Advanced Studies in Education (IASEs) and 104 Colleges of Teacher Education (CTEs), were sanctioned and all of these were functional. Of the 599 districts in the country, District Institutes of Education and Training (DIETs) were set up in 571 districts, of which only 529 are functional. Thus, 42 DIETs are yet to become functional. The main problem facing DIETs is nonavailability of qualified faculty. Presently, the faculty appointed does not possess qualifications or experience in elementary teacher education. A good number of CTEs face faculty shortage and poor library facilities, and spend more time on initial teacher education while research, development, and innovative activities are yet to take concrete shape. The same is the case with IASEs. The capacity of both CTEs and IASEs in performing their mandated roles has recently come under serious scrutiny.

and learning reproduced from textbooks. The reforms in the school education programs are not being reflected in such programs.

8.3 Teacher Preparation in Environmental Education

Teacher preparation in environmental education is a non-negotiable component to realize the goals and objectives laid down in the curriculum. Its importance cannot be overemphasized. As it is with other disciplinary subject, the key to successful implementation of environmental education in the classroom is the teacher—if teachers do not have the knowledge, skills, or commitment to "environmentalize their curriculum, it is unlikely that environmentally literate students will be produced" (Wilke 1985, 1 cited in Heimlich and Smith 2004, 14). Environmental literacy, here, does not mean having content knowledge about environmental issues. It refers to having the required knowledge, attitude, motivation, commitment, and skills to take informed decisions concerning the environment and its various issues. The prospective teachers, therefore, need to be environmentally sensitive individuals, who volunteer to solve environmental problems and develop positive environmental attitudes. Then only will they be able to educate their students in a similar vein (Genc 2015).

Teacher preparation is more so required in environmental education since it is comparatively a new focus which requires specific awareness, knowledge, and skills, along with an outlook which might not have been developed in the rest of the educational career of the student-teachers or the in-service teachers (Lahiry et al. 1988; Tilbury 1992 cited in Heimlich and Smith 2004, 15). It is not possible to expect teachers without the expertise to transmit environmental ideas to students in a manner that will stimulate the students to think holistically, regionally, and globally about the environment, rather than treating each topic as an isolated, discrete entity (Taylor 1988 cited in Heimlich and Smith 2004, 15). A study conducted by Plevyak et al. (2001) on the level of teacher preparation and the implementation of environmental education found a significant correlation between the levels of exposure of teachers to environmental education topics in the preservice preparation and their confidence about teaching environmental education and a greater understanding of what is involved in integrating environmental education into the curriculum. The study also found a higher rate of implementation of environmental education among teachers who had higher levels of exposure to environmental education such as participation in some preservice environmental organizations, workshops, or programs, and so on.

Tilbury (1997) suggested that professional development in environmental education is needed for the following purpose:

1. To learn about the purpose and goals of environmental education
2. To find out how the different approaches such as education 'about,' 'in,' and 'for' approach (or the head, heart, and hand approach) contribute toward the achievement of environmental education goals
3. To explore how the 'about,' 'in,' and 'for' dimensions can be integrated into the curriculum in practice

In the previous chapters, more specifically in Chapter 5, the issues with implementation of environmental education such as an incomplete or fragmentary way of approaching environmental education have been mentioned. It was pointed out that information-based education 'about' environment is found to be the most convenient and common way of doing environmental education. A major factor for such practice is attributed to lack of teacher education and professional development (Fien and Ferreira 1997; Lahiry et al. 1988). Without undergoing the basic course or training in environmental education, teachers do not completely understand the philosophies behind it and very few understand the purpose of EE. Studies have shown that teachers, in most cases, conceive environmental education as a body of knowledge rather than a learning process (Hawkins 1987 cited in Tilbury 1997). Hence, their objective of environmental education is limited to providing content knowledge on environmental topics and issues such as personal hygiene and environmental sanitation, water and air pollution, energy, material resources, forestry, climate and weather, populations, and so on. Neither are they concerned about helping students inculcate environmental attitudes or providing opportunities to participate in the resolution of environmental issues nor are they equipped to do so. It will not be, therefore, possible to implement environmental education meaningfully in schools unless teachers obtain adequate training. Not only is orientation of teachers essential, but intensive teacher education is a must for successful implementation of environmental education if the existing fragmented approaches of traditional education is to be done away with (Lahiry et al. 1988, 17).

However, this realization that teacher training and professional development is necessary for meaningful implementation of environmental education is not recent; it is as old as the concept of environmental education itself. For example, the Tbilisi Declaration in 1977 had clearly mentioned the steps to be taken regarding teacher preparation and professional development (UNESCO 1978, 35–36). The same is reproduced in Box 8.2.

8.3.1 Barriers in the Popularization of Environmental Education in Teacher Preparation

In spite of all the reasons discussed earlier on the need for teacher preparation in environmental education, what is being observed in reality is far from what is expected.

There is a glaring absence of environmental education courses at both the tertiary level and in preservice teacher education. Very few institutes are known to offer environmental education at the tertiary level. Several reasons have been put forth which act as a barrier in the popularization of environmental education in preservice courses. This may be due to the following:

1. Confusion in the terms of environmental education and environmental studies (EVS) even among the community of teacher educators (Harde 1982 cited in Monde 2011; Filho and O'Loan 1996 cited in Heimlich and Smith 2004).
2. Environmental education being limited by being placed in science as its disciplinary home (Disinger and Howe 1990).
3. Most educators and decision-makers about education consider environmental education to be a fringe activity (Briceno and Pitt 1988 in Heimlich and Smith 2004).
4. Within the curriculum of teacher preservice programs, environmental education must compete for time and space with many subjects and a series of interdisciplinary topics (Filho and O'Loan 1996 cited in Heimlich and Smith 2004).

BOX 8.2 TBILISI DECLARATION ON TEACHER PREPARATION AND PROFESSIONAL DEVELOPMENT

Training of Personnel

Recommendation No. 17

The Conference,
 Considering the need for all teachers to understand the importance of environmental emphasis in their teaching,

Recommends to Member States

- that environmental sciences and environmental education be included in curricula for pre-service teacher education;
- that the staffs of teacher-education institutions be assisted in this respect; and
- that teachers should get appropriate environmental training relating to the area, either urban or rural, where they are going to work.

Recommendation No.18

The Conference,
 Considering that the importance of in-service training is underlined by the fact that a great majority of present-day teachers were graduated from teacher-training colleges at a time when environ-mental education was largely neglected and thus did not receive sufficient education in environmental issues and the methodology of environmental education,

Recommends to Member States

- that they take the necessary steps to make in-service training of teachers in environmental education available for all who need it;
- that the implementation and development of in-service training, including practical training, in environmental education be made in close co-operation with professional organizations of teachers, both at the international and national levels;
- that in-service training take account of the area, either urban or rural, where the teachers are working;

Recommends to UNESCO

To promote the dissemination of ideas, programmes, and instructional material relevant to the promotion of in-service training in environmental education.

Besides these reasons, Heimlich and Smith (2004, 17) point out several philosophic barriers for the inclusion of environmental education into preservice programs such as the following:

1. The structure of preservice education limits environmental education;
2. The philosophic ways in which preservice teachers are taught—disciplinarily, content (not outcome) focused—and the models of instruction they receive do not demonstrate integration, multi- or transdisciplinary education;
3. Environmental education is not identified as such in those courses where it is taught;
4. The desire for incorporation of environmental education by the institution as evidenced by the inclusion of qualified EE teacher instructors (i.e., institutional interest);
5. Time in the classroom; and
6. Few opportunities to incorporate environmental education into practice for students in teacher preparation programs.

Ballantyne (1995 cited in Monde 2011, 20) clearly identifies problems with management of cross-disciplinary approaches or infusion and shortage of qualified and experienced environmental teacher educators as important barriers. However, Scott (1996 cited in Monde 2011, 20) adds lack of practice in terms of working with students and schools and the lack of opportunity to deliver environmental education goals through preservice courses as the additional limits for implementation of environmental education.

NCERT (1981, 55–56) had also identified teacher preparation as a barrier in the effective implementation of environmental education, going to the extent of labeling it as the 'greatest hurdle.' The issues with regard to noneffective implementation is not restricted to countries where environmental education is yet to catch momentum, but it is seen even in countries like the United States where the reason is attributed to lack of emphasis in preservice training in environmental education (Feinstein 2009, 36). The situation, however, is found to be improving as the current teacher preparation programs offer some form of environmental education (McKeown-Ice 2000 cited in Feinstein 2009, 37).

8.3.2 Course Content in Environmental Education for Teacher Preparation

Quality teacher preparation for environmental education will largely depend on the course content. Wilke, Peyton, and Hungerford (1987) suggest three ways in which teacher preparation programs could incorporate environmental education—specific course in environmental education methods, infusion into existing courses and additional courses in the curriculum which deal with foundational components. However, these are not alternate ways to incorporate environmental education: all the three are essential for effective implementation. This is because teachers or prospective teachers need to have foundational knowledge about environmental education, then they will need to learn about the methods and pedagogy to teach environmental education and finally through infusion into other courses they will be able to learn about infusion which they will apply in their classroom.

In Strategies for Developing an Environmental Education Curriculum, UNESCO (1980) provided guidelines for teacher preparation in environmental education, which is reproduced in Box 8.3. Looking at the guidelines and considering the purpose of professional development in environmental

---

BOX 8.3 GUIDELINES FOR TEACHER PREPARATION IN EE (UNESCO 1980)

Teacher preparation in environmental education should...

1. focus on and reflect the many-faceted and interdisciplinary nature of environmental education. In so doing, teachers should be provided with opportunities to acquire and apply the knowledge, skills, and attitudes inherent in environmental education. At the very minimum, this preparation should include:
   - basic training in ecology.
   - field and/or laboratory experiences for teachers in the area of environmental science.
   - knowledge of environmental issues and problems of resource management.
   - competencies in environmental problem identification, investigation, evaluation, and citizenship action.
   - opportunities to develop value clarification skills and knowledge of the roles of human values in environmental issues.
2. provide instruction and experience with environmental education multidisciplinary (infusion) models curriculum as well as instructional activities and methods similar to those they might utilize in their own classrooms.
3. provide for an opportunity for preservice teachers to experience a multidisciplinary or infusion model in their own training, that is, be a receiver in a tertiary infusion model of environmental education.
4. provide instruction on the philosophy and goals of environmental education and the nature of interdisciplinary and multidisciplinary (infused) environmental education curricula. Further, teachers should be trained in the implementation of these models.
5. provide specific training–particularly at the elementary level–in the use of environmental education content as a vehicle for teaching basic general education skills, e.g., in language arts, reading, and mathematics.
6. provide opportunities for teachers to develop skills in identifying, inventorying, and evaluating local resources for use in environmental education.

education as mentioned earlier, four basic essential elements can be identified so as to be included in all training programs in environmental education—pre-service and in-service. These elements are: (a) purpose and goals of environmental education, (b) functional knowledge of environmental sciences or how natural systems work, (c) educational methods and professional skills including value clarification and action-oriented abilities, and (d) exposure to actual situations in which learners can further strengthen their reservoir of skills. The latter three elements are further discussed in Environmental Education: A Process for Pre-service Teacher Training Curriculum Development (Lahiry et al. 1988). The same elements are true for professional development of practicing teacher educators or to-be-teacher educators and practicing teachers and to-be-teachers. This is because, to be able to implement environmental education successfully in schools, practicing teachers should be equipped with the necessary skills; and to equip practicing teachers or to-be-teachers, teacher educators need to master such skills themselves. There are many instances where programs for preparation of teacher educators do not adequately incorporate environmental education. Besides this, due to shortage of trained teacher educators in environmental education, these teacher educators, though lack the expertise, are engaged in professional development of teachers in EE. Therefore, professional development in environmental education for such teacher educators is also a must. In preparing a scheme for preservice teacher training, Stapp (1975 cited in Lahiry et al. 1988, 19) grouped the competencies required of a teacher into the following levels:

1. Environmental science competencies comprising (a) ecological foundations, (b) economic foundations, and (c) human ecosystem foundations.
2. Educational competencies comprising (a) psychological foundations and (b) educational foundations.
3. Environmental educational skills comprising (a) problem-solving, (b) handling of values and controversial issues, and (c) using materials and local situations pertaining to the environment.
4. Methods of teaching environmental education comprising (a) aims and objectives, (b) environmental education methods and techniques, (c) resources for learning and group dynamics, (d) curriculum design, and (e) fieldwork and environmental ethics.

(Lahiry et al. 1988, 19)

Standards for the Initial Preparation of Environmental Educators of the NCATE, which was prepared by the NAAEE (2007), included the following standards in the course:

1. Nature of environmental education and environmental literacy
2. Environmental literacy of candidates

3. Learning theories and knowledge of learners
4. Curriculum: standards and integration
5. Instructional planning and practice
6. Assessment
7. Professional Growth in Environmental Education

As part of the Environmental Literacy of candidates, this NAAEE document mentions that a candidate should demonstrate in-depth knowledge of the following topics: earth as a physical system, including processes that shape the Earth; changes of matter; energy and its transformations; living systems, including organisms, populations, and communities; heredity and evolution; systems and connections; flow of matter and energy; interface of environment and society, including consumerism, uses of land, ecosystem alteration, and energy and resource consumption, and human population growth; and roles that social, economic, political, and cultural systems play in issues such as resource depletion, environmental degradation, and sustainability.

Whether presented in the form of basic elements, competencies, or standards, what is important to note here is that teacher training programs necessitate careful planning by ensuring that every dimension, as discussed earlier, is addressed. The duration of the programs or the depth of dealing with each component may vary, depending upon the prior experiences and qualifications of the teachers. For example, a teacher/student-teacher who has been trained in biological science may not require much time to understand how ecological and natural systems function. However, it is important for every aspirant teacher to have a basic understanding of how ecological and natural systems function: simply put, functional knowledge of environmental science is a must for all. This requirement for content knowledge has also been clearly emphasized in the Report of the High-Powered Commission on Teacher Education Constituted by the Hon'ble Supreme Court of India, GoI (2012). Experts in the field have recommended different sets of course content. For example, Hungerford et al. (1994) listed the following:

> The Global Nature of Environmental Issues: the phenomenon called 'entropy,' an introductory overview of critical global issues including population, land use management, world hunger, energy resources, rainforest management, water resources, pollution, and wildlife management.
> Population: population dynamics, relationships between population, pollution, resource use, technology, sustainable development (SD), and health; the concept of a sustainable world population, human population control, variables conflicting with population control, critical issues to be resolved.
> Land Use Management: land use in developed and developing nations, the role of parks, wilderness, and wildlife refuges; urbanization and urban

growth, zoning, problems in the urban environment, strip mining and reclamation, the relationships between population and land use management from an SD perspective.

World Hunger: the relationships between food supplies and world hunger, relationships between population size and hunger, problems associated with various agricultural systems, benefits of various agricultural systems, problems associated with cultivating more land and increasing crop yields, problems associated with pesticide usage, the critical nature of soil erosion, and the limits to sustainable fisheries.

Energy Resources: types of energy resources, how man has applied various energy resources, benefits, and problems associated with technology and energy production, the limits to fossil fuels, alternatives to fossil fuels and attendant problems, the role of solar energy in all its forms, developing a regional and global energy plan.

The Tropical Rain Forest: distribution, ecological impact of the rain forest, economics of preservation vs. development, the rain forest as species habitat, development and extinction, management problems, and the potential for resolving these problems.

Water Resources: worldwide supply, the role of water in issues associated with SD, distribution and use of water, issues associated with water including soil salinization, use of fossil water supplies, water diversion, surface water pollution, groundwater pollution, and dams.

Air and Noise Pollution: types of pollution, effects of smog and other forms of air pollution, acid rain and its consequences, noise and its effects on human beings, regional issues associated with air and noise pollution.

Wildlife Management: the ecological role and benefits of wildlife, endangered species, habitat destruction, overutilization, extinction, the need for preserving gene pools, feral animal problems, protection and management of game and nongame species, regional issues associated with wildlife (including fisheries management).

Economics, Politics, and Environmental Ethics: national and international costs associated with environmental degradation, costs of resolving problems/issues, future costs if improvements are not made, the role of politics in environmental decision-making including SD, using the political process for initiating change, components of an environmental ethic, the need for appropriate life styles, influencing change at the local/regional levels.

However, Ballard and Pandya (1990 cited in Disinger and Howe 1990, 13–15) included the following as contents:

A. Natural Systems
   1. General

(a) Environment (b) Earth

2. Abiotic Components

    (a) Energy (b) Atmosphere

3. Biotic Components

    (a) Plant (b) Animal
    (c) Biosphere
    (c) Land and Soil
    (d) Water

4. Processes

    (a) Weather and Climate
        Biological Systems (a) Ecosystems
    (d) Population

B. Resources

   1. Natural Resources

      (a) General
      (c) Management and Conservation

   2. Abiotic Resources

      (a) Energy and Minerals (b) Water
      (b) Biogeochemical Cycles
      (b) Food Chains and Webs (e) Habitat and Niche
      (c) Evolution and Extinction (c) Community
      (c) Land and Soil (a) Forests (b) Wildlife and Fisheries (c) Biodiversity

   3. Biotic Resources

      (b) Distribution and Consumption (d) Sustainable Development

   4. Degradation of Resource Base

      (a) Limits to Systems (b) Pollution

C. Human Systems

   1. Humans and Environment

      (a) Humans as Part of Environment (c) Human Influence on Environment

   2. Technological Systems

      (a) Agriculture (b) Settlements
      (b) Human Adaptation to Environment (d) Population Factors
      (c) Manufacturing and Technology

3. Social Systems

    (a) Economic Systems (b) Sociopolitical Systems (c) Culture and Religion

4. Environmental Awareness and protection (a) Values and Ethics

    (b) Education and Communication
    (c) Participation/Voluntary Action
    (d) Legislation and Enforcement

As can be seen, most of the contents recommended in the two sets are overlapping. Both present the basic environmental knowledge required to be attained. However, keeping in view the current status of the environment and the prevalent issues of the day, it is pertinent to specifically include some present-day issues in the list. These include global warming and climate change, ozone layer depletion, consumerism, carbon footprint, toxic chemicals in food and appliances, natural and human-made disaster management, El Nino, La Nina, circular economy, and so on. Today, it has been recognized that most of the ecological or environmental crises that are seen have direct link with modern values and behavior patterns, and hence topics such as environmental ethics should also find adequate space. With almost all environmental issues, if not all, linked to economy, it will be appropriate to include a topic on environmental economics in the course.

When it comes to how best prospective teachers can learn, Kilinc (2010 cited in Genc 2015) suggested the project-based learning approach for environmental education programs since it enhances prospective teachers' environmental knowledge, attitudes, and behaviors. Hence, teacher preparation courses need to carefully incorporate such an approach. Even short-term project tasks are adequate for prospective teachers to attempt solving real social problems (e.g., garbage, water supply and sewers, abandoned land, erosion, paper recycling, and turtle protection) (Cheong 2005 cited in Genc 2015).

In addition to providing the basic essential elements during initial preparation of teachers, another concern facing teacher education programs pertains to the approach/model of environmental education that is to be followed in the curriculum. For example, in India, based on NCF-2005 school curriculum mandates that environmental education be taught as an infusion approach. However, with the introduction of a separate environmental education subject in Grade 10 as per NCF-SE 2023, preservice and in-service teachers will require training based on the curricular need. It is, therefore, essential that teachers are equipped in handling such an approach. The pros and cons of two models, interdisciplinary (separate subject) and multidisciplinary (infusion), have been discussed elaborately in Chapter 5. However, when it comes to actual classroom situations, infusion model can pose a problem compared to interdisciplinary model. Hence, all teacher training programs, both in-service and preservice, should adequately address this aspect for effective implementation of environmental education in schools. There are several other areas that need to be taken care of, such as details of teacher preparation for the early childhood, primary or secondary stage, strategies that can be adopted, evaluation of different teacher training programs, and so on. However, the details of such concerns are beyond the purview of this book and hence are not discussed here further.

8.4 Teacher Preparation in Environmental Education in India: Preservice

The preservice teacher education course aims at a complete development of the student-teacher, particularly in knowledge and skills, in individual care of the learner, and in methods and evaluation designed to facilitate learning. However, there remains several challenges in preservice courses. The Yashpal Committee Report (1993 cited in NCERT 2006) on 'Learning without Burden' attributed the cause for unsatisfactory quality of learning in schools to inadequate programs of teacher preparation. It highlighted the need to restructure the content of the program to ensure its relevance to the changing needs of school education. There are several preservice courses offered in the country to cater to different stages of school education. Some of the preservice courses are: Bachelor of Elementary Education (B.Ed.Ed.), Diploma in Elementary Education (D.El.Ed.), Bachelor of Education (B.Ed.), Master of Education (M.Ed.), Bachelor of Arts and Bachelor of Education (B.A.B.Ed.), Bachelor of Science and Bachelor of Education (B.Sc.B.Ed.), Master of Science and Bachelor of Education (M.Sc.B.Ed.), Bachelor of Physical Education (B.P.Ed.), Master of Physical Education (M.P.Ed.), etc. In order to bring about uniformity and quality in teacher education programs, these courses are being reconsidered and restructured in terms of the types of courses, duration, etc., such as introduction of the four-year integrated undergraduate program which will eventually replace the existing two-year B.Ed. course. This will be discussed in more detail later in the chapter.

Preservice courses are expected to cater to the current curricular concerns of school education. Any inadequacies and lapses in the preservice courses can in no way be compensated by any in-service program, however well-structured it may be. It is often seen that new focuses of learning or specific concerns are brought forth every time a new national curriculum framework for school education is brought out. For example, the NCF-2005 recommends infusion approach or infusion model to achieve the objectives of environmental education through the school curriculum (NCERT 2005). This is specific and needs special emphasis in the teacher education courses. However, it is quite alarming to find that in the NCFTE 2009 developed by the apex body for teacher education in the country, the National Council for Teacher Education (NCTE), environmental education itself is not reflected adequately, not to mention of the aspect of infusion approach. Hence, looking at the syllabi of the courses universities offer across the nation for preservice teachers, it is no more a surprise to see that courses on environmental education are rarely offered,[3] and when offered, it is almost always optional. And even when offered, infusion approach is hardly discussed[4] (NCERT 2012).

The complexities surrounding the inclusion of environmental education in school education in general and infusion approach of environmental education in particular is clear, and to understand such approach one needs to go through a systematically and meticulously designed course, as already discussed in Chapter 5. With this situation prevailing in the country, one can easily situate the status of environmental education in school education.

8.4.1 B.Ed. Syllabus at a Glance

Although environmental education[5] cuts across different stages, here B.Ed. syllabi will be the focus of discussion. As indicated by NCTE, the B.Ed. program is a professional course that prepares teachers for upper primary or middle level (Classes VI–VIII), secondary level (Classes IX–X), and senior secondary level (Classes XI–XII).[6]

In 2012, NCERT had brought out a syllabus titled "Syllabus for Two-year Bachelor of Education (B.Ed.)." It may be mentioned that NCERT has five regional institutions which offers preservice courses. One would expect this syllabus to be taken into consideration in the courses it offers in its regional institutions. While looking at this syllabus with respect to environmental education, it was found that the goals, objectives, nature, and scope of environmental education were not reflected in any way. Even when it comes to the content aspect, it was found to be limited to issues of conservation and environmental regeneration. While infusion approach of environmental education was proposed by NCERT in the NCF-2005, the syllabus did not reflect on this aspect. Pedagogy in environmental education did not find a place in the document. Nevertheless, a teacher educator having expertise in environmental education will still be able to cater to this aspect through other pedagogy courses such as in social sciences, biological sciences, physical sciences, etc.

A cursory study of the B.Ed. syllabi including the integrated four-year B.Sc.B.Ed. and integrated four-year B.A.B.Ed. offered in NCERT's four Regional Institute of Education located in Bhubaneswar, Mysuru, Ajmer, and Bhopal[7] was done to find out how far environmental education is reflected in the courses in general. For this, some broad areas were looked into such as clarity of goals and objectives, inclusion of content on environmental topics, and scope to develop pedagogical skills which include infusion in different subject disciplines. The same is provided in Table 8.1. This is being done since these colleges are affiliated to different universities and therefore will provide a sort of national picture.

Teacher Empowerment in Environmental Education **247**

TABLE 8.1 Comparative Study of B.Ed./B.Sc.B.Ed./B.A.B.Ed. Syllabus in the Regional Institutes of Education, NCERT

Regional Institute of Education	Objective	Content/Pedagogy	Detail	Credit
Bhubaneswar	Objectives focused on development of environmental content knowledge	• Mostly content • Some aspect of pedagogy reflected in the course detail	Ability Enhancement Compulsory Course AECC-III (environmental studies) in B.Sc.B.Ed. (Some aspect of content and pedagogy covered in Pedagogy of Biological Science in two-year B.Ed. program)	4/238
Mysore	Objectives focused on development of both content and pedagogy but pedagogy aspect could have been more elaborate	Both content and pedagogy	General Elective in Semester I in B.Sc.B.Ed. degree program B.A.Ed. and B.Ed.: nothing except in pedagogy in biological science such as 'developing professional competencies in dealing with environmental issues' and social science	2/209
Ajmer	Objectives focused on development of purely environmental content knowledge	Purely content	General Course: Environmental Education and Sustainable Development in BA.B.Ed. and B.Sc.B.Ed.	NA
Bhopal	Objectives focused on development of both content and pedagogy	Both content and pedagogy	PE-7: Environmental Education in Semester IV in B.Ed.	NA
	Objectives focused on development of purely environmental content knowledge	Purely content	Foundational Course: Environmental Education in Semesters 4 and 8 in B.Sc.B.Ed.	NA
	Objectives focused on purely environmental content knowledge	Purely content	Foundational Course: Environmental Education in Semesters 4 and 8 in B.A.B.Ed.	NA

The table clearly depicts the diverse ways in which environmental education is included in the courses. In general, development of environmental content knowledge appears to be the focus in most of the courses except for the B.Ed. course offered by RIE Bhopal which is found to be most comprehensive in terms of environmental education with adequate focus on both content and pedagogy. Another concern that can be gathered from these syllabi is that there is no emphasis or consideration on how environmental education is to be infused in different subject disciplines. At the most, students will learn how to infuse environmental concerns through pedagogy of biological science or social science.

UGC had prepared the model curriculum framework for B.Ed. course in which environmental education is included as one of the elective papers which is purely environmental content knowledge and awareness-based paper and not part of the pedagogy papers (Methods of Teaching).[8] The two-year credit-based B.Ed. syllabus of the University of Pune also includes "Environmental Education and Disaster Management" as one of the electives under the Foundation Course but it is purely content based which is for 2.5 credits if opted, and it also includes Environmental Education under Teaching Competency Courses for 0.5 credit out of the total 75 credits for the complete course.[9] In the two-year B.Ed. course offered by DU, environmental education is not part of the Foundation Courses or the pedagogy courses but just one of the elective courses, and it is purely awareness based for student-teachers which is also superficial in terms of content.[10] Even in the curriculum for B.Ed. mentioned in NCTE Regulation 2014, environmental education is not proposed to be one of the papers under Curriculum and Pedagogic Studies, which is restricted to Social Science, Science, Mathematics, and Languages. Environmental education is considered to be a side activity to be included as environment-based projects to address concerns of a particular village/city for a community in the pedagogy course on science.[11] What is common in these syllabi, and even in the syllabi discussed earlier, is that environmental education is included in the B.Ed. course mainly to develop environmental knowledge and awareness among the student-teachers. There is no denying that environmental knowledge and awareness is indispensable. However, if student-teachers are not trained how to transact environment-related concepts and concerns in the teaching–learning of different subject disciplines, how is it possible to prepare and nurture environmentally literate citizenry that have the knowledge and skills to tackle environmental challenges?

Course duration also used to be an issue up until 2014 when B.Ed. course could be for one-year or two-year duration. Such disparity in the course duration has been resolved beginning the academic year 2015–2016 with the introduction of a uniform duration of two-year B.Ed. course throughout the country by the NCTE Regulation of 2014.[12] However, the lacunae that is found in the syllabi with respect to environmental education does not have much to do with the course duration. It reflects more of a deliberate marginalization and treatment of environmental education as insignificant. This is evident from the fact that even the two-year B.Ed. curriculum brought out by NCTE (2015) does not discuss environmental education except for mentioning Environmental Studies (EVS) as a composite area of study at the primary stage that integrates science, social science, and environmental education. Another section where environmental education has found some relevance in this curriculum is where there is a mention that "in the pedagogy course on science may include environment based projects to address concerns of a particular village/city or a community." It remains to be seen how this idea of environmental education will be deciphered and taken forward by the teacher educators and put into practice in the course.

Although not analyzed in the syllabi, projects and activities will form the backbone of environmental education. And therefore this needs to be clearly spelt out in the syllabi. Providing opportunities to engage students in solving environmental issues also needs to find adequate space in the syllabus. This is essential for achieving one of environmental education's goals of preparing problem-solvers. For this, teacher training programs need to inculcate problem-solving skills through actual involvement in issues. Environmental education will only be meaningful when this aspect is fulfilled. It may be mentioned that teachers have cited the noninclusion of topics related to infusion of environmental education in different subjects in the D.Ed. and B.Ed. courses as the reason for their inability to effectively implement environmental education in classroom (CEE 1999, 31).

What is important to note is that the goals and objectives, their nature and scope, opportunities to be engaged in projects, and how environmental education is to be infused in the teaching–learning of different subject disciplines need to be clearly laid down in the syllabus.

Looking at the gaps that exist in the syllabi of different institutions, what is the need of the hour is a core syllabus with clear instructions for all syllabus developers on how environmental education is to be dealt with. With this in place, specific concerns such as infusion of environmental education in different subject disciplines, or other concerns that are new, will find place in the syllabus of every institution. A paragraph or two with a clear outline on 'what,' 'why,' and 'how' of environmental education will add value to the syllabus.

8.4.2 NEP 2020 and NCF-SE 2023 on Teacher Preparation

Any educational reform cannot happen without simultaneous changes in the teacher preparation component. As such, teacher preparation has been elaborately discussed in the NEP 2020.

As it was discussed in Chapter 6, NEP 2020 has some positive recommendations for teacher preparation—preservice and in-service. However, it is found that such recommendations are more applicable for subject-oriented teaching–learning and not so much for those cross-cutting areas which are infused or integrated in different disciplinary subjects but not taught as a separate subject such as environmental education. Currently, following NCF-2005, environmental education is not a subject, but infused in different subject disciplines. This approach is likely to change keeping in view the NCF-SE 2023, which recommends environmental education to be included as a cross-cutting area as well as a separate subject in Grade 10 and Grades 11 and 12 as already detailed in Chapter 6 (NCERT 2023). If these recommendations are to be effectively transacted, teacher training programs need to be put in place for both preservice and in-service, which so far has been as good as nonexistent except for teaching of EVS or Pedagogy of Environmental Science/Studies, which prepares teachers to teach the subject EVS from Classes III to V and are offered in courses such as D.El.Ed. and B.El.Ed.[13]

In order to move toward holistic empowerment of teachers as envisaged in NEP 2020, the NCTE brought out the norms and standards for Integrated Teacher Education Program (ITEP) in the National Council for Teacher Education (Recognition Norms and Procedure) Amendment Regulations, 2021.[14] As mentioned in the Regulations:

> …The ITEP programme emphasizes on preparing teachers as envisaged in Pedagogical and Curricular restructuring of school education under NEP 2020. Apart from preparing teachers for the school education system in the country, the disciplinary knowledge gained in different subjects would help the student-teachers to gain in-depth knowledge in their specific subject(s) which would ensure admission to higher studies in that disciplinary stream and for higher professional qualification… ITEP aims at the dual purpose of providing student teachers disciplinary knowledge along with the professional knowledge in an integrated manner. Since the program will be equivalent to an Undergraduate Degree (B.Sc./B.A./ B.Com.) and Teacher Education Degree, the curriculum of this program includes different courses and activities essential for both the degrees…The ITEP offered by multidisciplinary Higher Education Institutions (hereinafter referred to as 'HEIs') will be the minimal degree qualification for school teachers. The ITEP will be a dual-major holistic Bachelor's degree. This programme will prepare teachers for the new curricular and pedagogical structure of school education as reconfigured, to make it responsive and relevant to the developmental needs and interests of learners at different stages of their development, corresponding to the stages like Fundamental, Preparatory, Middle and Secondary guided by the 5+3+3+4 design…The ITEP shall be implemented in a phase wise manner starting from piloting in multidisciplinary Higher Education Institutions (HEIs)/ Teacher Education Institutions (TEIs) and thereby country wide expansion as per NEP 2020 timeframe.

The ITEP is being implemented across the country through the four-year integrated B.Ed. degree.

As the country gradually transitions into a four-year integrated B.Ed. degree as the minimum qualification for teaching by 2030 as recommended by NEP 2020 in the line of ITEP, the courses need to be prepared in such a way that environmental education is systematically included so that along with the necessary content knowledge, students are also provided adequate training in the area of pedagogy.

It may be noted that simply lodging B.Ed. courses in multidisciplinary institutions such as in the highly acclaimed Indian Institute of Technology (IIT) or any other university, for that matter, will not serve the purpose unless specific courses are offered for environmental education. What is needed is the revamping of the courses offered in the name of environmental education by bringing in the multidisciplinary aspects in the courses itself, such as bringing in various components like earth science, life science, social sciences (humanities included), language, arts, psychology, mathematics, technology, etc., as integral part of the course along with the indispensable pedagogy aspect. It is not the first time that the four-year integrated B.Ed. degree is being introduced in the country. It may be mentioned that the four Regional Institutes of Education (RIEs) of NCERT have been offering the four-year integrated course since decades. However, beyond getting two degrees (one Bachelor of Science degree and Bachelor of Education degree, i.e., B.Sc.B.Ed.) the real integration is hardly seen. The integration needs to be deliberate and purposeful so that actual integration happens and the outcome is visible in the quality of student-teachers that graduate from this newly introduced course.

However, the ITEP curriculum framework[15] and the syllabi brought out by the NCTE for the Middle[16] and Secondary[17] stages present a totally different picture with respect to environmental education. In these courses, environmental education is merely included as part of a two-credit course Citizenship Education, Sustainability, and Environmental Education under 'Ability Enhancement & Value-Added Courses' and not under 'Stage-Specific Content-cum-Pedagogy Courses.' This means that the course will enhance preservice students' environmental education knowledge but not prepare them on how to teach. This is despite the NCF-SE 2023 recommending the inclusion of environment as a crosscutting theme along with introduction of environmental education as a separate subject in Grade 10 and as one of the optional subjects in Grades 11 and 12 choice-based courses. As far as the course for The World Around Us in the preparatory stage is concerned, the syllabus[18] presents an impressive and exhaustive six-credit content-cum-pedagogy course that will span over three semesters. This suggests that the treatment of environmental education in these ITEP courses is no better than the existing ones. With ITEP courses in the present form, effective and meaningful implementation of environmental education will remain far-fetched since trained teachers will not be available to teach the newly introduced environmental education subject in Grades 10, 11, and 12.

From the above discussions, what needs to be answered is, 'with the existing preservice courses, how prepared are the teachers to handle environment-related concepts and concerns in the school curriculum?'

8.5 Teacher Preparation in Environmental Education in India: In-service

The lack of adequate preservice training opportunities in environmental education means that there are very few on-the-job teachers who have received environment-focused instruction, either pedagogical- or content-specific (Disinger and Howe 1990, 19). The situation was understandable during the 1990s since environmental education was still new then. But nothing much has changed even today and hence the imperative need for in-service environmental education programs.

In-service teacher education programs in general will serve the following purposes: One, it will update the teacher on the new trends and practices. Two, it will prepare the teacher to be able to meet the requirements of teaching–learning in accordance with the changes in the curriculum framework for schools as well as for teacher education. Three, those who have not undergone any kind of preservice course in environmental education, as is not uncommon in several parts of the country, will benefit the most in all areas of in-service professional development.

In the earlier discussions, it has been seen that preservice courses do not give much emphasis to environmental education in general, and hence they do not reflect infusion approach of environmental education adequately. It is not surprising that practicing teachers are, invariably, not aware or familiar with the philosophies, goals, and practices related to environmental education, and their understanding about 'infusion' or 'infusion approach' is limited to the literal meaning of the word. And so, whether the teachers know what and where environmental education has been infused and how it is to be transacted becomes irrelevant. At present, things do not look very bright for environmental education in preservice courses. Though not impossible, it might take some time, a few years, for environmental education to be reflected in such courses. While this transformation is taking place in the preservice sector, there are avenues for 'damage control' in the in-service sector. Most education committees and commissions have acknowledged the potential for radical shifts in the school practices and programs via effective in-service education programs. The Education Commission (1964–1966) strongly recommended that (a) large scale programs for in-service education of teachers should be organized by universities, and teacher organizations at all levels should enable every teacher to receive at least two or three months of in-service education for every five years of service, (b) continuing in-service education should be based on research inputs, and (c) training institutions should work on a 12-month basis and organize in-service training programs, such as refresher courses, seminars, workshops, and summer institutes.

In-service programs need to be paid equal attention as preservice courses, if not more, since these teachers will not be going back to attend another preservice course, unless it is made mandatory for the post/position they hold if they have not undergone such courses earlier. The Acharya Ramamurthi Review Committee (1990 in NCERT 2006) explicitly stated that, "in-service and refresher courses should be related to the specific needs of the teachers. In-service education should take due care of the future needs of teacher growth; evaluation and follow up should be part of the scheme."

Far from what has been recommended, there are just a few in-service teacher programs being offered in the country in environmental education. Mention may be made of the Green Teacher Diploma, a distance education program for in-service teachers offered occasionally by Centre for Environment Education (CEE) and Commonwealth of Learning (COL) Vancouver, Canada. There are no other regular programs, short term or long term, provided in environmental education. The needs of the teachers which were not addressed by the preservice course remain unaddressed due to lack of such programs. Feedback obtained from the nodal officers in environmental education of different states and UTs suggests that specific training or orientation in environmental education is required for the teachers. Most of them suggested a one-week program (Shimray, Hoshi, and Sasidhar 2014). Similar feedback on the need for capacity building in the area of environmental education was also obtained during the course of interaction with teachers teaching in DIETs in different parts of the country (Shimray 2015).

There are some institutes which offer an in-service B.Ed. course through distance mode such as the two-year B.Ed. degree by Maulana Azad National Urdu University for in-service graduate teachers[19]; Indira Gandhi National Open University (IGNOU)[20]; and Annamalai University. But such courses do not incorporate environmental education adequately.

The NCFTE 2009, however, mentions that systems are in place for imparting in-service trainings which are provided by institutes of advanced studies in education in chosen institutions and university departments of education, district institutes of education and training in each district, and SCERTs in states. It also mentions the continuous in-service teacher education program which requires each teacher to receive 20 days of training every year under the Sarva Shiksha Abhiyan (SSA) (NCTE 2009, 63). It is to be seen as to how much of environmental education components have been incorporated in such programs.

The NCERT had conducted a massive in-service teacher (including school heads) training programs such as National Initiatives for School Heads and

Teachers' Holistic Advancement (NISHTHA) at the elementary and secondary level covering the whole country not only in the pedagogy of subject disciplines but also in other areas such as art integration, health and physical education, assessment, etc.[21] One of the pedagogy courses in this program was Pedagogy of EVS. As per the information available on the website of Ministry of Education, 16,99,931 school heads and teachers were trained under NISHTHA in 2019–2020.[22] In a similar line, IMPACT (Integrated Multidisciplinary Professional Advancement Course for Teachers) was conducted specifically to train the untrained teachers in the Union Territory of Jammu and Kashmir. Pedagogy of EVS formed part of the training program. Considering the massive number of teachers who have been trained through these training programs, it can be assumed that a good number of teachers have been trained to cater to environmental education at the primary level, that is, Classes III to V through EVS subject. However, the training programs did not have scope to equip teachers to infuse environmental education as they transact their respective subject discipline especially after primary stage or from Class VI onwards. Unfortunately, environmental education is being equated with the subject EVS, which is learned in Classes III to V. Such a misunderstanding will reduce this important field of education to a primary-level subject. All in-service training programs should, therefore, necessarily include environmental education. If this is done, not only teachers will be trained to transact environmental concerns and concepts in any subject discipline, but the concerns of training teachers to teach EVS will also be automatically taken care. This concern is still relevant even as The World Around Us is introduced from Grades 3 to 5 as per NCF-SE 2023 instead of EVS.

8.5.1 Possibilities for In-service Teacher Empowerment

There are other possibilities to include environmental education in the training/orientation/refresher courses provided by different school systems such as Kendriya Vidyalaya Sangathan, Jawahar Navodaya Vidyalaya, Delhi Public School, DAV Schools, and so on, which conduct such programs for their teachers on an almost-regular basis. Another possibility to include environmental education is in the training programs organized as part of the government's initiative such as those conducted under Samagra Shiksha. However, in all these efforts one may bear in mind that it has been very difficult to follow the cascade model wherein a set of people are trained, who in turn train another set, and so on. Since environmental education is comparatively new to the teaching community, instead of focusing on cascade model it will be appropriate if the maximum possible numbers of teachers are directly exposed to the training programs conducted by the well-trained educators. This will also avoid possible dilution and ineffectiveness that could occur at every level of the cascade. This, of course, is going to be a very ambitious task and would require tremendous commitment by the government, huge funding, enormous human resource, and so on, to take the task ahead.

Though it will be challenging, mechanisms could still be worked out to train in-service teachers in government schools. A more serious concern is regarding the large chunk of para-teachers in government schools and teachers in private schools where certificates or degrees are not mandatory nor are there in-service training programs in place.

NEP 2020 clearly lays down its vision for Continuous Professional Development (CPD) with 50 hours of CPD opportunities which will be driven by their own interest in numerous areas covering latest pedagogies, learning outcomes, competency-based learning, etc. For effective implementation of environmental education, it will be crucial that it finds place in the CPD.

NEP 2020 also recommends a common guiding set of National Professional Standards for Teachers (NPST), which will cover expectations of the role of the teacher at different levels of expertise/stage, and the competencies required for that stage. It will also comprise standards for performance appraisal for each stage, which would be carried out on a periodic basis. It is to be seen how the Professional Standard Setting Body (PSSB), which will be responsible for the task, take into consideration environmental education in the whole gamut of the preparation of standards.

8.5.2 Some Systemic Issues

Motivation comes with confidence, confidence comes with training, and trainees are motivated by benefits and incentives—though not necessarily in that sequence. However, one thing is definite: teachers need motivation to make their class EE-oriented. With the workload that teachers have, most of the time their focus is on 'completing' the course. Moreover, the school administration and parents expect teachers to give 'results' in the form of marks. Why then would teachers follow the more elaborate and sometimes challenging route by considering environmental education? They would obviously encourage 'note' and 'rote' method by which students can still score marks, and score very high at that. However, if the government is ready to part with some of their exchequer, considering a mandatory certification program in environmental education with accompanying incentive for in-service teachers might be a step in the right direction.

8.6 Teacher Preparation in Environmental Education in India: Teacher Educators

Another area of concern related to teacher education is the lack of adequate professionally qualified teacher educators in environmental education. The issue with teacher educators is not only with environmental education, though. Similar concerns were pointed out by the Justice Verma Committee Report 2012

(GoI 2012, 17–18).[23] The situation is the same for teacher educators in general, as NCFTE 2009 (NCTE 2009, 75) points out:

> The need and importance of professionally trained teacher educators has been underscored in statements on educational policy, time and again, but the situation on the ground remains a matter of concern; there is a considerable shortage of properly qualified and professionally trained teacher educators at all stages of education and especially at the elementary stage. The shortage refers both to the inadequacy of required numbers as well as to mismatch in the qualifications of teacher educators and their job requirements.

In a similar line, NCERT (2006, 7) states, "There are also no established mechanisms to create a professional cadre of teacher educators, especially at pre-primary and the elementary stage. Most teacher educators, training pre-primary and elementary school teachers for example, are themselves trained in secondary education." Needless to say, the situation is worse when it comes to environmental education. There are no specific courses in higher education institutions which prepare qualified teacher educators in environmental education who would be capable of teaching the preservice or in-service courses. In a study undertaken among teacher educators from various district institutes of education and research of the country, more than half of the respondents mentioned that environmental education or related topics are taught by educators who have had no specific education or training in the area (Shimray 2015). This is quite alarming. All the respondents suggested the urgency to build the capacities of teacher educators in environmental education.

Therefore, the problem is about how to prepare such huge numbers of teacher educators to cater to the need of the whole nation? Who would provide them with such courses or training? Are there enough professionals to train them all? Wouldn't it be appropriate to look outward (trainers from other countries) for such academic support? Is the government ready to take up such an important step? The issue at hand is not even about the course content for training teacher educators but about coming up with a mechanism to set up such courses. The newly launched nationally sponsored scheme—Rashtriya Uchchatar Shiksha Abhiyan (RUSA), National Higher Education Mission—by the Government of India in 2013 would be the right platform to address concerns related to teacher educators. Crores of rupees will be spent each year on capacity-building, which is one of the goals of RUSA. It would be worth investing a portion of the budget in capacity building of teacher educators in the area of EE. For this to happen, either the government/concerned body of the government or some concerned teacher educators/institutes have to work out a plan strategically and ensure its implementation. Without a deliberate effort, the capacity building of teacher educators in the area of environmental education will not happen naturally. These are some of the many issues related to the area of teacher educators. This suggests that much is needed to be done when it comes to professional development of teacher educators in EE in India.

8.7 Teacher Preparation for Higher Education

In 2003, as per directives of the Hon'ble Supreme Court of India, the UGC had come out with a core module syllabus for compulsory implementation of EVS at the undergraduate level. Further, in 2017, the UGC framed an eight-unit module syllabus for the Ability Enhancement Compulsory Course (AECC-EVS) under the Choice-Based Credit System (CBCS). Similarly, in 2023, it brought out the four-credit environment education course at the undergraduate level titled "Guidelines and Curriculum Framework for Environment Education at Undergraduate level," as mentioned in Chapter 6. However, just as in the case of school education, there are no teachers who are specifically trained to teach the course in most cases. Often it is conveniently assigned to a botany or a zoology teacher, if not any teacher with a science background, in spite of the fact that Environmental Education is multidisciplinary covering earth science, botany, zoology, physics, chemistry, geography, psychology, political science, economics, history, law, mathematics, arts, humanities, etc. Therefore, the basic requirement to teach Environmental Education in colleges should be a qualified teacher who has a degree in the subject. In addition, it will also require the teacher to understand the goals of teaching Environmental Education as a mandatory course in higher education and thereby be able to customize the teaching–learning process accordingly. Therefore, some expertise in pedagogy will also be required.

8.8 Changing Names

Another concern that has come in the way of effective implementation of environmental education is about the change in focus and the change in names. Since the past decade, education for sustainable development (ESD) has gained popularity. While this should not have interfered in the implementation of environmental education but rather strengthened it, since the goals of EE and ESD are practically similar (Arjen 2009, 28–29), unfortunately, what is found is that ESD or SD has overshadowed environmental education, at least in documents. This is evident even in the NCFTE 2009 document which substantially covered SD, while the term 'environmental education' did not find even a mention. One might say that ESD or SD will ultimately take care of EE. Ideally it should. However, it will be apt to be reminded of the fact that environmental education did not get the focus it deserved even decades after it was introduced in the 1970s. For decades, the system has not succeeded in informing teachers what environmental education is, and now that the focus has suddenly shifted to ESD or SD, one can only keep guessing how many decades it would take to really implement it in letter and spirit. The details about ESD are discussed in the next chapter. However, interestingly, as mentioned in Chapter 6, in the National Curriculum for School Education 2023 the term 'environmental education' has been used, while ESD has been mentioned as a passing statement under the environment section (NCERT 2023, 171).

8.9 Conclusion

In spite of all the efforts that have been put into environmental education, serious issues exist in the area of teacher empowerment, including the teacher educators, which need immediate attention. As discussed in the chapter, environmental education has not been adequately reflected in the syllabi of preservice courses. Lack of quality teacher education curriculum with regard to environmental education coupled with very few primary teachers teaching EVS who had studied environmental education in their preservice education at B.Ed. was also found by Sharma (2018) in a study of research trends in Environmental Education in India. Some of the reasons could be that the curriculum developers missed out on the topic deliberately, or could not find adequate space and time to incorporate such topics, or did not understand the value and importance of environmental education. There could be many other reasons, but what is clear from this is that the courses need to be of adequate duration so that there is no room to make excuses for its noninclusion. The issues with in-service courses are also no less. It is known that without empowering teachers it is impossible to expect any positive result in the implementation of environmental education in schools. Indeed, in a huge nation like India where there are more than 95 lakh school teachers teaching at primary to higher secondary schools,[24] it is not going to be easy to think of professional development for each one of them. In this scenario, one might think that it would be too ambitious to think of working out a model for professional development in environmental education when even after decades a proper system could not be worked out for teacher education in general. But looking at the gravity of environmental issues that is spiraling out of human's control, there is no choice left but to work out a suitable model for professional development in environmental education—preservice and in-service.

Keeping this in view, there is an urgent need to review the syllabi of the existing professional development courses. Some of the suggestions that might be considered in such exercise are discussed below.

Preservice Courses

1. Inclusion of environmental education as one of the compulsory papers: Preservice courses such as B.El.Ed. and B.Ed. consist of many compulsory

papers which invariably include philosophy of education, basic concepts in education, and emerging areas. In such papers, environment-related education is mentioned only as passing statements. The issue is not so much with the primary stages because most of the courses in D.El.Ed. and B.El.Ed. offer pedagogy of EVS. It will not be an issue even with the implementation of The World Around Us based on NCF-SE 2023. The problem begins from upper primary stage or middle stage when the infusion approach or model of environmental education is being followed. The courses offered at present invariably caters only to the content aspect, that is, environmental concepts. It is, therefore, important to include environmental education as one of the compulsory papers or at the least; it can be part of a compulsory paper in all the preservice courses so that every student in the preservice program is introduced to the course. Such compulsory paper should address both content and pedagogy. NCERT (1981) had also brought forth this idea of introducing a compulsory paper in environmental education.
2. As far as pedagogy of environmental education is concerned, there can be two ways of addressing the concern: by having a separate paper on pedagogy of environmental education and by clearly highlighting how environmental education should be reflected in the pedagogy of different curricular subjects.
3. The role of NCTE will be crucial in the systematic inclusion of environmental education in all the preservice courses.
4. To foster quality assurance and sustenance, the National Assessment and Accreditation Council (NAAC) needs to ensure that environmental education is taken as one of the components in its process of quality assessment.

In-service Courses

1. In-service professional development courses in environmental education, which are recognized by competent authorities, need to be prepared. The government needs to formulate some ways to ensure that every teacher undergoes such a course. An incentive to those who complete such a course would enhance participation.
2. Routine in-service training programs for different subjects conducted at the national and the state level, or by different school system, need to include environmental education adequately in all such programs.
3. Inclusion of environmental education component in Teacher Eligibility Tests (TETs) and such other tests will go a long way in the process of recruitment of qualified teachers.
4. Distance Education Council (DEC) need to ensure that environmental education component is seriously considered in its in-service teacher education under the Open and Distance Learning (ODL) mode.
5. CPD as envisaged in the NEP 2020 will be crucial to enhance teachers' capacities in environmental education.

6. The role of National Council for Teacher Education will be crucial to prioritize environmental education in the NPST.

8.9.1 Training of Teacher Educators

The most neglected, yet the most important of all professional development programs is that of the teacher educators who teach preservice courses. Most of the teacher educators have not been trained in the area of environmental education. This is not surprising since, as mentioned earlier, environmental education is not compulsory in preservice professional development courses. Moreover, there is no mechanism in place for them for professional development in environmental education. It is therefore essential to empower these teacher educators with the emerging trends in the area of EE. The tasks sound enormous. However, it is workable. The following provides a simple way of organizing a short-term training program (which could be for five days) for teacher educators in DIET. There are approximately 630 districts in India. According to Education for All in India, as of 2021, there are 614 DIETs.[25] Two teacher educators from each DIET can be trained to be master trainers who would in turn train other faculty members. These master trainers can also be utilized to provide trainings to teachers working in schools located in the district.

Stakeholders need to wake up and take appropriate measures so that teacher preparation and empowerment in environmental education is seriously taken up. Or, as with the 1991 order from the Hon'ble Supreme Court of India to make environmental education compulsory in all stages of education throughout the country, will it require another order from the Hon'ble Court to make this aspect (teacher preparation and empowerment in environmental education) compulsory for all preservice and in-service teachers?

8.10 Summary

- Serious issues exist in the area of teacher empowerment, including teacher educators, in environmental education.
- Environmental education is not adequately reflected in the syllabi of preservice courses. Even when environmental education is included under the elective papers, it is kept an optional paper.
- Infusion approach of environmental education does not appear in any of the existing preservice or in-service professional development courses.
- Appropriate duration for various preservice courses need to be worked out to ensure that environmental education is highlighted sufficiently in the courses.
- There are also issues with in-service courses regarding environmental education. No system is in place to regularly provide training to in-service teachers in environmental education.

- There is no mechanism for the professional development of teacher educators, many of whom themselves have not received sufficient training in the area of environmental education.
- The existing mass training programs organized, under Samagra Shiksha, for different subjects can be used as a platform to train in-service teachers in environmental education throughout the country.
- In-service training programs organized by Kendriya Vidyalaya Sangathan, Jawahar Navodaya Vidyalaya Samiti, and so on may accommodate some sessions on environmental education.
- Lack of clarity on what exactly is being implemented—environmental education, SD, ESD, and so on—is becoming an issue in the implementation of environmental education.
- Implementation of the recommendations of NEP 2020 on teacher preparation such as four-year integrated B.Ed. degree as the minimum qualification for teaching by 2030 and professional development with special consideration for environmental education will go a long way in nurturing environmentally literate students.

Notes

1. In the chapter, teacher empowerment, teacher preparation, teacher training, and professional development have been used synonymously.
2. Kothari Commission, 1964-66: https://indianculture.gov.in/flipbook/1494 (Accessed on September 21, 2023).
3. http://www.ignou.ac.in/upload/programme/B.ED_.Progguide.pdf (Accessed on September 21, 2023).
4. https://cie.du.ac.in/userfiles/downloads/Academic/Syllabus/BED/Bed_syllabus.pdf (Accessed on September 21, 2023).
5. Environmental education as an area should not be confused with Environmental Studies subject which is taught in Grades 3 to 5.
6. https://ncte.gov.in/Website/PDF/regulation/regulation2014/english/appendix4.pdf (Accessed on June 8, 2023).
7. https://riebhopal.nic.in/downloads/BSc_BEd_Syllabus.pdf (Accessed on June 7, 2023; https://riebhopal.nic.in/downloads/BA_BEd_Syllabus.pdf (Accessed on June 7, 2023; https://riebhopal.nic.in/downloads/BEdSyllabus.pdf (Accessed on June 7, 2023).
8. https://www.ugc.gov.in/oldpdf/modelcurriculum/edu.pdf (Accessed on June 8, 2023).
9. http://www.unipune.ac.in/Syllabi_PDF/revised_2014/education/B_Ed_Syllabus_2014_Final_30-6-14.pdf (Accessed on June 8, 2023).
10. https://cie.du.ac.in/userfiles/downloads/Academic/Syllabus/BED/Bed_syllabus.pdf (Accessed on June 7, 2023).
11. https://ncte.gov.in/Website/PDF/regulation/regulation2014/english/appendix4.pdf (Accessed on June 8, 2023).
12. https://ncte.gov.in/Website/PDF/regulation/regulation2014/english/appendix4.pdf (Accessed on June 8, 2023).
13. https://scert.assam.gov.in/sites/default/files/swf_utility_folder/departments/scert_medhassu_in_oid_6/portlet/level_2/curriculum_syllabus_of_d.el_.ed_.pdf (Accessed on June 9, 2023); http://ihe.du.ac.in/wp-content/uploads/2021/12/Final_Prospectus_BElEd_2020-21.pdf; https://mscw.ac.in/LOCF/BElEd Handbook.pdf

(Accessed on June 9, 2023); http://ihe.du.ac.in/wp-content/uploads/2022/05/handbook-b.el_.ed_.pdf (Accessed on September 1, 2023).
14 https://ncte.gov.in/Website/PDF/regulation/509Regulations_2014.pdf (Accessed on June 7, 2023).
15 https://ncte.gov.in/website/PDF/ITEPCIRRICULUM.pdf (Accessed on February 26, 2024).
16 https://ncte.gov.in/website/PDF/Final_Middle.pdf (Accessed February 26, 2024).
17 https://ncte.gov.in/website/PDF/Final_Secondary.pdf (Accessed February 26, 2024).
18 https://ncte.gov.in/website/PDF/Final_PreparatoryA4.pdf (Accessed February 26, 2024).
19 https://manuu.edu.in/sites/default/files/2019-10/B.EdSyllabus201810.09.2018.pdf (Accessed on September 21, 2023).
20 http://www.ignou.ac.in/ignou/aboutignou/school/soe/programmes/detail/90/2 (Accessed on June 9, 2023).
21 https://itpd.ncert.gov.in// (Accessed on June 9, 2023).
22 https://www.education.gov.in/1699931-school-heads-and-teachers-have-been-trained-under-nishtha-2019-20-education-minister (Accessed on June 9, 2023).
23 https://www.education.gov.in/sites/upload_files/mhrd/files/document-reports/JVC Vol 1.pdf (Accessed on September 18, 2023).
24 https://www.education.gov.in/sites/upload_files/mhrd/files/statistics-new/udise_21_22.pdf (Accessed on September 21, 2023).
25 https://educationforallinindia.com/diets-in-india-present-status-challenges/#:~:text=In2009, the Rashtriya Madhyamik, DIETs in the Union Territories (Accessed on September 1, 2023).

References

CEE, Centre for Environment Education. 1999. *Environmental Orientation to School Education—A Programme of Ministry of Human Resource Development: A Documentation of the Scheme and Some Projects under the Scheme.* Edited by Meena Raghunathan and Mamata Pandya. Ahmedabad: CEE.

Disinger, J.F., and R.W. Howe. 1990. *Trends and Issues Related to the Preparation of Teachers for Environmental Education.* Environmental Education Information Report. Columbus, OH: ERIC Clearinghouse for Science, Mathematics, and Environmental Education. Available at: http://files.eric.ed.gov/fulltext/ED335233.pdf (Accessed on September 27, 2023).

Feinstein, Noah. 2009. *Education for Sustainable Development in the United States of America: A Report Submitted to the International Alliance of Leading Education Institutes*, University of Wisconsin-Madison.

Fien, John, and Jo-Anne Ferreira. 1997. "Environmental Education in Australia–A Review." *International Research in Geographical and Environmental Education* 6 (3): 234–259, Channel View Books/Multi-Lingual Matters Ltd. Available at: https://www.academia.edu/8161935/Environmental_Education_in_Australia_-_A_Review (September 27, 2023).

Genc, Murat 2015. "The Project-based Learning Approach in Environmental Education." *International Research in Geographical and Environmental Education* 24 (2): 105–117. DOI: 10.1080/10382046.2014.993169

GoI, Government of India. 2012. *Vision of Teacher Education in India: Quality and Regulatory Perspective, Report of the High-Powered Commission on Teacher Education*

Constituted by the Hon'ble Supreme Court of India. Ministry of Human Resource Development, New Delhi: Department of School Education and Literacy.

Heimlich, J.E., and L. B. Smith. 2004. *Preservice Environmental Education: What Do We Know?* A Report to World Wildlife Fund, US: Office of Environmental Education. Columbus, Ohio: Ohio State University Extension.

Hungerford, H.R., T.L. Volk, W.J. Bluhm, B.G. Dixon, T.J. Marcinkowski, and A.P.C. Sia. 1994. *An Environmental Education Approach to the Training of Elementary Teachers: A Teacher Education Programme (Revised)*. A Discussion Guide for UNESCO Training Seminars on Environmental Education. UNESCO-UNEP International Environmental Education Programme, Environmental Education Series 27. Paris: UNESCO.

Lahiry, D., Savita Sinha, J.S. Gill, U. Mallik, and A.K. Mishra. 1988. *Environmental Education: A Process for Pre-service Teacher Training Curriculum Development*. UNESCO-UNEP International Environmental Education Programme Environmental Education Series No. 26, edited by Patricia R. Simpson, Harold Hungerford, and Trudi L. Volk. Paris: UNESCO.

Monde, P.N. 2011. *Barriers to Successful Implementation of Environmental Education in Zambian High Schools: A Case Study of Selected High Schools of Central Province*. PhD Thesis: University of Zambia, 19. Available at: http://dspace.unza.zm:8080/xmlui/bitstream/handle/123456789/809/Monde.pdf?sequence=1 (Accessed on September 27, 2023).

NAAEE, North American Association for Environmental Education. 2007. *National Council for Accreditation of Teacher Education (NCATE) Standards for the Initial Preparation of Environmental Educators*. Washington, DC: NAAEE. Available at: https://studylib.net/doc/15380887/ee-standards---naaee--simmons--et.-al.- (Accessed on September 27, 2023).

NCERT, National Council of Educational Research and Training. 1981. *Environmental Education at the School Level: A Lead Paper*. New Delhi: NCERT.

———. 2005. *National Curriculum Framework 2005*. New Delhi: NCERT.

———. 2006. *Position Paper of the National Focus Group on Teacher Education for Curriculum Renewal*. New Delhi: NCERT.

———. 2012. *Syllabus for Two-year Bachelor of Education (B.Ed.)*. New Delhi: NCERT.

———. 2023. *National Curriculum Framework for School Education 2023*. New Delhi: NCERT.

NCTE, National Council for Teacher Education. 2009. *National Curriculum Framework for Teacher Education 2009*. New Delhi: NCTE.

NCTE, National Council for Teacher Education. 2015. *Curriculum Framework: Two-year B.Ed. Programme*. New Delhi: NCTE.

Plevyak, L.H., M. Bendixen-Noe, J. Henderson, R.E. Roth, and Richard Wilke. 2001. "Level of Teacher Preparation and Implementation of EE: Mandated and Non-Mandated EE Teacher Preparation States." *The Journal of Environmental Education* 32 (2): 28–36.

Sharma, Kavita. 2018. "Research Trends in Environmental Education." *Indian Educational Review* 56 (1): 7–52. Available at: https://ncert.nic.in/pdf/publication/journalsandperiodicals/indianeducationalreview/IER-JAN-18.pdf (Accessed on September 2, 2023).

Shimray, C.V., A.N. Hoshi, and R. Sasidhar. 2014. *Monitoring the Implementation of Environmental Education in Schools in States and UTs in Compliance with the Hon'ble Supreme Court's Order: Meeting of Nodal Officers—A Report* (Unpublished). New Delhi: NCERT.

Shimray, C.V. 2015. *Meeting of DIET Functionaries to Assess the Status of D.El.Ed. Syllabus in the Context of Environmental Education—Report* (Unpublished). New Delhi: NCERT.

Tilbury, D. 1997. "Environmental Education (EE) A Head, Heart and Hand Approach to Learning about Environmental Problems." *New Horizons in Education* 38: 1–11.

UNESCO, United Nations Educational, Scientific and Cultural Organization. 1978. *Intergovernmental Conference on Environmental Education*, Tbilisi, 14–26 October 1977, Final Report. Paris: UNESCO.

———. 1980. *Strategies for Developing an Environmental Education Curriculum: A Discussion Guide for UNESCO Training Workshops on Environmental Education*. Paris: UNESCO.

Wals, Arjen. 2009. *Learning for a Sustainable World: Review of Contexts and Structures for Education for Sustainable Development. United Nations Decade of Education for Sustainable Development (DESD, 2005–2014)*. Paris: UNESCO.

Wilke, R.J., R.B. Peyton, and H.R. Hungerford. 1987. *Strategies for the Training of Teachers in Environmental Education*. Environmental Education Series 25. Division of Science, Technical and Environmental Education. Paris: UNESCO-UNEP.

9
ENVIRONMENTAL EDUCATION VS EDUCATION FOR SUSTAINABLE DEVELOPMENT

9.1 Chapter Overview

The chapter discusses at length about the conception and nature of education for sustainable development (ESD) and thereafter about the decade of education for sustainable development (DESD) and the Global Action Program (GAP) that ensued as a follow-up to the DESD and also touching upon the Sustainable Development Goals (SDGs). All kinds of education that can contribute to sustainable development, such as on peace, human rights, gender, etc., are considered to be ESD. To clarify this, the chapter discusses on the types of sustainability education by trying to distinguish between sustainable development-related education and full-fledged ESD. Attempts have been made to bring out where and how ESD and environmental education converge or deviate. Further, it discusses whether environmental education (EE) should be continued alongside ESD. Will ESD be able to give enough emphasis to tackle the ever-increasing biophysical environmental issues? If so, will there still be a need to continue with environmental education? These are the concerns which the chapter will try to touch upon. Discussions on some of the ramifications that can be expected with the implementation of ESD have also been included.

9.2 Introduction

In the previous chapters, some discussions have gone into how ESD apparently came about. ESD is fundamentally about values, with respect at the center: respect for others, including those of present and future generations, for difference and diversity, for the environment, for the resources of the planet humans inhabit (UNESCO 2006). Since the Rio Conference in 1992, ESD gained enormous popularity. It has almost replaced environmental education in the process

DOI: 10.4324/9781003461135-10

of implementation in many countries. To a lay person ESD might sound like a totally new concept which could tackle all sustainability issues which environmental education has not been able to address. In this context, it is important to understand what exactly ESD is, how did it originate, what is DESD, what happens after DESD, and so on. Such discussions have become more so important with the global goals or SDGs in place for Agenda 2030, which is a plan of action for people, planet, and prosperity to be achieved by 2030.

9.3 Conception of ESD

Conception of ESDThe roots of ESD can be traced back to the history of two distinct areas of interest of the United Nations: (a) education and (b) sustainable development.

9.3.1 Education

Irina Bokova, director-general of UNESCO in 2012, had said, "Education is the most powerful path to sustainability. Economic and technological solutions, political regulations or financial incentives are not enough. We need a fundamental change in the way we think and act" (UNESCO 2014a).

In terms of education, the root of ESD goes back to the Declaration of Human Rights in 1948, which states, "Everyone has the right to education." The Convention on the Right of the Child (CRC), adopted by the United Nations General Assembly (UNGA) in 1989, reinforced this right to education by declaring that primary education should be compulsory and available free to all. The CRC further mentions that children may not be excluded from any right—including education—based on race, sex, disability, economic status.

Following this, in 1990, the Jomtien Declaration on Education for All (EFA) declared, "Basic education should be provided to all children, youth and adults. To this end, basic education services of quality should be expanded and consistent measures must be taken to reduce disparities." The declaration also made efforts to address the issue of gender disparity prevalent in the world by pointing out that utmost priority must be given to ensure access to, and improve the quality of, education for girls and women, and to remove every obstacle that hampers their active participation. It further added that all gender stereotyping in education should be eliminated.

Furthermore, international development targets (IDTs), a set of goals selected from the series of UN conferences held in the 1990s, include "by 2015, children everywhere, boys and girls alike, will be able to complete a full course of primary schooling."[1] Another very significant event in the area of education—the World Education Forum—took place in Dakar, Senegal, in 2000 (UNESCO 2000). The Dakar Framework for Action adopted during this Forum lists six important educational goals, which include: "Improving all aspects of the quality of education so that recognized and measurable learning outcomes are achieved, especially, in literacy, numeracy and essential life skills." Meanwhile, in the UN Millennium Summit (2000) held in New York, world leaders committed to achieve the Millennium Development Goals (MDGs) by 2015. Of the many goals the MDGs seek to address, the ones on education are: "Achieve universal primary education," "Promote gender equality and empower women," and "Ensure environmental sustainability." Furthermore, the UNGA declared 2003–2012 to be the United Nations Literacy Decade (UNLD) to support collective efforts to achieve the goals of EFA by 2015. It is evident from the discussion that the importance of EFA has been addressed by the United Nations repeatedly over its entire history (UNESCO 2005) with the momentum catching up markedly since the late 1980s.

9.3.2 Sustainable Development

Sustainable development has its roots in United Nations history in the environmental movement which goes back several decades (UNESCO 2005). In this long journey, mention may be made of the 1968 UNESCO Conference on Biodiversity and the landmark 1972 United Nations Conference on the Human Environment in Stockholm, Sweden, which led to the establishing of many environmental protection agencies and the United Nations Environment Program (UNEP) besides many environmental ministries and nongovernmental organizations (NGOs) working to conserve the planet's resources. Due to unprecedented growth and development taking place, especially beginning the second half of the 20th century, nations realized the urgency to tackle the issues collaboratively rather than adopting national approaches and solutions. Following the Stockholm conference, UNESCO came out with the Belgrade Charter and the Tbilisi Declaration (for details, see Chapter 2). Though holistic approach was envisaged, it was observed that while some attention was attached to the social and economic issues inherent in these environmental issues, the focus was largely on addressing the ecological impact of ever-increasing unrestricted development. The global community acknowledged the pressing need to explore the inter relationships between the environment and natural resources, and socio-economic issues of poverty and underdevelopment. It was increasingly realized that unless such issues are addressed, the environment will be subjected to ever more degradation. This formed the basis for the United Nations to hunt for a more encompassing strategy which would address both the needs of the society as well as the environment. The search finally ended with the report of the World Commission on Environment and Development or the Brundtland Commission Report (named after the head of the Commission)—Our Common Future—which came out in 1987 (UN 1987). Based on this report, sustainable development was endorsed by the United Nations as an overarching framework or construct for future development policy at all levels of government. It defined sustainable development as "development that meets the needs of the present without compromising the ability of future generations to meet their own needs." This definition is with reference to the capacity of the natural environment. It implies that development which is essential to satisfy human needs and improve the quality of life should occur in such a way that the capacity of the natural environment to meet present and future needs is not compromised. Though sustainable development began to be used extensively ever since the Brundtland Commission Report, references on the concept of sustainable development have also been indicated prior to this (Tortajada 2005). Several other definitions related to sustainable development have also been used by different professionals and researchers based on different context (Pezzey 1992). Some of those are provided in Box 9.1.

BOX 9.1 REFERENCES TO SUSTAINABLE DEVELOPMENT

Porritt (1984)—Director, U.K. Friends of the Earth
"All economic growth in the future must be sustainable: that is to say, 'it must operate within and not beyond the finite limits of the planet.'"
Repetto (1985)—Economist, World Resources Institute

1. The core of the idea of sustainability, then, is the concept that current decisions should not impair the prospects for maintaining or improving future living standards. This implies that our economic systems should be managed so that we live off the dividend of our resources, maintaining and improving the asset base. This principle also has much in common with the ideal concept of income that accountants seek to determine: the greatest amount that can be consumed in the current period without reducing prospects for consumption in the future.
2. This does not mean that sustainable development demands the preservation of the current stock of natural resources or any particular mix of human, physical and natural assets. As development proceeds, the composition of the underlying asset base changes.

Tolba (1987)—Executive Director, U.N. Environmental Programme

1. "[Sustainable development] has become an article of faith, a shibboleth: often used but little explained. Does it amount to a strategy? Does it apply only to renewable resources?
   What does the term actually mean? In broad terms the concept of sustainable development encompasses:

(i) help for the very poor because they are left with no option other than to destroy their environment;
(ii) the idea of self-reliant development, within natural resource constraints;
(iii) the idea of cost-effective development using different economic criteria to the traditional approach; that is to say development should not degrade environmental quality, nor should it reduce productivity in the long run;
(iv) the great issues of health control, appropriate technologies, food self-reliance, clean water and shelter for all;
(v) the notion that people-centered initiatives are needed; human beings, in other words, are the resources in the concept."

Turner (1988)—Academic Economist
"In this [sustainable development] mode...conservation becomes the sole basis for defining a criterion with which to judge the desirability of alternative allocations of natural resources."

Source: Pezzey (1992)

Following this development, a parallel concept of education to support sustainable development was visualized by the United Nations which finally materialized in the form of Chapter 36 of Agenda 21, 'Promoting Education, Public Awareness, and Training.' UNESCO was appointed to be the Task Manager for this chapter. This effort to promote ESD was further strengthened by embedding education as an enabling or implementation strategy in each of the 40 chapters of Agenda 21 (see Chapter 7), which was adopted by the participating nations in the Earth Summit held in Rio de Janeiro in 1992 (UN 1992). To further this initiative of identifying education to be inseparable from achieving sustainable development, it was in the Johannesburg World Summit on Sustainable Development (WSSD) in 2002 that the period 2005–2014 was proposed as the DESD (UNESCO, 2005).

9.4 What Is ESD?

ESD is "an emerging but dynamic concept that encompasses a new vision of education that seeks to empower people of all ages to assume responsibility for creating and enjoying a sustainable future" (UNESCO 2002, 5). It empowers everyone to make informed decisions for environmental integrity, economic viability, and a just society for present and future generations, while respecting cultural diversity (UNESCO 2014a). Further, "it is not so much education about sustainable development but education for sustainable development" (Pigozzi 2003).

9.4.1 Key Characteristics of ESD

ESD

- is based on the principles and values that underlie sustainable development;
- deals with the well-being of all three realms of sustainability—environment, society and economy;
- promotes life-long learning;
- is locally relevant and culturally appropriate;
- is based on local needs, perceptions, and conditions, but acknowledges that fulfilling local needs often has international effects and consequences;
- engages formal, nonformal, and informal education;
- accommodates the evolving nature of the concept of sustainability;
- addresses content, taking into account context, global issues, and local priorities;
- builds civil capacity for community-based decision-making, social tolerance, environmental stewardship, adaptable workforce, and quality of life;
- is interdisciplinary, i.e., no one discipline can claim ESD for its own, but all disciplines can contribute to ESD;
- uses a variety of pedagogical techniques that promote participatory learning and higher-order thinking skills.

These essential characteristics of ESD can be implemented in myriad ways, so that the resulting ESD program reflects the unique environmental, social, and economic conditions of each locality (UNESCO 2005).

9.4.2 Four Major Thrusts of ESD

Chapter 36 of Agenda 21 identified four major thrusts of education to support a sustainable future (UNESCO 2005):

- Improving access to quality basic education: The first priority of ESD is improving the access to and quality of basic education since the content and years of basic education differ greatly around the world. This recognition of the need for quality basic education sets ESD apart from other educational efforts such as environmental education or population education (McKeown et al. 2002). Retention is another area that is a priority. In this process, basic education must be reoriented to address sustainability and expanded to include critical thinking skills, skills to organize and interpret data and

information, and skills to formulate questions. Skill development to analyze local issues and lifestyle choices that do not erode the natural resource base or impinge on the social equity and justice of their neighbors should also be part of basic education. Such quality basic education alone can bring about sustainable societies.
- Reorienting existing education programs: Creating sustainable societies is at the heart of sustainable development. This can only be achieved by reorienting the content and relevance of education. ESD identifies questioning, rethinking, and revising education from preschool through university to include more principles, knowledge, skills, perspectives, and values related to sustainability in each of the three realms: environment, society, and economy. It envisages achieving this through a holistic and interdisciplinary context, engaging society at large, but carried out by individual nations in a locally relevant and culturally appropriate manner.
- Developing public understanding and awareness of sustainability: To make progress toward more sustainable societies requires a population that is aware of the goals of sustainability and has the knowledge and the skills to contribute toward those goals. A knowledgeable citizenry supports a more sustainable society in several ways—supporting government policy related to resource management and civic conduct, supporting measures related to sustainable development and politicians who introduce and support enlightened legislation, by becoming knowledgeable consumers taking into account environmental responsibility and sustainable business practices, and helping communities and governments enact sustainability measures and move toward more sustainable societies.
- Providing training: All sectors—including business, industry, higher education, governments, NGOs, and community organizations—should be encouraged to train their leaders in sustainability issues such as environmental management, equity policies, etc. and to provide training to their workers in sustainable practices. There needs to be collaboration between those in the formal education and nonformal education sector such as nature centers, NGOs, public health educators, and agricultural extension agents, etc.

The following seven strategies were identified for ESD:

1. Vision building and advocacy
2. Consultation and ownership
3. Partnership and networks
4. Capacity building and training
5. Research and innovation
6. Use of information and communication technology (ICT)
7. Monitoring and evaluation

9.4.3 Dimensions of ESD

Based on its characteristics, thrust areas, and strategies, the focus of the implementation of ESD can be placed under the following four dimensions:

- Learning content: Integrating critical issues such as climate change, biodiversity, disaster risk reduction (DRR), and sustainable consumption and production (SCP), and others into the curriculum.
- Pedagogy and learning environments: Designing teaching and learning in an interactive, learner-centered way that enables exploratory, action-oriented, and transformative learning; rethinking learning environments—physical as well as virtual and online—to inspire learners to act for sustainability.
- Learning outcomes: Stimulating learning and promoting core competencies, such as critical and systemic thinking, collaborative decision-making, and taking responsibility for present and future generations.
- Societal transformation: Empowering learners of any age, in any education setting, to transform themselves and the society they live in.
  - Enabling a transition to greener economies and societies.
    - Equipping learners with skills for 'green jobs.'
    - Motivating people to adopt sustainable lifestyles.
  - Empowering people to be 'global citizens' who engage and assume active roles, both locally and globally, to face and to resolve global challenges and ultimately to become proactive contributors to creating a more just, peaceful, tolerant, inclusive, secure, and sustainable world.

(UNESCO 2014b)

9.5 Decade of Education for Sustainable Development: 2005 to 2014

UNESCO was identified as the lead UN agency for DESD. The overall goal of the DESD is to integrate the principles, values, and practices of sustainable development into all aspects of education and learning (UNESCO 2005). Some of its key goals are provided in Table 9.1.

9.5.1 Relationship of DESD with Other International Initiatives

As discussed earlier under the sub-heading Genesis, DESD shares several concerns with other international initiatives such as MDGs, EFA, and UNLD. The common objectives shared by these are as follows:

- A concern to improve the quality of life: All of them aim to reduce poverty and improve health;

TABLE 9.1 Key Goals of the DESD

Promoting ESD	ESD is about engaging and empowering people in sustainable development. The former seeks people's commitment to sustainable development; the latter gives people the power to make decisions and bring changes.
Introducing lifelong learning perspectives	All possible spaces of learning—formal, nonformal, and informal—with a lifelong learning perspective should be considered.
Promoting quality education and learning	Quality education and learning are a requirement in our current system. Teacher training and educators' retraining are important components.
Seeking new governmental structures and support	Governments are playing a very important role in the DESD's success. At governmental level, policies, strategies, and action plans in ESD need to be established. The first half of the DESD focuses on this particular goal.
Engaging stakeholders (including those not already involved)	The DESD should engage not only the stakeholders who are currently working toward ESD objectives but also those stakeholders who are less aware about sustainable development issues.

Source: Mulà and Tilbury (2009).

- The promotion of human rights: All of them see education as a right, and they aim to increase the equality of women and men, as well as advance the human rights of all, particularly minorities and other marginalized communities;
- A commitment to education: All believe that education is a key to development, as a way of enabling people to fulfill their potential and take increasing control over decisions that affect them. The MDGs and DESD focus on broader purposes beyond education, whereas the purposes of EFA and UNLD are about making sure that basic education, and literacy within that, is available to all;
- Primary education: All four recognize that primary education plays an important foundational role in development;
- The participation of everyone in education and development: All of the initiatives call for not only governmental engagement but also the active involvement of organizations, civil society, the private sector, communities, and individuals

(UNESCO 2007)

Hence, the International Implementation Scheme for UNDESD framed by UNESCO reflects the initiatives to promote education, not only those concerning ESD but all other global initiatives as well (UNESCO 2014a).

While the DESD shares common ground with other international initiatives, it differs from them by the very virtue of its mission in that while other initiatives ensure the right to EFA and address the needs of all learners, and especially those who are excluded from access to quality basic education, the DESD stresses the need and relevance of ESD for all, within and beyond the formal sphere of education. Besides, the outreach of the DESD is broader than other initiatives as it not only tackles education but also addresses the way humans live, and their attitudes and values that impact the sustainability of not just the societies but also the planet (UNESCO 2007).

9.5.2 Impact of DESD

The 2014 Global Monitoring and Evaluation Report, Shaping the Future We Want–UNDESD (2005–2014) brought out the outcomes of ten years of work around the world to advance education as a critical tool for moving societies toward sustainability. It also provides insights on the impact of the call for a UNDESD on all levels and areas of education, and it charts the major lessons that will inform future work. It lays down ten key findings and trends that have emerged which will guide ESD into the future (see Table 9.2).

At the end of the DESD, the report said, a solid foundation has been laid for ESD being achieved by raising awareness, influencing policies, and generating significant numbers of good practice projects in all areas and levels of education and learning. However, several challenges have also been identified in the report. For example:

TABLE 9.2 Ten Key Findings of 2014 Global Monitoring and Evaluation Report

ESD, an enabler for sustainable development	ESD is galvanizing pedagogical innovation
1. Education systems are addressing sustainability issues	6. Whole-institution approaches help practice ESD
2. Sustainable development agendas and education agendas are converging	7. ESD facilitates interactive, learner-driven pedagogies
Importance of stakeholder engagement for ESD	ESD has spread across all levels and areas of education
3. Political leadership has proven instrumental	8. ESD is being integrated into formal education
4. Multi-stakeholder partnerships are particularly effective	9. Nonformal and informal ESD is increasing
5. Local commitments are growing	10. Technical and vocational education and training advances sustainable development

Source: UNESCO (2014a).

1. While much has been done to advance the ethos and values of ESD, a full integration of ESD into education systems has yet to take place in most countries.
2. It mentions the need for further alignment of education and sustainable development sectors.
3. Major work remains to ensure full policy coherence between the education sector and the sustainable development sector.
4. ESD is not integrated coherently across relevant sectorial or sub-sectorial policies.
5. ESD implementation requires enhanced capacities among policy makers, curriculum developers, school leaders, assessment experts, and, most importantly, teachers.

(UNESCO 2014a)

9.6 Global Action Program (GAP)

The GAP on ESD, as a follow-up to the United Nations DESD after 2014, was developed by UNESCO, and it was endorsed by the UNESCO General Conference in 2013. GAP was launched at the World Conference on Education for Sustainable Development in Aichi-Nagoya, Japan, in November 2014 and adopted by the member states as part of the Aichi-Nagoya Declaration on Education for Sustainable Development.[2] Included in the Declaration was to "Reflect and strengthen ESD in the post-2015 agenda and its follow-up processes, ensuring, first, that ESD is maintained as a target in the education goal and also integrated in SDGs as a cross-cutting theme…" This, to some extent, has been taken care of with the inclusion of ESD as part of Target 4.7 under Sustainable Development Goal (SDG) 4: Quality education, which requires that

> By 2030, ensure that all learners acquire the knowledge and skills needed to promote sustainable development, including, among others, through education for sustainable development and sustainable lifestyles, human rights, gender equality, promotion of a culture of peace and non-violence, global citizenship and appreciation of cultural diversity and of culture's contribution to sustainable development

Milestones leading to ESD, and thence to DESD, and thereafter is provided in Table 9.3.

9.6.1 Goals and Objectives

The GAP contributes to achieving the vision put forward by the Decade of ESD: "a world where everybody has the opportunity to benefit from education and learn the values, behavior and lifestyles required for a sustainable future

TABLE 9.3 Milestones in ESD

Year	Event
1968	UNESCO Conference on Biodiversity UNESCO organized the first intergovernmental conference to reconcile environment and development. It led to UNESCO's Man and the Biosphere (MAB) program. It was a significant step in the process that led to the United Nations Conference on the Human Environment. As a follow-up of this conference, the UNEP was established.
1972	United Nations Conference on the Human Environment held in Stockholm, Sweden This led to the establishing of many environmental protection agencies and the UNEP besides many environmental ministries and NGOs working to conserve the planet's resources
1987	**'Our Common Future'** (Report of the World Commission on Environment and Development, also known as the Brundtland Report) published. It defined sustainable development as "development that meets the needs of the present without compromising the ability of future generations to meet their own needs."
1992	United Nations Conference on Environment and Development (UNCED)—Rio Earth Summit held in Rio de Janeiro, Brazil Agenda 21 and the Rio Declaration on Environment and Development were adopted by 178 governments. Agenda 21 is a GAP for sustainable development. UNESCO was designated Task Manager of Chapter 36 of Agenda 21 on education, , and public awareness, as well as Chapter 35 on Science for sustainable development.
2002	WSSD (Johannesburg Summit, Rio+10) held in Johannesburg, South Africa Member states and global stakeholders reviewed the outcomes of the 1992 Earth Summit and made recommendations for future actions including recommendations to the UNGA to consider adopting a DESD, starting in 2005.
2002	57th session of UNGA held in New York Adopted resolution 57/254 that declared the period between 2005 and 2014 as the UNDESD and designated UNESCO as lead agency.
2005	UNDESD (2005–2014) Officially launched at UN Headquarters in New York.
2009	UNESCO's mid-DESD World Conference on Education for Sustainable Development held in Bonn, Germany The Bonn Declaration provided the international community with an action plan on ESD and outlined steps for implementing the remainder of the DESD. To guide its work, UNESCO developed a UNESCO Strategy for the Second Half of the UNDESD.
2009	First DESD Global Monitoring and Evaluation Report Completion of the first phase of the DESD monitoring and evaluation process: 2007–2009 provided a review of contexts and structures for ESD.

(*Continued*)

TABLE 9.3 (Continued)

Year	Event
2012	UN Conference on Sustainable Development (Rio+20), Rio de Janeiro, BrazilThe Rio+20 outcome document, *The Future We Want*, contained commitments made to education as important for a green economy, for work and social protection, and for training for sustainability. Member states resolved to 'promote education for sustainable development and to integrate sustainable development more actively into education beyond the DESD.' Tbilisi+35 commemorates 35 years of global educational efforts toward a sustainable world An Intergovernmental Conference (Tbilisi+35) in Tbilisi, Georgia, brought together delegates from all over the world to carry forward the global appeal for environmental education as a means for sustainable development. Second DESD Global Monitoring and Evaluation Report Completion of the second phase of the DESD monitoring and evaluation process: 2009–2012 provided a review of processes and learning for ESD.
2013	37th session, UNESCO General Conference, Paris Adopted 37 C/Resolution 12, which endorsed the GAP on ESD as the follow-up to the DESD.
2014	ESD included as a target in the Muscat Agreement adopted at the Global Education For All Meeting (GEM) and in the proposal for Sustainable Development Goals (SDGs) adopted by the Open Working Group (OWG). UNESCO World Conference on Education for Sustainable Development, Aichi-Nagoya, Japan Learning Today for a Sustainable Future Conference has the following four objectives: (a) celebrating a decade of action; (b) reorienting education to build a better future for all; (c) accelerating action for sustainable development; and (d) setting the agenda for ESD beyond 2014. The Conference marks the end of the DESD, celebrating its achievements and launches the GAP on ESD. Final Global Monitoring and Evaluation Report Completion of the third and final phase of the DESD global monitoring and evaluation process: 2005–2014. This focuses on the impacts and outcomes of the DESD.
2015	All member states of the United Nations in 2015 adopted the 2030 Agenda for Sustainable Development. At the heart of this Agenda, there are 17 SDGs with 169 associated targets which are an urgent call for action by all countries. SDG 4: Quality educationOf the ten targets to be achieved under this SDG, Target 4.7 includes ESD to ensure that all learners acquire the knowledge and skills needed to promote sustainable development by 2030.

and for positive societal transformation." The overarching goal of the GAP is "to generate and scale up action in all levels and areas of education and learning to accelerate progress towards sustainable development." The GAP will deploy a twofold approach to multiply and to scale up ESD action: (a) integrating sustainable development into education and (b) integrating education into sustainable development. Corresponding to this overall approach, the program has the following two objectives:

- To reorient education and learning so that everyone has the opportunity to acquire the knowledge, skills, values, and attitudes that empower them to contribute to sustainable development
- To strengthen education and learning in all agendas, programs, and activities that promote sustainable development

(UNESCO 2014b)

9.6.2 Priority Areas of Global Action Program

To enable strategic focus and foster stakeholder commitment, the GAP has identified five priority action areas to advance the ESD agenda:

1. Advancing policy: Mainstream ESD into both education and sustainable development policies, to create an enabling environment for ESD and to bring about systemic change
2. Transforming learning and training environments: Integrate sustainability principles into education and training settings
3. Building capacities of educators and trainers: Increase the capacities of educators and trainers to more effectively deliver ESD
4. Empowering and mobilizing youth: Multiply ESD actions among youth
5. Accelerating sustainable solutions at local level: At community level, scale up ESD programs and multi-stakeholder ESD networks.

(UNESCO 2014b)

9.7 Types of Sustainability Education

As brilliant as the concept of ESD may sound, it is not without limitations and ambiguities. There exists lack of clarity on whether ESD as a concept or an approach is different from any form or practice of education 'for'/'leading to' sustainable development. If they are different, how does it affect the education process aimed to bring about sustainable development or sustainability. Some aspects of this will be explored in the following discussions.

UNESCO identifies two types of sustainability education. They are:

1. SD-related education ('adjectival' educations), which includes peace education, global education, development education, HIV and AIDS education,

citizenship education, and intercultural education, human rights education, as well as long-existing educations such as environmental education and health education, and so on (Wals 2009, 9, 72). The list of such SD-related education will be numerous and each of such types of SD-related education will invariably contribute to one of the dimensions of SD.
2. Full-fledged ESD which essentially requires the integration of all the dimensions of SD: environmental, social (cultural dimension included), and economic (Wals 2009, 28). UNESCO (2014b) also clearly mentions the integrated, balanced, and holistic approach to environmental, social, and economic pillars of sustainable development in ESD. The key here is 'integration,' and therefore any issue discussed under this will always include the environmental, social, and economic aspects.

However, it is important to note that SD-related education and ESD cannot be totally separated since the broader the interpretation of a particular SD-related education, the more it resembles ESD (Wals 2009, 28).

In this context, it might be appropriate to elaborate on how SD-related education continues to remain as SD-related education and when the same becomes ESD-like. Let us take, for example, health education. As long as the focus of health education is on 'health' by concentrating on topics such as how to eat healthy, how to live healthy, how to take preventive measures from diseases, how to prevent the spread of diseases, first aid, and so on, then such health education is considered SD-related education. To maintain a sustainable society, this aspect definitely counts, but, here, health education is done in isolation. However, when the discussion is broadened to include its environmental dimensions such as pollution of air, water, soil, solid wastes, scarcity of potable water, and economic dimensions related to health—such as inability to procure nutritious food, maintain healthy surroundings (such as inability to afford smokeless *chulha*, i.e., hearth or inability to construct toilet), or avail basic medical facility due to poverty, and even other social issues such as alcoholism leading to health and other problems—then it can be said that it has taken the form of ESD, because now all the dimensions of ESD such as environment, society, and economy are brought in the purview of health education and is done holistically. In such a situation, there will be an integration of all the dimensions, and each will impact the course of action of the other. And finally, what is being seen to be practiced in ESD is an integration of all the three dimensions, often reinforcing the other while also accepting a 'compromised' stand many a time. However, every issue related to SD-related education cannot take the form of ESD. Discrimination based on race or caste or disability, for example, is purely a social issue, and it will be difficult to give it the form of ESD. Another example is of the natural extinction of flora and fauna, many of which occur even before scientists could identify them or even know that they exist (not to be confused with the increased rate of extinction due to exploitation of nature by humans). This phenomenon is purely environmental in nature and hence can only fall in the purview of SD-related education.

An important point to be noted here is that though every SD-related education contributes in some way to ESD, the sum of all SD-related education does not give rise to ESD.

Similarly, every sustainable action with respect to environment, society, or economy contributes in some way to sustainability or sustainable development. However, the sum of all sustainable actions carried out independently of other parts does not give rise to sustainable development of a whole. In sustainability or sustainable development, integration of the three dimensions is essential while addressing issues. To illustrate this view more explicitly, let us consider sustainability or sustainable development as a coat. As mentioned earlier, SD-related actions do contribute in some way in the process of sustainability or SD. However, since the different actions are not correlated or linked with other sustainable development actions, what is obtained is a weird-looking coat which is disproportionate in every respect, as shown in Figure 9.1. For example, environmental education, health education, population education, gender education, and so on, taken up independently in isolation, will give rise to such a situation which is chaotic and shapeless. However, in Figure 9.2 all the pieces have been arranged in proportion to the other parts, thus giving a perfect shape to the coat. This represents a situation wherein during the process of taking up a specific SD-related education, all dimensions of sustainability are addressed holistically. That means, it has taken the form of ESD. However, all the types of SD-related education are not necessarily linked directly with each other as arranged in the figure, and their placement in the coat does not indicate their functional proximity in reality. Nor does the shape and size of each patch which indicates a specific SD-related education in the figure represent the proportion of its relative role in sustainability. The figure has been used only for the purpose of illustrating the concept so as to differentiate between SD-related educations and ESD.

In the Figures 9.1 and 9.2, only some SD-related education has been mentioned. Besides these, there are many other forms of SD-related education. Interestingly, UNESCO also included environmental education, which is considered to be the base for ESD, under the SD-related education. However, at the same time, it also acceded that the relationship of ESD with environmental education is more striking compared to other SD-related education signifying the conceptual proximity of the two. This is because the founding documents of both environmental education and ESD are practically the same. The Tbilisi Declaration was the founding document for environmental education while for ESD it was Chapter 36 of Agenda 21—education, public awareness, and training—for which the Tbilisi Declaration provided the fundamental principles for the proposals in the Chapter 36 document. Therefore, labeling environmental education as SD-related education is not as much to do with the nature of

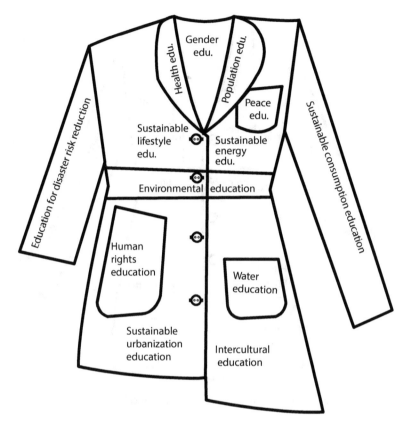

FIGURE 9.1   SD-Related Educations Done in Isolation.

environmental education but more so to fortify the identity, existence, and relevance of ESD.

Based on the above discussion, it will be interesting to figure out what kind of education is being imparted in India in reality: Is it Environmental education, ESD or Sustainable Development-related Education?

9.8 Is Environmental Education Very Different from ESD?

The question that has been asked ever since ESD was implemented is, "Is EE very different from ESD?" In the earlier discussion, the view of UNESCO was presented wherein it was projected that environmental education and ESD are sufficiently distinct. Yet the answer seems to be subjective as the ensuing discussion will reveal. Besides, there also appear to be a total disconnect in the interpretation of environmental education based on its origin and nature and when interpreted based on how it is practiced. It is found that what environmental education actually is, is totally different from how it is practiced, the

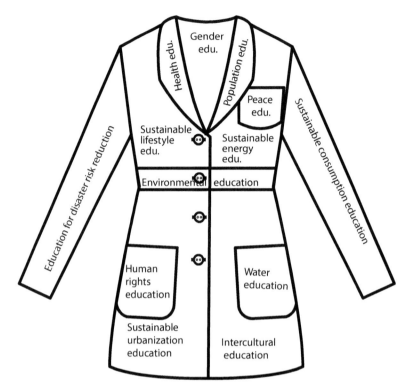

FIGURE 9.2 SD-Related Educations Taking the Form of ESD.

reasons for which will also be discussed in this section. Whatever may be the reason, such indistinctiveness has surely paved the way for ESD. Such lack of clarity or difference in interpretation of terms is not restricted to environmental education. Similar debates were observed around ESD in the initial years of its implementation and eventually agreed that the differences were necessary to make it locally relevant and culturally appropriate (Wals 2009, 25–26).

Clearly, there are differing views about environmental education and ESD. Some argue that environmental education has in fact become ESD (Arlemalm-Hagser and Sandberg, 2011 and Eilam and Trop, 2010 cited in Kopnina 2012).

There are also those who maintain that ESD is a dominant perspective of environmental education, while, according to supporters of the concept of sustainable development, environmental education is just one of the tools for sustainable development (Sauvé, 2005). Gough (2006), while comparing the objectives of the Belgrade Charter of 1975 and the UNDESD, summarizes that both environmental education and ESD have many elements in common—both are concerned with reforming educational processes and with balancing quality of human life, environmental protection, and economic growth—and hence, the path for both are essentially same.

With the same document (i.e., the Tbilisi Declaration) guiding both environmental education and ESD, it is obvious that the two will be similar in principle. As such, it is no surprise that in many countries, including India and the United States, environmental education is still firmly established, especially in formal education systems. However, ESD is slowly catching up in such countries, and other countries have gone ahead with various variants of sustainability education such as education for sustainability, sustainability education, and ESD. This parallel existence and development of environmental education and ESD has given rise to questions about the relationship between the two and the call for distinctions by some or for convergence by others. Toward this confusion, pro-ESD proponents claim that ESD is intended to build on the lessons of environmental education and not to simply perpetuate environmental education under another name. They maintain that SD-related educations, including environmental education, continue to contribute to ESD in terms of content and pedagogy.

UNESCO (2005, 26) mentions of programs initiated under the UNEP, of which environmental education was a major initiative, as: "while some attention was attached to the social and economic issues inherent in these environmental issues the focus was largely on addressing the ecological impact of ever increasing unrestricted development." This view is also shared by many others. For example, McKeown et al. (2002) argue that equal attention is not focused on the social and economic strands in environmental education. These observations, however, did not imply that the concept of environmental education itself was flawed or lacking holistic approach. All that they indicate is that there were drawbacks in the implementation. As a matter of fact, it would be nonsensical for one to contest that environmental education was incomplete since all the guiding documents of environmental education clearly talk about its holistic and interdisciplinary nature. Recall the first guiding principle of environmental education programs of the Belgrade Charter, which states, "Environmental education should consider the environment in its totality—natural and man-made, ecological, political, economic, technological, social, legislative, cultural and esthetic" (UNESCO–UNEP 1976). Similarly, the Tbilisi Declaration characterizes environmental education as "interdisciplinary and holistic in nature and application" with one of its goals being "to foster clear awareness of, and concern about, economic, social, political and ecological interdependence in urban and rural areas." Further, the guiding principle of the Tbilisi Declaration states that "EE should consider the environment in its totality—natural and built, technological and social (economic, political, cultural-historical, moral, esthetic)" (UNESCO–UNEP 1978). The Belgrade Charter or the Tbilisi Declaration does not signal even a slightest indication that social and economic dimensions should be kept secondary or given lesser importance. The fact that environmental education presents a holistic view is reiterated by many professionals in the field such as Jenkins (1994 cited in

Gough 2008), who argues that "environmental education exposes with particular clarity the complex interactions among social, economic, personal and other value positions associated with almost any environmental issue." In the light of these discussions and arguments, it may be agreed that environmental education is indeed holistic in approach, and if it is felt that equal attention is not focused on the social and economic aspects, then it has to do with flaws in implementation. This can be supplemented by studies undertaken by many researchers. For example, Braus and Wood (1993) observed that educators continue to link environmental education exclusively with science education in spite of the fact that environmental education is interdisciplinary in nature and that it requires the understanding of economics, math, geography, ethics, politics, and other subjects. As a result of this, the focus turns out to be on providing scientific content knowledge, leaving little space for discussion on social and economic issues.

Therefore, the issue with environmental education is to be attributed to implementation. Environmental education 'done right' serves the objectives of ESD equally well. However, instead of holistically approaching environmental education, practitioners have been implementing environmental education according to their convenience. The reasons for such undesirable deviation from what is expected could be many—lack of government support, method of dealing with environmental issues were more confrontational, and skills were provided accordingly—and hence environmental education apparently became less interdisciplinary; skills to communicate with officials, understand environmental issues, persuade, lobby, and boycott became part of the curriculum; challenging and controversial issues which are at the core of environmental education were dropped; and, most importantly, environmental education became more focused on teaching science-based information about ecosystems and conservation (Monroe 2012). An altogether different meaning of environmental education was, therefore, presented to the world. These ultimately resulted in the need to explore for a more encompassing, broader, and more-inclusive alternative which was eventually discovered in the concept of ESD. With the 'three pillars—society, environment and economy'—clearly defined in ESD, it is envisaged that practitioners will naturally consider all the 'pillars' when dealing with any issue or topic. But this will be easier said than done. Many factors will come into play, such as level of training of the practitioners, motivation factors, monitoring factors, political pressure, and so on. Having seen what environmental education went through during the past more than three decades, it is now feared that ESD could also see the same fate unless special measures are kept in place.

In the light of the earlier discussions, the practical difference between environmental education and ESD, if they are indeed different or considered to be different, might be summed up in the following words: In environmental education, the 'environment' component is still not clearly defined, while in ESD 'environment,' as one of its pillars, is explicitly about the biophysical environment. Further, in environmental education issue identification invariably begins with biophysical problems. It then considers the holistic approach to resolve the issue. For example, degradation of soil due to use of chemical fertilizers is a biophysical issue for which productivity of the farmland, and poverty of the farmers and their social life also form important concerns which are taken into account while resolving it. With ESD, issue identification has no boundary. It may begin with biophysical environmental problem, social problem, or economic problem but the holistic approach to resolve the issue remains the same as in environmental education. Hence, productivity of the farm due to use of fertilizers (economic in nature), poverty of farmers and their social life (social in nature), or degradation of soil due to use of chemical fertilizers (environmental or biophysical in nature) can all be associated with ESD. However, the above view might be contested by many environmental educators who also consider social problems for issue identification as mentioned in Chapter 2 (Glasser et al. 1972; Stapp and Cox 1974). If this view is accepted, then there will be practically no difference between environmental education and ESD.

9.9 Do Away with Environmental Education?

Another matter of debate arises with the wide endorsement of ESD. Where does environmental education stand in the context of ESD? Does focusing on full-fledged ESD mean doing away with SD-related education including environmental education? Like other SD-related educations, the fate of environmental education will be settled with this. A plausible answer to this could be, rather than doing away, synergies need to be created between ESD and other SD-related educations, which should mutually support rather than compete with each other. With the root of ESD established in EE (Wals 2009), environmental education might well be retained viewing it "as indispensable to achieving the broader goals of ESD" (Jenkins and Jenkins 2005), as 'environment' represents one of the three 'pillars of sustainable development' (UNESCO 2006, 14) or as one of the three spheres of sustainability (UNESCO 2005, 28). Besides, it has also been established that EE and ESD are complementary to each other (McKeown and Hopkins 2003; Monroe 2012).

Although it is understood that ESD would address both the needs of the society and the environment, environmental education need not be discontinued. The reason is, environmental education, whether practiced with a focus on biophysical environment or with equal emphasis on the biophysical, social, or economic aspects, it would contribute in the move toward sustainable development. Further, the Brundtland Commission Report—Our Common Future—based on which the whole concept of sustainable development became popular, itself encourages the implementation of environmental education, as it says in Chapter 4 of the Report:

> Environmental education should be included in and should run throughout the other disciplines of the formal education curriculum at all levels—to foster a sense of responsibility for the state of the environment and to teach students how to monitor, protect, and improve it.[3]

Besides, environmental education continues to receive enormous attention even after the concept of sustainable development or ESD became established globally. For example, the role of environmental ESD was widely recognized at the WSSD (Boojh 2003). Similarly other conferences on environmental education remain to be conducted with the same vigor and purpose, though sustainable development became an unavoidable suffix in all such endeavors. Mention may be made of the Fourth International Conference on Environmental Education Toward a Sustainable Future, which was held in Ahmedabad, India, which looked into the current status of environmental education and its development to meet the challenges of sustainability and the objectives of the DESD and an Intergovernmental Conference (Tbilisi+35), which commemorates 35 years of global educational efforts toward a sustainable world was held in 2012 during which the delegates carried forward the global appeal for environmental education as a means for sustainable development (UNESCO 2014a).

From the above discussions, it can be concluded that whether only ESD or both ESD and environmental education are practiced and professed is not the issue. As Monroe (2012) writes:

> We need quality education that prepares people to understand multiple views; to listen and communicate with others; to vision and evaluate options; to collect, synthesise and understand data; to learn how others have balanced contentious elements of an issue; and to be able to adopt actions. Both environmental education and ESD have the potential to provide exactly that.

9.10 Ramifications of Implementation of ESD

Professionals have been raising concerns about the possible fallout of implementing ESD if practitioners are not cautious. This is because, nature, in the notion of sustainable development, is conceived as a resource and reflects anthropomorphic and even economic motives (Bonnett 2004a, 2004b; Sauve 1999 cited in Hadzigeorgiou and Skoumios 2013). The ramifications of implementation of ESD could be many, a few of which are discussed here.

(i) ESD is more issue-based, or challenge-based, or problem-based, while environmental education is an approach to learning environmental concepts and is not limited to issues and problems. This whole approach to learning may entirely be neglected with the implementation of ESD. As a result, deeper understanding of environmental concepts may not occur in schools. Practitioners are most likely to superficially deal with the environment components in ESD.

(ii) Another concern of implementation of ESD is that the pluralistic perspectives of ESD might not be truly democratic as the discourse on sustainable development is dominated by the perspectives of the political and corporate elites. Considering the power of political or corporate elites and the glaring influence of industrial capitalism in shaping the discourse on development, with its clear emphasis on human welfare, the chances for the students to develop ecocentric values is far from certain. But what is most likely is that the environment could be considered nothing more than a resource to be exploited in the name of development. Keeping in view the influence of the corporatists, it is feared that such perspectives may find way in the school in the form of hidden curriculum and further encourage development and discourage ecocentrism.

(iii) The pluralistic perspective of ESD will not be able to address the real-world problems arising as a result of continuing exploitation of the environment that need urgent attention (Bonnett 2013 and Fien 2000 cited in Kopnina 2014).

(iv) Professionals and researchers have voiced their concerns on the increased focus on social issues as a result of implementation of ESD. This is because in such issues which involve both the environment and the society, human's natural tendency would be to first attempt to alleviate the concern of the society. Invariably such decisions will always be biased and inclined toward the society. As a result, environmental concerns would become secondary.

In the situation the world is in today, any education toward sustainability is welcome, and ESD is definitely one such approach that will cater toward this end. But, it will also be worthwhile to specially ponder on the serious damage it has done to its environment and to look for ways for its restoration as well as for prevention of further damage. In this context, apprehensions have been raised especially on the nature of ESD and its pluralistic views. There are concerns that suggest that ESD presents a radical change of focus from prioritizing environmental protection which is the essence of environmental education and gravitate toward mostly social issues, which may or may not be related to environment. As Kopnina (2012) in ESD: the turn away from 'environment' in environmental education argues:

> Recent ESD debate does not fully realize the problematic nature of economic development for the ecological health of the biosphere. Pluralistic perspectives on ESD can lead practitioners into an essentially anthropocentric

paradigm which can be counter-productive to the effort of fostering environmentally concerned citizenry.

There is also a concern that the pluralistic anthropocentric orientation in ESD will weaken human's moral obligation toward nonhuman species. In line with this view, Kopnina (2014) supports education for deep ecology so that the intrinsic value of nonhuman species is recognized and argues that ecocentric educators need to advocate by being the 'voice' of these nonhuman species so that they are protected. Interestingly, the Hon'ble Supreme Court of India, in its judgment dated April 15, 2013, in Centre for Environment Law, WWF-I Vs. Union of India and Others (I.A. No. 100 in Writ Petition (Civil) No. 337 of 1995 (I.A. No. 3452 in WP(C) No. 202 of 1995), had also reiterated that sustainable development is anthropocentric with little concern for the rights of other species on earth and hence suggested a move toward ecocentrism which is nature-centered, where humans are part of nature and nonhumans have intrinsic value.

This is especially true in terms of environmental justice. Environmental justice refers to equitable distribution of environmental goods such as natural resources, clean air, water, and so on, among human populations as well as between species. This can be broadly grouped into anthropocentric environmental justice and ecological justice. The issue here is that, in both the cases, it is human beings who have to stand up to raise concerns of both human and non-human species. While anthropocentric environmental justice has its own issues (such as an economically weaker section of the society having to bear the adverse impacts of environmental issues, for example industrial waste, while not receiving proportionate good out of it), when it comes to priority between anthropocentric environmental justice and ecological justice, it is most likely that the former will prevail. This is supported by a study in which participants saw current developments as essential in alleviating poverty and improving standards of living, and felt that if given a choice, they would put development ahead of environmental concerns (Almeida and Cutter-Mackenz 2011) In the process of unprecedented development and growth of population with increasing demand for resources, it is but expected that ecological justice will not find enough space and place as part of human priorities. That is, the ecocentric perspectives will not be addressed adequately, if not neglected entirely. This will lead to a situation which will do more harm to the already deteriorating environment which will, in turn, ultimately impact human life.

This suggests that conscious and deliberate efforts need to be taken while implementing ESD so that ecological justice is given equal priority. A huge responsibility rests on the practitioners and educators so that ESD is implemented fairly and justly without any biases. It must be remembered that human life can only be sustained when the ecosystem is sustained and not the other way round. The ecosystem can exist sans humankind!

9.11 Conclusion

The concept of ESD is no more new to the world. However, when it comes to its implementation, there still appears to be lack of clarity. ESD covers such a vast area that it might appear that there would be no issue with implementation. In fact, hardly any topic under the sun can be beyond the purview of ESD. But this feature itself seems to have become a hindrance to its implementation. The idea that education should be aimed at bringing about sustainable development is yet to be understood by practitioners in relation to their curriculum; how they should do it is a whole different issue to be addressed. While ESD itself is a unique approach to education, there are also other forms of sustainable development-related education. These two broad categories of education focused at bringing about sustainable development—ESD- and SD-related education—will have to be clearly interpreted for the sake of practitioners.

While proponents of ESD might claim that environmental education is ecocentric and that social and economic concerns are not taken care of through environmental education, there are valid concerns that ESD could sideline or downplay the concerns related to the biophysical environment. Many are of the opinion that ESD is anthropocentric and that ecological justice may not be achieved with the implementation of ESD. If this is true, the dangers to human life and survival of humankind will be at a greater risk than ever, the inconvenient truth which humans fail to seriously consider.

One might sometimes wonder if it has been really worth debating whether environmental education is better or ESD should be the way. Many, probably, might have also wasted years in their effort to transit from environmental education to the fancier term ESD, and many will still struggle in their attempt to transition, not doing any good to either in the process.

9.12 Summary

- ESD came about to cater to the two broad areas of interest of the United Nations: Education and Sustainable Development.
- ESD is envisaged to contribute toward other initiatives of the United Nations such as the EFA, the MDGs, and the UN Decade of Literacy.
- To further the implementation of ESD, 2005–2014 was declared by the UN as the DESD.
- The GAP was initiated to take forward the vision of DESD. GAP is envisaged to generate and scale up action in all levels and areas of education and learning to accelerate progress toward sustainable development.
- Sustainability education is not limited to ESD but is also done through different forms of education, which are collectively called SD-related education.

- ESD and environmental education are fundamentally similar as both environmental education and ESD share the same footing in the document Tbilisi Declaration of 1977. And that both environmental education and ESD will lead to the same result that we strive for—sustainable future.
- Due to inconsistencies in the implementation, environmental education is thought to be more ecocentric, giving little importance to social and economic issues, and hence the need for a more encompassing concept was felt which ESD was believed to provide.
- Many are of the opinion that ESD is anthropocentric and that ecological justice may not be addressed with the implementation of ESD.

Notes

1 https://www.un.org/millenniumgoals/education.shtml#:~:text=Ensurethat,by2015,children,agewereoutofschool. (Accessed on September 21, 2023).
2 https://sustainabledevelopment.un.org/content/documents/5859Aichi-Nagoya_Declaration_EN.pdf (Accessed on September 2, 2023).
3 https://sustainabledevelopment.un.org/content/documents/5987our-common-future.pdf (Accessed on September 2, 2023).

References

Almeida, Sylvia, and Amy Cutter-Mackenzie. 2011. "The Historical, Present and Future Ness of Environmental Education in India." *Australian Journal of Environmental Education* 27 (1): 122–133. DOI: 10.1017/S0814062600000124

Boojh, Ram. 2003. "Is a Sustainable World Possible?—The WSSD: An NGO Report." *Connect, UNESCO International Science, Technology & Environmental Education Newsletter* XXVIII (1–2): 7–9.

Braus, J.A., and D. Wood. 1993. *Environmental Education in the Schools: Creating a Programme That Works!* Manual M0044. Washington, DC: Peace Corps Information Collection and Exchange.

Glasser, R., B. William Stapp, and J. James Swan. 1972. *Urban Environmental Education—Demonstration. Final Report.* Michigan University, School of Natural Resources, Ann Arbor, Michigan.

Gough, Annette. 2006. "A Long, Winding (and Rocky) Road to Environmental Education for Sustainability in 2006." *Australian Journal of Environmental Education* 22 (1): 71–76.

———. 2008. "Towards More Effective Learning for Sustainability: Reconceptualising Science Education." *Transnational Curriculum Inquiry* 5 (1): 32–50.

Hadzigeorgiou, Y., and M. Skoumios. 2013. "The Development of Environmental Awareness Through School Science: Problems and Possibilities." *International Journal of Environmental & Science Education* 8: 405–426.

Jenkins, Edgar. 1994. "Public understanding of science and science education for action." *Journal of Curriculum Studies*, 26(6): 601–611.

Jenkins, K.A., and B.A. Jenkins. 2005. "Education for sustainable development and the question of balance: Lesson from the Pacific." *Current Issues in Comparative Education* 7 (2): 114–129. Available at: https://files.eric.ed.gov/fulltext/EJ853853.pdf (Accessed on September 27, 2023).

Kopnina, H. 2012. "Education for Sustainable Development (ESD): the Turn Away from 'Environment' in Environmental Education?" *Environmental Education Research* 18 (5): 699–717.

———. 2014. "Future Scenarios and Environmental Education." *The Journal of Environmental Education* 45 (4): 217–231.

McKeown, R., and C.A. Hopkins. 2003. "EE ≠ ESD: Diffusing the Worry." *Environmental Education Research* 9 (1): 117–128.

McKeown, R., C.A. Hopkins, R. Rizzi, and M. Chrystalbridge. 2002. *Education for Sustainable Development Toolkit*. Knoxville, TN: University of Tennessee. Available at: http://www.esdtoolkit.org/esd_toolkit_v2.pdf (Accessed on September 27, 2023).

Monroe, M.C. 2012. "The Co-evolution of ESD and EE." *Journal of Education for Sustainable Development* 6 (1): 43–47. https://doi.org/10.1177/097340821100600110

Mulà, Ingrid, and Daniella Tilbury. 2009. "A United Nations Decade of Education for Sustainable Development (2005–2014)—What Difference will it Make?" *Journal of Education for Sustainable Development* 3 (1): 87–97.

Pezzey, John. 1992. *Sustainable Development Concepts–An Economic Analysis*. World Bank Environment Paper No. 2. Appendix 1. Washington, DC.

Pigozzi, M.J. 2003. "UNESCO and the International Decade of Education for Sustainable Development (2005- 2015)." *Connect, UNESCO International Science, Technology & Environmental Education Newsletter* XXVIII (1–2): 1–7.

Sauvé, Lucie. 2005. "Currents in Environmental Education: Mapping a Complex and Evolving Pedagogical Field." *Canadian Journal of Environmental Education* 10 (Spring): 11–37. Available at: http://cjee.lakeheadu. ca/index.php/cjee/article/view/175/9 (Accessed on September 28, 2014).

Stapp, William B., and Dorothy A. Cox. 1974. *Environmental Education Activities Manual, Book 3: Middle Elementary Activities*. Dexter, MI: Thomson–Shore. Available at: https://files.eric.ed.gov/fulltext/ED119946.pdf (Accessed on September 26, 2023).

Tortajada, Cecilia. 2005. "Sustainable Development (SD): A Critical Assessment of Past and Present Views." In *Appraising Sustainable Development—Water Management and Environmental Challenges*, edited by Asit K. Biswas and Cecilia Tortajada, 1–17. New Delhi: Oxford University Press.

UN, United Nations. 1987. *Report of the World Commission on Environment and Development: Our Common Future*. New York: UN.

———. 1992. *Agenda 21: Programme of Action for Sustainable Development Earth Summit*. United Nations Conference on Environment and Development (UNCED), Rio de Janeiro, 3–14 June 1992. New York: UN.

UNESCO, United Nations Educational, Scientific and Cultural Organization. 2000. *The Dakar Framework for Action Education for All: Meeting our Collective Commitments*. Paris: UNESCO.

———. 2002. *Education for Sustainability—From Rio to Johannesburg: Lessons Learnt from a Decade of Commitment*. Paris: UNESCO.

———. 2005. *UNDESD International Implementation Scheme*. Paris: UNESCO.

———. 2006. *Framework for the UNDESD International Implementation Scheme*. Paris: UNESCO.

———. 2007. *The UN Decade of Education for Sustainable Development (DESD 2005–2014)—The First Two Years*. Paris: UNESCO.

———. 2014a. *Shaping the Future We Want – UN Decade of Education for Sustainable Development (2005–2014) Final Report*. Paris: UNESCO.

———. 2014b. *Roadmap for Implementing the Global Action Programme on Education for Sustainable Development*. Paris: UNESCO.

UNESCO-UNEP, United Nations Educational, Scientific and Cultural Organization-United Nations Environment Programme. 1976. "The Belgrade Charter." *Connect, UNESCO-UNEP Environmental Education Newsletter* I (1): 1–2.

———. 1978. "The Tbilisi Declaration." *Connect, UNESCO-UNEP Environmental Education Newsletter* III (1): 1–8.

Wals, Arjen. 2009. *Learning for a Sustainable World: Review of Contexts and Structures for Education for Sustainable Development*. United Nations Decade of Education for Sustainable Development (DESD, 2005-2014), Paris: UNESCO.

10
CLIMATE CHANGE EDUCATION

10.1 Chapter Overview

The unprecedented impacts of climate change have forced the world to come together to address this global challenge. Although climate change education is part and parcel of environmental education, keeping in view the urgency of the problem, this chapter on climate change education has been especially included so that the issue can be presented systematically in the curriculum in addition to other environmental issues. The chapter presents a broad picture of climate change education globally with special emphasis on India, keeping in view the new National Education Policy 2020 (NEP 2020) and the new curriculum frameworks that have been prepared in the light of NEP 2020. This is especially important since whatever is implemented based on these documents will shape what students learn about climate change for at least a decade or two to come. The chapter discusses the importance of climate change education and brings out the need for its systematic inclusion in the curriculum of school and teacher preparation programs. It suggests ideas for curriculum developers about the various aspects that need to be addressed and provides some strategies for its implementation in the school and teacher education programs.

10.2 Introduction

Today the world is convinced that climate change is a threat to human well-being and planetary health (IPCC 2023). However, one of the earliest warnings about global warming can be traced back to 1912 in *Popular Mechanics*

Magazine, March 1912 issue, which shows a photograph of a coal plant with the caption:

> The furnaces of the world are now burning about 2,000,000,000 tons of coal a year. When this is burned, uniting with oxygen, it adds about 7,000,000,000 tons of carbon dioxide to the atmosphere yearly. This tends to make the air a more effective blanket for the earth and raise its temperature. The effect may be considerable in a few centuries.
>
> *(Molena 1912, 41)*

Tucker and Sherwood (2019, 6–7) presented the history of the study of greenhouse effect and climate change wherein they mentioned that

> the earliest recorded thoughts about greenhouse effect go back to the 1820s in France when Jean Baptiste Joseph Fourier (1768–1830) calculated that an object the size of the Earth should not be as warm as it was, given its distance from the Sun. He reasoned that something else must be affecting our planet's temperature. He theorized that the light coming from the Sun was able to pass through our atmosphere, but radiant heat coming from Sun-warmed surfaces must somehow be trapped.

It is now universally known that it is the greenhouse gases that 'trap' the reradiated heat from the surface of the earth. They went on to mention the evidence observed by John Tyndall (1820–1893) during the 1860s that northern Europe was once covered by ice sheet and his experiments with heat-trapping gases like water vapor and carbon dioxide. Tucker and Sherwood (2019, 7) then referenced the work of a Swedish scientist Svante Arrhenius (1859–1927), who concluded in 1896 that if atmospheric CO_2 levels doubled to 560 ppm (from preindustrial levels of 280), then surface temperature levels would rise several degrees. Arrhenius and Arvid Högbom (1857–1940) were the first to suggest that the burning of fossil fuels for heat could add enough CO_2 to the atmosphere to make a difference, although "they didn't have a concept of how this increased heat could affect the overall climate of the planet—only how it might melt glaciers" (Tucker and Sherwood 2019, 7–8). Later with the advancements of knowledge about carbon and the role of CO_2, in the mid-1950s, researcher Charles David Keeling (1928–2005) started measuring more accurately the amount of CO_2 in the atmosphere by positioning sensors at the 13,600-foot-high Mauna Loa Observatory in Hawaii, the data obtained being used extensively by scientists. Tucker and Sherwood (2019, 8) also touched upon in their book a brief background about the beginning of the usage of the terms such as 'global warming' and 'climate change.'

Most of us are now aware of the impacts of climate change such as increasing average global surface temperature, extreme weather events in the form of more intense rainfall, cyclone, drought, melting of glacier, loss of biodiversity, increase in the duration of heat wave, etc. The challenge posed by climate change is enormous. Hence, there is a global attempt to specifically address climate change and not consider it as just-another-environment-issue. Similarly in the education sector, special emphasis is being given and hence climate change education is introduced so that its importance is specifically highlighted while environmental education caters to all environmental issues in general.

In Chapter 1, the global initiatives to tackle climate change such as the setting up of Intergovernmental Panel on Climate Change (IPCC) and their role or that of the Kyoto Protocol or the Paris Agreement have been discussed. However, in spite of all the initiatives taken so far, there is no respite from climate change as is indicated in the latest IPCC Sixth Assessment Report (AR6), which came out in 2023 (IPCC 2023). The Synthesis Report (SYR) of AR6 summarizes the state of knowledge of climate change, its widespread impacts and risks, and climate change mitigation and adaptation. This report recognizes the interdependence of climate, ecosystems and biodiversity, and human societies; the value of diverse forms of knowledge; and the close linkages between climate change adaptation, mitigation, ecosystem health, human wellbeing, and sustainable development, and reflects the increasing diversity of actors involved in climate action. It clearly points out the impact of human activities, principally through emissions of greenhouse gases, causing the global surface temperature to reach 1.1°C above 1,850–1,900 in 2011–2020. The extensive rapid changes in the atmosphere, ocean, cryosphere, and biosphere due to human-caused climate change are already affecting many weather and climate extremes in every region across the globe. This has led to widespread adverse impacts and related losses and damages to nature and people. With the present nationally determined contributions (NDCs) announced in October 2021, AR6 warns that warming will exceed 1.5°C during the 21st century and that it will be harder to limit the warming to below 2°C. It also warns that every increment of global warming will intensify multiple and concurrent hazards—which means regional changes in mean climate and extremes will become more widespread and pronounced. This suggests that the difference in terms of resolution and impacts will be drastic between 1.5°C and 2°C increase. Although some future changes are unavoidable and/or irreversible, it is encouraging to know that it can be limited by deep, rapid, and sustained global greenhouse gas emissions reduction. What is important to point out is that adaptation options that are feasible and effective today will become constrained and less effective with increasing global warming. And the worst can be avoided if warming can be limited to 1.5°C for which human-caused global warming needs to be limited to net zero CO_2 emissions. The report also says that there is a rapidly closing window of opportunity to secure a livable and sustainable future for all. As mentioned earlier, deep, rapid, and sustained mitigation and accelerated implementation of adaptation actions in this decade would reduce projected losses and damages for humans and ecosystems, and deliver many co-benefits, especially for air quality and health. The cost of delayed mitigation and adaptation action will be worst. Accelerated and equitable action in mitigating and adapting to climate change impacts is critical to sustainable development. Prioritizing equity, climate justice, social justice, inclusion and just transition processes can enable adaptation and ambitious mitigation actions and climate resilient development (IPCC 2023). Therefore, as Al Gore used in his keynote address at the 2018 Nobel Peace Prize Forum on "How to Solve the Climate Crisis?," 'all hands on desk' is the need of the hour to tackle this daunting challenge facing humanity.

Ironically, while India ranks at number 5 (in 2018) and 7 (in 2019) among the most affected countries globally in the Global Climate Risk Index 2021, according to Germanwatch (2021),[1] climate change did not receive adequate attention in the daily public conversations till recently, not even in educational institutions. This is in spite of the fact that the Government of India (2020) acknowledges the enormous impacts climate change is going to have on India. The Government of India in its report titled 'Climate Change and India: A 4×4 Assessment – A Sectoral and Regional Analysis for 2030s' mentioned that no other country in the world is said to be as vulnerable, on so many dimensions, to climate change as India (MoEF 2010). Thanks to the unprecedented disasters that hit different parts of the country during the past few years, as discussed in Chapter 1. Such unprecedented events have woken everyone's consciousness about climate change so much so that every disaster is now conveniently, unscientifically, and indiscriminately attributed to climate change! For example, in the case of the Joshimath disaster (see Chapter 1) developmental works were undertaken haphazardly, and when disaster struck, climate change was conveniently blamed for it. It may be mentioned here that many of the environmental disasters for which climate change is assumed to be the reason are rarely caused by it. Climate change only exacerbates the issues. For example, cyclones will still occur even in the absence of climate change. But with climate change, cyclones are more severe or more intense. Interestingly, in order to stress and highlight India's concern for climate change, it has also renamed the Ministry of Environment and Forests as Ministry of Environment, Forest and Climate Change (MoEFCC). It is also evident from India's Intended NDC document that climate change is certainly a priority area (MoEFCC 2015). As recent as in February 2, 2023, MoEFCC mentioned in its press release that "India is part of the solution and is doing more than its fair share to address climate change" in addition to other initiatives undertaken by India under the Paris Agreement.[2] Similarly, India's rank (number 8) in the Climate Change Performance Index 2023 by Germanwatch (2022) reveals that India is performing appreciably well.[3]

Discourses on climate change have definitely increased tremendously over the past two decades globally in the academia including schools and colleges, in government, public space, etc. India is catching up as well. However, in spite of all the clear warnings, little is done—globally, nationally, or individually. One only wonders what could be the possible reasons for such passivity or inaction. Is it sheer ignorance? Is there vested interest economically? Aren't the evidences enough? Did scientists fail to communicate the message well? Has education failed us when it comes to climate change? There are several aspects that a can be discussed. How school and teacher education caters to climate change will lead us to the answers to some of the aforesaid questions. For successful implementation of climate change education in school education, a few aspects must necessarily be in place—the school curriculum needs to be robust in terms of inclusion of climate change, teachers must have adequate content knowledge as well as appropriate pedagogy, availability of appropriate resources and, a conducive school environment.

10.3 Goal of Climate Change Education

Before diving into the details about climate change education in the curriculum, it is important to understand the goal of climate change education. In the simplest term, the goal of climate change education is to nurture climate-literate students. How a climate-literate student is defined may vary. In this context, the following characteristic features of a climate-literate person provided by the US Global Change Research Program (USGCRP 2009) will be helpful. The same has been slightly reframed to accommodate a few other points.

A climate-literate person

- understands the essential principles of Earth's climate system,
- knows how to assess scientifically credible information about climate,
- relates the cause and effect of climate change at different levels and dimensions,
- communicates about climate and climate change in a meaningful way to different audience, and
- is able to make informed and responsible decisions with regard to actions that may affect climate and also with regard to mitigation and adaptation strategies.

In short, climate literacy is an understanding of human's influence on climate and climate's influence on humans so that appropriate action can be taken that is socially just and climate-friendly. Therefore, having the knowledge about climate science alone will not suffice but acquiring the aforesaid characteristic features in its entirety is the key. This is what is attempted to be achieved through climate change education. How different schools, school systems, or countries will go about it will depend upon various factors such as possibilities, opportunities, flexibilities, facilities, capabilities, etc.

10.4 Literature Review on Climate Change Education

Education is a powerful tool to transform societies and so also nations. The need for climate change education cannot be overemphasized. To recognize and emphasize its importance, the National Science Teaching Association had to even issue a statement[4] so that climate change is given its due emphasis in the curriculum (NSTA 2018). Chang (2014) discussed the link between lack of knowledge about climate change and apathy for climate change issues. Further, a study conducted by Jie Li and Monroe (2019) also found that knowledge about climate change and understanding the causes empower students to perceive that they can act in meaningful ways. This validates the need to develop appropriate strategies to teach the issue of climate change (Chang 2015). The need to adapt climate change education, its content, frame, and method, to the particular conditions of the respective target group, that is, to know the audience and to tailor the education program to their preconditions, was also reiterated by Kuthe et al. (2019). Several studies have been undertaken in the area of climate change education with respect to students, teachers, or the curriculum.

A review of literature in the different aspects of climate change education for students and teachers is presented here.

10.4.1 Curriculum and Students' Knowledge

Review of literature reveals that a wide range of studies related to climate change education in formal education system have already been undertaken by researchers.

Studies from different countries indicate that students' knowledge about climate change is poor or superficial with erroneous information or misconceptions, for example Singaporean students not being able to connect its causes with impacts and holding misconceptions (Chang 2014; Chang and Pascua 2016) and poor knowledge exhibited among high school students in Austria and Denmark (Harker-Schuch and Bugge-Henriksen 2013). Many of the literature available have been found to be on 'what students know about climate change' or 'how aware they are.' For example, Kuthe et al. (2019) conducted a study about teenagers' climate change awareness in Germany and Austria, which was found to be poor. Similarly, Shepardson et al., (2011) in their study about students' conceptions about the greenhouse effect, global warming, and climate change among secondary students, found that students are confused about the greenhouse effect as well as the kind of radiation involved in the greenhouse effect. Other studies were also conducted by Boon (2010); Liarakau, Athanasiadis, and Gavrilakis (2011); Vinuesa et al. (2022). When it comes to 'what are they taught in science,' a study conducted by Kastens and Turrin (2008) for different states in the United States found that causes of climate change which is crucial to be taught in science were covered lightly as compared to the impacts. Similarly, a study in Singapore by Chang and Pascua (2017) discussed what is taught in economics, social studies, and science. However, it did not provide a comprehensive way to include climate change in the curriculum. Studies, in general, did not focus on topics to be taught in different grades or subjects. For example, a study conducted by Plutzer et al. (2016) found that climate change was widely taught in US public schools. They also found that teachers are covering the essential topics but did not specify the grades or the subject nor did the study include teachers who teach other nonscience subject disciplines. One of the most comprehensive studies undertaken on what students should know and understand about a climate system was done by Shepardson et al. (2012) wherein they proposed a climate system framework for teaching about climate change. However, this is only for the secondary students. With regard to 'what they want to learn,' a study of 16–19–year-olds from Asia and Europe by Tolppanen and Aksela (2018) found that "even in a scientific context, students do not ask questions merely related to science: on the contrary, students ask a wide range of questions, ranging from politics to psychology and from economics to individuals' behavior." Most of their questions were of multidisciplinary nature.

Another concern observed from review of literature is that of climate change education not seemingly prioritized despite climate action and adaptation being an immediate national priority as is pointed out to be the case in the UK national school curriculum where climate receives little mention (Guest post: The climate-change gaps in the UK school curriculum posted on 15 September 2021[5]). However, encouraging trends are being seen in different countries as they make amends in the curriculum so that climate change education is prioritized. For example, the UK government came out with a policy paper—sustainability and climate change: a strategy for the education and children's services systems which was published on April 21, 2022, with a vision to make the United Kingdom the world-leading education sector in sustainability and climate change by 2030. This policy is applicable to all stages of education—early users to higher education to children's social care. However, this policy applies only to England.[6] India's implementation strategy for climate change in the curriculum will be discussed a little later in this chapter.

Although it was with reference to informal science institutions, Spitzer (2014) pointed out the need for systematic approach to climate change in the curriculum which equally applies to formal education. Other studies have also pointed out such cumulative, coordinated climate change curricula for different grades and subjects (Plutzer et al. 2016). One of the few studies that identified what should be taught was conducted by Shepardson et al. (2012) wherein they not only identified what students know about climate change but they also proposed a climate system framework that include several key elements or constructs that need to be addressed in order to develop students' conceptualizations of climate change within the context of a climate system by primarily emphasizing on Earth's energy budget. Although the suggested framework provides useful information for curriculum developers, this will not be sufficient and would require a more comprehensive content laid out for the users.

While there are several aspects of climate change that need to be incorporated in the curriculum, it is crucial to incorporate those aspects which are important not only in terms of the concepts but also in terms of age-appropriateness. In this context, Monroe et al. (2017) raised an important question, "Are some impacts of climate change more relevant and meaningful to learners of different ages?"

10.4.2 Teachers' Preparedness

Studies pertaining to teachers include their climate change knowledge (Ratinen 2013; de Sousa, Hay, and Liebenberg 2019; Anyanwu and Le Grange 2017); their pedagogical content knowledge (Clausen 2018; Plutzer et al. 2016a); what do they teach about climate change, their motivation, beliefs, or barriers in teaching climate change (Higde, Oztekin, and Sahin 2017; Wise 2010; McBean and Hengeveld 2000; Seow and Ho 2016); how they should be prepared or those related to professional development programs (Higde, Oztekin, and Sahin 2017; Buhr 2011; Boon 2010; Drewes, Henderson, and Mouza 2018; Sullivan et al. 2014; Hestness et al. 2014); information related to their sources of information about climate change (Puttick and Talks 2021); how they address misconceptions (Monroe et al. 2017). Teachers may feel strongly about climate change education but for effective transaction; it is crucial for teachers to be prepared or be confident to teach climate change. However, this was not the case among teachers in the United Kingdom. A guest post—the climate-change gaps in the UK school curriculum posted on September 15, 2021—writes of a survey of teachers conducted by Teach the Future campaign group, which found that while nine out of ten teachers agree that climate change should be compulsory in schools, only three feel properly equipped to teach it.[7] They feel that they have not received adequate training to educate students on climate change, its implications for the environment and societies around the world, and how these implications can be addressed.[8] Similar trends were observed among US teachers indicating the dire need for teacher training on content knowledge and pedagogy (Plutzer et al. 2016; Plutzer et al. 2016a).

An important consideration in teachers' preparedness pertains to the source of information teachers use to enhance their knowledge or pedagogy. This is crucial because resources on climate change are in abundance, particularly online. Teachers need to know where such resources can be found or how to get to the kinds of resources that are authentic and how to use them. However, it may be mentioned that only 2% of all teaching materials produced actually get used in classrooms (UNESCO 2009). This is also consolidated by a scoping review of teachers' sources of information about climate change by Puttick and Talks (2021), which also found that there is limited research on the sources of information about climate change that teachers use, and of the few studies that was found to be relevant to their study; they found four types of sources of information frequently mentioned—the internet, government sources, mass media, and professional development courses. This suggests that information available on such sources will play an important role as teachers engage in the teaching–learning process. Hence, it will be instrumental to develop appropriate resources, which can be made available on such sources for effective climate change education.

10.4.3 Inclusion in Different Subjects

Another important aspect regarding climate change education relates to the curriculum in different subject disciplines. Many of the studies were found to discuss climate change with specific subject or a few subjects such as science, geography, and economics (Chang and Pascua 2017; Ho and Seow 2017; Roman and Busch 2016; Chang 2015) and how disciplinary boundaries can impact discourses in climate change education (Ho and Seow 2017). The power of science fiction, in shaping or mirroring society, with regard to environment was pointed out in several studies (Fagan 2017; Hulme 2009; Weldes 2003, 11; Leavenworth and Manni 2021). In a study conducted among teachers in England by Howard-Jones et al. (2021), it was found that direct reference to climate change in the National Curriculum was confined to secondary science and geography. However, although climate change was explicitly mentioned only in these two subjects, they found that most teachers were already teaching the topic or talking to their students about it, which is in contrast to teachers in the United States whose interaction with students on the topic was found to be much less. It was interesting to find climate-based maths questions by MetLink.[9] Other than that, literature on how climate change can be incorporated in the teaching–learning of math, history, and other subjects is not easily available.

10.4.4 Contextualization

Several studies have also pointed out the importance of making climate change personally relevant and meaningful (CRED 2009; Dilling and Moser 2007; Wibeck 2014; Monroe et al. 2017; Monroe, Oxarart, and Plate 2013). For example, in coastal India in Puducherry, climate change information was embedded in a unit on water quality for middle school students. However, studies related to contextualization of climate change in the curriculum in India's context in terms of visible impacts, such as Himalayan glacial melting, more frequent and intense cyclones, increase of mosquito populations in colder places, etc., were not found.

Studies have also found that students are engaged in schools using different strategies such as using an experiential, inquiry-based, or constructive approach, debates, group discussions with worksheets, hands-on labs, field trips, music and graphics, role-play, simulations, etc. The power of visual imagery and videos to capture interest was also found to be effective (Vethanayagam and Hemalatha 2010; Mutlu and Tokcan 2013). Similarly, simple drawings and cartoons were used to convey information about global warming (Oluk and Özalp 2007; Reinfried, Aeschbacher, and Rottermann 2012). Interestingly, although infographics has been in use extensively, studies related to their effectiveness to learn about climate change are hardly found. Moreover, in general, most of the studies on the effective ways of teaching climate change are in US context as is evident from the finding of the review conducted by Monroe et al. (2017) to identify effective climate change education strategies in which out of the total 49 publications found relevant to the study, 26 were from the United States alone. Further, as pointed out by Howard-Jones et al. (2021), the contexts and challenges for furthering high-quality CCE are likely to vary greatly across different nations and educational jurisdictions. For example, beliefs among teachers and students about human-induced climate change could still be a common area of research in the United States (e.g., Plutzer et al. 2016), while in countries like India, there is no debate or issue of beliefs related to human-induced climate change. Similarly, there is a high level of belief in anthropogenic climate change among a teacher workforce in England (Howard-Jones et al. 2021). Differences such as in beliefs itself will impact 'what' and 'how' climate change is to be taught.

10.5 Present Status of Climate Change Education in India

There is very limited research on Indian students' knowledge about climate change and their preparedness to tackle the issues associated with climate change by way of mitigation or adaptation. Of the few studies that have been conducted in relation to India, mention may be made of the following studies: by Alexandar and Poyyamoli (2012), in which students' willingness to engage was assessed by embedding climate change information in a unit on water quality for middle school students in coastal India; by Vethanayagam and Hemalatha (2010), who found an increase in attention and responses to global warming content after an animated educational video was shown to 10- and 11-year-old students in India; and, more recently, by Shimray and Shirol (2020), on students' knowledge about climate change wherein they found that students in general have some knowledge about climate change and not extensive knowledge "because the existing curriculum is not robust enough to drive students to be climate literate." They also found that students who had manifested interest in science did not have better knowledge about climate change compared to other students who did not have manifested interest in science. Although not for students, one that can also be cited here is a study conducted among Indian adults by Leiserowitz et al. (2013) of Yale University. They found that only 19% were aware and convinced of the reality and danger of climate change and highly supportive of national actions to mitigate the threat, while a huge chunk (16%) of the participants have never heard of climate change and have no opinion about it, even when it was described to them.

Nevertheless, the existing curriculum for schools and colleges will provide a fair idea about the integration of climate change in different stages—how much students can learn about climate change in the best scenario and what aspects of climate change have been focused and at the same time reveal the gaps, if any.

10.5.1 Current School Curriculum on Climate Change at a Glance

An analysis of the existing syllabus and textbooks prepared in the light of the National Curriculum Framework 2005 (NCF-2005) by the National Council of Educational Research and Training (NCERT 2005), New Delhi, an apex body for school education in India, also reveals that several topics related to climate change have been incorporated in the syllabi (NCERT 2006a, 2006b) and textbooks especially in disciplinary subjects such as science, geography, and biology. Topics such as greenhouse effect, global warming, and carbon cycle were the focus in science and biology syllabi and textbooks, while those related to atmospheric science were mostly considered in geography. However, systematic inclusion of concepts or concerns are found to be missing. It was also found that the same concepts were included in different stages (e.g., carbon cycle is included in Class IX science and also in Class XII biology in the prerationalized textbooks) without any visible clarity in the depth of the content. Climate change is yet to be streamlined in the curriculum unlike other 'established' concepts. For example, looking into the syllabus developed by NCERT (NCERT 2006a, 2006b), the concept of photosynthesis has been systematically introduced spirally in the curriculum of science for Classes VII and X and further in biology for Class XI with increasing depth. Similar pattern is followed for other concepts as well, such as reproduction, digestion, sound, motion, electricity, chemical reactions, etc. Unlike these streamlined concepts, a systematic approach to bring about climate literacy is missing in the curriculum. Topics related to climate change are included haphazardly and in piecemeal. More than focusing on the process, facts and information are provided. For example, many textbooks carry information like "Greenhouse gases (GHGs) causes global warming which in turn causes sea level rise, more intense weather events such as cyclone, melting of glacier, biodiversity loss, etc." Along with this information, at the most, greenhouse effect is explained. All other aspects, such as how different GHGs impact differently, how increase in GHGs increases ocean acidification, how global warming causes more intense weather events or sea-level rise or glacier melting, permafrost thawing or biodiversity loss, etc., are rarely explained.

In addition, most of the very important topics fundamental to learning climate change do not find place in the curriculum. For example, the basic idea of how scientists measure climate so as to arrive at the global average temperature, what does a one-degree increase in average surface global temperature even mean, how has temperature changed over the past two centuries which is attributed to anthropogenic activities, or what are the evidences of climate change or why polar regions are getting warmer faster, how different sectors in India will be impacted, etc., are yet to find place in the curriculum. This could be the reason why students' performance was not found to be satisfactory in a study conducted to find out their knowledge on climate change (Shimray and Shirol 2020).

Given the emergency situation that is approaching due to climate change, one would expect that climate change education would form the overarching theme in the curriculum. On the contrary, very few topics have been covered but without much coherence. One may conclude that, at best, bits of information have been provided without the necessary explanation—cause and effect. How well such information will be transacted will purely depend on how equipped the teacher is. However, it is important to point out that, as mentioned earlier, the existing school curriculum was developed based on the National Curriculum Framework 2005. Much of the data about climate science that is available today was not available then. That could be one valid reason that the curriculum did not emphasize on climate change education. While textbooks are reviewed regularly before every reprint, patchwork by randomly adding some topics related to climate change would not be helpful. It would require a complete reorganization of the curriculum in different subject disciplines if climate change is to be incorporated systematically, which can be expected only after a new curriculum framework is brought out by the country (Shimray 2020). A new curriculum framework has been introduced recently which was guided by the NEP 2020. How climate change education has been envisaged to be implemented is discussed in Section 10.4 of this chapter.

10.5.2 Curriculum on Climate Change for Higher Education

Of late, it is encouraging to find that environmental science departments are being added in different universities. Such departments provide avenues for in-depth course at the undergraduate and postgraduate level and research on climate change. Students can opt for such courses according to their choice and eligibility. A six-month compulsory core module course in environmental studies was also introduced in all the universities/colleges of India by the University Grants Commission (UGC) in compliance to the Hon'ble Supreme Court's order (six-month module syllabus for environmental studies for undergraduate courses[10]). Although the course includes classroom lectures and some scope for fieldwork, the focus was primarily on 'knowledge' about the environment and environmental issues. Such an approach to the course will be of little benefit to the students or the environment. A better approach would have been to engage students in the area they can contribute to address environmental issues since they have acquired sufficient knowledge about the environment or environmental issues till their 12th grade (Shimray 2016). Specifically on climate change, the course indeed includes climate change and global warming as one of the umpteen number of topics in the course. However, the concern is whether students are able to contribute, or are even given opportunity to make efforts, in some way to mitigate or adapt to climate change, through this compulsory course. Therefore, it is to be seen how such inclusion of climate change will serve any purpose. Seriousness, or the lack of it, is another matter of concern for this compulsory course. As rightly pointed out in the syllabus document, the success of the course will depend on the initiative and drive of the teachers and the students. More recently, the UGC brought out a new guideline and curriculum framework for a four-credit environmental education course at the undergraduate level titled "Guidelines and Curriculum Framework for Environment Education at Undergraduate level," which has been discussed in Chapter 6. Although the curriculum included climate change as one of the nine units, the focus of the unit is on enhancing 'knowledge' aspect of climate change.

10.6 Climate Change Education in the National Education Policy 2020 and Thereafter

In this section, the focus will be on the latest national education documents such as the NEP 2020 and the National Curriculum Framework for School Education 2023 (NCF-SE 2023).

10.6.1 National Education Policy 2020

Specific to climate change, the NEP 2020 recognizes the need to prepare the nation through the medium of education and research with climate change increasingly impacting every aspect of life—social, economic, and environmental. In view of this, it has recommended measures which will contribute toward adaptation or mitigation through different forms of education. For example, it recommends that all higher education institution (HEIs) will include environmental education as a credit-based course which "will include areas such as climate change." Further, it recommends agricultural education to be cognizant of critical issues such as declining land productivity, climate change, food sufficiency for the growing population, etc. It also emphasizes the need for a robust ecosystem of research keeping in view the rapid changes occurring in the realm of climate change, population dynamics and management, biotechnology, artificial intelligence, etc., and therefore advancing international research efforts to address global challenges such as healthcare, agriculture, and climate change using AI (artificial intelligence). However, there is no specific reference to climate change for school education in the NEP 2020. Nevertheless, this in no way suggests that climate change will not be included in the school curriculum since the document clearly mentioned that "Concerted curricular and pedagogical initiatives, including the introduction of contemporary subjects such as…Environmental Education…at relevant stages will be undertaken to develop these various important skills in students at all levels" (Section 6.18). This opens up endless scope to include climate change in the school curriculum. The following section will reveal how much this has been reflected in the NCF-SE 2023.

10.6.2 National Curriculum Framework for Foundational Stage 2023 (NCF-FS 2023)

As one would expect, there is no specific mention about climate change education in the document. However, it is envisaged that relevant elements will find place in the teaching–learning process as students enhance their capacities of curiosity, critical thinking, empathy, compassion, awareness of the immediate environment, etc.

10.6.3 National Curriculum Framework for School Education 2023

The first mention of the term 'climate change' or its variation in the national curriculum framework first appeared in the NCFSE 2000 (NCERT 2000, 64) as 'climatic changes.' However, there was no direct reference of the term or its variation in the National Curriculum Framework 2005 (NCF 2005). The NCF-SE 2023 vis-à-vis environmental education has been discussed in Chapter 6. As mentioned in the introduction, although climate change is an integral part of environmental education, it is being given a special emphasis due to the urgency to tackle it. Since climate change encompasses a very broad area, it is possible to relate climate change with every environmental issue. Table 10.1 presents how environmental education in general and specific mention of climate change has been made in the NCF-SE 2023 in the curriculum of different subjects and stages.

The NCF-SE 2023 document recognizes the challenges of climate change and environmental degradation (NCERT 2023, 20, 34). As evident from the table, the document, without a doubt, has quite adequately incorporated climate change in different stages in different subject disciplines of school education, including philosophy, which is much-appreciated. Although rightly pointed out in the document that "…the problems of sustainability and climate

Climate Change Education 307

TABLE 10.1 Integration of Environmental Education and Climate Change in the NCF-SE 2023

SL. NO.	Stage	Mechanism
1	Foundational	As a cross-cutting theme 'Learning about and Caring for the Environment' (NCERT 2023, 177)
2	Preparatory	1. As a cross-cutting theme 'Learning about and Caring for the Environment' (NCERT 2023, 178) 2. Through the curricular area 'The World Around Us' (NCERT 2023, 390-398)

3	Middle	1. As a cross-cutting theme 'Learning about and Caring for the Environment' (NCERT 2023, 178)
		2. Science education
		   CG-3 Explores the living world in scientific terms
		   • C-3.1 Describes the diversity of living things observed in the natural surroundings (insects, earthworms, snails, birds, mammals, reptiles, spiders, diverse plants, and fungi), including at a smaller scale (microscopic organisms) (NCERT 2023, 300)
		   • C-3.3 Analyses patterns of relationships between living organisms and their environments in terms of dependence on and response to each other (NCERT 2023, 300)
		   CG-5 Understands the interface of science, technology, and society
		   C-5.1 Illustrates how science and technology can help to improve the quality of human life (healthcare, communication, transportation, food security, mitigation of climate change, judicious consumption of resources, applications of artificial satellites) as well as some of the harmful uses of science in history (NCERT 2023, 300)
		3. Social science education
		   CG-6 Understands the spatial distribution of resources (from local to global), their conservation, the interdependence between natural phenomena and human life, and their environmental and other implications
		   • C-6.1 Explains key natural phenomena such as climate, weather, ocean cycles, soil formation, the flow of rivers, and how they are spatially distributed (NCERT 2023, 326)
		   • C-6.3 Analyzes Indian perspectives on and efforts toward conservation and sustainability in society, and advocates the importance of the same, and what more needs to be done in these directions including in the context of global climate change (NCERT 2023, 326)
		   • C-6.4 Correlates the existence of different patterns of livelihoods with different types of landforms, availability of resources, and climatic conditions and changes (in local, regional, national, and global contexts) (NCERT 2023, 326)

(*Continued*)

TABLE 10.1 (Continued)

SL. NO.	Stage	Mechanism
4	Secondary	Social science education Grades 9 and 10 CG-4 Develops an understanding of the interrelationship between human beings and their physical environment and how that influences the livelihoods, culture, and the biodiversity of the region • C-4.3 Draws interlinkages between various components of the physical environment, such as climate and relief, climate and vegetation, and wildlife (NCERT 2023, 329) • C-4.5 Critically evaluates the impact of human interventions on the environment, including climate change, pollution, shortages of natural resources (particularly water), and loss of biodiversity; identifies practices that have led to these environmental crises and the measures that must be taken to reverse them (NCERT 2023, 329) CG-8 Evaluates the economic development of a country in terms of its impact on the lives of its people and nature • C-8.5 Appreciates the connections between economic development and the environment, and the broader indicators of societal well-being beyond GDP growth and income (NCERT 2023, 330)
	Grade 9 Grade 10	As a cross-cutting theme 'Learning about and Caring for the Environment' (NCERT 2023, 179) 1. As a cross-cutting theme 'Learning about and Caring for the Environment' (NCERT 2023, 179) 2. Through the Essential Course 'Environmental Education' (under interdisciplinary areas as one of the curricular areas) CG-1 Understands key issues and challenges related to climate change, pollution, and biodiversity collapse • C-1.1 Explains how climate change, pollution, and biodiversity collapse affect human well-being (economic activity, migration, cultural practices) and the well-being of plant and animal species (NCERT 2023, 409) • C-1.2 Understands connections between and the causes underlying pollution, climate change, and biodiversity collapse (NCERT 2023, 409) CG-2 Appreciates the need for interconnectedness, balance, and harmony between human society and nature – the essence of '*Vasudhaiva Kutumbakam*' • C-2.1 Describes the place of humans within ecosystems, and illustrates how humans and natural ecosystems are interconnected and must co-exist (NCERT 2023, 409)

Climate Change Education 309

- C-2.2 Illustrates actions at the individual, local, community, national, and international level towards mitigation of issues related to environmental damage (NCERT 2023, 409)
- C-2.3 Identifies actions that can be taken at the level of the school or local community to counter environment-related concerns (NCERT 2023, 409)

Grades 11 and 12

1. As a cross-cutting theme 'Learning about and Caring for the Environment' (NCERT 2023, 179)
2. Through 'Sustainability and Climate Change,' which is one of the choice-based disciplines (NCERT 2023, 504)

Related to Sustainability and Climate Change discipline, the document provides certain principles for Designing the course which is provided below:

The aim of teaching sustainability and climate change is to enable in students a deeper engagement with environmental education and explore the interconnectedness with sustainability and climate change grounded in the Indian context. The courses for sustainability and climate change must be designed keeping the following in mind:

- Students will engage with complex environmental problems without being overwhelmed by them.
- They will describe and summarize environmental challenges linking society and the environment.
- They will understand trade-offs and ethical dimensions of sustainability and climate change challenges.
- They will develop environmental literacy, enabling them to engage in environmental action. (NCERT 2023, 504)

3. Biology

Content Area 1: Biodiversity and biogeography of India
Students will engage with units on the impact of climate change and the importance of conservation efforts. (NCERT 2023, 483)

Content Area 3: Organismal biology
…Food production, food security (including challenges of climate change and diseases, the role of biotechnology), and sustainability (resource use, environmental impact) will be discussed. (NCERT 2023, 484)

4. Philosophy

Content Area 5: Environmental philosophy
Through this content area, students will be able to think abstractly about questions related to environmental issues, such as: Who is to blame for climate change, and are current solutions ethical?… (NCERT 2023, 478)

Source: Shimray (2023).

change are not merely informed by the Sciences, but also by our understanding of Social Sciences and Mathematics" (NCERT 2023, 57), yet its goals, objectives, and systematic inclusion in different subject disciplines are not spelt out in the document. It is a fact that climate change is complex, covers a vast area, and is complicated to teach. Therefore, it is crucial to systematically work out how the aspects of climate change related to science, social science, humanities, literature, etc., are spread over different grades, which will be age-appropriate. Everything about climate change cannot be taught in one particular grade or two as is seemingly envisaged in the document, for example in Grade 10 as Essential Course: Environmental Education. Similarly, although 'Sustainability and Climate Change' course has all the essential components of climate change, since it is a choice-based discipline in Grades 11 and 12, it will be opted by only few students. Therefore, in spite of all the efforts that have been made in the document to highlight the importance of climate change, such lack of systematic inclusion will be a huge barrier to nurture climate-literate students.

10.7 Curriculum for Climate Change Education in School

For effective implementation of climate change education, the first step would be to figure out what students need to know about climate change or what should be taught about climate change, where it should be taught and how it should be taught. As mentioned earlier, the curriculum should be such that it brings about climate literacy among the students, which is understanding of one's influence on climate and climate's influence on them and society. This implies that climate change is not only a subject matter of science but is interdisciplinary in nature. While the science provides the basic understanding of how the climate works, the social sciences can provide the necessary knowledge about the economics and its social implications and empower students with understanding about polity and climate change, historical perspective of climate change, indigenous knowledge and climate change, climate justice, and implications of climate change on language, literature, and culture. Arts, too, have unique ways to portray climate change through different art forms. While the best curriculum for climate change education would be to discuss it holistically, unfortunately the existing school structures do not support such interdisciplinary approach (Chang and Pascua 2017a). Hence, systematic approach through various disciplinary areas such as science, social science, language, arts, and humanities remains the best available option.

Irrespective of the what, when, where, and how, there are different dimensions of climate change which need to be considered in the curriculum. There are concepts, topics, or contents that have to be considered. Then there are challenges that need to be addressed. These are discussed in the ensuing sections.

10.7.1 Dimensions of Climate Change

Climate change is best understood based on its impact on different sectors or dimensions. In spite of its complexity, much is known about climate science today and more keeps unraveling as new findings are added by researchers each day. If humans were the only ones to deal with 1-degree Celsius rise in average surface global temperature, then it would not have been so much a problem. They would have invented for themselves certain technologies that would help them cope with that increase in temperature. However, as will be agreed by all, it is much more complicated and far-reaching than that. That simple sounding 1-degree Celsius rise in temperature will result in the worsening of the issues already prevalent today. For example, cyclones becoming more intense, more rainfall in lesser time, flood becoming more frequent and severe, etc. Therefore, climate change is known to be a threat multiplier. Such ramifications that climate change can have must necessarily form part of the curriculum. Shimray (2020) listed eight dimensions necessary to be considered while incorporating climate change education in the curriculum. Those are reproduced here with some modifications.

10.7.1.1 Agriculture

It is an established fact that due to global warming leading to climate change, not only oceans but even lands will get warmer and drier, which will impact the soil quality. There will be more frequent or erratic droughts and floods. Warming of higher altitudes is going to have its own impact in terms of crop production. What is increasingly worrying is that pest dynamics are going to change with global warming, and this will require innovations and development of safe and nonpolluting pesticides to meet the new challenges. Carbon dioxide increase will reduce nutrients in wheat, rice, etc (Ujiie et al. 2019). Reduction in nutrients in crops can impact the health of those who are already vulnerable, undernourished, and malnourished. These will have impacts on different dimensions such as food security, which could result in tensions within and between countries through manipulation of import and export of food items; there will be issue of internally displaced persons (IDPs) due to movement of farmers to bigger towns and cities or even migration to and from other neighboring countries in search of livelihood due to uncertainty in the agriculture sector. This will in turn change the demographics of such towns and cities and put pressure on the limited available resources. In this situation, scientists are likely to come up with different kinds of genetically modified (GM) crops to tackle food scarcity and security due to climate change, which could lead to other issues such as biodiversity loss, ecosystem dynamics, etc.

10.7.1.2 Health

Health is another sector where climate change is expected to severely impact. There will be increase in the incidence and geographical range of climate-sensitive infectious diseases such as malaria, dengue, tick-borne diseases, etc. (USGCRP, 2009). Mortality rate will increase due to increasing heat-induced deaths among those with existing critical medical conditions. For example, those with respiratory diseases such as asthma or those vulnerable to suffering from other diseases will be hit hardest. These will be exacerbated by poverty.

10.7.1.3 Sea-Level Rise and Ocean Acidification

India has a long stretch of coastline touching 13 states and union territories. Although coastal India will not be soon inundated under water due to sea-level rise like what is seen in Kiribati in the Pacific or Bangladesh, coastal life will definitely be impacted by global warming. Sea will be closer to the mainland, thus affecting settlements close to it. New levies will have to be built. More seawater will get into the mainland affecting agriculture and drinking water. The marine ecosystem will be most affected due to ocean acidification from increased carbon dioxide in seawater. Marine fishing industry will also be impacted, thereby affecting livelihood. Governments will have to invest more in the coastal region toward mitigation and adaptation to global warming and climate change, thereby impacting the country's economy.

10.7.1.4 Water

Climate change will bring about severe water-related issues. In fact, an unusual rainfall pattern which is more erratic is already being experienced. As this continues, it will cause some places to be drier and some places to be wetter. This will be aggravated by warming atmospheric temperature that will cause the lands to be drier. In turn, it will impact the availability of water for agriculture, domestic use, industries, etc. Forest-fed rivers are likely to be drier with lesser rain. Water-related disputes are already taking place between states due to sharing of river water. On the other hand, rivers which are also fed by glacier to some extent may show some changes in its characteristics. For example, if the Himalayan glacier recedes drastically, it will impact rivers such as the Ganga, which could be disastrous.

10.7.1.5 Biodiversity

The impact of climate change on biodiversity is a matter of huge concern. Biodiversity loss already happening due to habitat loss will now be aggravated by temperature rise. More organisms will be lost in the process, especially those sensitive to temperature since they are not likely going to adapt to the temperature shock so fast. As such, conservation strategies will change and will be more complicated by the addition of the complex climate change factors. Conservation strategies will have to reorient. Conservation of some species might have to be compromised, while focus could be shifted on select organisms. Prey–predator dynamics will change, impacting the ecosystem. Changes in phenology are likely to affect many plant species, which will in turn affect animals which are dependent on those plants.

10.7.1.6 Economy

The economy of the country will be impacted due to the adverse effects of climate change. At the same time, business strategies will change eventually. For example, in coastal areas, insurance companies could give its customers the option to get insurance for their houses due to sea-level rise, etc. However, with an increase in risk, insurance companies are likely to change its policies to ensure profit for the companies. As a result, customers or property owners will end up paying more to buy insurance. As discussed earlier under Section 10.7.1.1., import–export, especially of food and its products, will be drastically impacted and strategically negotiated.

10.7.1.7 Climate Justice

Climate change will have the worst impact on vulnerable populations—those with physical or mental disability, marginalized populations, indigenous populations, technologically handicapped citizens, economically weak sections of the society, small islands, those living in places with poor medical facilities, outdoor workers, etc. Therefore, climate change becomes more of an ethical and social justice issue and hence the need for global climate justice to bring about ethical and adequately responsive climate change education (Kagawa and Selby 2010).

10.7.1.8 Climate Refugees

With climate change, there will be an increase in refugees in places where water, food, and land are available. This will lead to conflict between the refugees and the original inhabitants due to competition for food, space, water, and other resources. Such competition will put pressure on the resources and eventually impact its availability permanently. There will be issues of IDPs resulting from the impact of climate change on agriculture, as discussed earlier.

Although the dimensions discussed may not be sacrosanct, it sends out a warning that every dimension of human life will be impacted by climate change. Therefore, these concerns need to be reflected in the curriculum. Given the enormous consequences it will have, teaching of climate change in science, or geography alone as it is presently practiced, cannot be continued but included in every discipline. As mentioned earlier, every discipline has something to offer to make students climate-literate.

10.7.2 Content Outline for Climate Change Education

Identifying the content to be included in the curriculum will be the first step in the implementation of climate change education. Figure 10.1 broadly outlines the topics that must find place in the curriculum for climate change. These need to be incorporated appropriately in different disciplines and stages so that students are given the opportunity to understand the various aspects of climate change (Shimray 2018). The topics are grouped under the following themes:

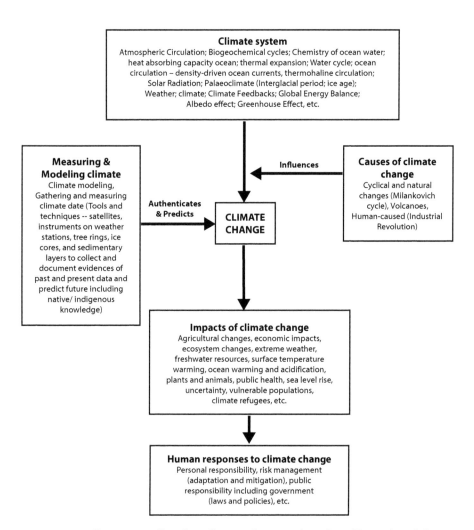

FIGURE 10.1 Content outline for climate change education (Reproduced from: Shimray 2018).

1. Climate System
2. Causes of Climate Change
3. Measuring and Modeling Climate
4. Impacts of Climate Change
5. Human Responses to Climate Change

As shown in Figure 10.1, the topics included under each theme are numerous. Systematic mapping of the topics/concepts will be required so that they are appropriately reflected at relevant places in different subjects and grades. The figure clearly depicts the interdisciplinary nature of climate change. Climate literacy cannot be achieved through one subject. It will require the collective contribution of different subject disciplines. However, this is easier said than done. Nevertheless, it might be easier when climate change is considered as a standalone discipline and more complicated when it is to be incorporated in different subject disciplines.

10.7.3 Challenges in Climate Change Education

While environmental education is more or less streamlined, there will be several challenges when it comes to implementation of climate change education. Shimray (2020) listed some of the challenges that can be anticipated, especially in India, which are discussed here.

10.7.3.1 When to Start Teaching?

As studies have shown, the science behind climate change is complex (Tolppanen and Aksela 2018), and it requires some level of mental maturity to understand it. Therefore, what will be the appropriate grade to start teaching about climate change is a reasonable question to ask. However, the prior experiences and knowledge required to understand climate science can be addressed from the foundational stage through simple activities, for example experiencing or measuring the difference in temperature inside the classroom and outside on a sunny day.

10.7.3.2 What to Teach Where?

The interdisciplinary nature of climate change has been discussed earlier. In the content outline for climate change education in Figure 10.1, what to teach have been broadly listed, and clearly it has elements of different subject disciplines. It will be a herculean task to work out a feasible curriculum to incorporate different elements of climate change in different subject disciplines and to ensure that students get the 'whole' even as they are fed in 'pieces.' This may not be such a challenge if a standalone approach of climate change education is introduced. Different countries have been found to include climate change differently in their curriculum. In England, direct reference to climate change in the National Curriculum is confined to secondary science and geography (Howard-Jones et al. 2021), while currently in India direct reference to climate change can be seen in the middle stage science curriculum and in the secondary stage geography curriculum in addition to 'Sustainability and Climate Change' as a choice-based discipline at the secondary stage Grades 11 and 12 (NCF-SE 2023). Whether a cross-curricular approach should be favored as found in a study of teachers in England (Howard-Jones et al. 2021) or an interdisciplinary framework should be opted (Hawkey, James, and Tidmarsh 2019) will be crucial to decide.

10.7.3.3 What Should Be the Focus?

There needs to be clarity on what the focus should be—knowledge, attitude, behavior, action, mitigation and adaption skills and competencies, learning outcomes, etc.—so that appropriate curriculum can be prepared such as appropriate resources, pedagogy, and at the same time teachers can be oriented accordingly. It may be noted that the NCF-SE 2023 have listed the competencies to be developed in students in different grades and subject subjects. The learning outcomes for different grades for different subject disciplines have already been prepared by NCERT for the elementary stage (NCERT 2017),[11] secondary stage (NCERT 2019),[12] and higher secondary stage (draft).[13]

10.7.3.4 How to Make It Relevant and Tangible?

Climate change is often considered to be an issue which is irrelevant to us. Therefore, the first and foremost point to be remembered in the teaching–learning of climate change is to make it relevant. For this, examples or case studies which directly relate or impact the students need to be included in the curriculum. Coastal region may consider sea-level rise or more intense and frequent cyclones. The Himalayan region may consider glacier melting. Those in colder and higher altitudes may consider an increase in disease-causing vectors such as mosquitoes. Those in the plains may consider the increase in the number of deaths due to heat. Where agriculture is prominent, the students may consider changes in insect, pest dynamics, drought, etc. Unless they are convinced that climate change impacts them, students are less likely to be motivated to learn about climate change. By using probing questions, students may also be given opportunities to share their experience about climate change. This will set a positive stage to take forward teaching–learning on climate change.

Although the question as to whether climate change is real or not is settled, since the impacts of climate change are not directly seen or felt personally by many, it is a challenge to present it convincingly to students. The issues associated with climate change such as those related to time frame (e.g., the 1-degree Celsius rise in average surface global temperature that happened gradually over more than a century) and scale (e.g., the impact a 1-degree Celsius rise in average surface global temperature has on the climate system globally) are hard for students to conceptualize. As a result, students perceive the climate change to be a distant threat or is not relevant to them (Chang 2014; Newstadt 2015). What makes the matter worse is that climate change is discussed in terms of decades and not necessarily in terms of what is happening at the moment. For example, a particular year may be exceptionally cold compared to other years, yet it does not mean that there is no global warming. Further, the impact of climate change is different in different parts of the country or the world. Temperature is also not uniformly increasing in different parts of the world but the average global temperature is increasing. Therefore, the real challenge is to scale down the climate data, or the impact of climate change for that matter, so as to make it relevant to a smaller geographical area instead of fixating the issue to a global scale. This will help students comprehend and contextualize the information better. It cannot be denied that climate change itself is a complex phenomenon—the intriguing result of increase in greenhouse gases, the impact on the average global temperature, atmosphere, and oceans, the effects on precipitation, on sea-level rise, and on lives and livelihood, etc. Unless an attempt is made to make these as tangible as possible, climate change will remain too abstract to students that they may lose interest about the issue.

10.7.3.5 How to Communicate about Climate Change?

Climate change is complex, and communicating about it is even more complicated. The hundreds of factors that contribute to climate change, the different possible models, data and graphs generated, the various predictions brought forth, etc., are not easily understood by all (Shimray 2020). Therefore, communicating about climate change will have to address the following: (i) resources—availability and appropriateness, (ii) misconceptions, (iii) misinformation, (iv) disinformation, and (v) uncertainties.

Availability of appropriate resources is found to play a crucial role in the effective transaction of climate change as in the case of teachers in England whose feeling comfortable delivering climate change education was correlated with availability of resources (Howard-Jones et al. 2021). Resources should be prepared in such a way that the information/concepts to be disseminated are made quantifiable or comprehensible, tangible (as discussed earlier) and tailor-made for different audience in the form of easy-to-understand tables and graphs, animations on various aspects of climate science or its impacts, simplified diagrams, simulations, augmented reality, virtual reality, etc. The persuasiveness of the message or content will also play an important role (Kazdin 2008). Preparation of such resources for teaching–learning or self-learning will be crucial. Scientists alone cannot do this daunting task. Teachers, teacher educators, students, engineers, graphic designers, etc. have to come along and work in collaboration with scientists to accomplish the task. Such collaborations to some extent are, in fact, already happening in some countries as, for example, resources developed by the National Oceanic and Atmospheric Administration (NOAA) under Teaching climate,[14] National Aeronautics and Space Administration (NASA),[15] PhET Interactive Simulations project at the University of Colorado, Boulder,[16] and various climate-based resources developed by MetLink—Royal Meteorological Society for teaching, assessment, etc., for different stages and subject disciplines including maths.[17] The Climate-Based Questions for students and teachers under Maths for Planet Earth have been developed by a team of students, Madeleine Ratcliffe, Lucy Fellingham and John Allen, and academics at the Environmental Change Institute, School of Geography and the Environment, and Department of Physics, University of Oxford.[18] Such climate-focused resources related to school curriculum are hardly prepared by HEIs or national institutes and organizations in India barring very few referable resources uploaded on DIKSHA portal.[19]

The misconceptions that can arise because of lack of appropriate or clear information from authentic sources is well known as it was seen in the case of the 2018 Kerala flood. Without authenticity, the flood was attributed to climate change by many including media. However, this claim has been refuted and the flood has been, to some extent, attributed to the ecological mis-management (Mishra and Shah 2018). Several other misconceptions could also arise from everyday experience (Bentley, Petcovic, and Cassidy 2019). For example, students often get to hear from different sources, such as uninformed political leaders and others, that global warming is caused due to ozone hole. Another example is that of some winters being colder than the previous winter and hence concluding that there is no global warming. Such incorrect information tends to cause more confusion about climate change. Dispelling misconceptions, therefore, becomes crucial.

One of the major reasons for misconceptions related to climate change is misinformation. Numerous studies have been done on the prevalence of misinformation which are disseminated through different platforms, very prominent among those is the YouTube (Hossler and Conroy 2008; Bentley et al. 2019). Such misinformation could become a deterrent in our strive to tackle climate change. For example, misconceptions on the possible effects and severity of the issue can lead to adoption of ineffective mitigation actions (Huxster, Uribe-Zarain, and Kempton 2015). And it is especially important for teachers to be free from misconceptions or misinformation because if they do, the same will be transmitted to all the students in their classrooms (Khalid 2003).

Some misinformations are deliberately disseminated for vested interest and are termed 'disinformation.' Therefore, students should also be prepared to be able to identify disinformation so that they do not consume such distorted information which are deliberately put out in the public domain.

It is also equally important to cautiously deal with the uncertainties associated with climate change. Although any amount of global warming is dangerous, "there remain great scientific uncertainties about how the ice sheets will respond to increased global warming" (Leiserowitz 2005). Such "uncertainties in the risks that climate change poses make it challenging for laypersons to understand its causes, perceive its impacts, and take actions that might help alleviate future warming" (Dunlap 2013). However, such uncertainties are bound to be seen when it comes to climate change as is reflected even in IPCC documents. For example, the IPCC calibrated language uses five qualifiers to express a level of confidence: very low, low, medium, high, and very high, and typeset in italics, for example *medium confidence*. It also uses the following terms to indicate the assessed likelihood of an outcome or a result: virtually certain 99–100% probability, very likely 90–100%, likely 66–100%, more likely than not >50–100%, about as likely as not 33–66%, unlikely 0–33%, very unlikely 0–10%, exceptionally unlikely 0–1%. Additional terms (extremely likely 95–100%; more likely than not >50–100%; and extremely unlikely 0–5%) are also used when appropriate. Assessed likelihood is typeset in italics, for example *very likely* (IPCC 2023). Such usage of seemingly uncertain terms like 'likely,' 'medium confidence,' etc., is simply indicative of the possible outcome or risks associated with climate change so that adequately preparations can be made. Scientists could easily exaggerate the outcomes or risks to the maximum but that will put people and countries into more risks. For example, if scientists advise restricting global warming well below 1.5°C by 2050 from preindustrial levels to avoid catastrophe, then countries have to take more stringent measures. Therefore, such qualifiers are necessary for countries to enable them to take appropriate measures.

It is no secret that attempts are made by the fossil industry lobbyists and conservatives to highlight uncertainties in climate science and thereby questioning the causes and consequences of climate change (Jang and Sol Hart 2015). Therefore, care needs to be taken while using such terms in the classroom to ensure that the seriousness of the issue is not diminished in the minds of the students. It may be noted that climate change is influenced by numerous factors, and there are inherent uncertainties when it comes to weather or climate (Dupigny-Giroux 2010). Students need to be made aware of such uncertainties. What also needs to be communicated is that through science attempts are made to make the uncertainties more certain. As more is unraveled about climate science and better technologies are developed, it will be possible to communicate about climate impacts or risks in more certain terms.

10.7.3.6 What Should Be Assessed?

Reid (2019) had included "How might climate change education be assessed?" as one of the key questions about climate change education. This is a valid question since what is assessed is taught and what is not assessed is not taught in most cases. It has been pointed out that if it is not part of the national assessment, teaching about civic engagement with climate change might be tackled only if time and space allows (Chatzifotiou 2002).

Assessment regarding climate change education can be done on different dimensions. It could be content knowledge; skills, competencies, or learning outcomes; attitudes and behavior; contribution in solving climate-related problems; and many other aspects. While assessment of each of this will be vital, the most important consideration should be whether they contribute in achieving the goal of climate change education such as understanding of the Earth's climate system, assessing the credibility of climate information, relating cause and effect of climate change, communicating about climate change meaningfully in school and outside, making informed and responsible decisions with regard to action, adaptation, and mitigation which is socially just and climate-friendly. Therefore, whatever may be the format or dimension of assessment, as long as it is linked to the goal, it should be good.

10.7.3.7 Are Teachers Prepared?

Climate change is a fairly new topic for many teachers. While some teachers in India are already teaching some aspects of climate change in the course of teaching science or geography, teachers in general have not been trained to teach climate change specifically in their preparatory courses (preservice course) or in their degree courses. Let alone climate change, teachers are not even prepared to teach environmental education, as it was seen in Chapter 8. Such lack of training or limited training leads to climate confusion among teachers, which ultimately reflects in their teaching (Plutzer et al. 2016). There are two aspects that have to be looked into when it comes to assessing teacher preparedness: content knowledge and pedagogy. Researches have shown that teachers hold misconceptions about the scientific aspects related to climate change (Tolppanen and Aksela 2018).

Pointed efforts need to be made to prepare teachers based on their requirements. Trainings—preservice or in-service—should not use one-size-fits-all approach. Teachers teaching language or humanities may not require so much of climate science knowledge as science or geography teacher would. Similarly, the pedagogy for different stages and subject disciplines will be different from when it is taught as a standalone subject discipline, and hence training strategies will also vary accordingly. Depending upon the requirements, different programs and courses need to be developed for preservice and in-service teachers.

Broadly, teacher preparation for climate change education can be under two categories:

(i) Development of content knowledge: One can be a lighter version for teachers (preservice or in-service) who would not require in-depth knowledge about climate change. For example, language teachers who would not be delivering the content per se. The other would be a more rigorous course for teachers who will be teaching content, for example, teachers teaching climate change in science or geography. With the introduction of credit-based system in many colleges and universities, those who have already earned adequate credits on climate change or those who have already studied courses which had the necessary content on climate change may be exempted from taking the course. Alternatively, a separate refresher course may be prepared for such teachers.
(ii) Development of pedagogical knowledge: As mentioned earlier, development of pedagogical knowledge will be different when it is to be taught via different subject disciplines compared to when it is to be taught as a standalone subject. Also, the pedagogy to teach via different subject disciplines will be different since every subject discipline has their unique nature. Undoubtedly, when taught as a standalone subject, it will be more holistic and meaningful for students.

10.7.4 Some Suggestions to Incorporate Climate Change in the School Curriculum

As discussed earlier, incorporating climate change in different stages and different subject disciplines will not be easy, and it will require meticulous planning. The following briefly discusses how climate change can be more effectively incorporated in the curriculum. In order to achieve this, several aspects have to be taken into consideration. For example, which topics have to be included in the curriculum for which class, what resources should be used, which strategy or approach should be used, etc. As per a study conducted by Howard-Jones et al. (2021), teachers in England supported an action-based climate change curriculum including issues of global social justice, beginning in primary school with mitigation projects such as conservation, local tree-planting, and family advocacy; local campaigning (e.g., legal demonstration) around the primary/secondary transition, and most teachers supporting inclusion of civil disobedience beginning at secondary school (11+ years). The role of students as climate advocates to bring about awareness and social change is also an aspect that is being considered globally with family advocacy in the primary stage and community advocacy as students grow older (Trott 2019a, 2019b). Such involvement of students to bring about social change also has positive impacts on children (Sanson, Burke, and Van Hoorn 2018) who have negative emotional response (Ojala 2012) in relation to climate change. However, the negative impact of involving students in social justice activities has also been pointed out in that activism can be stressful, and some students may not be able to handle them (Ballard and Ozer 2016; Kahne and Westheimer 2006).

Foundational stage: Getting students familiarized with their immediate surrounding will suffice at this stage such as getting to know about the plants, animals, soil, water, heat, cold, etc., and learning to care, share, empathize, etc. Emphasis may be given on hands-on experiential learning.

Preparatory stage: The primary stage should be marked by the involvement of students in different activities and sharing of ideas and experiences about the world around them. It is not advisable to introduce scientific terminologies at this stage which are used in the context of climate change. Instead, students may be introduced to the ideas they can relate with, such as those of rainfall and changes in the pattern, absorption of light by darker objects or reflection of light by light-colored objects, variation in temperature during a day or seasons, giving them an experience of a greenhouse, vegetables, and flowers found in different seasons, scarcity of water, etc. Familiarizing them by providing opportunity to experience themselves or giving them opportunity to share their experience or what they learn from the community/society will be a good way to start. At this stage, children should be introduced only to local environmental problems that they see or experience and, hence, as mentioned earlier, they could be engaged in 'family advocacy' such as working out a climate action plan of their family or of their school and taking action on those. Depending on the nature of the activities, they may be part of literacy, numeracy, or environmental studies.

Middle stage: At the middle stage, students may be introduced to different concepts of climate system as listed in Figure 10.1. They can also be introduced to the concept of natural and human-caused climate change, impacts of climate change and human responses at the state or national level, and also some aspects of measuring and modeling climate. The cause-and-effect aspect of climate change should be introduced at this stage. Different concepts can be incorporated in different subject disciplines such as science, social science, math, or language, depending upon their appropriateness. At this stage, it is crucial to involve them in climate action—what they, and others, can do to reduce or adapt to climate change at the community level, that is, in a more public form of involvement. Students need to be engaged in a lot of critical thinking tasks: for example, what will happen to crops and farmers if it gets warmer and warmer, what happens to people in small islands and in the coastal areas if sea level continues to rise, how much more energy will be consumed in their school or home if the temperature keeps on increasing, what kinds of laws and policies should be implemented, etc. Opportunities should be provided at this stage so that students are engaged in debates and discussions. Students should also learn to communicate about climate change to create awareness in their community and begin to be agents of change. Simulations, videos, pictures, etc., can be used in addition to hands-on experiences (Shimray 2020) to enhance awareness and learning among students.

Secondary stages 1 and 2: The learnings of the previous stage can be strengthened further as students learn deeper about the concepts and concerns introduced in the middle stage. Measuring and modeling may be emphasized in this stage. They should learn to analyze and verify facts and information related to climate change. Cause and effect of climate change may be discussed at a deeper level. They may be introduced to global climate issues, challenges, efforts in different countries, United Nations, etc. Opportunities may be given to develop analytical and critical thinking skills by discussing and debating about scientific findings, policies, case studies, etc. With a focus on problem-solving, they may be given an opportunity to come up with a comprehensive plan to tackle climate change, which could be in terms of policy, laws, governance, agriculture, transportation, communication, energy production, risk management, zoonotic diseases, etc. This can be given as an individual task or a group task. Beginning from the early secondary stage, social justice and ethical dimensions may be introduced. The focus at this stage should be to nurture students to become informed and responsible citizens.

With the recommendation of an optional subject 'Sustainability and climate change' at the secondary stage 2 in the NCF-SE 2023, a holistic and systematic curriculum can be prepared keeping in view the contents mentioned in Figure 10.1. This course should prepare students to not just acquire knowledge about the different concepts and dimensions, but it should prepare them to be climate-literate citizens in the real sense who is able to contribute in solving climate-related problems of the society.

10.8 Conclusion

Climate change education is not an option but a necessity in the world's efforts to tackle climate change. The need to nurture generations of students who are able to adapt to the changing world and contribute in solving climate-related challenges is an understatement given the climate crises facing us. Schools throughout the world are increasingly introducing climate change education in their curriculum. How it is being implemented greatly varies, though. India is making an attempt in this direction with the launch of its new NEP 2020 and the subsequent introduction of new curriculum frameworks for different stages of school education. Although environmental education has been reflected fairly well in the documents, the same is not in the case of climate change education. Systematic inclusion of the concepts and concerns is wanting till Grade 10. Such gaps and shortcomings will now have to be taken care in syllabus, resources such as textbooks, supplementary resources, and the teacher training programs. In addition to what is included in the syllabus and textbooks of different subject disciplines, other possibilities must also be explored to boost climate literacy. The ten-day bagless period suggested by NEP 2020 could be one such avenue where students are engaged in activities that will enhance their capacities on climate change.

How students are motivated to be climate literate will also be crucial. Contrary to conclusions drawn from past research that outdoor experiences in 'nature' or 'natural areas' are significant to raise/increase concern and interest in climate change and their mitigation and action, Howell and Allen (2019) conclude from their study that

> EE specifically directed towards promoting engagement with climate change need not entail promoting outdoor experiences, nature connectedness, or biospheric values and motivations for action, and that there is a case to be made for avoiding framing climate change education as 'environmental' education.

Howell and Allen found social justice concerns to have inspired climate action in their study about climate change educators' significant life experiences, motivations, and values. Such considerations will also be crucial in the implementation of climate change education.

Although climate change education is now pretty much an integral part of the curriculum around the world, it might as well be taken more seriously if how well countries incorporate climate change education in their curriculum is considered as one of the criteria for measuring different countries' commitments to address climate change.

10.9 Summary

- Climate change is a threat to human well-being and planetary health.
- Education is an important and crucial medium to address climate change.
- There is a need for clarity about the goals of climate change education.
- Literature review reveals that globally teachers are not prepared adequately to incorporate climate change in the curriculum.
- There needs to be clarity on which aspects of climate change should be included in different subject disciplines.
- Contextualization is key to making climate change relevant to students.
- Climate change has been part of the curriculum in India. However, systematic inclusion is found wanting for its holistic understanding.
- The latest education policy and the curriculum frameworks introduced in India strongly advocate for climate change education. However, the documents fall short of explaining or clarifying how to systemically address different aspects of climate change in different stages and grades.

- Different dimensions of climate change need to be considered while designing curriculum for climate change education. How such dimensions are included in different stages and grades will be crucial for successful implementation of climate change education.

Notes

1 https://www.germanwatch.org/sites/default/files/GlobalClimateRiskIndex2021_2.pdf (Accessed on September 2, 2023).
2 https://pib.gov.in/PressReleaseIframePage.aspx?PRID=1895857#:~:text=InAugust 2022,Indiaupdated,basedenergyresourcesby2030 (Accessed on April 27, 2023).
3 https://ccpi.org/wp-content/uploads/CCPI-2023-Results-3.pdf (Accessed on September 2, 2023).
4 https://www.nsta.org/nstas-official-positions/teaching-climate-science (Accessed on September 24, 2023).
5 https://www.carbonbrief.org/guest-post-the-climate-change-gaps-in-the-uk-school-curriculum/ (Accessed on April 22, 2023).
6 https://www.gov.uk/government/publications/sustainability-and-climate-change-strategy/sustainability-and-climate-change-a-strategy-for-the-education-and-childrens-services-systems#leadership-engagement-and-next-steps (Accessed on April 22, 2023).
7 https://www.carbonbrief.org/guest-post-the-climate-change-gaps-in-the-uk-school-curriculum/ (Accessed on April 22, 2023).
8 For details, see Teaching the Future: Research with UK teachers on the current stage and future of climate education conducted by Teach the Future in March 2021: https://uploads-ssl.webflow.com/5f8805cec9a94e60b31d616b/6045e0f11d947afbc651a21d_TeachingtheFutureSummaryReport.pdf (Accessed on April 22, 2023).
9 https://www.metlink.org/maths-for-planet-earth/ (Accessed on May 9, 2023).
10 https://www.ugc.gov.in/pdfnews/2269552_environmentalstudies.pdf (Accessed on April 29, 2023).
11 https://ncert.nic.in/pdf/publication/otherpublications/tilops101.pdf (Accessed on September 19, 2023).
12 https://ncert.nic.in/pdf/publication/otherpublications/learning_outcomes.pdf (Accessed on September 19, 2023).
13 https://ncert.nic.in/pdf/publication/otherpublications/Draft_LO.pdf (Accessed on September 19, 2023).
14 https://www.climate.gov/teaching (Accessed on May 10, 2023).
15 https://climatekids.nasa.gov/; https://science.nasa.gov/learners/wavelength; https://www.giss.nasa.gov/edu/res/ (Accessed on May 10, 2023).
16 https://phet.colorado.edu/en/simulations/filter?subjects=earth-science&type=html,prototype (Accessed on May 10, 2023).
17 https://www.metlink.org/ (Accessed on May 9, 2023).
18 https://www.metlink.org/maths-for-planet-earth/ (Accessed on May 9, 2023).
19 https://diksha.gov.in/ncert/explore/1?key=climatechange&selectedTab=all (Accessed on May 10, 2023).

References

Alexandar, R., and G. Poyyamoli. 2012. "Activity-based Water Resources and Climate Change Education among School Students in Puducherry." In *Climate Change and the Sustainable Use of Water Resources*, edited by Walter Leal Filho, 557–578. Climate Change Management series. New York: Springer.

Anyanwu, R., and Lesley Le Grange. 2017. "The Influence of Teacher Variables on Climate Change Science Literacy of Geography Teachers in the Western Cape, South Africa." *International Research in Geographical and Environmental Education* 26 (3): 193–206. DOI: 10.1080/10382046.2017.1330039

Ballard, P. J., and E. Ozer. 2016. "The Implications of Youth Activism for Health and Well-Being." In *Contemporary Youth Activism: Advancing Social Justice in the United States*, edited by J. Conner & S. M. Rosen. Westport, Connecticut: Praeger.

Bentley, Andrew P. K., Heather L. Petcovic, and David P. Cassidy. 2019. "Development and Validation of the Anthropogenic Climate Change Dissenter Inventory." *Environmental Education Research* 25 (6): 867–882. DOI: 10.1080/13504622.2016.1250150

Boon, H. J. 2010. "Climate Change? Who Knows? A Comparison of Secondary Students and Pre-service Teachers." *Australian Journal of Teacher Education* 35 (1): 104–120. http://dx.doi.org/10.14221/ajte.2010v35n1.9

Buhr, S. 2011. *Navigating climate science in the classroom: Teacher preparation, perceptions, practices and professional development*. Washington DC: National Research Council Board on Science Education.

Chang, C. 2014. *Climate Change Education: Knowing, doing and being*. Abingdon: Routledge.

Chang, Chew-Hung. 2015. "Teaching Climate Change – A Fad or a Necessity?" *International Research in Geographical and Environmental Education* 24 (3): 181–183.

Chang, Chew-Hung, and Liberty Pascua. 2016. "Singapore Students' Misconceptions of Climate Change." *International Research in Geographical and Environmental Education* 25 (1): 84–96. DOI: 10.1080/10382046.2015.1106206

———. 2017. "The Curriculum of Climate Change Education: A Case for Singapore." *The Journal of Environmental Education* 48 (3): 172–181. DOI: 10.1080/00958964.2017.1289883

———. 2017a. "The State of Climate Change Education – Reflections from a Selection of Studies Around the World." *International Research in Geographical and Environmental Education* 26 (3): 177–179. DOI: 10.1080/10382046.2017.1331569

Chatzifotiou, A. 2002. "An Imperfect Match? The Structure of the National Curriculum and Education for Sustainable Development." *The Curriculum Journal* 13 (3): 289–301. DOI: 10.1080/0958517022000014673

Clausen, S. W. 2018. "Exploring the Pedagogical Content Knowledge of Danish Geography Teachers: Teaching Weather Formation and Climate Change." *International Research in Geographical and Environmental Education* 27 (3): 267–280. DOI: 10.1080/10382046.2017.1349376

CRED (Center for Research on Environmental Decisions). 2009. *The Psychology of Climate Change Communication: A Guide for Scientists, Journalists, Educators, Political Aides, and the Interested Public*, Center for Research on Environmental. Decisions. New York.

de Sousa, L. O., E.A. Hay, and D. Liebenberg. 2019. "Teachers' Understanding of the Interconnectedness of Soil and Climate Change When Developing a Systems Thinking Concept Map for Teaching and Learning." *International Research in Geographical and Environmental Education* 28 (4): 324–342. DOI: 10.1080/10382046.2019.1657684

Dilling, Lisa, and Susanne C. Moser. 2007. "Introduction." In *Creating a Climate for Change*, edited by Susanne C. Moser and Lisa Dilling, 1–28. Cambridge, NY: Cambridge University Press.

Drewes, A., Joseph Henderson, and Chrystalla Mouza. 2018. "Professional Development Design Considerations in Climate Change Education: Teacher Enactment and Student Learning." *International Journal of Science Education* 40 (1): 67–89. DOI: 10.1080/09500693.2017.1397798

Dunlap, R. E. 2013. "Climate Change Skepticism and Denial: An Introduction." *American Behavioral Scientist* 57 (6): 691–698. DOI: 10.1177/0002764213477097

Dupigny-Giroux, Lesley-Ann L. 2010. "Exploring the Challenges of Climate Science Literacy: Lessons from Students, Teachers and Lifelong Learners." *Geography Compass* 4/9 (2010): 1203–1217. DOI: 10.1111/J.1749-8198.2010.00368.X

Fagan, Madeleine. 2017. "Who's Afraid of the Ecological Apocalypse? Climate Change and the Production of the Ethical Subject." *British Journal of Politics and International Relations* 19 (2): 225–244. DOI:10.1177/1369148116687534

Germanwatch. 2021. *Global Climate Risk Index 2021.*

———. 2022. *Climate Change Performance Index 2023.*

GoI, Government of India. 2020. *National Education Policy—2020*, Ministry of Education, Government of India.

Harker-Schuch, Inez, and Christian Bugge-Henriksen. 2013. "Opinions and Knowledge About Climate Change Science in High School Students." *Ambio* 42 (6): 755–766. DOI: 10.1007/s13280-013-0388-4

Hawkey, K., J. James, and C. Tidmarsh. 2019. "Using Wicked Problems to Foster Interdisciplinary Practice Among UK Trainee Teachers." *Journal of Education for Teaching* 45 (4): 446–460. DOI: 10.1080/02607476.2019.1639263

Hestness, E., R. Christopher McDonald, Wayne Breslyn, J. Randy McGinnis, and Chrystalla Mouza. 2014. "Science Teacher Professional Development in Climate Change Education Informed by the Next Generation Science Standards." *Journal of Geoscience Education* 62 (3): 319–329. DOI: 10.5408/13-049.1

Higde, E., Oztekin, C., and Sahin, E. 2017. "Turkish Pre-Service Science Teachers' Awareness, Beliefs, Values, and Behaviours Pertinent to Climate Change." *International Research in Geographical and Environmental Education* 26 (3): 253–263. DOI: DOI: 10.1080/10382046.2017.1330040

Ho, Li-Ching, and Tricia Seow. 2017. "Disciplinary Boundaries and Climate Change Education: Teachers' Conceptions of Climate Change Education in the Philippines and Singapore." *International Research in Geographical and Environmental Education* 26 (3): 240–252. DOI: 10.1080/10382046.2017.1330038

Hossler, E. W., and M. P. Conroy. 2008. "YouTube as a Source of Information on Tanning Bed Use." *Archives of Dermatology* 144 (10): 1395–1396. DOI: 10.1001/archderm.144.10.1395

Howard-Jones, Paul, David Sands, Justin Dillon and Finnian Fenton-Jones. 2021. "The Views of Teachers in England on an Action-Oriented Climate Change Curriculum." *Environmental Education Research* 27 (11): 1660–1680. DOI: 10.1080/13504622.2021.1937576

Howell, R. A., and S. Allen. 2019. "Significant Life Experiences, Motivations and Values of Climate Change Educators." *Environmental Education Research* 25 (6): 813–831. DOI: 10.1080/13504622.2016.1158242

Hulme, M. 2009. *Why We Disagree about Climate Change: Understanding Controversy, Inaction and Opportunity*. Cambridge: Cambridge University Press.

Huxster, Joanna K., Ximena Uribe-Zarain and Willett Kempton. 2015. "Undergraduate Understanding of Climate Change: The Influences of College Major and

Environmental Group Membership on Survey Knowledge Scores." *The Journal of Environmental Education* 46 (3): 149–165. DOI: 10.1080/00958964.2015.1021661

IPCC (Intergovernmental Panel for Climate Change). 2023. *Synthesis Report of the IPCC Sixth Assessment Report (AR6)—Summary for Policymakers*. Available at: https://www.ipcc.ch/report/ar6/syr/downloads/report/IPCC_AR6_SYR_SPM.pdf (Accessed on May 10, 2023).

Jang, S. Mo, and P. Sol Hart. 2015. "Polarized Frames on 'Climate Change' and 'Global Warming' Across Countries and States: Evidence from Twitter Big Data." *Global Environmental Change* 32: 11–17.

Jie Li, C., and Martha C. Monroe. 2019. "Exploring the Essential Psychological Factors in Fostering Hope Concerning Climate Change." *Environmental Education Research* 25 (6): 936–954. DOI: 10.1080/13504622.2017.1367916

Kagawa, Fumiyo, and David Selby. 2010. "Introduction." In *Education and Climate Change: Living and Learning in Interesting Times*, edited by Fumiyo Kagawa and David Selby, 1–11. London: Routledge.

Kahne, J., and J. Westheimer. 2006. "The Limits of Political Efficacy: Educating Citizens for a Democratic Society." *PS: Political Science & Politics* 39 (02): 289–296. DOI: 10.1017/S1049096506060471

Kastens, K., and Margaret Turrin. 2008. "What Are Children Being Taught in School About Anthropogenic Climate Change?" In *Communicating on Climate Change: An Essential Resource for Journalists, Scientists, and Educators*, edited by Bud Ward. Rhode Island, USA: Metcalf Institute for Marine & Environmental Reporting.

Kazdin, Alan E. 2008. *Society's Grand Challenges—Insights from Psychological Science*. Washington, DC: American Psychological Association. Available at: https://www.apa.org/science/programs/gc-climate-change.pdf (Accessed on June 19, 2023)

Khalid, T. 2003. "Pre-Service High School Teachers' Perceptions of Three Environmental Phenomena." *Environmental Education Research* 9 (1): 35–50.

Kuthe, A., Lars Keller, Annemarie Körfgen, Hans Stötter, Anna Oberrauch and Karl-Michael Höferl. 2019. "How Many Young Generations Are There? – A Typology of Teenagers' Climate Change Awareness in Germany and Austria." *The Journal of Environmental Education* 50 (3): 172–182. DOI: 10.1080/00958964.2019.1598927

Leavenworth, Maria Lindgren, and Annika Manni. 2021. "Climate Fiction and Young Learners' Thoughts—A Dialogue between Literature and Education." *Environmental Education Research* 27 (5): 727–742. DOI: 10.1080/13504622.2020.1856345

Leiserowitz, Anthony. 2005. "American Risk Perceptions: Is Climate Change Dangerous?" *Risk Analysis* 25 (6). DOI: 10.1111/j.1540-6261.2005.00690.x

Leiserowitz, Anthony, Jagadish Thaker, Geoff Feinberg, and Daniel K. Cooper. 2013. *Global Warming's Six Indias*. Yale Project on Climate Change Communication. New Haven, CT: Yale University.

Liarakau, Georgia, Ilias Athanasiadis, and Costas Gavrilakis. 2011. "What Greek Secondary School Students Believe About Climate Change." *International Journal of Environmental and Science Education* 6 (1): 7998.

McBean, Gordon A., and Henry G. Hengeveld. 2000. "Communicating the Science of Climate Change: A Mutual Challenge for Scientists and Educators." *Canadian Journal of Environmental Education* 5 (1): 9–23.

Mishra, V., and H. L. Shah. 2018. "Hydrological Perspective of the Kerala Flood of 2018." *Journal of Geological Society of India* 92 (5): 511–650.

MoEF (Ministry of Environment and Forests). 2010. *Climate Change and India: A 4×4 Assessment – A Sectoral and Regional Analysis for 2030s*. Ministry of Environment & Forests, Government of India.

MoEFCC (Ministry of Environment, Forest and Climate Change). 2015. *India's Intended Nationally Determined Contribution: Working Towards Climate Justice.* Ministry of Environment, Forest and Climate Change, Government of India. Available at: https://ksdma.karnataka.gov.in/storage/pdf-files/IndiaINDC.pdf (Accessed on September 27, 2023).

Molena, F. 1912. "Remarkable weather of 1911 - The Effect of the Combustion of Coal on the Climate - What Scientists Predict for the Future." *Popular Mechanics Magazine* March issue; 339–342.

Monroe, Martha C., Annie Oxarart, and Richard R. Plate. 2013. "A Role for Environmental Education in Climate Change for Secondary Science Educators." *Applied Environmental Education & Communication* 12: 4–18. DOI: 10.1080/1533015X.2013.795827

Monroe, Martha C., Richard R. Plate, Annie Oxarart, Alison Bowers and Willandia A. Chaves. 2017. "Identifying Effective Climate Change Education Strategies: A Systematic Review of the Research." *Environmental Education Research* 25 (6): 791–812. DOI: 10.1080/13504622.2017.1360842

Mutlu, Mehmet, and Halil Tokcan. 2013. "Success Effect of Documentary Use in Teaching of Global Warming Subject." *International Journal of Academic Research* 5(5): 263–268.

NCERT (National Council of Educational Research and Training). 2000. *National Curriculum Framework for School Education.* National Council of Educational Research and Training, New Delhi.

NCERT, National Council of Educational Research and Training. 2005. *National Curriculum Framework.* National Council of Educational Research and Training, New Delhi.

———. 2006a. *Syllabus for Classes at the Elementary Level.* National Council of Educational Research and Training, New Delhi.

———. 2006b. *Syllabus for Secondary and Higher Secondary Classes.* National Council of Educational Research and Training, New Delhi.

———. 2017. *Learning Outcomes at the Secondary Stage.* National Council of Educational Research and Training, New Delhi.

———. 2019. *Learning Outcomes at the Elementary Stage.* National Council of Educational Research and Training, New Delhi.

———. 2023. *National Curriculum Framework for School Education.* National Council of Educational Research and Training, New Delhi.

Newstadt, M. R. 2015. *The Complexities, Persistence, and Relationships among Middle School Students' Climate Change Stances and Knowledge.* A dissertation submitted in partial fulfillment of the requirement for the degree of Doctor or Philosophy (Educational Studies) in the University of Michigan.

NSTA. 2018. *NSTA Position Statement: The Teaching of Climate Science*, National Science Teaching Association.

Ojala, M. 2012. "Regulating Worry, Promoting Hope: How Do Children, Adolescents, and Young Adults Cope with Climate Change?" *International Journal of Environmental and Science Education* 7: 537–561.

Oluk, Sami, and Işılay Özalp. 2007. "The Teaching of Global Environmental Problems according to the Constructivist Approach: As a Focal Point of the Problem and the Availability of Concept Cartoons." *Educational Sciences: Theory & Practice* 7 (2): 881–896.

Plutzer, Eric, A. Lee Hannah, Joshua Rosenau, Mark McCaffrey, Minda Berbeco, and Ann H. Reid. 2016. *Mixed Messages: How Climate is Taught in America's Schools.*

Oakland, CA: National Center for Science Education. Available at: http://ncse.com/files/MixedMessages.pdf (Accessed on May 15, 2023).

Plutzer, Eric, Mark McCaffrey, A. Lee Hannah, Joshua Rosenau, Minda Berbeco, Ann H. Reid. 2016a. "Climate Confusion among U.S. Teachers - Teachers' Knowledge and Values Can Hinder Climate Education." *Science* 351 (6274): 664–665. DOI: 10.1126/science.aab3907

Puttick, Steven, and Isobel Talks. 2021. "Teachers' Sources of Information About Climate Change: A Scoping Review." *The Curriculum Journal* 00: 1–18. https://doi.org/10.1002/curj.136

Ratinen, I. J. 2013. "Primary Student-Teachers' Conceptual Understanding of the Greenhouse Effect: A Mixed Method Study." *International Journal of Science Education*, 35 (6), 929–955. DOI: 10.1080/09500693.2011.587845

Reid, Alan. 2019. "Key Questions About Climate Change Education and Research: 'Essences' and 'Fragrances'." *Environmental Education Research* 25 (6): 972–976. DOI: 10.1080/13504622.2019.1662078

Reinfried, Sibylle, Urs Aeschbacher, and Benno Rottermann. 2012. "Improving Students' Conceptual Understanding of the Greenhouse Effect Using Theory-based Learning Materials That Promote Deep Learning." *International Research in Geographical & Environmental Education* 21 (2): 155–178. DOI: 10.1080/10382046.2012.672685

Roman, Diego, and K. C. Busch. 2016. "Textbooks of Doubt: Using Systemic Functional Analysis to Explore the Framing of Climate Change in Middle-School Science Textbooks." *Environmental Education Research* 22 (8): 1158–1180.

Sanson, A. V., S. E. L. Burke, and J. Van Hoorn. 2018. "Climate Change: Implications for Parents and Parenting [Article]." *Parenting* 18 (3): 200–217. DOI: 10.1080/15295192.2018.1465307

Seow, Tricia, and Li-Ching Ho. 2016. "Singapore Teachers' Beliefs about the Purpose of Climate Change Education and Student Readiness to Handle Controversy." *International Research in Geographical and Environmental Education* 25 (4): 358–371.

Shepardson, Daniel P., Dev Niyogi, Soyoung Choi, and Umarporn Charusombat. 2011. "Students' Conceptions About the Greenhouse Effect, Global Warming, and Climate Change." *Climatic Change* 104 (3–4): 481–507.

———, Anita Roychoudhury, and Andrew Hirsch. 2012. "Conceptualizing Climate Change in the Context of a Climate System: Implications for Climate and Environmental Education." *Environmental Education Research* 18 (3): 323–352. DOI: 10.1080/13504622.2011.622839

Shimray, C. 2018. *A study of strategies adopted for climate change education in K-12 and teacher education programs in the U.S. and development of model curriculum frameworks—A report* submitted to the National Council of Educational Research and Training, New Delhi.

Shimray, Chong. 2016. "Redesigning Environmental Courses for Effective Environmental Protection." *Current Science* 110 (4): 499–501.

———. 2020. "Climate Change and Climate Literacy in India—Some Key Aspects for Consideration in the Curriculum." *School Science* (1): 24–37. Available at: https://ncert.nic.in/pdf/publication/journalsandperiodicals/schoolscience/SchoolScienceMarch2020.pdf (Accessed on February 14, 2024).

———. 2023. "An Analysis of the National Curriculum Framework for School Education 2023 in the context of Environmental Education." *School Science* 61 (4): 1–15.

Shimray, Chong, and Shrishail Shirol. 2020. "A Study of Students' Knowledge about Climate Change Science in India." *School Science* 58 (2): 65–78 Available at: https://

ncert.nic.in/pdf/publication/journalsandperiodicals/schoolscience/SchoolScience june2020.pdf (Accessed on February 14, 2024).

Tolppanen, Sakari, and Maija Aksela. 2018. "Identifying and Addressing Students' Questions on Climate Change." *Journal of Environmental Education* 49 (5): 375–389. DOI: 10.1080/00958964.2017.1417816

Trott, C. D. 2019a. "Children's Constructive Climate Change Engagement: Empowering Awareness, Agency, and Action." *Environmental Education Research* 26 (4): 532–554. DOI: 10.1080/13504622.2019.1675594

—— 2019b. "Reshaping Our World: Collaborating with Children for Community-Based Climate Change Action." *Action Research* 17 (1): 42–62. DOI: 10.1177/1476750 319829209

Tucker, Laura and, Lois Sherwood. 2019. *Understanding Climate Change—Grades 7-12*. NSTA Press, Arlington, VA.

Ujiie, K., K. Ishimaru, N. Hirotsu, S. Nagasaka, Y. Miyakoshi, M. Ota, T. Tokida, H. Sakai, Y. Usui, K. Ono, K. Kobayashi, H. Nakano, S. Yoshinaga, T. Kashiwagi, and J. Magoshi. 2019. "How elevated CO_2 affects our nutrition in rice, and how we can deal with it." *PloS One* 14 (3): e0212840. DOI: 10.1371/journal.pone.0212840

UNESCO. 2009. *UNESCO International Seminar on Climate change Education*. UNESCO, Paris—Report. Available at: https://www.uncclearn.org/wp-content/uploads/library/unesco45.pdf (Accessed on September 21, 2023).

USGCRP. 2009. *Climate Literacy: The Essential Principles of Climate Science*. U.S. Global Change Research Program.

Vethanayagam, Anand Lenin, and F. S. R. Hemalatha. 2010. "Effect of Environmental Education to School Children through Animation Based Educational Video." *Language in India* 10 (5): 10–16.

Vinuesa, Antonio García, Serafino Afonso Rui Mucova, Ulisses M. Azeiteiro, Pablo Ángel Meira Cartea and Mario Pereira. 2022. "Mozambican Students' Knowledge and Perceptions About Climate Change: An Exploratory Study in Pemba City." *International Research in Geographical and Environmental Education* 31 (1): 5–21. DOI: 10.1080/10382046.2020.1863671

Weldes, J. 2003. "Popular Culture, Science Fiction, and World Politics: Exploring International Relations." In *To Seek Out New Worlds*, edited by J. Weldes, 1–30. New York: Palgrave Macmillan.

Wibeck, V. 2014. "Enhancing Learning, Communication and Public Engagement about Climate Change-Some Lessons from Recent Literature." *Environmental Education Research* 3: 387–411.

Wise, S. 2010. "Climate Change in the Classroom: Patterns, Motivations, and Barriers to Instruction Among Colorado Science Teachers." *Journal of Geoscience Education* 58 (5): 297–309. DOI: 10.5408/1.3559695

11
WAY FORWARD

11.1 Chapter Overview

India has a constitution that strongly favors environmental education (EE). Policies and curriculum frameworks also support and promote the ideas contained in the constitution and other contemporary environmental issues. To top it up, the Hon'ble Supreme Court mandates environmental education to be taught as a compulsory subject. In spite of all the efforts put in by different agencies, governmental and nongovernmental, the outcome of implementation of environmental education in the country is far from satisfactory. Looking at the ineffectiveness of the present status of implementation of environmental education in India, this chapter of the book attempts to work out a comprehensive roadmap for its implementation. The chapter points out that implementation of environmental education will require the contribution of different stakeholders—governmental and nongovernmental. Their contribution has been enormous and will remain wanted, and this aspect has been provided in the chapter in brief. Any such attempt to improve the implementation of environmental education can only happen which is supported by rigorous research in different aspects concerning environmental education. Keeping this in view, some possible areas for research have also been provided here.

11.2 Introduction

The chapters discussed so far in the book reveal a picture about the status of implementation of environmental education in schools especially in India, the barriers in the implementation, and the issues related to teacher education and many other relevant areas as well. This suggests that successful implementation will require taking into consideration various elements and putting each one of them in place. The elements could include the policy documents, different stakeholders, training, research, and so on. Concerns put forth in the policy documents or the curriculum framework need to be in sync with the efforts made in professional development courses and in the teaching–learning process in the classrooms. The collective efforts of different stakeholders, including the nongovernmental organizations (NGOs), are key to the successful implementation of environmental education. One organization or institute with its all-out efforts cannot make environmental education work. For example, even if teacher education institutes give the best of trainings, but the school syllabus or routine does not give space for teachers to apply their knowledge, experiences, and expertize then nothing substantial can be achieved. Similarly, even if the school syllabus and routine provides opportunities to implement environmental education, if the teachers are not trained in the area, then there will be no result. Hence, implementation in patches or piecemeal will do no good. What is needed is concerted efforts simultaneously in all aspects to make environmental education work. To effectively deal with the issues and for successful implementation, systems need to be in place. For a system, which may be as big as a nation or as small as a school, it is necessary to have a plan for implementation to achieve the set goals.

Besides government agencies, other major contributors in the implementation of environmental education in India are those in the nongovernmental sectors and institutes of higher education. The role of these organizations and institutes cannot be overemphasized. They will continue to play an important role in the future as well, and, hence, they have been prominently featured in the proposed roadmap which will be discussed in the chapter. Therefore, before discussing the roadmap a brief description of major agencies—governmental and nongovernmental—in environmental education have been provided to highlight and understand the contributions they have made so far in strengthening environmental education in India.

Notwithstanding the many issues en route its implementation, we can acknowledge the fact that environmental education as a discipline or as an approach to education has now seeped into the education system world over, including India. The problem related to its implementation is not limited to India but is seen to be prevalent even in the most developed nations. It will be impossible to figure out what exactly was not done right or suggest measures to address the issues facing the rest of the world.

However, there definitely seems to be a ray of hope when it comes to India. The reason being, there are issues related to the organization and functioning of different systems which have not been given much attention up until now. Addressing these could possibly pave way to make some headway in the implementation of environmental education with more impact. Some feasible modalities for doing this are suggested in this concluding chapter. It is especially crucial to consider them with the launch of the National Education Policy 2020 and the introduction of new curriculum frameworks, syllabi, textbooks, and other curricular materials. Whether India will continue implementing environmental education or whether it wants to switch over to ESD model, the same strategy, which is presented in this chapter, can be adopted.

In spite of the many issues related to the implementation of environmental education in India, very few studies have been undertaken to look into the reasons and suggest the means to overcome the barriers which could be related to curricular materials, pedagogy, administrative issues, issues related to policies, and so on. Such studies are necessary to provide inputs for improving the system. In view of the importance of research, the chapter reiterates the role of research and also discusses some specific areas for focus, even as research has been mentioned as one of the important areas in the road map for implementation of environmental education in India. This will guide the stakeholders and researchers to identify the areas to take up appropriate studies.

11.3 Brief Description of the Roles and Contributions of Stakeholders

Undoubtedly, hundreds of agencies throughout the country have contributed in the implementation of environmental education in India. The contributions of these agencies have been portrayed to be even more crucial in the proposed roadmap. It is, therefore, imperative to understand the nature of contributions of these agencies. In the following, a brief description of the activities of some prominent agencies—both governmental and nongovernmental—is provided. However, this in no way undermines the contributions of the many other agencies not mentioned here but have otherwise made tremendous contributions and are solicited to continue in their endeavor.

11.3.1 Government Agencies

11.3.1.1 Ministry of Environment, Forest and Climate Change

Various initiatives have been taken up by the Ministry of Environment, Forest and Climate Change (MoEFCC) for the promotion of environmental education in both formal and nonformal sectors of which is the Environmental Education, Awareness, and Training (EEAT)—a flagship scheme of the ministry for enhancing the understanding of people at all levels about the relationship between human beings and the environment and for developing capabilities/skills to improve and protect the environment. The objectives of this scheme are being realized through the implementation of the following programs:

(i) National Environment Awareness Campaign (NEAC): Through this program, environmental awareness is created at the national level by providing nominal financial assistance to NGOs, schools, colleges, universities, research institutes, women and youth organizations, army units, government departments, and so on, from over the country for conducting awareness-raising and action-oriented activities. Thirty-four Regional Resource Agencies (RRAs) appointed by the ministry are involved in conducting, supervising, and monitoring the NEAC activities. During NEAC 2013–2014, 11,754 organizations participated from across the country.

(ii) National Green Corps (NGC): This scheme was operated through eco-clubs established in schools across India. About 100,000 eco-clubs were established in the country, making it one of the largest conservation networks. A monetary support of Rs 2,500 was provided to each school per annum. The amount was later raised to Rs 5,000.[1] The program has a unique partnership between the MoEFCC and the state government agencies, along with the dedicated NGOs working in the field of environmental education. Recognizing the fact that children can be catalysts in promoting a mass movement about the ensemble of the environmental issues, this scheme envisaged that inculcation of environment-friendly attitudes and behavioral patterns among them could make a significant difference to the long-term efforts for protection of environment. As a result, children could trigger a chain reaction, making a difference at the local and community level, which in due course could lead to awareness at village, city, state, country, and global level.

Realizing the need to also mobilize the participation of youth in environmental conservation activities, the program support was extended to colleges during 2019–2020.[2] Some of the activities commonly undertaken as part of eco-club include waste management, water harvesting, cleaning public places, planting of trees, visits to nature centers, and wildlife parks. The NGC program was implemented as the flagship program of MoEFCC for nonformal environment education till 2021–2022. The Central Board of Secondary Education (CBSE) has also issued circular in 2019 instructing all the schools to mandatorily create eco-clubs in schools. The Department of School Education and Literacy (DoSEL), Ministry of Education (MoE), also extends support inter alia for youth clubs and eco-clubs under Samagra Shiksha, a centrally sponsored scheme for government schools. Formation of eco-clubs and nature clubs is promoted by various state/UT governments as well.[3]

(iii) Environment Education, Awareness, Research and Skill Development (EEARSD): In 2022, MoEFCC launched the Environment Education Program (EEP), which is a component of the revamped central Sector scheme 'Environment Education, Awareness, Research and Skill Development (EEARSD).' The aim of EEP is to supplement the efforts of the MoE in the formal education front, through varied pedagogical initiatives to impart nonformal environment education. It will leverage the eco-clubs formed under NGC and also scale up activities from symbolic ones to focused training/campaigns which would bring about a long-lasting change of lifestyle and behavior that will be in harmony with nature. This will be achieved through varied pedagogical initiatives like workshops, projects, exhibitions, campaigns, competitions, nature camps, summer vacation program, etc. Implementing agency will include various organizations/institutions of MoEFCC, State Nodal Agencies (SNAs) designated for the previous EEAT Scheme, Nehru Yuva Kendra Sangathan (NYKS) or any such body under Department of Youth Affairs (DoYA), Kendriya Vidyalaya Sangathan (KVS), Navodaya Vidyalaya Samiti (NVS) or other such body under the MoE, associated organizations of Ministry of Women and Child Development (MoWCD), Panchayati Raj institutions/Urban Local Bodies, etc. A nonrecurring grants-in-aid will be provided for the approved proposals which will be limited to a ceiling of Rs. 15 lakh per district. However, this program is not open to any other agency/body/institute other than those of central government/state government/UT administration.[4]

(iv) Seminars/Symposia/Workshops/Conference: These programs provide a forum to professionals, scientists, environmentalists, and other groups of the society to share knowledge and experience on various aspects of the environment. Under these programs, financial assistance is provided to universities, academic institutions/colleges, NGOs, government departments and so on, to create mass environment awareness for the organization of seminars/symposia/workshops/conferences on identified thrust areas related to the environment, or any emerging area impinging on technology and innovation with regard to the environment which can be taken up at the state, national, or international level.

(v) Other awareness programs, such as vacation programs, quiz/essay/debate/poster/slogan competitions, training programs and so on, are outside the purview of the aforementioned programs. Different stakeholders such as NGOs and other organizations may propose such awareness activities.

MoEFCC has also listed three centers of excellence devoted to environmental education. They are:
1. Center for Environment Education (CEE), Ahmedabad: Activities of CEE will be discussed in more detail later in the chapter.
2. CPR Environmental Education Center (CPREEC), Chennai: Activities of CPREEC will be discussed in more detail later in the chapter.
3. Center for Animals and Environment, CARTMAN, Bengaluru: The main objective of the project is to study the mutual dependence and interrelationship between the animals (livestock) and the environment (plant life) and initiate steps to preserve environment and to improve the health and welfare

of animals by making them more productive. Another activity envisaged is to eliminate pollution of the environment caused by city-based abattoirs by providing alternate locations where animals are born and reared. This would also result in development of rural areas by retaining the value added in the process in villages and nearby towns. Other centers of excellence of MoEFCC include the following:

- Center of Excellence in Environmental Economics
- Foundation for Revitalization of Local Health Traditions
- Center for Ecological Sciences
- Center for Environmental Management of Degraded Ecosystem
- Center for Mining Environment
- Salim Ali Center for Ornithology and Natural History
- Tropical Botanic Garden and Research Institute

11.3.1.2 Ministry of Education

Besides working through institutions under the ministry such as National Council of Educational Research and Training (NCERT), CBSE, NVS, KVS, and so on, the ministry has also taken specific programs to promote environmental education. One such program it had initiated was the scheme of Environmental Orientation to School Education (EOSE) in 1988 (GoI 1988). This scheme was introduced in the light of the National Policy on Education, 1986 (revised in 1992), which stated that protection of the environment being a value must form an integral part of curriculum at all stages of education and also highlighted the need to create a consciousness of the environment. The rationale of this scheme was:

> One set of syllabi and textbooks are used in a State whereas the environmental conditions and environmental concerns vary from one region of the State to the other...It has, therefore, been decided to take up a centrally sponsored scheme of Environmental Orientation to School Education which will allow educational programmes in the schools to be fully harmonized with the local environmental situation and concerns.

The centrally sponsored scheme was proposed to be implemented through the education departments in the states/union territories (UTs) and the voluntary agencies having expertise and interest in environmental education. It was proposed that the scheme would assist the voluntary organizations for taking up programs for increasing awareness about environmental issues and for taking up activities for improving environment. Some of the activities suggested under the scheme were adoption of monuments for upkeep and maintenance, preparation of informative brochures, and so on; nature study; study of ecological problems of a village, educating people on the hazards of environmental pollution, advocating construction of sanitary toilets, and participation in the conservation efforts of the community; preparation of textbooks/instructional materials, and so on. Though the scheme could not be implemented through the education departments of states/UTs as proposed, the ministry appointed three organizations as the nodal agency for implementation of the scheme. They were CEE, Ahmedabad; CPREEC, Chennai; and Uttarakhand Seva Nidhi, Almora (CEE 1999; Sonowal 2009).

However, the EOSE scheme is no longer implemented as was laid down in the initial implementation framework. It was later transferred to NCERT and is no longer implemented through the nodal agencies. However, with the infusion of environmental education throughout the curriculum in the light of the National Curriculum Framework 2005, the program has remained dormant.

The MoE must now try to make most of the massive training/orientation programs organized for in-service teachers such as those conducted under the Samagra Shiksha umbrella. Since it has not been possible to train teachers separately for environmental education so far, due to administrative or other reasons, the MoE must tap these nationwide programs by keeping special sessions for environmental education in all such programs, if not come out with special training/orientation programs only for environmental education.

Besides, the MoE may consider initiating a scheme wherein teachers who completes a diploma or certification course in environmental education are provided some kind of incentives. For this, an appropriate course may be developed and the same may be provided through nodal institutions.

11.3.1.3 Other Government Agencies

There are a few other important government agencies, such as the NCERT, State Council of Educational Research and Training (SCERT)/State Institute of Education (SIE)/State Institute of Educational Research and Training (SIERT), National Council for Teacher Education (NCTE), and University Grants Commission (UGC), which have specific roles.

NCERT's role in this task is undoubtedly enormous, being the apex body for school education in the country. Beginning with its role in preparing the national curriculum framework, development of curricular materials, training programs it organizes for preservice and in-service, and so on, to its role in policymaking as an advisory body, it has a huge responsibility at hand. The challenges that will be associated with each activity that it undertakes will be tremendous. How prepared it is to overcome such challenges is a matter of concern. If environmental education is a priority in the country, then it becomes NCERT's responsibility to see to it that the same is reflected in all its activities. For that, first and foremost, it should see that it has requisite experts in the area of environmental education to ensure effective implementation. We had discussed in the previous chapters, especially in Chapter 7, how NCERT has contributed so far in the implementation of environmental education. Besides considering environmental education in the curriculum as a contemporary area as part of its routine activity of curriculum revision, it is also legally binding on the part of NCERT to ensure its implementation in all the schools throughout the country, as we had seen in the Hon'ble Supreme Court's order. Hence, how the NCERT highlights environmental education through the curriculum framework or through the curricular materials it develops will be an indicator to gauge the success of the implementation of environmental education in the country. This is because states and UTs adopt or adapt the curriculum framework developed by NCERT, and they have to abide by the instructions that are given to them with regard to environmental education, in compliance with the Hon'ble Supreme Court's order. NCERT also has to ensure that the state and UT functionaries are equipped to implement environmental education in their states and UTs. At the state level, the SCERT/SIE/SIERT or its parallel body will be responsible for taking up similar activities as NCERT.

The NCTE has the challenge of bringing out a curriculum framework for teacher preparation to meet the challenges in the area of environmental education reflected in the curriculum framework for schools and in the development of appropriate curricula for preservice and in-service courses so that environmental education is given adequate space and time. It is high time NCTE considers including environmental education as one of the compulsory papers in all its courses, instead of the optional paper it offers in some of its preservice courses. The UGC has a similar role in bringing out an appropriate model curriculum for the teacher preparation courses besides introducing courses related to environmental education at the tertiary level. While we have seen in the previous chapters about the disconnect in the school curriculum and the teacher education courses, we know that how these organizations reflect environmental education in their activities will go a long way in the implementation of environmental education.

11.3.1.4 Central and State Boards and School Systems

The role of central boards such as the CBSE, Council for the Indian School Certificate Examinations (CISCE), and other state boards is crucial for the success of implementation of environmental education. Their contribution could be through curricular materials, training, examination, and so on. Besides, school systems such as KVS and NVS also can play an important role in this process. They can ensure that their teachers get sufficient training in the area of environmental education and consider environmental education as an important component of their training programs.

11.3.2 Nongovernmental Organizations and Other Institutes

There are several organizations, outside of the government, whose contributions in the area of environmental education are immense. Some of the organizations are briefly introduced in the following sections.

11.3.2.1 Center for Environment Education

CEE is another organization whose contribution has been immense in the area of environmental education, in both the formal and the nonformal sector. It is committed to ensuring that due recognition is given to the role of environmental education in the promotion of sustainable development. CEE develops innovative programs and educational material, and builds capacity in the field of education and communication for sustainable development. As a center of excellence of the MoEFCC, it provides technical support to the nodal agency in implementing the NGC program in 15 states and 2 union territories. Mention may be made of its popular program 'Paryavaran Mitra Programme,' a nationwide ESD school program.[5] As a nodal agency for the EOSE scheme of the MoE, CEE had taken up several projects through its various centers located in different parts of the country and through collaboration with other NGOs. The projects included (a) development of locale-specific print material, (b) audiovisuals, (c) capacity building through training programs/workshops, (d) training/camps, and (e) adaptation and translation of existing environmental education materials (CEE 1999).

11.3.2.2 Center for Science and Environment

The Center for Science and Environment (CSE) is a nongovernmental research and advocacy organization that researches, lobbies for, and communicates the urgency of development that is both sustainable and equitable. Its environment education unit targets the future inheritors of this earth and tomorrow's planners and administrators by bringing out quality resource material and programs for school, college, and university students as well as environment educators and parents to bring about awareness about our environment. The Green Schools Program is a practical tool for environmental education that involves teachers and students in assessing the environmental performance of their own school.[6]

11.3.2.3 C.P.R. Environmental Education Center

With a mission to increase awareness and knowledge of key target groups (school children, local communities, woman, and so on) about the various aspects of environment, CPREEC has been a pioneer in environmental education efforts in South India and has conducted a variety of programs to spread awareness and interest among the masses.[7] Some of its activities include developing curricular materials, imparting training to teachers in different states on how to integrate environmental education into the school curriculum, and framing curriculum for environmental education in schools at the state and national level. CPREEC is also a center of excellence of the MoEFCC.

11.3.2.4 Institute of Environment Education and Research, Bharati Vidyapeeth University, Pune

The Institute of Environment Education and Research, Bharati Vidyapeeth University (BVIEER) is a unique educational and research institution. It is probably the only postgraduate environment science center in the country to have a large extension division that implements school environmental education programs. BVIEER began its environmental education programs in 1995 with three-day workshops conducted for teachers of the Bharati Vidyapeeth schools, numbering more than a hundred spread over western Maharashtra. The same year it initiated the School Environment Education Program (SEEP) with a focus on capacity building of teachers in environmental education, giving special emphasis on 'infusion approach' so that teachers are equipped to incorporate environmental education in the existing curricula. BVIEER thereby developed a manual for teachers using the 'infusion approach'—a first for India. This 200-page manual in English and Marathi was closely linked to the textbooks of Maharashtra and provided suggestions and ideas for activities, games, field visits, and school projects. It contained basic information on natural resources, biodiversity, nonconventional energy, and pollution. This task was significant because it was done at a time when most environmental education activities where through nature clubs which were optional and seen as 'extracurricular' or 'nonserious.'

To further its efforts to integrate environmental education into the school curricula, BVIEER initiated a SEEP within urban schools of the city of Pune and rural schools in the Mawal and Mulshi regions of the Western Ghats, with funding from the Confederation of Indian Industries and Tata Power Company, respectively. The school program that was evolved includes developing a set of modules using various interactive methods focusing on activity-based learning that were implemented in the schools by trained teachers with assistance from educators of the BVIEER. This program culminates into an academic year-end environment fair for all the students involved in the program, wherein schools and teachers not only display the action projects they have implemented but also participate in a host of competitive events.

Over the last 15 years, BVIEER has implemented this model in more than 600 schools in Pune and Ahmednagar districts of Maharashtra as well as in schools in Madhya Pradesh and Uttar Pradesh with the support of various funders and by maintaining close cooperation with the state education departments. The program implemented in the new schools today has a strong linkage to community environment action.

In 1998, BVIEER was assigned the task to review the status of environmental infusion in the school curriculum and suggest strategies for the same. This mammoth task involved analyzing 1,848 textbooks from all the states of India. This in-depth study provided interesting insights into the present status of environmental information in school textbooks, as well as the mode of delivery of environmental concepts in schools. Following the textbook analysis, the Ministry of Environment, Forest and Climate Change selected eight states for rewriting of textbooks taking into consideration the suggestions from the BVIEER study.

In its bid to improve textbooks, BVIEER also conducts workshops specifically targeted at orienting textbook writers across India to infuse concepts related to sustainable development into their textbooks. It has provided training to textbooks writers from 33 states, who were deputed by the respective SCERT.

BVIEER also contributed to the development of the existing undergraduate environmental studies curriculum as mandated by the Hon'ble Supreme Court. The course is implemented across the country. It also provides a diploma course for in-service teachers in environmental education and a master's degree course in education for sustainable development.

BVIEER has been appointed as the resource agency for Maharashtra for the NGC program of the MoEFCC, Government of India, since 2003. This program reaches out to 9,050 schools and involves 4,57,500 students across the state of Maharashtra. Through this program, it provides training to teachers across the states and supports the program with educational material in the form of innovative low-cost posters that communicate project ideas to be implemented in schools. It has also initiated a 'gray to green school' concept that involves rating the green level of the school through specific projects and measurable indicators, through the medium of well-designed posters.

The distinctive characteristics of BVIEER are its wide mandate of teaching, research, and extension. It has worked in the field of environmental policy building and furthered academic excellence through various collaborations with international universities and organizations. The notable achievements of the institute include its projects and programs that have led to influencing policy and implementation of environmental education at the school and college level and infusion of sustainability issues in school textbooks across India along with strategies for protected area management.

11.3.2.5 The Energy and Resources Institute

With a vision to creating innovative solutions for a sustainable future, The Energy and Resources Institute (TERI) has also been working in the area of environmental education through various activities such as providing training, developing relevant materials, working on specific projects to create awareness, facilitate information exchange, as well as capacity building activities in different parts of the country for students, teachers, school communities, and the society at large on different issues, and so on.[8]

11.3.2.6 Toxics Link

Toxics Link is a Delhi-based environmental NGO, dedicated to bringing toxics-related information into the public domain, relating to both struggles and problems at the grassroots and global information to the local levels. Toxics Link also engages in ground work, especially in areas of municipal, hazardous, and medical waste management, and food safety among others. They work at the state and central levels to help create solutions, which are driven by the needs of people through networking and utilizing community outreach and education, policy analysis, research, training, and program development. Through persistent campaigns, the organization has been able to make a strong awareness among the public and stakeholders about toxicity and pollution. It also contributes in policymaking by directing concerned people through interaction about pro-people and environment-friendly policies.[9]

11.3.2.7 Uttarakhand Seva Nidhi Paryavaran Shiksha Sansthan or Uttarakhand Environmental Education Center (UEEC)

Initially appointed as a nodal agency by the Department of Education, MoE, to undertake locale-specific environmental education programs both in rural schools and in villages in the hill districts of Uttarakhand, Uttarakhand Seva Nidhi Paryavaran Shiksha Sansthan (USNPSS) is now a full-fledged organization handling all the environmental activities of the organization. USNPSS supports the educational activities of rural schools, NGOs, and community-based organizations by organizing training programs and discussion meetings, supplying teaching/learning materials, village and school visits for on-the-spot guidance and problem-solving, and providing honoraria to preschool teachers and small project grants. Besides its many other contributions, with the cooperation of the state's department of education, USNPSS has designed and introduced environmental education course focused on village land rehabilitation and sustainable management into the regular school curriculum in Classes VI, VII, and VIII.

11.3.2.8 World-Wide Fund for Nature–India

Education has been an integral part of the World-Wide Fund (WWF)'s global activities since the very beginning. Through its environmental education program, which began in 1969, the vision of World-Wide Fund for

Nature–India (WWF-India) has been to inform, inspire, and empower India's children and youth to take action for a healthy planet. The organization has been working to build an environmentally aware generation through both formal and nonformal approaches in education. With a wide range of programs meant for teachers, students, and policy makers, WWF-India has always endeavored to use creative and participatory ways of reaching out to its varied audiences.

Through the Nature Clubs of India, which set the tone for the eco-clubs, the Wild Wisdom Quiz, the National Nature Camps Program, and many other activities, WWF-India has been engaging school children in myriads of exciting ways for nature conservation and environmental awareness. The 'Aqua Symphony' drew participation from school bands who composed original songs on water conservation and came together to win the prize for the best song on World Wetland Day.

The Wild Wisdom, which started in 2008, is India's only national and Asia's biggest wildlife quiz. The objective of the quiz is to raise awareness about Indian flora and fauna in India and inculcate a sense of pride among students about India's rich natural heritage. So far, more than 700,000 students from over 90 countries have participated in the quiz.

In the formal realm, WWF-India has been working to embed ESD in the entire educational framework of the country through a four-pronged approach. This approach includes policy intervention, training national and state educational authorities on ESD, creating resource material for teachers and students, and developing ESD model schools.

The organization has adopted 12 schools near the protected forest areas in Assam, Chhattisgarh, Madhya Pradesh, and West Bengal to demonstrate the practical implementation of the ESD approach to the government and community members. The schools have been created as models using the 'whole school approach,' which works to develop the schools holistically in five areas that include the following: school estate, pupils, teaching and learning, communities, and monitoring and evaluation. WWF-India has also trained over 3,000 master trainers from 95 District Institutes for Education and Training and 4 State Councils for Education Research and Training to build their capacity in ESD.

The backbone of all these programs has been the rich and varied educational resource material that has been created through books, audiovisuals, and manuals in English, Hindi, and many other local languages of India. WWF-India had also developed a handbook in Locally Relevant Themes (LO-RET), a portfolio of local curricula to guide teachers in individual schools that will also inspire teachers elsewhere. This pedagogical tool integrates issues of sustainable development into subject teaching and connects this teaching to nonformal education that targets key developmental issues in the local community and, at the same time, satisfies the demands of the national curricula. Several other programs are also being undertaken such as Ek Prithvi, One Planet Academy, People for Planet, etc.[10]

11.4 Road Map for Implementation of Environmental Education in India

This section provides a broad road map or blueprint for action in the form of a flow chart for the implementation of environmental education in India (see Figure 11.1). It elucidates how different agencies working at different levels can contribute individually as a body as well as collaboratively and collectively, or how their nature of collaboration can be. The flow chart is self-explanatory, and detailings have been avoided.

The flow chart presents various activities which can be grouped under the following heads: (a) administrative and academic setups, (b) development of curriculum and curricular materials, (c) training, (d) research, (e) monitoring, (f) evaluation, (g) networking, (h) implementation, and (i) web portal. Each of these is explained briefly here.

11.4.1 Administrative and Academic Setups

One of the most important factors that hinder the implementation of environmental education can be attributed to lack of appropriate administrative and academic setups. Environmental education has not been taken seriously by organizations and institutes working in the area of school education and hence in most cases, it is not reflected in their organizational setups. For example, the NCERT, which is the apex body in school education for the country till date, has been managing with a make-shift arrangement to look after all concerns related to environmental education. The situation in other institutes is expected to be no better. Hence, the first task to begin implementation of environmental education would be to remedy this issue. The first step in this direction would be to set up a steering committee for EE by the MoE consisting of members who are experts in the field. This committee would guide the MoE in its implementation of environmental education. This will be followed by the setting up of cells/departments in relevant bodies such as the MoE, SCERTs/SIEs/Boards, NCTE, UGC, and NCERT. These cells/departments will be governed by requisite numbers of administrative staff and academicians. This should not be a make-shift arrangement but a permanent structure. A team will also be formed by the MoE at the national level, to be headed by an expert. Members may include concerned people from the relevant ministries, university faculty members, teacher educators, SCERTs/SIEs/Board, NCTE, NIOS, UGC, NCERT, NGOs, and school teachers. This team will be instrumental in taking up all academic tasks.

11.4.2 Development of Curriculum and Curricular Materials

This is another very crucial step in the implementation of environmental education. What we want to achieve through our school curriculum, with respect to environmental education, needs to be first worked out—that is, defining goals.

346 Way Forward

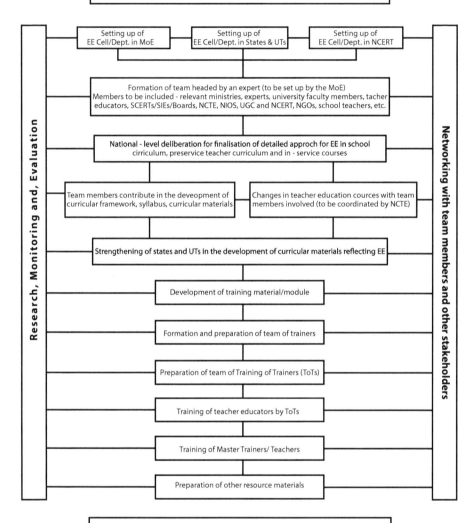

FIGURE 11.1 Road Map for the Implementation of Environmental Education in India.

Based on this, the teacher education curriculum will be prepared. However, we have seen that the school curriculum suggests a few things while teacher education courses do not reflect such suggestions at all. For example, the National Curriculum Framework, 2005, recommended that environmental education should be taught in an infusion model, but the same is not considered in the teacher education courses. First, environmental education is not reflected in the compulsory courses. Besides, there is no mention of infusion approach in the optional courses as well. The reason for such discrepancies is that the school curriculum and teacher education curriculum (preservice courses) are developed independently of each other, and, hence, there is no coherence in the two. Therefore, measures must be taken so that these activities occur simultaneously so that concerns of both can be considered and sorted out. India is at a very crucial juncture in terms of education as it rolls out new curriculum frameworks for school and teacher education in the light of the National Education Policy 2020. While this could tackle issues related to preservice courses, measures also need to be taken for the courses for in-service programs. This is necessary since most of the in-service teachers have not received any training in environmental education.

Development of curricular material is another very important activity that requires special attention. If environmental education is to be infused in different subject areas, it is imperative that the teachers should be able to identify what has been infused, where it has been infused, and how it has been infused. These should be clearly reflected in the curricular materials. The material should be such that teachers should be able to make use of it to achieve the goals of environmental education. Hence, experts in environmental education should be involved in all the developmental activities of curricular materials for different subject areas. Appropriate materials for preservice and in-service courses should also be prepared accordingly.

Countless number of resources have already been prepared by different organizations in India. In order to avoid duplication of the resources, it will be appropriate to curate the resources and also upload them in one platform so that they are easily accessible to different stakeholders.

11.4.3 Training

This will form the backbone of the whole process in the implementation of environmental education. The stronger and durable the trainings, the better the implementation. Training will be at different levels and depths. It will necessarily include the following steps: (a) development of training modules for each level; (b) preparation of a team of trainers; (c) training of trainers (ToTs); (d) training of teacher educators by ToTs; (e) training of master trainers/in-service teachers.

11.4.4 Research

This is another indispensable component in the implementation of environmental education. Research will regularly provide feedback on the status of implementation. It will also suggest ways to improve implementation at every step. This can be taken up by any of the stakeholders, as mentioned in the plan of implementation. The results of such a study should be shared on a common platform which can be accessed by all.

11.4.5 Monitoring

Strict monitoring will ensure that all the stakeholders are serious in the implementation of environmental education. The Hon'ble Supreme Court had directed the NCERT to monitor the implementation of environmental education throughout the country. Strategies need to be worked out so that monitoring is effective. Regular assessment of the monitoring report should also be conducted, which could be done annually or biannual. This will enable timely action to fix issues in the process of implementation.

11.4.6 Evaluation

Evaluation of the activities undertaken should form an important component of the implementation strategy. Besides research and monitoring, meetings of all the stakeholders should be organized at regular intervals so that each stakeholder is aware of the latest status of implementation. This will also bring about transparency in the functioning of different stakeholders. State-level or national-level seminars, workshops, and conferences should also be organized regularly, which will provide inputs toward improvement of the strategies.

11.4.7 Networking

In a huge country like India, successful implementation of environmental education, or any plan or program for that matter, will depend heavily on how well the networking is done. This appears to have been one of the drawbacks in the implementation of environmental education in India. There is no dearth of organizations, mostly nongovernmental though, working for the environment throughout the country, yet so little impact is seen in terms of success. There is no mechanism to share each other's works and success stories. In the present scheme of implementation being proposed, we can see the involvement of several organizations, institutes, departments, ministries, state bodies, school systems, and so on, each functioning as an important part of a larger body. Without systematic networking, it is impossible to expect that each of these will be able to contribute meaningfully. A system needs to be in place so that there is constant coordination and cooperation between all the parts that will enable the body as a whole to be effective and productive. Stray initiatives, however good they may be, cannot have any visible impact. Only when such initiatives are shared and collectively implemented, then only will it make the efforts worthwhile.

Perhaps it is this lack of networking that is the reason for the present sorry state of affairs in environmental education where there is complete lack of coherence between what is proposed in the school curriculum and what is being implemented in the professional development courses and also by the different school systems and boards of school education. As a result of these, the actual classroom practices do not reflect any elements of environmental education.

11.4.8 Implementation

Implementation of the proposed strategy needs to be coordinated by an agency. As represented in the flow chart, the NCERT, being the apex body in school education, is found to be most appropriate to be the nodal agency for the whole exercise and coordinate all the programs, except wherever specified. It will network and collaborate with all stakeholders in all the matters concerning the implementation of environmental education in the formal education system and should also be answerable for the lapses. Besides the NCERT, all stakeholders should also be made accountable for their respective share of activities.

11.4.9 Web Portal for Environmental Education

It is often not possible to share every material with all the stakeholders or it might happen inadvertently. To avoid such a situation, it is important that a website is created so that all relevant documents, materials, and reports can be uploaded. A space can be created for all the stakeholders to update their activities by uploading on the proposed website. This site can not only be accessed by the stakeholders but is open for access for viewing online to all, the only difference being that the stakeholders will be able to modify the contents. This website can also be used for many other activities such as alerting about upcoming events in environmental education, and other relevant information.

11.5 Areas for Research in Environmental Education in India

Research is the foundation or basis on which any idea or thought stands. It is fundamental for taking any field or area of study forward or for improving upon any existing situations and practices. Excellence and qualitative improvement in the teaching–learning can be brought about by policy makers, teacher educators, and practicing school teachers by utilizing the findings of educational research. Policy documents are guided by research findings, so also is the curriculum—pedagogy, syllabus, teaching–learning materials, and so on. However, research in the area of environmental education is few and far between. As is evident from the previous chapters, environmental education is no more a new field in India. But it is also true that the field has not progressed with time. Not much has been done to improve pedagogy in schools and professional development programs or to ensure implementation at the grassroots level. At the same time, no data base or research findings are available based on which necessary changes can be brought about. Qualitative as well as quantitative research remains the answer to improve the prevailing situation. Evidence-based practices such as those that "has been implemented and evaluated, and there is evidence of some kind, based on data that have been systematically collected and analyzed, and are available for public inspection, to support the view that it achieves all (or at least some) of its intended outcomes" (Evidence-based Practice in Science Education Research Network, 2003, cited in Lucas 2008) need to be promoted. However, such practices may be implemented under specific conditions and in the context of some specific content and generalization may not be possible due to diversity in cultures, and hence the focus of research should also be to explore ways how evidence-based practices "can be sustained, identify the conditions which would have to be met to make it possible, and explore its strengths and limitations as a strategy for improving practice" (Evidence-based Practice in Science Education Research Network 2003 cited in Lucas 2008). Keeping in view the importance of research in strengthening environmental education in India, this section will focus on some of the areas where researchers in environmental education can focus on. The same is discussed under different heads based on their relevance to school education.

11.5.1 Trends and Practices

It is said that nothing in this world is static—change is the norm. This is also true with academic subjects and areas. It is evolving. It is therefore important to understand how environmental education is evolving in different parts of the world, what causes it to move to certain direction, and how and why different countries are implementing environmental education the way they are implementing. This could be called micro-evolution since the changes will not be drastic but mostly contextual/local-specific. Researchers can also look into the more drastic changes taking place in the area of EE which could be called macro-evolution. For example, environmental education has its roots in nature study, conservation education, and so on, and some are of the opinion that environmental education has now evolved into ESD. Given this trend, what is the form environmental education going to take in the near future would be an important area of research.

11.5.2 Policy Documents

We know that implementation of any philosophy or area or concern begins with the same being reflected in the policy documents. In matters related to education, we have the National Policy on Education documents which are again formulated based on the recommendations of various committees and commissions. Then there are the national curriculum frameworks for school and teacher education. Based on these documents, states/UTs come out with an adapted version for their state/UT. In this regard, research can focus on how environmental education is reflected in such documents and how the same can be better incorporated. These tasks go through an elaborate process which is worth researching. Findings of such studies can be feeders in the development of such documents.

11.5.3 Curricular Materials

The syllabus, textbooks, and other complementary and supplementary books developed from time to time by different states, UTs, boards, private publishers, and so on demand serious research. Comparative analysis of all the syllabi may be conducted with respect to environmental education. It is also necessary to find out the age-appropriateness of the concepts provided for different classes. Similarly, textbooks and other curricular materials can be analyzed to find out how environmental concepts have been discussed and how useful they are for classroom transaction. At the same time, ways for improvement can also be suggested through such studies. Results obtained from such studies can be made available to the concerned state, UT, board, publisher, and so on. Umpteen number of resources are produced by different organizations—government, NGOs, private publishers. It will be interesting to find out what kinds of resources are produced, how useful the resources are, what kinds of resources are required by students, teachers, and other stakeholders, where do students or teachers look for resources—websites, books, journals, etc. This will enable need-based development of resources.

11.5.4 Pedagogy

The pedagogy adopted by teachers in classrooms for different subjects is another area where research needs to be focused. This can be considered the most important aspect for research since it involves the actual implementation of environmental education. The success of implementation of environmental education is heavily dependent on this aspect. Studies in this regard will bring out the barriers teacher encounter in the process of implementation, which could be due to academic, administrative, or many other issues. Based on this, appropriate measures can be taken to overcome such barriers.

11.5.5 Information and Communications Technology

The application of Information and Communications Technology (ICT) in the teaching–learning process is gaining momentum in all disciplines. The use and abuse of technologies is well known in general. Even in the area of environmental education one is often tempted to entirely focus on ICT due to its convenience, attractiveness, and hassle-free nature, since one need not get exposed to the hot sun, biting cold, polluted air, stinking locality, and so on. Though ICT can be used to address some aspects of environmental education such as providing information, enriching knowledge, collecting and sharing data, and so on, it cannot entirely replace hands-on activities and field-based tasks. Hence, to what extent and in which areas ICT can be and should be used in environmental education has become a serious concern. It is therefore essential to find out the possibilities and limits of use of ICT in the implementation of environmental education through research.

11.5.6 Impact of Implementation

Regular study needs to be undertaken so as to find out how far the goals and objectives of environmental education are achieved. This will help us find out the gaps and problems in different states and UTs, and the interventions required and work for possible solutions of the same. Impact of implementation of environmental education in terms of behavioral change would form an important area of research. This can be done in terms of the programs initiated by the government. For example, eco-club, a program initiated by the MoEFCC under the NGC which is also now supported by the Department of School Education and Literacy (DoSEL), Ministry of Education (MoE) under Samagra Shiksha, has been running for decades in over one lakh schools. Evaluation of this program, on whether students who are part of such clubs exhibit some change in their attitude and behavior during their involvement in such activities or whether such experiences produce lasting effect, would give us some idea on the effectiveness of the program, and the same can be used for further improvement of the program.

11.5.7 Functioning in States and UTs

States and UTs are the ones that are actually going to implement environmental education. For this, it is essential that they have a system set up for the same. This is in terms of not only administrative setup but also an academic one. It is therefore imperative to find out the situation in the states and UTs—whether there is any system that is in place to ensure implementation or promote EE; if not, what are the issues and limitations or what are the possible ways to address the same.

11.5.8 Assessment and Evaluation

This is a very important area for research. We had already mentioned in earlier chapters about the importance of linking environmental education with 'scores.'

Though it will be challenging, it is important to study the existing assessment pattern of environmental education by different boards and also to formulate assessment methods which are practical. The challenge will lie in coming out with an appropriate assessment measures for different subjects as an infusion approach of environmental education is followed in the country. Another challenge will be in terms of research related to behavior change which is developed over time.

11.5.9 Professional Development

This is another area that researchers can focus on. Unless teachers are empowered, environmental education will never see the light of day. Despite UGC's core curriculum for teacher education courses, like the B.Ed. course, there is so much disparity in the syllabi of teacher education courses throughout the country. It is evident that there is little focus on environmental education. Researchers may find out how best environmental education can be reflected in the syllabi of such courses without adding additional burden to the student–teacher. Another area that researchers can explore is the duration of preservice courses. It is unclear whether the duration of the courses is based on research findings. One might wonder why the duration for the same course could be different. For example, while the majority offered a one-year B.Ed. course, some offered the same course for two years. And what is more surprising is that this went on years after years, till recently, when it was decided that the course would be offered by all as a two-year course. The basis of such fixing of duration can be looked into in the context of environmental education. Researchers can also look more closely at the integrated courses such as B.Sc.Ed. (bachelor's in science education) and M.Sc.Ed. (master's in science education):Are they really integrated or are two separate courses offered simultaneously so as to call integrated course? Besides, the effectiveness of other professional development courses such as B.El.Ed. (bachelor's in elementary education), D.El.Ed. (diploma in elementary education), D.Ed. (diploma in education), and so on, or the effectiveness of open and distance learning can also be studied. Researchers can also focus their study in the in-service courses in environmental education. What exists, what works, what doesn't work, and why it doesn't work are some of the areas they can look out for. It can even be on the qualifications of teacher educators at present and what should be the essential qualification for different professional development courses to be an environmental educator. It will be especially interesting to undertake research on different aspects of ITEP with respect to environmental education—the course content, in terms of preparedness to offer the course, challenges, etc.

11.5.10 Roles of Institutions

The roles and functions of organizations such as NCERT, NCTE, UGC, CBSE, and other boards are very crucial in the implementation of EE. While NCERT formulates the curriculum for school education, NCTE does it for the teachers.

UGC directs colleges and universities, CBSE directs schools under it, and other boards and institutes direct schools under their jurisdiction to implement them. Hence, each body has its specific role. Any lapse on the part of any one of them is going to impact the implementation of EE. Besides, being specific in the nature of their roles, these institutions cannot work in isolation. They need to take into consideration what the rest are doing. Hence, coordination and consultation with each other will be the mantra for effective delivery of their functions. How do they collaborate, what is the nature of their collaboration, how effective is their collaboration, and so on will form important areas for research.

11.5.11 Government Agencies

School education is under the purview of the MoE. It is therefore very important that this ministry has a very strong environmental education base. The success of implementation of environmental education, or failure for that matter, will to a large extent depend on how strong and serious this ministry is about environmental education. Its organizational setup in the context of environmental education, its mode of instruction or functioning with states and other national bodies, and so on will form an important area of research. Environmental education, by virtue of its name, has also been a 'commodity' of MoEFCC. Whether MoE and MoEFCC work in the area of environmental education independent of each other, or whether there are some areas where they work together, and so on, is another important area for research. The effectiveness of the different programs and activities undertaken, and the materials developed by MoEFCC as mentioned earlier, can also form a good area for research.

11.5.12 Nongovernmental Organizations

The role of NGOs in the implementation of environmental education has been instrumental and will remain very crucial. Their contribution has been enormous. Many NGOs have adopted schools in different places and are working with them while others collaborate with schools in different ways. However, it has not been possible to assess how far their contribution has been, whether they are getting enough support from the government, whether they collaborate with other educational bodies, what are the activities they take up in schools, what the barriers are in their functioning, and so on. All these areas can be looked into by researchers.

11.6 Conclusion

Implementation of environmental education successfully in a huge and populous country like India will indeed require extraordinary efforts. While the country makes all possible efforts to ensure that every child till the age of 14 receives free and compulsory education through its universalization of primary and secondary education programs, to push for effective implementation of environmental education somewhat seems to be a little overambitious. Besides, there are other disciplines which are considered more important. Yet, we are also aware that so much depends upon the health of the environment. There is so much at stake if we fail to take appropriate and timely measures to take care of the environment. Given this situation, a well-thought-of way of implementation needs to be worked out, wherein the role of each stakeholder is clearly defined. The proposed road map has tried to clearly identify the role of each stakeholder. Laxity on the part of any one of the stakeholders and the proposed activities in the road map will affect the effectiveness of the rest of the stakeholders, which will ultimately render all the efforts to naught. With the launch of the National Education Policy 2020 and the introduction of new curriculum frameworks, syllabi, textbooks, and other curricular materials, this is a perfect time to implement the road map so that environmental education is so strongly rooted in the school system that it nurtures environmentally literate students.

Research is certainly one area where India needs to focus and promote. It is the research findings that will guide policy makers, curriculum developers, educators, practitioners, and so on to take environmental education where it should be headed. Therefore, in order to strengthen environmental education in the country, it is inevitable that researchers in colleges, universities, education institutes, and NGOs working in the area of environmental education are encouraged to take up serious research. In the chapter, the focus was only on some possible areas for research. It will be much broader and deeper as researchers begin to explore. Many other areas of greater importance will unravel. Meaningful research studies can be taken up in research leading to Ph.D. or postdoctoral research, which basically will form a long-term research. In that case, it can also be taken up in parts by students as part of project assignments during their teacher development course or as part of their masters dissertation. There are various other ways to work at it. Dissemination of research findings will also be instrumental in taking environmental education forward. It will be a good idea to set up an online portal where thesis, dissertations, reports, research articles, other relevant results, and so on, in the area of environmental education, can be posted which can be utilized by other researchers or stakeholders.

11.7 Summary

- Implementation of environmental education will require the contribution of different stakeholders—governmental and nongovernmental.
- A road map proposed for implementation of environmental education in India has been provided.
- There are six broad areas that have to be taken into consideration for successful implementation of environmental education in the country, such as administrative setup, development of curriculum and curricular materials, training, research, monitoring, and evaluation.

- Different agencies and stakeholders, such as the state functionaries, different school systems, boards, institutes, NGOs, policymaking bodies, and so on, have been instrumental in the implementation of environmental education in India, and their contribution will continue to be very significant to take environmental education forward.
- The lacunae in the system, such as issues of infusion approach, assessment, monitoring, teacher empowerment, and so on, could be due to lack of coordination, collaboration, and networking between these organizations.
- Research findings will guide policy makers, curriculum developers, educators, practitioners, etc., so as to take environmental education in the right direction. However, there is little evidence of research undertaken in India in the area of environmental education.
- Since sufficient data is not available in India which it can refer to implement appropriate measure, it may have to look outward and tap on the research undertaken in other countries where environmental education has received tremendous attention in terms of research.

Notes

1. https://pib.gov.in/PressReleasePage.aspx?PRID=1882835 (Accessed on September 21, 2023).
2. https://ecoclub.mp.gov.in/uploads/files/Guidelines-of-EEP-English.pdf Accessed on September 21, 2023).
3. https://ecoclub.mp.gov.in/uploads/files/Guidelines-of-EEP-English.pdf Accessed on September 21, 2023).
4. https://ecoclub.mp.gov.in/uploads/files/Guidelines-of-EEP-English.pdf Accessed on September 21, 2023).
5. https://www.ceeindia.org/paryavaran-mitra-nationwide-esd-school-network-programme-education-for-children (Accessed on September 20, 2023).
6. http://www.cseindia.org/node/252 (Accessed on September 20, 2023).
7. https://cpreec.org/ (Accessed on September 20, 2023).
8. https://www.teriin.org/ (Accessed on September 20, 2023).
9. https://toxicslink.org/ (Accessed on September 29, 2023).
10. https://www.wwfindia.org/about_wwf/environmental_education/ (Accessed on September 20, 2023).

References

CEE, Centre for Environment Education. 1999. *Environmental Orientation to School Education—A Programme of Ministry of Human Resource Development: A Documentation of the Scheme and Some Projects under the Scheme*, edited by Meena Raghunathan and Mamata Pandya. Ahmedabad: CEE.

GoI, Government of India. 1988. *Scheme of Environmental Orientation to School Education*, Ministry of Human Resource Development, Department of Education, Government of India, New Delhi.

Lucas, A.M. 2008. "Evidence-based Practice and the De-professionalization of Practitioners." *Studies in Science Education* 44 (1): 83–91.

Sonowal, C.J. 2009. "Environmental Education in Schools: The Indian Scenario." *Journal of Human Ecology* 28 (1): 15–36.

12
AFTERWORD

In this day and age, using the word 'environment' as a prefix or suffix has become the trendiest practice in all public speeches and discourses. Should it be the policy makers, economists, bureaucrats, educationists, personalities in the field of arts, culture and literature, and so on, none seem to have spared. The word is 'sexy,' and so it 'sells'! But do we really mean what we say as we blabber about the environment? Has it done any good to the environment? Hardly. The fact is, we have not only used and abused the environment in words, but have done the same in action as we have exploited and deteriorated it to the extent that is unprecedented, and there seems to be no end to it.

Isn't it about time we now 'do' something for the environment? But where do we start? More importantly, how do we deal with it in our school curriculum? Toward this, efforts are being made and the buzzword now seems to be 'climate change' and, of course, a very important one at that. With July 2023 set to be the hottest month ever recorded in human history, which eventually did, Secretary-General of the United Nations Antonio Guterres at a press conference held on July 27, 2023, had said, "The era of global warming has ended; the era of global boiling has arrived."[1] Rightly so, and such warming's possible adverse impacts are beyond our imagination, and it is in our hands how we want to deal with it. The situation is grim, but there is no hope lost since every step we take, big or small, will count. The more positive steps we take, the lesser the adverse effects will be and vice versa.

Climate change is largely manifested as a result of global warming, which is contributed, to a great extent, by human activities especially in the form of greenhouse gas emissions such as carbon dioxide, methane, nitrous oxide, and so on. No doubt, the rise in average global surface temperature as well as the

DOI: 10.4324/9781003461135-13

rise in ocean temperature at the present rate is going to affect—in fact, it has already affected—the economy, agricultural production, weather pattern throughout the world, health and safety, security, and many other dimensions, putting the survival of human race itself at risk. And we have put in all our 'energy' to address this issue by focusing on energy use—how to reduce emissions of greenhouse gases, how to tap renewable sources of energy such as wind and solar energy, and everything else related to energy. That's all fine and good. We definitely must focus on that. However, there are issues with this and the issues are twofold. First, there are issues concerning our approach as we try to address climate change, global warming in particular, by focusing only on vehicular emission of greenhouse gas. Second, there is a lopsided emphasis on climate change, as if environmental education is all about climate change and climate change is all that matters in environmental education.

Let us assume that we (the whole world) have succeeded in our efforts to rely only on renewable sources of energy for all means of transportation. Should that mean that we can now buy as many vehicles as we want or can effort? Should that be the end of environmental problems related to greenhouse gas emissions? The manner in which focus has been given to global warming by trying to address vehicular emission issue is likely to backfire in our attempt to address environmental issues as a whole. This is because environmental issues are much more complex than they appear. Unfortunately, the cause (greenhouse gas from vehicular emissions)—effect (global warming)—solution (renewable energy) sequence of events is what is presented to students while explaining global warming. This is not only simplification, but it is trivialization of the understanding about global warming. Besides these events, there are other factors which need to be taken into consideration. It is very important that students are able to link their consumption pattern of food products, their modes of transportation, their energy consumption, their lifestyle in terms of clothing, housing, and so on, with emissions. They need to know that the clothes factories which release greenhouse gases manufacture clothes because there is demand. So the more we buy, the more the factories are going to manufacture. The same is true with processed food where it requires a lot of resources to preserve, pack, and transport them to distant places, consuming a lot of fuel in the process. If the demand for processed food decreases, the production of the same will also reduce automatically and thereby reducing the use of fuel. The same is also true with our vehicles. We talk so much about vehicular exhaust that we hold it as the culprit for global warming to a large extent. Even if we use clean and green fuel to run the vehicles, we still have to use a lot of resources, including energy, in the manufacture of vehicles. These 'unaccounted' causes of environmental issues in general, and global warming in particular, need to be emphasized in the school curriculum.

The argument here is that we fail to focus on the source where the problem actually started. The point source of global warming is not vehicular pollution which releases greenhouse gases. It all started during the construction of the manufacturing units for different parts of motor vehicles, and then during the manufacturing process of the vehicles which are the cause of pollution. We might not be even aware that pollutions from factories, in fact, are aggravated because we have no control over our purchase tendency. If we can afford it, we simply purchase it, irrespective of whether we need it or not, thereby contributing in more production leading to more pollution. Ships and cargoes transport food commodities and releasing greenhouse gases in the process, all because we love consuming processed foods and any other foods from other far-off states or countries. At this point, one might say that that is how economy functions and that the more our purchasing capacity increases the more a nation is considered to economically develop. But 'at the cost of what' deserves an explanation. These topics should form the basis for discussion while talking about global warming.

Besides, a lopsided emphasis on climate change is clearly evident in environmental education which is sending out a wrong message about our approach to environmental education. However, some might argue that the curriculum needs to specially include climate change due to the urgency to tackle it. But the fact is, environmental education was not introduced to tackle climate change, but environmental issues in general. In fact, climate change is comparatively a fairly new environmental issue which began to be talked about after the 1990s in the curriculum. More importantly, environmental education is an approach to education as a whole and is not issue-specific. Focusing on climate change alone will do much harm to the environment since there are many other environmental issues, besides climate change, that would be neglected. Even if we miraculously wake up to a morning where we find that the greenhouse gas level has gone down to the preindustrial era and the Earth's climate system is back to normal, and climate change becomes a thing of the past, even then we will continue deal with biodiversity loss, waste management, overexploitation of natural resources, etc. Therefore, all environmental issues including climate change have to be given equal emphasis. However, this is not to suggest that climate change should be ignored in the curriculum. In fact, it should be catered for with utmost seriousness but without undermining other environmental issues.

Having said that, we are yet to arrive at the ultimate source of all the environmental problems and issues that are prevalent today. Looking closely, we will realize that it all begins with our attitude, our value system, and our ethics. As long as we think that it is alright to buy as many cars as we can afford, as long as we think that it is alright to buy imported foods instead of buying local foods, as long as we have money, as long as we think it is alright to change our electronic gadgets as often as possible, as long as we think it is alright to waste domestic energy, as long as we are able to pay the bills, as long as we think that it is alright to convert agricultural lands into housing complexes in the name of development, as long as…and the list goes on. Unless we change our attitudes and our way of thinking, all our efforts to address climate change or any environmental problem for that matter can never bear fruit and sustainable development will remain a distant dream. Though one may rightly argue that such an attitude does not guarantee the resolution of environmental problems (we have discussed 'attitude' at several places in the book), it definitely guarantees that without it there can be no resolution. It is based on the simple logic that unless we think right, we cannot act right. And the education system has a huge role to play in shaping this 'attitude' aspect of young minds.

While we set ambitious goals at the 'big' global-level meetings to curb the emission of greenhouse gases or ozone-layer depleting gases, efforts to address attitudinal problems at individual level, which is more realistic, should not be undermined. In fact, this should receive priority if we are looking for a solution that will sustain. It is possible to achieve such efforts, not at the so-called meetings of the mighty and powerful people of the world but within the lowly classrooms of schools. It is in this context that if at all we want to achieve anything in our efforts to tackle environmental problems, it has to begin in schools.

Till date, it appears that our attempts have only been top-down, wherein decisions are taken at the highest international level and the instructions are passed down. When instructions are passed down, however true or good they may be, there is no sense of belongingness or lack of excitement or motivation to act. However, when the approach is bottom-up, there will be an increasing surge in our sense of responsibility to take an appropriate action. People are more motivated in a situation where they want to take action because they know and have the right attitude, and not because somebody else is instructing them to do so. For example, people are more likely to use public transport when they are personally committed to reduce pollution as they tell themselves, 'I will use public transport as much as possible because I want to reduce pollution,' than when they are given instruction, 'Use public transport as much as possible because that will reduce pollution.'

The issue facing us is not so much about climate change or any other environmental problem *per se*, but it is to do with our mindset, our attitude, our value system, and our lack of compassion or empathy for our fellow humans and nonhuman species. Therefore, the topical treatment that we have been applying so far is only skin-deep and cannot be an answer for a long-term solution. We need to look for something that heals from within, which in our context is changing our mindset through the medium of education.

Education systems in general, and school education in particular, will be instrumental in tackling environmental problems effectively, whether those at the top accept this or deny. Those of us in the education system may have to go out of our way so that environmental education is given its due importance in the curriculum. Unfortunately, 'environment' has become a public property which is nurtured by none. And hence, we might as well adopt it and make it an integral part of our education system sincerely and provide all the care it needs by educating our students. We, as educators, have a huge responsibility on our shoulders. We may take the challenge forward as an educator who is concerned for the environment or, as has been a practice, brush the responsibility aside like an escapist, blaming the curriculum developers for not incorporating the concern enough in the syllabus. We should know that curriculum developers may never incorporate environmental concerns adequately in the curriculum because there are other subjects which are considered 'more important.' In this situation, what we can do is to look beyond the prescribed syllabus, employ our innovative ideas, and work out the curriculum accordingly to address environmental concerns wherever relevant and possible. Should we take the easy route which is ritualistic and conventional or should we take the more challenging and inspiring route to do our bit to integrate environmental concerns meaningfully in our curriculum? It will definitely be a challenge since educators have a larger task at hand to complete the course and comply with the administration in various other tasks as well. On top of that, educators have to satisfy the school and parents with 'good results.' Yet, we also know that we are best placed to nurture students to become environmentally conscious citizens. We might not get all the support we need and might also have a convincing list to shy away from this noble endeavor. Even so, let our conscience lead us…

Note

1 https://www.un.org/sg/en/content/sg/speeches/2023-07-27/secretary-generals-opening-remarks-press-conference-climate (Accessed on August 8, 2023).

INDEX

Pages in *italics* refer to figures, pages in **bold** refer to tables

Acharya Ramamurthi Review Committee 253
Aichi-Nagoya Declaration on ESD **56**, 275

Basic Education Movement 145
Belgrade Charter: environmental education definition 30–31; goal of environmental education 93; Gough view 282; guiding principle 283; important events **55**; in India 200; International Environmental Education Workshop 29, **55**, 199–200; statement 37; Stockholm conference 267; The Belgrade Charter 38–41; totality, of environment 48
Brundtland Commission Report 52, **55**, 267–268, **276**, 285–286

Centre for Environment Education (CEE) 253, 340
Chattopadhyaya Commission 233
climate change education: challenges 315–321; climate literacy 297, 310, 315, 323; communicating 317–319; content outline *314*, 315; contextualization 301; dimensions 310–313; goal 297; in India, present status 302–305; integration in NCF-SE 2023 **307–309**; IPCC 295; literature review, different aspects 298–303; National Education Policy 2020, recommendations 305–306; nationally determined contributions 295; school curriculum, suggestions 321–323; student's knowledge 298–299; teachers' preparedness 300–301
climate-literate 297, 313, 32
Convention on the Right of the Child (CRC) 266
Convention on Wetlands 19
COVID-19 7, 10–11, 21
Curriculum for the Ten-Year School: A Framework (1975): environmental education, recommendation of 149–151

Dakar Framework for Action 266
Decade of Education for Sustainable Development (DESD): adoption **276–277**; impact of 274; international initiatives 226, **227**; key goals 227; period 2005–2014 as the UNDESD 202; relationship with other initiatives 272; report, key findings 274
descriptive norm 97–98
disciplinary areas: nature of 63; boundary 65; social science 65

Index **363**

District Institute of Education and Training (DIETs) 218, 234, 253, 256, 344

Earth Summit 52, 202, 269, **276**
education for all (EFA): Jomtien Declaration 266; United Nations Literacy Decade 266
education for sustainable development (ESD): Aichi-Nagoya Declaration 229–231; conception 266; define 269; dimensions 272; education 266–267; environmental education, differing view 281–285; Global Action Program (GAP) 275; key characteristics 270; milestone **276–277**; ramifications implementation of 286–288; SDG 277; sustainable development 267; thrusts 270–271
environmental concerns: as global issue 62
environmental education (EE): approaches 113; areas for research 262; bio-physical issue 28, 48–50, 57, 182; Caldwell statement 68; characterization of 45; definitional problem Disinger, J.F. 118; different disciplines, examples 126–135; Disinger and Monroe statement 68; environmental literacy 80, 169, 173–174, 214, 234, 240–241, **309**; environmental values development, emphasis on 66; goals 41; guiding principles 42; holistic approach 68; Hon'ble Supreme Court of India, intervention 110–111; important events, chronology of 25, 26; India vis-à-vis global initiatives 119–123, 128; Lucas perspective on EE 30, 34–35, 43–44, **55**, 76–78, 98, 118; multi-perspectives of 43–52; nature of 66; objectives 41–42; road map for implementation in India 334, 345; roots of 33; skills development 67–68; syllabus of 2004 161–162; trends in India 197; undergraduate level, guidelines 176
environmental education-environmental science-environmental studies: comparison **83–85**; environmental education and environmental science 79; environmental science and environmental studies 80

environmental issues: climate change 18, 295, 304; *see also* climate change education; dealing with 27; effects *16*; exploitation, of environment 8; industrial revolution 7; human-induced 9; initiatives, India 21–23; initiatives, international 17–21; initiatives to address 16–17; Intended Nationally Determined Contribution 23; Intergovernmental Panel on Climate Change (IPCC) 17, 295; paradox 13–16; technological developments 6–8
environmental science: Carter and Simmons statement 79–80; concern of 79; Davis argument 79
environmental studies: characterization of 80; Davis indication 82; Nash argument 80
environmental problems: areas, deal with 81; issue of depletion, presented as 66

Guidelines and Curriculum Framework for Environment Education at Undergraduate level 176, 305

Hon'ble Supreme Court of India order: promoted environmental education 178, **212**; syllabus, in pursuance of 161–162
Hand-Print CARE 137, *138*, 13

Indian Education Commission—Education & National Development: aim of 147; Kothari Commission, known as 147; recommendations 147–148
information and communications technology (ICT): application 352; research, of use 352
infusion/multidisciplinary approach: advantages 120–121; different stages, examples 136; EE infusion, all subjects into 119; Hungerford et al. views on 119–120; illustration, of infusion 122–123; implementations, barriers in 218; interdisciplinary, comparison with 126, **127–128**; meaning 119; model *120*; Monroe (1991) and Engleson suggestions 121; Monroe and Cappaert views on 120; Monroe recommended activities 121; preservice courses, inadequacies and

lapses in 245; *see also* teacher empowerment in environmental education; pros and cons **124**; support by professional environmental educators 120
injunctive norm *96*, 97–98
International Conference on Environmental Education 286, 59n1
international development targets (IDT) 219
International Environmental Education Program (IEEP): activities in India 200–201; created **56**; first phase 37; phases of 17; second phase 43; third phase 43
International Environmental Education Workshop 29, **55**, 199–200
International Union for Conservation of Nature (IUCN) 33–34, **55**, 197
Ishwarbhai Patel Review Committee (1977) 151–152,157

Johannesburg World Summit: on Sustainable Development in 2002 54, 202, 269, **276**
Jomtien Declaration 266

Kyoto Protocol 12, 18, 206, 295

learning without burden 157, 245; *see also* Yashpal Committee Report
LiFE 24

Millennium Development Goals (MDGs) 267
Ministry of Environment, Forest and Climate Change (MoEFCC): creation 198; initiatives in EE 334–337; renaming 296; single-use plastic ban 23
Ministry of Education (MoE): eco-clubs 335; Environmental Orientation to School Education, launch of **212**; IMPACT, EVS pedagogy 254; initiatives in EE 337–338; in-service training 338; NISHTHA, EVS pedagogy 254
Montreal Protocol 17

Namami Gange Program 22
National Council of Educational Research and Training (NCERT): apex body, school education 338; environmental education, opinion about 30; environmental education, role 338–339; nodal agency, implementation of EE 162, 349; road map, EE implementation *346*
National Curriculum for Elementary and Secondary Education: A Framework 90
National Curriculum Framework 2005 (NCF- 2005): environmental education, statement about 163; science 164; social science 165; work and education 165–166
National Curriculum Framework for School Education, 2000 92, 122, **127**; 'Frontline Curriculum' 157; Environmental education, integration of 158–160
National Curriculum Framework for Foundational Stage 2023: capacities, enhancement 306; environment, curricular goal 173–174; five domains 173
National Curriculum Framework for School Education 2023: climate change, integration of 207, 306–310, **307–309**; definition 44–45; environmental education, aims 174–175; environmental education, integration of 175, **176**; environmental literacy 80, 169, 173, 174, 214, 234, 240, 241, **309**; The World Around Us 175, **176**, **213**, **307**
National Curriculum Framework for Teacher Education (NCFTE) 166–168
National Education Policy 2020: Continuous Professional Development (CPD) 255; environmental education, key recommendations for 169–171; in-service 171–172; preservice 172
National Green Tribunal: Act, 2010 199; Bill 44
National Mission for Clean Ganga 22
National Policy on Education (NPE-1968 document) 148, 150
National Policy on Education (NPE-1986 document): statements of 153–154
National Solar Mission 23
nationally determined contributions 18, 23, 295
natural science: limitations of 65

non-governmental organizations (NGOs): environmental education, implementation of 340–341
norm-based persuasive communications: Cialdini's observations 98

Ozone Layer Depletion 16–17, 244

Paris Agreement 18
People's Biodiversity Registers 24
professional development 218, 233, 236–237, 240, 253, 258–259, 260; *see also* teacher empowerment in environmental education; teacher preparation
project-based environmental education: advantages 219–220; in India 220–221; pilot study 221–227; practicability 219

responsible environmental behavior (REB): cognitive factors *96*–97, 99, 103; complexity of 98–99; intention to act *96*–100; lack of intention 98; Lucas perspective 111; mindset of 100; models *96*; personality factors *96*, 97, 99; significance of 103–104; traditional thinking models *94*; variables, categorization 99–101
Rio Declaration on Environment and Development 202–206, **276**

Samagra Shiksha 254, 335, 338
Science: nature of 64
science education, converging with EE: categories of 77–78; Feinstein and Kirchgasler study 75; Gough view about 76; Lucas perspective 76–77; possibilities and limitations 75–78; reasons for 77
science–technology–society (STS): and socio-scientific issues (SSI) 71–75
Secondary Education Commission: recommendations 146–147
separate subject (Interdisciplinary) Approach: Braus and Wood view 115–116; holistic approach 116; pros and cons **116**; model *115*; systemic thinking 117; team-teaching 117; interdisciplinary, the term 59n2
single use plastic: In India, ban of 23
social science: nature of 65; normative responsibility 65

Stockholm Conference 17, 29, 39, 51, 198–199, 267
STS education: application/design 71; characterization of EE 72; Hadzigeorgiou and Skoumios indications 74; Harms view 72; implementation strategies, lack of 75; limitations of STS 72; logical reasoning 73; Lucas review 71; movement 71; Pedretti and Nazir indication 73; *Science Education* by Jim Gallagher 71; socioculture context 73; socio-ecojustice 73; STSE education, currents in 73; theory and practice, gaps between 72; value-centered 73; words by Rubba 72–73
sustainability education (SE): full-fledged 278–279, *282*; SD-related 278, *281*; types of 278
sustainable development (SD) 267–268
sustainable development goals (SDGs) 20–21, 51, 176, 207–208, **277**
Swachh Bharat 22

Tbilisi Conference 29, 37, **55**, 200
Tbilisi Declaration: Agenda 21, founding document of 280; EE characterization as 283; in 1977 48; on teacher preparation 237
teacher empowerment in environmental education: barriers 236; comparative study of B.Ed. syllabus 246–248; competencies required, Stapp view 240; course content, by Ballard and Pandya 242–244; course content, by Hungerford et al. 241–242; higher education 257; in-service, in India 252–254; ITEP 250–251; NCATE standards 240–241; need of 235; NEP 2020 and NCF-SE 2023 249–252; possibilities, in-service 254–255; preservice, in India 245; systemic issues 255; Tbilisi declaration 237; teacher educators 255–257
teacher preparation 233, 238–239, 257; *see also* teacher empowerment in environmental education; professional development
technological developments 6, 24
traditional and indigenous knowledge/practices 8, 135, 177

UN Decade of Education for Sustainable Development (UNDESD) 22, 54, **56**, 202, 273–274, **276**
United Nations conference: on human environment organized in Stockholm in 1972 198
United Nations Convention on the Law of the Sea 19
United Nations Environment Programme (UNEP) 18–19, 35–37, **55**, 199, 267, **276**, 283

Water Convention 20
Water Pollution Control Act of 1974 199
World Commission on Environment and Development 14, 52, **276**; *see also* Brundtland Commission Report
World Summit on Sustainable Development (WSSD) 54, 202, 269; *see also* Johannesburg World Summit

Yashpal Committee Report 245

Printed in the USA
CPSIA information can be obtained
at www.ICGtesting.com
LVHW021123170924
791293LV00002B/371